MEDIA AND SYMBOLS:
THE FORMS OF EXPRESSION,
COMMUNICATION, AND EDUCATION

Officers of the Society
1973-74
(Term of office expires March 1 of the year indicated.)

JEANNE CHALL
(1974)
Harvard University, Cambridge, Massachusetts

LUVERN L. CUNNINGHAM
(1976)
Ohio State University, Columbus, Ohio

N. L. GAGE
(1975)
Stanford University, Stanford, California

JOHN I. GOODLAD
(1976)
University of California, Los Angeles, California

ROBERT J. HAVIGHURST
(1974)
University of Chicago, Chicago, Illinois

KENNETH J. REHAGE
(Ex-officio)
University of Chicago, Chicago, Illinois

HAROLD G. SHANE
(1975)
Indiana University, Bloomington, Indiana

Secretary-Treasurer
KENNETH J. REHAGE
5835 Kimbark Avenue, Chicago Illinois 60637

ii

MEDIA AND SYMBOLS:
THE FORMS OF EXPRESSION,
COMMUNICATION, AND EDUCATION

*The Seventy-third Yearbook of the
National Society for the Study of Education*

P A R T   I

By

THE YEARBOOK COMMITTEE
and
ASSOCIATED CONTRIBUTORS

Edited by

DAVID R. OLSON

Editor for the Society

HERMAN G. RICHEY

19 NSSE 74

Distributed by THE UNIVERSITY OF CHICAGO PRESS • CHICAGO, ILLINOIS

The responsibilities of the Board of Directors of the National Society for the Study of Education in the case of yearbooks prepared by the Society's committees are (1) to select the subjects to be investigated, (2) to appoint committees calculated in their personnel to insure consideration of all significant points of view, (3) to provide appropriate subsidies for necessary expenses, (4) to publish and distribute the committees' reports, and (5) to arrange for their discussion at the annual meeting.

The responsibility of the Society's editor is to prepare the submitted manuscripts for publication in accordance with the principles and regulations approved by the Board of Directors.

Neither the Board of Directors, nor the Society's editor, nor the Society is responsible for the conclusions reached or the opinions expressed by the Society's yearbook committees.

Library of Congress Catalog Number: 6-16938

Published 1974 by

THE NATIONAL SOCIETY FOR THE STUDY OF EDUCATION

5835 Kimbark Avenue, Chicago, Illinois 60637

Copyright, 1974, by KENNETH J. REHAGE, Secretary

The National Society for the Study of Education

First Printing, 10,000 Copies

Printed in the United States of America

The illustration above pictures the contributors to this volume. Identification may be found on the following page.

Not shown: Gerbner
Complete identification may be found on pages vii to ix.

The Society's Committee on Media and Symbols: The Forms of Expression, Communication and Education

RUDOLF ARNHEIM
Professor of the Psychology of Art
Harvard University
Cambridge, Massachusetts

JEROME S. BRUNER
Watts Professor of Psychology
Oxford University
Oxford, England

N. L. GAGE
Professor of Education and Psychology
Stanford University
Stanford, California

GEORGE GERBNER
Professor of Communications and Dean
The Annenberg School of Communications
University of Pennsylvania
Philadelphia, Pennsylvania

NATHAN MACCOBY
Professor
Stanford Institute for Communication Research
Stanford University
Stanford, California

DAVID R. OLSON
(Chairman)
Professor of Applied Psychology
Ontario Institute for Studies in Education
Toronto, Canada

HARLEY PARKER
Professor, Kern Chair of Communications
Rochester Institute of Technology
Rochester, New York

GAVRIEL SALOMON
Lecturer
The Hebrew University
Jerusalem, Israel

Associated Contributors

JOHN B. CARROLL
Senior Research Psychologist
Educational Testing Service
Princeton, New Jersey

HENRI DIEUZEIDE
Director, Division of Methods, Materials and Techniques
UNESCO
Paris, France

HOWARD GARDNER
Research Associate
Harvard Project Zero
Cambridge, Massachusetts

E. H. GOMBRICH
Professor of the History of the Classical Tradition
Director of the Warburg Institute
University of London
London, England

LARRY GROSS
Associate Professor of Communications
Annenberg School of Communications
University of Pennsylvania
Philadelphia, Pennsylvania

V. A. HOWARD
Visiting Associate Professor of Philosophy
Graduate School of Education
Harvard University
Cambridge, Massachusetts

T. R. IDE
Chairman, The Ontario Educational Communications Authority
Toronto, Canada

BRUCE JOYCE
Professor of Education
Teachers College, Columbia University
New York, New York

JOHN M. KENNEDY
Assistant Professor of Psychology
University of Toronto
Toronto, Canada

EDWARD L. PALMER
Vice President for Research
Children's Television Workshop
New York, New York

DAVID N. PERKINS
Director, Harvard Project Zero
Graduate School of Education
Harvard University
Cambridge, Massachusetts

I. A. RICHARDS
University Professor Emeritus
Harvard University
Cambridge, Massachusetts

OLEG K. TIKHOMIROV
Professor of Psychology
Institute of Psychology, Academy of Science of the U.S.S.R.
Moscow, Russia

SOL WORTH
Professor of Communications; Director, Media Laboratories;
Chairman, Undergraduate Program in Communications
Annenberg School of Communications
University of Pennsylvania
Philadelphia, Pennsylvania

Preface

True to its spirit, this yearbook served as a means for exploring a profound theoretical and practical problem, the problem of the nature and educational consequences of communication and its technologies. It began with some rough conjectures based on Bruner and McLuhan about the nature of communication and about the ways in which technologies of communication, once invented, could alter the cognitive processes of those who used them. These conjectures were ones, as some readers will recognize, that had become central to the book *Cognitive Development: The Child's Acquisition of Diagonality*, which I was just completing at the time.

Independently, the National Society for the Study of Education was interested in producing a yearbook devoted to communication, its last systematic attention having been paid two decades earlier in a yearbook entitled *Mass Communication and Education*. N. L. Gage, a member of the Society's board of directors, had taken responsibility for examining the possibilities of producing such a yearbook. The fact that I was a visiting fellow at the Stanford Center for Research and Development in Teaching of which Gage was codirector made possible the contingency between Gage's and my concerns. The NSSE, it was decided, would be an ideal sponsor for the systematic presentation of this important problem, much of which lay outside my own or anyone else's competence. At Gage's suggestion, a more substantial proposal was prepared for the consideration of the NSSE and for a special committee consisting of Drs. Maccoby, Gage, Havighurst, Gerbner, and Calfee, which met at Stanford in the spring of 1970. Thus from its outset to its completion the NSSE board, its executive, and its editor, Dr. Herman G. Richey, served a critical role in the production of the yearbook.

At the Stanford meeting, it became clear that communication media and education could not be examined as psychological problems alone but that they involved important social and economic problems as well. The meeting also resulted in my being invited to serve as editor and in the selection of the editorial committee consisting of R. Arnheim, J. S. Bruner, N. L. Gage, G. Gerbner, N. Maccoby, H. Parker, and G. Salomon. They served well and I am indeed grateful for their help and advice.

Further private discussions with particular scholars, most of whom subsequently became contributors to the yearbook, made me realize that the nature and consequences of media could not be studied directly but could be examined through the types of symbol systems utilized by these media.

The three following conceptions amplified and clarified at an editorial committee meeting in New York in February 1971 served as the major foci of the yearbook; they were essentially our underlying assumptions:

1. The psychological and educational consequences of the media cannot be understood outside of the nature of the symbol systems they permit or utilize.

2. Each symbol system and the medium underlying it may be considered as "tools" which amplify man's powers in particular ways and communicate a partially unique aspect of reality; each medium therefore must have its own set of instructional potentials and limitations.

3. There is an interaction between a society (including its institutions) and any communication technology such that institutions, including schools, are altered by the invention of new technologies, but the institutions themselves put severe restrictions upon the uses of those technologies.

These themes and the supporting arguments which made up the final proposal, much of which appears in the introduction to this yearbook, were sent along with an invitation to the various authors whose papers appear in this volume.

Because of the pioneering nature of this venture, it was considered vital that the authors have an opportunity to confront each other before the final versions of the papers were prepared. To this end, financial assistance was sought from the Division of Research and Development of the Ontario Institute for Studies in Education and the Research Department of the Ontario Educational Communications Authority to cosponsor a working conference. We are pleased to acknowledge the generous support of these agencies as well as the fine arrangements that were made by June Armstrong and Bill Ford. That three-day conference, held at the Guild Inn in Toronto in March 1972, resulted in a wealth of discussion and, more important for the yearbook, a willingness on the part of the authors to revise their papers in the light of the proceedings and of my editorial suggestions. These revisions and my introduction were completed before the end of 1972. I am grateful to these scholars both for their important theoretical contributions and for their cooperation in helping to increase the coherence of the yearbook.

Although E. H. Gombrich was one of the authors originally invited to prepare a paper for the yearbook, he was unable to do so because of previous commitments. However, with his approval and the generous consent of W. H. Freeman and Company, owners of the copyright, we are able to include in this volume a paper which is highly relevant to this yearbook, entitled "The Visual Image", which appeared in a recent issue of *Scientific American*. We are pleased to record our gratitude to them.

Finally, I am pleased to acknowledge the many forms of support I have obtained through my home institution, The Ontario Institute for Studies in Education, both through the Department of Applied Psychology and the Editorial Division, as well as the assistance of my colleagues and students, including Carl Bereiter, Cliff Christensen, Debbie Cooper, Susan Dalfen, Bill Ford, Angela Hildyard, Ruth Pike, Frank Smith, and Ed Sullivan, and from my competent and patient secretary, Carolyn Dundas.

DAVID R. OLSON
Toronto, December 1973

Table of Contents

        Media, Modes, and Symbol Systems: The Forms of Expression and Communication. The Educational Potential of Various Media: How Media Inform, Instruct, and Influence. Technology and Institutions: The Nature of Education in a Changing Culture.

SECTION I

Media, Modes, and Symbol Systems: The Forms of Expression and Communication

        Introduction to a Theory of Symbols. Research on Symbol Systems and Notationality. Educational Implications. Concluding Remarks.

        The Aims of Education. The Multimodal Nature of Symbolic Thought and Action. Varieties of the Symbolic Experience. The Acquisition of Skills and Competencies. Educational Policies and Technological Imperatives.

        Special Uses of Language. Translation into Alternative Signs. Depiction. Exploratory Activity. The Art of Conscious Comparing.

SECTION III

Technology and Institutions: The Nature of Education in a Changing Culture

CHAPTER I

Introduction

DAVID R. OLSON

To the educationists who attended the Great Exposition of London in 1851, the wide array of new and "revolutionary" educational materials must have been impressive indeed. The industrial revolution which was radically altering both the work patterns and the cultural patterns of Western Europe was, apparently, about to revolutionize its educational patterns as well. The educational devices offered there served primarily to weaken the monopoly of knowledge held by teachers and by books—through inexpensive books which could be widely distributed, through "technologizing" the recitation technique by means of workbooks, and through the impressive assortment of pedagogic devices that persist to this day—number blocks, form boards, nesting cubes, charts, models, and other visual displays.

The beginnings of technological support to socialization in general and to education in particular are, of course, lost in antiquity. Some "mental tools" must have marked mankind from its beginnings—a shared spoken language, songs and ryhmes to summarize experience and to aid the memory, games to master the social and practical skills of a culture, and so on. But the origins of pedagogic devices, actual tools that had particular pedagogic purposes, can be traced back at least to the development of writing surfaces. The earliest of these, dating from the fifteenth century B.C., is a small flat rectangular piece of stone found at Thera that is described in the catalogue as "the earliest example of the present-day slate used by school children on which they scratched designs and learned their first letters." [1] While this may be an overinterpretation, cer-

1. Professor Marinatos (in his catalogue of the Thera exhibit in the National Museum at Athens) in Eric A. Havelock, *Prologue to Greek Literacy*

I

tainly some technological developments have had radical consequences on both the aims and processes of schooling.[2] As Eric Havelock impressively shows, Plato's *Republic* represents in part an
educational reform movement away from the oral Homeric poetry
and towards a reliance on literacy,[3] a development made possible
largely by the invention of a phonetic alphabet. This was a revolution that was to repeat itself in Western Europe after the invention
of printing.

Gutenberg developed the technology of printing from move-
able type about 1450, but it was almost a century later that Peter
Ramus (1515-1572) led his successful reform movement in higher
education towards a radical dependency upon printed books. Schools
were seen as agents of the press; printed books provided the medium
through which all experience had to pass before it became available
for "use" in intelligent action.[4] The common or elementary schools
of the time were primarily concerned with training in religion and
etiquette; most of what we would call education was left in the
hands of the craft guilds, who passed on their skills through appren-
ticeships. The ABC's were, however, taught more widely, often by
means of a hornbook, a tiny board with a handle suitable for a
child's hand. On one side was a piece of parchment on which were
printed the ABC's and other rudiments, the whole surface of which
was protected by a thin transparent sheet of horn.[5] Although the
purpose of teaching the alphabet was to enable the child to read and
write, it often became an end in itself, precipitating Rabelais's
famous satirical comment to the effect that the schoolmaster had
succeeded in teaching Gargantua the alphabet backwards in five years
and three months. When children did approach actual reading, they
were exposed to whatever was at hand. Two types of books stood
out because of their importance and simplicity: one was the "manual

---

(Lectures in Memory of Louise Taft Semple, Second Series, University of
Cincinnati, 1971), p. 7.

2. Eric A. Havelock, *Preface to Plato* (New York: Grosset & Dunlap,
1967).

3. Ibid.

4. Walter J. Ong, "Ramist Classroom Procedure and the Nature of Reality," in *Studies in English Literature, 1500-1900*, 1 (Winter 1961): 31-47.

5. Mitford M. Mathews, *Teaching to Read* (Chicago: University of Chicago Press, 1966).

of etiquette" [6] and the other was the layman's prayer book or primer [7] which gave its name to the books published subsequently as textbooks for the education of young children. The publication of textbooks for the use of children in the schools undoubtedly altered both the conception of education and the patterns of schooling, but to my knowledge these results have never been carefully analyzed. Comenius (1592-1670), who in Piaget's words "is thus among the authors who do not need to be corrected . . . to bring them up to date" [8] is usually celebrated for his belief that children must learn by doing, that is, by direct experience. It must be noted, however, that he was the author of over a hundred textbooks for children, among them *Janua Linguarum Reserata* or *Gate of Languages Unlocked* (1631), the first Latin grammar for children; the *Palatium* or the *Thesaurus*, excerpts from classical authors to be used as readers; and *Orbis Sensualium Pictus* or *The World of Sense Objects Pictured* (1658), said to be the first illustrated textbook for children. Although his textbooks were adopted or imitated all over Europe, his theoretical writings remained virtually unknown until the nineteenth century.[9] He thus inadvertently reformed the lower schools in the same way that Ramus did the universities, all the while advocating the exact opposite—more reliance upon direct experience.

Printed pictures as well were in existence in the early fifteenth century. These early pictures served simply for decoration or edification and not for conveying information. The first known use of printed pictures for the deliberate communication of information and ideas was in Valturius's *Art of War*, printed in Verona in 1472, which showed by means of many woodcuts the construction and use of machines of war. A few years later the first illustrated botany book with repeatable prints appeared; and, as Ivins [10] suggests, it was

6. Philippe Ariès, *Centuries of Childhood: A Social History of Family Life* (New York: Vintage Books, 1962), p. 291.

7. *Webster's Third New International Dictionary*, ed. Philip B. Gove (Springfield, Mass.: G. & C. Merriam Co., 1966), p. 1801.

8. Jean Piaget, *John Amos Comenius: Selections* (Paris: UNESCO, 1957), p. 30.

9. Ibid.

10. William M. Ivins, Jr., *Prints and Visual Communication* (Cambridge, Mass.: Harvard University Press, 1953).

these repeatable prints that made the science of botany possible—
hand-drawn copies of pictures tended to lose the distinguishing features of the plants. Comenius, as we have mentioned, was the first
to put pictures to the task of instructing young children. Each chapter (*Orbis Pictus*) was headed by a picture in which the various objects were numbered with reference to a certain part of the text—a
clear case of the requirements of the medium outdistancing the message conveyed.

In the Middle Ages, writing was not to be taught in the schools;
to do so would have violated the monopoly held by the guild of the
master scribes. However, the use of writing spread rapidly with the
development of printing and the production of paper. Although the
French High Court of 1661 passed a decree that scribes must not
on any account teach reading and that schoolmasters must not teach
writing and that neither be allowed to teach mathematics,[11] in less
than a century all three had been added to traditional studies of religion and etiquette as the basis of an enlarged and extended elementary school; education was increasingly a matter for the schools.
With classrooms established as social units with set objectives, the
advancing industrial revolution provided an unending string of inventions of better writing and drawing instruments and writing surfaces, books, models, and so on, culminating in the mechanical devices that looked so revolutionary in 1851.

By present standards, however, the communication revolution
had barely begun. Alternative media were just beginning to challenge the monopoly of the printing press. In about 1830 Daguerre
discovered that a permanent photographic image could be produced
by casting a camera image on an iodized silver plate. By 1877 shutters and film were improved sufficiently to permit Edward Muy-
bridge, with the sponsorship of Leland Stanford, to make his famous
photographs which showed the stopped action of a galloping horse,
by triggering serially twenty-four different cameras. Less than
twenty years later Edison's Kinetoscope permitted individuals to
glimpse a fifteen-second film of people and objects in lifelike action, thus heralding the beginnings of motion pictures. In the mean-
time a technology for recording and reproducing sound was advanced in Edison's phonograph, invented in 1877. Bell's improved
version, the Graphophone, appeared only a few years later.

11. Ariès, op. cit., p. 297.

But the most important of these developments came from the technological application of such advances in the understanding of electromagnetic phenomena. Telegraph, telephone, and radio were all developed between 1835 and 1900. Public broadcasting by radio began only in the decade 1920–30, followed by television in the 1940s. Computers and other automata and technological developments such as cable television, video recorders, and satellites are competing for a niche in the contemporary world, just as they are competing for a place in contemporary education.

The fact that evolving technologies have regularly found their way into the schools and survived there suggests that they have served some pedagogic purpose. When media were attacked, it was usually in terms of their content—the horrors of the tales told by the brothers Grimm, the violence in comic books or on children's television, immorality in the movies—and rarely in terms of the medium itself: fairy tales, cartoons, movies, or television.

It is interesting to note that the primary concerns with the mass media in the 1954 Yearbook of the National Society for the Study of Education were those of control of the media—particularly by totalitarian governments—and the possibility of "harmful influence," both of which might be counteracted, it was claimed, by "cultivating discriminating tastes" and by censorship.[12] Censorship, of course, applied *only* to the contents of a medium. Similarly, in current educational theory the use of a medium is considered exclusively in terms of the content it conveys; hence, television is used to teach people how to read books without regard to the effects of developing either "TV literacy" or "print literacy." Further, the psychological effects of relying on one medium to teach about another medium are not known. We must consider the possibility urged on us by McLuhan and more recently by the "film-literacy" and "media-literacy" advocates that more important effects are produced by the medium itself than by its content.

As we pointed out earlier, at least some reform movements in education have centered on the introduction of a new technology. While Dewey was contemporary in his reforms against the reliance on printed-book knowledge (as was Comenius), his reform move-

---

12. *Mass Media and Education*, Fifty-third Yearbook of the National Society for the Study of Education, Part II (Chicago: Distributed by the University of Chicago Press, 1954).

ment took, as an alternative, the simpler "learning by doing." In contrast, the current movement for educational reform, while attacking the same enemy that Dewey attacked, advances as an alternative "learning by viewing," a reliance upon the newer communication technologies including film, television, computers, and cathode ray tubes. Of course, it has been the case with this reform movement, as with all reform movements, that the rhetoric accompanying its advancement far outstrips the general effects it produces. Silberman [13] carefully examined several of the most prominent educational reforms of the past two decades: administrative reorganization such as nongraded schools and team teaching, the curriculum reform movement, educational television, and computerized, individualized instruction. "While some worthwhile if restricted effects have been attained, they have made a pitifully small impact on classroom practice." Either the effects are small or our theories and research have failed to render them visible.

The widely shared belief in the profound effects of technological change is based on our widely shared experiences of the advantages of rapid communication technology, whether in distant-early-warning lines, in weather predicting, in forecasting business trends or school enrollments, in making rapid calculations, and so on. Furthermore, communication technology has improved innumerable other enterprises both in increased productivity and in reduced costs. Similar effects are expected in regard to schooling.

There is almost universal sentiment that, as the Report to the President by the Commission on Instructional Technology [14] put it, "technology can make education more productive, individual, and powerful, making learning more immediate; give instruction a more scientific base; and make access to education more equal." Yet, it is an indictment of our present state of knowledge that we know neither how to assess the psychological effects of these technologies nor how to adapt them to the purpose of education. *The impact of technologies both ancient and modern on children's learning is either negligible or unknown.*

13. Charles E. Silberman, *Crisis in the Classroom* (New York: Random House, 1970), p. 172.

14. *To Improve Learning*, A Report to the President and the Congress of the United States by the Commission on Instructional Technology (Washington: U.S. Government Printing Office, 1970), p. 7.

That the impact is negligible is suggested not only by surveys such as those of Silberman but also by almost a half century of research associated with the audiovisual movement. Although summaries vary in their estimates of the outcome of this work, which consisted largely of experimental comparisons of different treatments, such as film vs. print vs. live teachers, etc., the overwhelmingly common result is that "no significant differences were found among the groups." [15] Furthermore, if modern media are having an effect on educational programs, it certainly is not noticeable in terms of an increase in measurable output. Reports by Oettinger [16] have shown that higher education's costs per student have been increasing at 5 to 7 percent per year for many years, while productivity in terms of output per man-hour has increased only 1.9 percent a year for all services, including education. Indeed, Oettinger makes a case for taking seriously the repeated findings that there are no significant differences between various methods or technologies of instruction. He concludes that "learning as now measured is largely independent of the details of means." [17] It follows that decisions on instructional effectiveness can be made on other grounds, such as cost, availability, individual preferences, and so on.

The report by the Commission on Instructional Technology represented a much more optimistic if conventional view of the future of technology in education: "learning might be significantly improved if the so-called second industrial revolution—the revolution of information processing and communication—could be harnessed to the tasks of instruction." [18] That view suffers from the fact that its projections fall halfway between the two conceptions of educational technology it advocates. The first and more conventional conception of educational technology involves the application of the media of communication, such as television, films, and computers, to instructional goals. But it is this conception of technology that

15. Paul Saettler, *A History of Instructional Technology* (New York: McGraw-Hill Book Co., 1968), chap. 15.

16. Anthony G. Oettinger and Nikki Zapol, "Will Technology Help Learning?" (Prepared for the Carnegie Commission on Higher Education, December 1971).

17. Ibid., p. 6.

18. *To Improve Learning*, op. cit., p. 6.

has led to the disappointing empirical findings of no significant differences referred to earlier. The alternative conception of educational technology is not related to particular technological devices at all, but rather to a method for program development—the manipulation of techniques for the achievement of fixed ends. In the past such a method has led to the improvement of existing means—rewriting instructional programs, revising texts, and so on, but as a technique for achieving preset ends such as universal grade-twelve literacy or a high level of moral judgments, the power of the technological or systems approach is unknown.

A third possibility, overlooked by that report, is that the communications revolution necessitates a new, more broadly construed conception of the educational process. Perhaps the function of the new media is *not* primarily that of providing more effective means for conveying the kinds of information evolved in the last five hundred years of a book or literate culture, but rather that of using the new media as a means of exploring and representing our experience in ways that parallel those involved in that literate culture. In this sense, media are not to be considered exclusively as means to preset ends but rather as means for reconstruing those ends in the light of the media of expression and communication.

A fourth possibility, raised by Gerbner,[19] Katz,[20] and Cremin,[21] is that the means do in fact exist but are not implemented because such implementation would alter society. As Gerbner puts it, "no society trains its young to live in a different society." We shall return to this social issue.

In any case, the basis for advocacy of educational technology remains bounded by the antinomy of widely shared beliefs in the power of the new technology to substantially improve learning and by almost complete absence of empirical support for that belief

19. Gerbner, this volume; see also George Gerbner, "Communication and Social Environment," *Scientific American* 227 (1972): 3, 153-60.

20. Michael Katz, *Class, Bureaucracy, and Schools: The Illusion of Educational Change in America* (New York: Praeger Publishers, 1971).

21. Lawrence A. Cremin, *American Education: The Colonial Experience, 1607-1783* (New York: Harper & Row, 1970). Cremin promises a future volume on American education which will stress "the radical changes in the architecture of education wrought by the evolution of the new media of communication" (p. xii).

despite almost half a century of both theoretical research and pragmatic reform.

The absence of such empirical knowledge has not lessened the problems and conflicts on either the practical or theoretical side of the educational enterprise. In regard to practice, planners view the communication media as the new basis for the democratization of education; instruction can be widely shared by means of broadcast television, for example. This is already a reality for some aspects of college-level programs such as the Open University in Great Britain and the Tellekolleg in West Germany and for the highly successful "Sesame Street," even if the media have had little effect on actual classrooms. These successful cases are, however, at the margins of the established school systems; it is this marginal position that is now being challenged by reformers. As Illich has put it, "Proponents of recorded, filmed and computerized instruction used to court schoolmen as business prospects; now they are itching to do the job on their own." [22]

Knowledge about the effects of media and their relation to the educational process would contribute in an important way to the decision which, without that information, shows signs of being made on the basis of a power struggle between publishers, broadcasters, and schoolmen. Which functions could be assumed by producers and which ones could not is not known.

At a more theoretical level, both educational and psychological research is severely limited by the absence of a theory of the structure of the symbols that make up such an important part of our environment, the media that propagate those symbols, and the cognitive consequences of exposing children to them. Research on media, without this framework, has already shown this limitation. [23]

In educational and psychological thought the structure of information in symbols, excepting some aspects of language, has remained unspecified. For example, it is not clear how the structure of information in film differs from that in language or from that in static pictorial representation. Lacking such a theory, psychologists

22. Ivan Illich, "The Breakdown of Schools: A Problem or a Symptom?" *Interchange* 2 (Winter 1971): 4, 5.

23. William H. Allen, "Instructional Media Research: Past, Present and Future," *AV Communication Review* 19 (Spring 1971): 5-18.

and educators are forced to approach the consequences of new media either with a simple empiricism, or else in terms of the structure of direct experience, as in learning theory, or in terms of the structure of language. One result has been to think of media in terms of "aids" to instruction rather than as means of conveying various kinds of information. Few advances are possible until some scheme is evolved for specifying how information is structured by various symbol systems, how that structuring is influenced by the various media that are used for instructional purposes, and the psychological consequences of relying on these structurings.

It is in this context that the planning and writing of this yearbook occurred. The strong belief that communication technology is of profound significance to the culture in general and to education in particular was coupled with the equally strong belief that the practical advocacy of a "media revolution" was poorly founded and that the conventional categories for the empirical study of the effects of these media were either too narrow or else misconstrued.

Although the solutions to these important problems were not available, the questions themselves were quite clear, a widely shared mode of attack existed, and the scholarship was available. The sponsorship of the National Society for the Study of Education provided the occasion for bringing these together. The intention was to provide a general conceptualization of the nature of media and symbols that would reflect their important place in our conception of man and his culture and, at the same time, would indicate, if in a preliminary way, their uses and effects in the educational enterprise.

Our attack on the problem is in three parts. The first concerns the general structure of the symbolic world that is created by our media of expression and communication. The second section concerns the particular potentials and limitations of several media for educational purposes. The third examines the social context of educational technological reform. These sections will be introduced successively.

Media, Modes, and Symbol Systems: The Forms of Expression and Communication

To further set the stage for what is to follow, it is necessary to provide some more explicit conception of media, modes, and symbol systems. To facilitate remembering the descriptions, consider the following rough natural history of symbols. Like all biological creatures, man is equipped with many automatic or easily learned adaptive responses in terms of which he carries on his commerce with the environment. But sometime in the course of his evolution he discovered that his adaptability was increased by the use of tools, a discovery that many animals have also made—chimpanzees use a straw to probe and to extract termites, for example. All tools or technologies served to amplify man's powers over the environment. Some tools, however, were used not directly on nature but, rather, communicatively; the resulting cooperation in turn facilitated his adaptiveness. Tools that have a communicative function may be called media. "Rounding up" one's prey was greatly facilitated by having a set of verbal signals or symbols that could be used to coordinate the activities of the group. Ernst Mayr, in his *Animal Species and Evolution*, says:

> The assumption that rather small-brained hominids were experienced tool users and manufacturers raises at once the question of the nature of that (tremendous) selection pressure which caused an increase of brain size during the mid-Pleistocene at an unprecedented rate. Average cranial capacity rose from a thousand to 1,400 cubic centimeters in less than one million years. . . . It seems likely that the ability to make tools contributed far less to this selection pressure than did the need for an efficient system of communication, that is, speech. Foresight and capacity for leadership would be greatly enhanced by an ability for articulate communication. Many aspects of intelligence and planning would have little survival value without a medium of communication far more efficient than that of the anthropoid apes.[24]

It was the sharing and improving of both the practical and communication tools and the skill in their use which, when transmitted to the young, made culture possible—culture became "man's adaptive dimension" in Ashley Montagu's phrase.[25] Devices or artifices evolve to more adequately serve their functions as any examination of the development of technology will show. Clubs differentiated into swords and sledges. Signal systems differentiated into the patterns

24. Ernst Mayr, *Animal Species and Evolution* (Cambridge, Mass.: Harvard University Press, 1963), pp. 634-35.

25. M. F. Ashley Montagu, ed., *Culture: Man's Adaptive Dimension* (New York: Oxford University Press, 1968).

of ordinary language—the complexities of which we are still trying to unravel—as well as into various visual symbols such as gestures and icons with varying sets of properties. Some of these symbol systems, including both spoken language and cattle brands, may be characterized in terms of a small set of elements with highly constrained rules for their combination. These symbol systems may be described as lexical, linguistic, or notational. Others, including poetic language and the visual arts, cannot be analyzed in terms of such categories. The invention of new communication technologies results in the development of new symbolic systems or at least in the modification of existing ones. Thus, the invention of transcribing spoken language into written language apparently had the additional consequences of making language analytic and logical. For example, while ordinary discourse may be possible with only oral language, logic and mathematics may be dependent upon the invention of writing surfaces. At first, written language was used to record only poetry that had already been composed in the oral tradition— Homer and the "Books of Moses" were written down. Only later did creative writing develop, as in the works of Aristotle.[26]

Such a conception underlies the following tentative definitions:

1. *Technology*—any tool or artifice that amplifies or extends man's muscular or intellectual abilities
2. *Medium*—a technology (not necessarily mechanical) for informing, for recording, sharing, and distributing symbols, usually consisting of a restricted sensory utilization combined with a certain structuring of information, e.g., print, drawings, sound recordings, TV, and so on
3. *Instructional technology*—any medium employed for instructional purposes
4. *Symbols*—diverse materials that can be used in a referential way and which can potentially be organized into systems, e.g., +, stop
5. *Symbol system*—a set of symbols so organized as to form a system of interrelated options which are correlated with a field of reference, e.g., language, music, numbers
6. *Symbolic code*—a subset of symbolic systems restricted to a particular medium
7. *Symbolic mode*—a family of symbolic systems that is characterized by nontranslatability into other symbolic systems, e.g., lexical, pictorial, gestural, musical

26. Havelock, *Preface to Plato*, op. cit.

8. *Symbolic form*—modes of knowledge, perception and experience, e.g., myth, arts, sciences, history, religion (cf. Cassirer)

The differences in the structure of information in different symbolic systems conveyed by different media may be discussed in terms of their "information potential." The naïve view assumes that the information potential of all media is the same, that the symbol systems may be different as may the means of transmission but that the information conveyed is the same. For example, this view holds that for every picture there is a sentence that is informationally equivalent, while the surface form of conveying the information differs in the two cases. McLuhan [27] has been primarily responsible for the alternative hypothesis, namely, that the information potential of different media differs; the critical problem thus becomes that of differentiating these potentials and exploiting them for purposes of communication and education. A hint as to the character of these differing potentials is suggested in Panofsky's [28] view that the unique potential of film (or any medium that employs moving visual images) is the dynamization of space and the spatialization of time. The other informational aspects of film could, presumably, be found in still pictures or perhaps in ordinary language. Conversely, various media are presumably characterized by their own unique range of limitations. In Carpenter's words: "Each medium, if its bias is properly exploited, reveals and communicates a unique aspect of reality".[29]

A parallel concern is with an examination of the extent to which the child's mastery of "skill in a medium" is an educational objective in its own right.[30] In Bruner's words: "Man's use of mind is dependent upon his ability to develop and use 'tools' or 'instruments' or 'technologies' that make it possible for him to express and am-

27. Marshall McLuhan, *Understanding Media: The Extensions of Man* (New York: Signet Books, 1964).

28. Erwin Panofsky, "Style and Medium in the Motion Pictures," *Critique* 1 (1947): 3.

29. E. Carpenter, "The New Languages," in *Explorations in Communication*, ed. E. Carpenter and Marshall McLuhan (Boston: Beacon Press, 1960), pp. 173-74.

30. David R. Olson, *Cognitive Development* (New York: Academic Press, 1970).

plify his powers." [31] To examine how such effects occur requires the "systematic study of symbols and symbol systems and the ways they function in our perceptions and actions and arts and sciences and, thus, in the creation and comprehension of our worlds." [32] The general structure, the potentials and limitations of various symbolic systems and technologies, their role in the culture, and their consequences on human development are the focus of the first section of the book. An introduction to the individual papers and their authors follows.

Howard Gardner, David Perkins, and Vernon Howard—a psychologist, a mathematician, and a philosopher—whose cooperative efforts spring from Harvard's *Project Zero*, headed by Nelson Goodman, advance in their paper a theory sufficiently general to account for all symbolic activity. Drawing on the work of Goodman,[33] they specify a set of dimensions that may be used to analyze all symbol systems. One such dimension marks the differences between "notational" systems (such as musical scores) and "nonnotational" or "nonlinguistic" systems (such as pictures). They argue and examine the evidence that it is these differences among symbolic systems that account for such important factors as the psychological processes that are built up, utilized, and modified in dealing with particular symbol systems.

Larry Gross, a second-generation communication psychologist from the Annenberg School of Communications, begins his analysis not with the range and possible dimensions of the symbolic environment, but rather with the categories of human competence, that is, social and intellectual skills that our culture develops and values. He relates these competencies to major "modes" of processing our symbolic environment: the lexical, social-gestural, iconic, logico-mathematical, and musical. Competence is dependent upon the mastery of skills relevant to each of these modes, and the primary means of developing these competencies is active performatory attempts in that mode. Media are primarily distributional systems in his analy-

31. Jerome S. Bruner et al., *Studies in Cognitive Growth* (New York: John Wiley & Sons, 1966), p. 24.

32. Nelson Goodman, *Languages of Art* (Indianapolis and New York: Bobbs-Merrill Co., 1968), p. 265.

33. Ibid.

sis. While it is not known to what extent such technologies as educational TV can short-cut these acquisition processes, Gross is not optimistic that they can replace the child's basic experiences of learning through active performances, a view he shares with Piaget. The most general activities that develop these basic categories of human competence are in the arts.

Harley Parker, an artist, designer, and scholar of the University of Toronto's Center for Culture and Technology, which is directed by Marshall McLuhan, argues that our conception of intelligence as well as our conception of schooling has been shaped almost exclusively by a reliance on one medium—print—with its psychological consequences of literacy. This "bias of the eye," while it has permitted the development of logical analysis and formal systems of organization, is losing its dominance in a culture shaped by the "all at once" character of electric technologies. Yet, the role given to electric media in educational practice is simply that of bolstering the old literate culture—teaching children to read via television. Rather than fight to preserve the values of the older literate culture with its fragmented sensibilities, Parker argues that education's role should be that of "reorchestrating" and balancing our senses primarily through a more general education in the arts.

I. A. Richards, whose first book with C. K. Ogden, *The Meaning of Meaning*, has been required reading for four generations of graduate students in many disciplines, and whose efforts over forty years have been devoted to the study of the uses of language for educative purposes, devotes his paper to an examination of the centrality of meanings in human cognition. He shows that the development, preservation, and refinement of these meanings is the primary concern of the educative process. To this end, teaching requires a specialized use of language different from, say, that of politicians or admen, namely, the use of signs that are both memorable and yet call for further exploration. Exploration, analysis, and comparison of meanings are facilitated through the use of many signs functioning contrastively and through different types of signs specified through such diverse activities as enactions, visual depictions, and verbal statements. These meanings make the generalized apprehension of experience possible, and make thinking—the comparison of meanings—possible. The important role they serve makes children's acquisition and use of meanings the primary concern of the schools while the development of techniques that enhances these functions, such as those of visual depiction, becomes one of the chief tasks confronting educators.

The Educational Potential of Various Media: How Media Inform, Instruct, and Influence

The second section of the yearbook is concerned primarily with how the media may be utilized to improve children's learning. It is a commonplace that children learn at least some things better from concrete objects and from visual representations of experience than they do from language. Further, it is generally believed that considerable learning can be managed through the arrangement of reinforcement contingencies, that is, through direct experience guided by reinforcement. Further, learning occurs through modeling, through the imitation of a successful performance. To these must be added print, pictures, films, television, sound recordings, computers, and a whole range of media that serve to mediate the symbols in our environment. Yet, not knowing the structure of these media, that is, their information potential, it is difficult or impossible to indicate the general consequences of exposure to these media or the most appropriate uses of these various media for educational purposes. Education has used such rules of thumb as "the more media or channels, the better" and "go from the concrete to the abstract." One critical need at this point is to make some theoretical analysis of the "potential" of various media for various intellectual and scholastic purposes. Each of the authors of the chapters of this section was asked the following questions:

1. How is information coded in the particular medium? (To what symbol system is it appropriate?)
2. What basic skills are required and what degree of "literacy" is required for use of this medium?
3. What are the intellectual consequences of exposure to that medium? (For example, is ability to imagine an action in slow motion dependent upon having seen slow-motion film?)
4. To what scholastic goals is the medium most appropriate?
5. Is there an asymmetry between its educational value to producers and consumers?
6. How may knowledge and skill (intelligence) in this medium be assessed?

Jerome S. Bruner and David R. Olson were at one time (1964-66) colleagues at the Harvard Center for Cognitive Studies, of which Bruner was codirector. Jerome Bruner, whose most recent book on education is *The Relevance of Education*, is now the Watts Professor of Psychology at Oxford University. David R. Olson, whose book *Cognitive Development: The Child's Acquisition of Diagonality* led directly into the planning of this yearbook, is Professor of Applied Psychology at The Ontario Institute for Studies in Education.

The paper by Bruner and Olson is an attempt to conceptualize children's learning in such a way as to highlight the possible effects of the whole spectrum of educational experiences. The most general question in regard to children's learning, then, becomes that of how does one code or represent his experience so that it has the widest generalizability and is most readily shared with learners. Both these constraints implicate symbolic systems directly. The very symbolic codes that render experience generalizable, or applicable to new experiences, render that experience communicable. The communicability of these experiences, however, must not be taken as complete. The Bruner and Olson paper goes on to show that the content, the "knowledge" as coded and communicated in various symbolic systems through various media, is widely generalizable; for example, there are many ways to learn about the circulatory system of the frog. On the other hand, the skills or activities that are utilized in extracting that particular information or content are unique to each medium experience. Whether they are discovery skills, reading skills, or diagrammatic skills, they are largely independent of each other. They are usually overlooked in tests measuring "content," even though they make up the most important aspects of what we normally call intelligence. In Bruner and Olson's words, "Media converge as to knowledge conveyed, but they diverge as to the skills they assume and develop." Instructional media, therefore, cannot be chosen simply in terms of their ability to convey certain kinds of content, but must also be chosen in terms of their ability to develop the processing skills that make up such an important part of human intelligence.

John B. Carroll, Senior Research Psychologist and Chairman of the Human Learning and Cognitive Research Group of the Educational Testing Service, has made many important contributions to the fields of language and language development as well as to that of teaching and instruction. Carroll examines the role that the print medium has played in education and the culture generally. While that medium has some characteristic limitations and misuses, he shows why its central role in the education process is not likely to be seriously challenged: it plays an important part in the formation and communication of the abstract ideas so essential to science and philosophy and, therefore, plays an important role in any democratic society. It serves as an important source of vicarious experience and it can guide and interpret direct experience as well as the experience portrayed in other media. Also, it is accessible to everyone, as producers as well as receivers.

Rudolf Arnheim is widely recognized as the foremost authority on the psychology of art, a reputation carved out by two of his books, *Art and Visual Perception* and *Visual Thinking*. He analyzes the world of images in order to find the principal criteria by means of which visual images may be assigned to particular educational functions. What kinds of effects can be achieved through the use of such features of visual media as their realism, form, size, color, animation, abstraction, and so on? Images are always a selection from the real event. This provides them with their powers to select aspects of situations which are critical, while deleting all the rest, and of transforming a world of action into a world of contemplation. It also lays the ground for their limitations—the selection and organization is done for the viewers, thereby tending to minimize the mental activity of probing, questioning, and so on.

Arnheim's paper is full of practical suggestions as to how images may be made more interesting and instructive: let the demonstration experiments go wrong occasionally to add a degree of reality; use questions rather than a redundant commentary to accompany a documentary or instructional film; select a degree of abstraction suitable to the information intended but within the limits of the skills of the audience, and many others.

John Kennedy, a psychologist who studied with James Gibson and who has devoted a considerable part of his time to the design and study of illustrations for books and magazines, attacks the question of how icons or images give information. In so doing he briefly considers the range of representational displays available in our culture and the roles they are called upon to play: to motivate, to inform, to facilitate memory, and to evoke further thinking.

Rather than theorize about the whole range of representational visual displays, the diversity of which prohibits the formulation of general rules in any case, Kennedy provides a careful analysis of one kind of display—line drawings. While line drawings may be used to represent a very wide range of visual features, they all have one fundamental property—they reflect the discontinuities that occur naturally in the optic array. It follows that pictures make minimal assumptions about children's "literacy"; the rules for their perception are the same ones that are involved in the direct perception of the world.

It is true, however, that one can grossly overestimate what information the uninitiated will extract from a picture. In his beautifully illustrated paper, E. H. Gombrich, Director of the Warburg Institute at the University of London and author of several books, including *Art and Illusion*, examines the visual image in terms of the communication functions of language. While visual images are highly successful in serving the function of arousing our emotions, they are limited in serving the functions of making explicit statements. Further, reading information from pictures, "like the reception of any other message, is dependent upon prior knowledge of possibilities; we can only recognize what we know." But given these limitations, Gombrich shows the range of informative purposes visual images may serve when the code, the caption, and the context are appropriate.

Sol Worth, an artist, film-maker, and anthropologist at the Annenberg School of Communications, University of Pennsylvania, and author of the recent book *Through Navajo Eyes: A Study in Film Communication and Anthropology*, begins his examination of the nature of film and its potential roles in education by criticizing three of the most popular bases of film advocacy. The "visual primacists," he argues, lose track of the importance of symbols in human thinking; the "film theorists" tend to lose track of communication, the conveying of intended meanings; and the "film teachers" tend to lose track of education, the development of a set of human competencies.

A consideration of the nature of film communication permits

Worth to conclude that the currently predominant uses of film in education—teaching "through" film and teaching "about" film— must be supplemented and in some cases replaced by teaching film- making. "Making a film cannot only help a child learn how films are made or why they are art, but can help him to learn how to manipulate images in his head, how to think with them, and how to communicate through them."

Ed Palmer, vice-president for Research of Children's Television Workshop, the producers of "Sesame Street" and "The Electric Company," examines CTW's success in using the medium of tele- vision for the achievement of a set of specified educational goals. As such, his chapter constitutes a case study of the development of the new "technology of education." His concern is not with the technology per se, but rather with the achievement of planned effects. Palmer describes the methodology involved in producing these effects in terms of formative evaluation, and the resulting generalized knowledge in terms of theory of presentational learn- ing, which links program attributes such as appeal and potential for elicitation of intellectual activity to particular effects upon the viewer. Formative evaluation, he maintains, offers the possibility of linking the science and the technology of learning.

T. R. Ide, who is responsible for, among other things, the pro- duction and broadcasting of educational television in Ontario, has critically examined the range of educational effects that have either been attained by means of television or that may be expected to be attained in the future and contrasts these with the relatively mar- ginal place currently given to television in the public schools. Many of the major potentials of educational television, such as its edu- cational effectiveness, its wide distribution, its possibilities for indi- vidualization, and its economy, can be achieved, however, only by continuing the trend towards the realignment of functions and re- sponsibilities which have traditionally been monopolized by schools, teachers, and other socializing agencies.

Oleg Tikhomirov, Professor of Psychology at Moscow Univer- sity, contrasts human thinking with computer thinking and con- cludes that while they may arrive at similar goals, they do so by different means. Human thinking is as much problem-forming as problem-solving. Therefore, the conception that computers add to or replace human intelligence, as in the "artificial intelligence" movement, is poorly founded.

Rather, Tikhomirov holds that computers are "tools" which alter man's psychological processes: "Man alters external things; but afterward, these alterations influence his internal psychological processes." Man's role in a man-machine system is, then, one of transforming an informal, concrete, contextual problem into a formal one; the computer's role is to solve the formal problem by means of its available heuristic programs. Man and computer roles are therefore complementary. He concludes by noting that the general psychological and pedagogical study of such a system is greatly needed.

Gavriel Salomon, Education and Communication Psychologist at the Hebrew University of Jerusalem, attempts to provide a summary characterization of the relationships between what children learn and how they are taught, that is, the medium of instruction. Statements of this relationship, he argues, must specify the structure of the symbol system employed, the inherent properties of the medium of transmission, the educational goals served, and the characteristics of the learners. Optimal instruction must capitalize on the coincidence between the particular information to be conveyed and the inherent properties of the medium. This is particularly important in serving goals concerned with the development of mental skills. In this case, the medium may perform overtly the very skills the child is to subsequently perform covertly, thereby "supplanting" them. For other educational goals, educators are free to choose media of instruction on the basis of quality, efficiency, cost, and student preference. Optimally, forms of instruction may be chosen to simultaneously "maximize the knowledge acquired and the skills developed" by tailoring them "to the level of skill and knowledge of the individual learner."

Technology and Institutions: The Nature of Education in a Changing Culture

The invention of media, particularly mass media, has important social consequences. To quote George Gerbner, "The rise of mass media communications created a new cultural force whose educational functions rival those of the school." How does the function of the school change under the impact of mass media? From this perspective, mass media have their effect less through the differential cognitive consequences (discussed in the preceding sections) than through the important different social forces they either create or serve.

How may the schools be expected to change under the further influence of the mass media? What functions which were classically assigned to the schools are being, or may be, taken over by the mass media? Is the conventional school obsolete? Undoubtedly, more efficient means of communication make a more powerful educational system possible. New media make possible a new concept of education with altered roles for both teacher and student.

Bruce Joyce, Professor of Education at Teachers College, Columbia University, and author of several books, including *Models of Teaching*, devotes his paper to the problem of designing an educational system that is more compatible with the "contemporary media ecology" than is the traditional classroom. He suggests that the educational functions such as individualized personal growth, social development, skill acquisition, and so on, be assigned to "learning centers," each of which would be equipped with the human and technological or media support systems necessary for the achievement of their goals, from beginning levels to adult competence. Such a design would permit a more appropriate distribution of the technological and human resources of the community while adding the qualities of individualization and continuing education.

Henri Dieuzeide, Directeur de la Division des methodes, materiels et techniques d'education a l'UNESCO, in Paris, examines the role that the media of communication and instruction are coming to play in education, particularly in developing countries. The fundamental incentive for change is the fact that under the impact of new communication technologies the schools and schoolmen have lost their monopoly on knowledge and must therefore establish new roles. In planning new alternatives large-scale operations are more justifiable economically than piecemeal changes. Dieuzeide considers how technologies may be adopted and modified to serve their purposes by taking a systems approach to educational design—the development of a self-correcting system that is directed to the achievement of planned educational effects. The

achievement of these goals, particularly in developing or industrial-
izing countries, demands the use of existing technologies and the
invention of "intermediate technologies" which would permit the
education of children to keep pace with their rapidly changing
society.

Universal education for a society of equals appears as an attainable goal. But, as George Gerbner points out in his chapter, the
social context not only is altered by new and powerful educational
technologies, it puts limits on those changes.

As we have seen in a preliminary way, the invention of technology has changed schooling in the past. There is an important
precedent for fearing the success of the educational revolution. In
the late sixteenth century, a movement began to deal with the poverty, laziness, and immorality of the itinerant poor of England by
the combined tactics of the English poor laws and the establishment
of free education for poor children—in Ariès's words, "an attempt
to make pious, serious workers out of what had been depraved ad-
venturers." [34] About the time there was some indication that the
process might succeed not only in teaching the poor to read and
write, but also in preparing them to go on to secondary schools—
the traditional ground of the rich—the poor were excluded from
the Latin schools by the development of the boarding school system, which was largely restricted to richer pupils. In both France
and England the "result was that what had been a virtually un-
restricted secondary education became a class monopoly, the symbol of a social stratum and the means of its selection." [35]

George Gerbner, Dean of the Annenberg School of Communications, University of Pennsylvania, devotes his paper to showing
that the symbolic environment, particularly that propagated by the
mass media, provides an unexamined and largely unconscious framework, a mythology, for structuring our ordinary experience. Elsewhere, he has written: "The highly predictable scenarios of news,
fiction, drama, and 'intimate' conversations watched by millions can
easily pass for the rituals, cults, passion plays and myths of modern
life." [36] Socialization is largely a matter of the adoption of this

34. Ariès, op. cit., p. 303.

35. Ibid., p. 313.

36. Gerbner, "Communication and Social Environment," op. cit., p. 158.

framework, this mythology, and it is achieved primarily by means of what Gerbner calls "the hidden curriculum . . . the lesson plan that no one teaches but everyone learns." By analyzing in detail the images portrayed in such media as TV, film, and fiction, Gerbner is able to uncover some aspects of the underlying conception of learning, of teachers and students, of educational institutions, and of the use of power that pervades our society. He concludes that "no school or culture educates children for some other society." Giving teachers a messianic mission and having schools soak up all the dreams and aspirations citizens have for their children doom the enterprise to failure. No social order can "afford" to make good such a promise. The illusion itself contains the seeds of the "noble but impractical" image. It becomes only "reasonable" and "realistic" to show teachers "full of goodness but sapped of vitality and power." The optimism of some of the earlier chapters as to the future of educational technology and its ability to solve social problems must be tempered by Gerbner's findings.

But these comments are intended primarily to launch the important discussions which follow. We rely on the strength of those arguments and on those added by the readers to approach the other shore, the enlightened use of communication technology for educational purposes.

MEDIA, MODES, AND SYMBOL SYSTEMS: THE FORMS OF EXPRESSION AND COMMUNICATION

CHAPTER II

Symbol Systems: A Philosophical, Psychological, and Educational Investigation

HOWARD GARDNER, VERNON HOWARD, AND DAVID PERKINS

Introduction to a Theory of Symbols

That words, images, gestures, and other symbols constitute an important aspect of human cognition has long been asserted, but only in the past few decades has the nature of these symbols and their role in psychological processes been studied by philosophers, psychologists, and educators. Many interesting findings about the nature of symbol use, the relationship between symbols and referents, and the modalities of communication have emerged in the course of these investigations. Yet, in the absence of a logical analysis of the range of symbol systems, considerable confusion and contradiction continues to characterize the area. In this paper an approach to a theory of symbol systems, inspired by the work of Nelson Goodman and carried on by an interdisciplinary research group at Harvard Project Zero, will be described. Goodman's classification of diverse symbol systems, based on the concept of notationality, will be introduced; psychological and philosophical research stemming from this theory will be reviewed; educational implications will be touched upon. Two complementary goals will motivate the presentation: to describe a potentially productive approach to the investigation of symbol systems; to demonstrate the fruitfulness of an interdisciplinary approach to educational questions.

In the following pages, the term *symbol* has been construed broadly to include diverse materials which can be used in a referential way, and which can potentially be organized into systems. Because of our view that certain kinds of symbols employed in the arts have not been adequately studied and our conclusion that the

properties of such symbols have important implications for psychological and educational questions, we will concentrate here on those
symbol systems involved in the arts. However, the results of our
studies appear relevant to other domains of knowledge.

FROM SYMBOLIC FORMS TO SYMBOL SYSTEMS

The approach to symbols taken here can perhaps be best appreciated through a brief description of earlier work. Two broad perspectives have characterized philosophical studies of symbols. The
cultural-epistemic approach has stressed the origins and genesis of
symbolic forms of cognition and knowledge such as art, science,
language, myth, and religion interpreted as cultural and historical
achievements. Cassirer's monumental *Philosophy of Symbolic
Forms* [1] is the single most influential work of this kind. Combining
cultural anthropology with Kantian epistemology, Cassirer constructs a "philosophical anthropology" through examination of the
ontogenetic relations between language and myth, magic and religion, art, science, and other "symbolic forms" of human experience. The second or *semiotic* approach,[2] less historically oriented,
has focused instead on specific differences and kinships between
linguistic, logico-mathematical, pictorial, diagrammatic, gestural,
musical, and other sorts of symbol systems construed as so many
ways of using one thing to refer to another. Until recently, dramatic advances in the linguistic sciences virtually eclipsed the study
of nonlinguistic symbol systems. With Goodman's elaboration of
a general theory of linguistic and nonlinguistic symbols,[3] a major
step was taken towards correction of that imbalance.

Though often complementary, the cultural-epistemic and semiotic approaches to the study of symbols differ in essential ways.
For Cassirer and his followers, "symbolic form" tends to refer

1. E. Cassirer, *The Philosophy of Symbolic Forms*, 3 vols. (New Haven:
Yale University Press, 1953-57).

2. An example of the semiotic approach is the work of Charles W. Morris.
See, for example, C. W. Morris, "Foundations of the Theory of Signs," *International Encyclopedia of Unified Science*, vol. 1, no. 2 (Chicago: University
of Chicago Press, 1938).

3. N. Goodman's work is presented in *Languages of Art* (Indianapolis:
Bobbs-Merrill Co., 1968). The summary which follows is taken from this
work.

to historically and culturally acquired modes of knowledge, such as "art" and "science," "history" and "religion." The basic task is to reveal the conditions of mind and culture, peculiar to the *animal symbolicum*,[4] which have made possible the evolution of these ways of comprehending man and his world. A "symbol system," on the other hand, is defined in terms of certain syntactic and semantic features of the specific items being used symbolically; for example, letters in an alphabet, the notes and staff of a score, the gestures of a dancer, or the patterns of color and line in a painting.

Not only do the two approaches differ in method and stress, but, more importantly, there is no general correspondence between symbolic forms and symbol systems. Myth, science, and art alike utilize language, while the symbols of religion may be pictorial, auditory, gestural, or linguistic. Thus, as suggested in the following pages, an analysis of symbol systems often reveals unexpected contrasts within, say, the arts or sciences and equally startling kinships between them, having the effect of disrupting traditional classifications by "subject matter," "symbolic forms," or "media."

An important early development in semiotic studies is Peirce's classification of "signs" as *icons, indices,* or *symbols* according to whether they signify by resemblance (pictures, statues), a causal connection (symptoms of a disease, smoke and fire), or convention (words, numerals).[5] This same general taxonomy was taken over and elaborated by Langer and Morris in several books.[6] The notion of the iconic sign in particular has been used extensively by critics and philosophers of art in attempts to explain representation, expression, onomatopoeia, and other types of aesthetic reference. However, the fact that replicas of coins or toots of a whistle are not normally considered signs of their respective objects is sufficient to undermine the notion of iconicity as the core of a certain type of

4. E. Cassirer, *An Essay on Man* (New Haven: Yale University Press, 1944), p. 26.

5. C. S. Peirce, "Logic as Semiotic: The Theory of Signs," in J. Buchler, ed., *Philosophical Writings of Peirce* (New York: Dover Publications, 1955), p. 102.

6. S. Langer, *Philosophy in a New Key* (Cambridge: Harvard University Press, 1942); C. W. Morris, *Signification and Significance* (Cambridge: M.I.T. Press, 1964).

symbolic relation; an amorphous relation of similarity between a symbol and its referent explains neither how certain objects get to be symbols nor in what respects they resemble their referents.[7] After all, any two elements have an indefinite number of elements in common and hence are "similar" to one another.

In all, the semiotic tradition produced broad taxonomies of symbols without devoting sufficient attention to the formal, identifying features of particular symbol systems. This left the comparison of symbol systems, the relation between symbol and referent, and the various symbolic uses of objects at a primitive stage. Consequently, despite an accumulated wealth of insight into the arts, relatively little progress has been made in our theoretical understanding of nonlinguistic symbols until Goodman's recent work.

Certain confusions still recur in general discussions of symbol use. Thus, psychologists and educators often treat "symbolic behavior" as if it were somehow all of a piece, or confined only to linguistic systems. Yet, a theory of symbols clearly should differentiate among symbols, encompassing not only linguistic but also nonlinguistic systems. Even as different entities have been lumped together, untenable dichotomies have occasionally been defended. For example, the distinction between the "verbal" and the "visual" is often emphasized, despite the obvious consideration that verbal materials can be visual as well as auditory, and visual materials verbal or nonverbal. Finally, there has been a growing tendency to equate the notions of *medium* and *symbol*. Yet, examination reveals that these two terms have rather different applications.

The *medium* is generally treated as a stimulation of one or more senses plus informational content. Thus a church bell announces to the ear that services will soon begin, or traffic lights signal the eye that one should "stop" or "go." This characterization should make clear that symbol systems and media are different, complementary concepts. The same medium (e.g., radio) may be a vehicle for different symbol systems (language, music), even as the same symbol system (e.g., natural language) may occur in different media (radio,

7. E. Nagel, "Review of *Philosophy in a New Key*," *Journal of Philosophy* 40(1943): 323-29; R. Rudner, "On Semiotic Aesthetics," *Journal of Aesthetics and Art Criticism* 10 (1951): 66-67; N. Goodman, "Seven Strictures on Similarity" in *Experience and Theory*, ed. L. Foster and J. W. Swanson (Amherst: University of Massachusetts Press, 1970), pp. 19-29.

print). Important differences between language and other sorts of symbol systems are blurred in a classification by medium which stresses differences in sense appeal over more fundamental syntactic and semantic features; an analysis in terms of symbol systems is required for an understanding of media.

NOTATIONALITY: A MEASURE OF SYMBOL SYSTEMS

How, then, may we describe, perhaps even measure, the differences among symbol systems? What, for instance, distinguishes pictures from paragraphs, graphic representation from linguistic description? It cannot be anything intrinsic to the symbols themselves if only because "oo" may function as letters in the alphabet in one system and as Little Orphan Annie's eyes in another. One means of analysis proposed by Goodman is the concept of notationality, in particular the various independent conditions of notational as opposed to nonnotational symbol systems. Briefly put, a notational system consists of a set of separate, discontinuous characters (e.g., a musical score) correlated with a field of reference which is similarly segregated (e.g., sounded pitches) so that any character in the system isolates the object or objects it stands for, or, conversely, an object isolates the character that is correlated with it. Notationality contrasts with a continuous, unsegregated (e.g., pictorial) system for which no alphabet or set of disjoint characters exists. A more formal account of this intuitive distinction between symbol systems runs as follows.

A symbol *scheme* consists of the *characters* of a symbol system irrespective of their reference or what they stand for. Thus, the characters a, b, c, and so on, and combinations of them (also called characters) constitute the symbol scheme of English, the staff and various note and clef signs that of music, and so on. A character may be formally defined as the class of all inscriptions or utterances of it, so that each of a, A, and a is said to be an a-inscription or to "belong to" the character A. To be notational, a symbol scheme must satisfy two syntactic conditions. First, it must be *syntactically disjoint*; that is, no inscription can belong to more than one character. This condition eliminates confusion about the character to which a particular inscription belongs, assuring textual identity—sameness of spelling, as it were—across a variety of shapes due to differences in handwriting or typeset.

Although an a-inscription of any other shape is still a "true copy" or "replica" of an A, it must nevertheless be possible to distinguish it from other marks which are not a-inscriptions. This second condition is called *syntactic finite differentiation* (or "articulateness"), which stipulates that for any two characters of the scheme (say, *A* and *B*) a given utterance or written inscription which does not belong to both can be determined to belong to neither or at most to one of them. As Goodman observes, "The syntactic requirements of disjointness and finite differentiation are met by our familiar alphabetical, numerical, binary, telegraphic, and basic musical notations; and by a variety of other describable notations, some of them having purely academic interest." [8]

Pictorial systems, on the other hand, typically violate both syntactic requirements inasmuch as their visual surfaces are not composed of readily identifiable inscriptions assignable to characters in a notational scheme. On the model of a notational scheme, a system of picturing is *syntactically dense* because it "provides for infinitely many characters so ordered that between each two there is a third," such that "no mark can be determined to belong to one rather than to many other characters." The same is true of analogue computers or undifferentiated pressure gauges and temperature scales.

A symbol scheme becomes a symbol *system* by the addition of a field of reference. Such a system is notational if and only if it meets three additional semantic requirements. First, the system must be *unambiguous*. A character is ambiguous if different inscriptions of the character can have different referents, like the word *cape* meaning either cloak or headland.

Second, like the characters of a notational scheme, the referents of a notational system are entirely segregated or *semantically disjoint*. No two characters in the system have any referents in common. This amounts to the prohibition of class inclusion (e.g., "All cats are mammals") and class intersection ("Some cats are white")—two conspicuous and economical features of most natural languages. Natural language (spoken as well as written) meets the conditions of a notational scheme but does not constitute a notational system. Among other things, this means that "while a good definition always unequivocally determines what objects conform to it, a definition is seldom in turn uniquely determined by each of its instances." [9] A given man may conform simultaneously to "featherless biped" and "English gentleman" and numerous other descriptions none of which is uniquely *the* description which denotes him. A musical score, on the other hand, is recoverable from the sounded pitches and durations it uniquely determines, barring some redundancy in the scheme (e.g., C♯, D♭) and nonnotational instructions (e.g., dynamics marks, figured bass, linguistic instructions).[10] This mu-

8. Goodman, *Languages of Art*, op. cit., p. 140.

9. Ibid., p. 120.

10. Ibid., pp. 151, 181-85.

tual recoverability of score and performance, possible only in unambiguous and disjoint systems, serves the double purpose (as do most art
notations) of guiding performance as well as *identifying* a work through
good and bad performances by many performers.

Third, *semantic finite differentiation* parallels but does not follow
from syntactic articulateness and stipulates that for any two characters
of the system, and any object *t* which does not belong to both, it must
be possible to determine that *t* complies with at most one of those characters. For example, if musical tradition did not limit minimum dura-
tional difference at the 1/128 note, a sounded pitch could then belong
to an infinite number of note-inscriptions for all that we could determine. In fact, many modern methods of scoring music, devised in quest
of maximum or minimum control over performance, are neither syntactically nor semantically differentiated and are, therefore, strictly
speaking, nonnotational.

Given the bewildering array of symbols and kinds of reference, the
extreme syntactic and semantic requirements of strict notationality provide a convenient measure of various symbol systems which may be distinguished by "violations" of certain combinations of the notationality
conditions. There may also be significant differences in the psychological
mechanisms involved in the manipulation of notational and nonnotational
systems which experimental study, combined with a precise taxonomy of
symbol systems, can clarify. Indeed, the characteristics of notationality
provide a way of assessing both the symbol systems within a culture and
the nature of the psychological processes used in dealing with these elements; accordingly, we will examine both "external" symbols and the
"internal cognitive mechanisms," any of which may conform to or violate conditions of notationality.

SOME IMPLICATIONS OF NOTATIONALITY

In addition to providing a clear way of distinguishing among
various symbol systems, Goodman's theory illuminates a number of
perennial questions in the areas of semiosis and aesthetics. Already
mentioned was his demonstration that similarity is an unreliable and
inadequate explanation of the relationship between a symbol and its
referents, and his consequent rejection of the "iconic" view of
symbols. Here we shall mention briefly only two applications of
the theory, both of which follow from the concept of notationality:

The question of artistic authenticity. Why is it that a copy of
Rembrandt's *Head of Christ*, however exact, is not considered a
genuine instance of the work, while there are many (good and bad)
performances of Beethoven's *Pastoral Symphony*, each no less genuine or authentic than another? The answer seems to lie in the

amenability of an art to a notation which determines the "constituent" (identifying) properties of a work while leaving other properties contingent and variable. In those arts for which notations
have been devised (e.g., music, dance), authenticity or work-
identity (though not "the spirit of the work" or "aesthetic merit")
consists in performances complying with a score rather than "identification of the actual object produced by the artist." [11] The latter
can be forged, whereas the former cannot. Those works and arts
which admit the possibility of forgery are said to be "autographic,"
while those which do not are called "allographic." Whether this
logical distinction has psychological validity—whether the individual operates in a different way with autographic and allographic
works, with fakes, copies, or originals—is a separate question merit-
ing investigation.

The difference in domain between art and science. The concept
of notationality points to significant differences in the characteristics
of the symbol systems of art and science. Rather than a fixed set
of criteria, Goodman suggests four "symptoms" of the aesthetic:
syntactic and semantic density discussed previously, as well as syntactic repleteness and exemplificationality. Syntactic repleteness is
what distinguishes a sketch from a diagram or "the more representational among semantically dense systems from the more diagrammatic" by the number and variety of constituent features. In a line
drawing, for example, all surface features are relevant, whereas in
a graph or cross-sectional diagram the only relevant feature is the
exact location of points along a line. Exemplificationality refers to
the properties which are literally exhibited (e.g., trochaic footing,
sonata-allegro form) or expressed (e.g., melancholy) by a work as
contrasted with those a symbol may describe, name, or represent.
Together the four symptoms may be conjunctively sufficient or
disjunctively necessary for the aesthetic; taken separately, they are
neither necessary nor sufficient. It should be noted that, by this
analysis, literature and music qualify as aesthetic; though these systems meet syntactic characteristics of notationality, they exhibit the
aesthetic symptoms of repleteness and exemplification.

All this is quite distinct from the question of aesthetic merit.
Whether an experience or symbol is aesthetic depends less upon

11. Ibid., p. 118.

what we feel or the quality of the work or performance than upon
the presence or absence, dominance or subordinance of certain sorts
of symbol relations.

SYMBOLS AND THE PERCEPTION OF THE WORLD

Given the task of wedding a theory of symbols to a psychology
of perception and symbol use, it is appropriate to ask how symbols
mediate our perception of the world. Widely diverging views on
this question have been defended. Whorf, for instance, claimed that
in acquiring a language we dissect reality in ways that are "codified
in the patterns of our language." [12] In this view, the world appears
to be the arbitrary construct of an infinitely creative perception
strongly constrained by the particular symbol systems at its disposal. At the opposite extreme is the view that at least certain
symbol systems incorporate incorrigible standards of fidelity that
transcend differences in style, culture, or learning. Thus, Gibson
has argued that laws of perspective in pictorial representation are
not merely conventional but reproduce on flat surfaces significant
aspects of the light patterns that originate from the world of objects.[13] This suggests that our perception should require less interpretive activity as our symbol systems become increasingly accurate,
culminating in a veridical passive form of perception of the world
as it really is. Direct perception and perception via a symbol system would ultimately become equivalent in their essential aspects.
Our own view, reflected in the research described below, is that
there is no *one* way that things really look, nor any one way that
the world really is; rather the world is as many ways as it can be
accurately described.[14] In other words, the fidelity of a symbol
system depends upon the accuracy of the information about the
world that can be obtained from knowing how to use and understand the system. This holds for pictures quite as much as for natural languages or musical scores. The theory of symbols described

12. B. L. Whorf, "Science and Linguistics," in J. B. Carroll, ed., *Language,
Thought, and Reality: Selected Writings of Benjamin Lee Whorf* (Cambridge:
M.I.T. Press, 1957).

13. J. J. Gibson, *The Senses Considered as Perceptual Systems* (Boston:
Houghton Mifflin Co., 1966).

14. N. Goodman, "The Way the World Is," *Review of Metaphysics* 14
(1960): 48-56.

herein is most compatible with a view of perception as an active, constructive process which can give us information about the world without creating it *ex nihilo* or merely copying it.

In this context we should record our own hesitancy in contrasting "symbols" with "real objects" or "the *real* world." Though the child's initial commerce with the world may seem devoid of symbolic overtones, symbols rapidly come to play an important and perhaps determining role in one's knowledge of the world. Symbols are part of the real world, though they need not be as physical as Dr. Johnson's rock; and even the rock will function as a symbol when it refers to or exemplifies sundry properties (such as solidity, thrust, or prudence). To regard an object in a nonsymbolic way may become as difficult as to perceive that object with an innocent eye. And even when dealing with "direct" action and experience, our behavior appears to be mediated through internal symbol systems—the codes and cognitive processes to which considerations such as notationality are highly relevant. *Rather than divorcing the symbolic from the real, we seek to demonstrate the reality and pervasiveness of symbol systems.*

POSSIBLE INTERPRETATIONS AND MISINTERPRETATIONS

The conceptual framework summarized here is a novel one which has sometimes been misinterpreted by those accustomed to traditional approaches in semiotics. We would like to review some of the points where confusions have arisen.

1. We are not interested in notationality alone. Notationality is but one of the many kinds of symbolic references, including description, representation of various sorts, and literal and metaphorical exemplification. Indeed, strict notationality as a measure of symbol systems is an *ideal construct* which, like Boyle's law, refers to an extreme combination of factors. There are many permutations or departures from the various conditions of notationality and we are interested in examining these departures and the psychological consequences which follow from them (e.g., the problems encountered in working with dense symbol systems in the arts).

2. Notational symbol systems are neither better nor worse than non-notational ones. Diverse symbol systems have different possibilities and limitations; if there are problems encountered in working with "dense media," there are also fresh possibilities inherent in such systems. As later sections demonstrate, such highly nonnotational mat-

ters as picturing, imitation, and style perception are very much our focus, and the particular challenges which they pose for perceivers and producers are a matter of great interest.

3. Similarly, notational systems are neither inherently easier nor more difficult to "read" or "learn" than other symbol systems. It is sometimes proposed that children are better at interpreting pictures than language, and, by implication, that notational symbol schemes are more difficult to assimilate than dense ones. However, there appears to be nothing inherent in the pictorial mode which makes it easier to read. There can be complex pictures which are very difficult to "read" as well as simple notational schemes (such as one consisting of only two characters) which pose no problems. Furthermore, the fact that an individual is viewing a picture is no proof that he is treating the picture as a dense, nonnotational scheme. Indeed, children often will treat a certain class of pictures as equivalent characters denoting a cat or a bird, while failing to take into account the dense and replete aspects of the pictorial symbol. Difficulty of learning and reading seems more likely to be due to the complexity of a realm than to its notationality.

4. *Notational systems must not be confused with practical or "working" notations.* Neither is notationality limited to "practical" notations (like print or scores), nor do all "practical notations" fulfill the requirements of notationality. Practical notations are responses to various exigencies rather than attempts to fulfill fine logical requirements. Some notations, such as certain of those devised for avant-garde music, deviate in part or in toto from the semantic and syntactic requirements for notationality; other systems not usually called notations, such as cattle brands, are notational.

5. Notationality is neither limited to nor equivalent with what has been written down. Both spoken (or "sound") and written English are notational schemes, while neither fulfills the semantic requirements for a notational system. Traditional Western music would fulfill the requirements for notationality (with the exceptions noted above) even if scoring had not developed in its present form.

Are there, nonetheless, certain domains which lend themselves particularly well to the devising of a "notational notation"? As a practical matter a notation can be devised for any domain that can be digitalized—separated into sets of discrete elements. The crux is whether such a digital demarcation reflects the factors which have been regarded as important within a culture. Thus, in dance, an antecedent classification of performances into performances of the same work existed before the advent of Labanotation, which thus codified important facets of a tradition. In contrast, no such antecedent tradition or codifying of identifying features exists for painting. Any selection of features in a painting (size, location, etc.) could be made the basis for a notational system, but such "arbitrary" notations would ignore the repleteness of paintings which make every feature of the painted surface essential. Any domain can be notationalized; at issue is the utility of such an exercise.

6. Finally, *no inscription is in itself notational or nonnotational.* It is the system of symbols which is notational or nonnotational and the same artifact may participate in different systems. For instance, a pictured silhouette seen as a traffic warning sign is part of a notational system; all that is relevant is its clear reference to one of a few hazards. The same picture hung in an art gallery is seen as highly nonnotational; subtleties of contour, nuances of form become central constituents of the symbol in its gallery setting. More generally, any visual, auditory, tactile, or even multisensory element may function in a dense, partially dense, or notational system. What is crucial is not its physical dimensions but rather its relation to other symbols and the particular way in which the perceiver elects to process and view it.

In the pages that follow we will review research which has sought to ferret out the psychological and educational implications of the theory of symbols. Of the numerous strands of research undertaken by the several members of Project Zero, we will focus on those lines which deal most directly with questions of notationality. And we will apply the concept of notationality in two ways: as a means of classifying the various kinds of symbol systems which figure in human activity; as a model of the way in which certain "psychological" or "cognitive" mechanisms may operate. We are concerned, in other words, with the interactions between the individual who possesses a range of perceptual and motor skills and the symbols with reference to which these skills are built up, utilized, and modified. We begin by reviewing evidence on a possible fit between psychological processing and symbol systems— and in doing so we shall contrast "linguistic" or notational schemes with "nonlinguistic" or nonnotational schemes.

Research on Symbol Systems and Notationality

SYMBOL SYSTEMS AND BRAIN ORGANIZATION

Our logical analysis has raised the possibility that different psychological processes may be involved in working with systems which are essentially "linguistic" and with systems which are dense, replete, and "nonlinguistic." In an effort to test this hypothesis, the literature of psychology and education was reviewed, and some support in favor of the division between linguistic and nonlinguistic systems was gathered from an unexpected area: study of the effects of brain damage.

A large body of evidence, gathered from normal subjects, brain-damaged subjects, and individuals whose hemispheres have been disconnected for medical reasons seemed to indicate that the bifurcation between linguistic and nonlinguistic systems is honored by the brain. The left hemisphere, dominant in a great majority of individuals, appears to be involved principally in dealing with verbal material, with material that is easily codable, with abstract and logical forms of thought. In contrast, while extensive damage in the right hemisphere leaves these faculties relatively unimpaired, such damage affects an individual's ability to make subtle kinds of discriminations between patterns, to process and remember strange visual forms, to exhibit appropriate emotional reactions to situations—in general, to deal adequately with dense symbol systems.[15]

Initial acquaintance with neurological evidence suggested that the distinction between linguistic and nonlinguistic systems was a property of the human nervous system. However, a more thorough review of relevant case studies has indicated the extreme difficulty of documenting the "psychological reality" of a logical bifurcation between linguistic and nonlinguistic systems. Most of the studies can be explained by an alternative theory that the right hemisphere deals primarily with unfamiliar material, while the left hemisphere is dominant for the processing of familiar (and hence easily codable) materials. The apparent right hemisphere superiority in processing subtle patterns can be explained by the unfamiliarity (and lack of available encodings) of such designs. One implication of this position is that, at first, all patterns may be processed by both hemispheres, or by the right hemisphere alone, with the left hemisphere gradually taking over the function of dealing with patterns as they become familiar (and more subject to notational differen-

15. B. Milner, "Laterality Effects in Audition," in *Interhemispheric Relations and Cerebral Dominance*, ed. V. B. Mountcastle (Baltimore: Johns Hopkins University Press, 1962); A. R. Luria, *The Higher Cortical Functions in Man* (New York: Basic Books, 1966); D. Kimura, "Functional Asymmetry of the Brain in Dichotic Listening," *Cortex* 3 (1967): 163-78; R. W. Sperry et al., "Interhemispheric Relationships," in *Handbook of Clinical Neurology*, vol. 4, ed. P. J. Vinken and G. Bruyn (Amsterdam: North Holland Publishing Co., 1969), pp. 273-90.

tiation). The fact that language is so overlearned and familiar a means of dealing with the world makes a crucial test between the "linguistic" and the "familiarity" hypotheses of hemispheric specificity difficult to envision.[16]

Examination of the mnemonic capacities of brain-injured persons cast further doubt on the accuracy, in its strict form, of a description of the left hemisphere as the linguistic one. Earlier studies had suggested that memory was "material specific"; subjects who had difficulty dealing with "verbal" materials failed irrespective of the modality (visual or auditory) of presentation, while subjects who had difficulty with "nonverbal, meaningless patterns" failed on both auditory and visual presentation. This position supports the model of brain specialization outlined above. When subjects were tested on short-term memory, however, the results were different. Asked to recognize or recreate patterns a few seconds after initial exposure, subjects gave evidence that their memories were "modality specific"; one group of subjects had difficulty with auditory input, whether the material was linguistic or not, while another group, suffering from a different type of brain damage, had difficulty with visual material, again independent of the "verbalness" or density of the presented material. In these studies, there was prior determination that the difficulty lay in retention of information, not in initial processing and recognition of the stimuli.[17]

Based on this limited evidence, we have hypothesized that symbolic material may initially be processed on a modality-specific basis, with the traces of this initial processing persisting in short-term memory. In contrast, longer-term storage and the capacity to deal with this material on subsequent presentation may reflect the nature of the material and, in particular, its degree of notationality or "linguisticness." The complex picture which is emerging indicates that the nervous system, as manifest in psychological processes, may not faithfully reflect any single logical analysis. The roles played by language, notationality, familiarity, and codability remain to be sorted out. Nonetheless, it is through the kind of examination of symbol systems undertaken by Goodman that a test

16. Cf. H. Gardner, "A Psychological Investigation of Goodman's Theory of Symbols," *The Monist*, in press.

17. I. Samuels, N. Butters, and P. Fedio, "Short-term Memory Disorders Following Temporal Lobe Removals in Humans," *Cortex* 8 (1972): 283-98.

of the psychological organization of symbol processing becomes possible. And despite the intricate picture that is emerging, the basic point that the brain processes linguistic and nonlinguistic forms of information at different loci and in a different manner seems well supported at the present time. That these differences have pedagogical consequences seems likely, but little direct evidence exists on this issue.

Supplementing investigation of the general relevance of the theory of symbols to psychological processing, several studies have focused on particular symbol systems and on the uses of notations in the investigations of psychological processes. We turn first to research which has examined the dense and replete systems prominent in the arts. One example of this effort to elucidate dense symbols is a consideration of how pictorial symbols inform, that is, how they give information about that to which they refer.

HOW PICTORIAL SYMBOLS INFORM

Examples of informing are very straightforward. A painting of George Washington informs us that he wore a wig, had piercing eyes, and so on. A sentence, "John is short, fat, and bald," informs us of John's physique. A number of commentators have discussed perception of pictures in terms of the information they offer without, however, offering a comprehensive account of what "information" means.[18] The aim of recent work by Roupas has been to achieve some formalization of this slippery concept.[19]

The examples given suggest a simple formalization which proves remarkably useful for many problems: the information a symbol conveys is taken to be the properties of the referent that can be inferred from the symbol. One pregnant concept that readily follows is that of "imitative" informing, which occurs when a property of the symbol implies the very same property of its referent. For example, a black and white photograph is (roughly speaking) imitative with respect to relative whiteness, but a photographic negative is not.

This notion of "imitative" finds its strength in the context of the

18. Cf., e.g., J. J. Gibson, "The Information Available in Pictures," *Leonardo* 4 (1971): 27.

19. G. Roupas, "Logical Problems in the Definition of Pictures" (Ph.D. diss., Harvard University, in preparation).

many misguided attempts to construe pictures, sculpture, etc., as "imitations" of reality without explaining any rigorous sense of imitative and without accounting for the fact that representational art obviously differs in many respects, such as often being on a flat surface, from the objects represented. Accordingly, pictures cannot be strictly imitative with respect to spatial depth properties because such properties obviously do not apply—or apply only trivially—to the flat surface of the picture. But surface properties such as color, relative brightness, profile, shading, and the like, may be imitatively given by the picture.

How, then, can one read pictures for depth? To cite one example, recent research by Perkins [20] has revealed that although people tend to see spatial corners as right-angular (i.e., having three right angles), not all drawn corners formed by the meeting of three lines could geometrically be images of right-angular spatial corners. And those that could not be are not generally interpreted by viewers as representing right-angular corners. In other words, in this experiment the human eye respects the geometry of the situation. In implicational terms, "not meeting certain angular inequalities" for the picture yields the inference "does not represent a right-angular corner." Many traditional depth cues, occlusion, perspective convergence, etc., lend themselves to similar framing.

The discussion has been proceeding implicitly in the context of a "projective" system of picturing. This is of course just one of many pictorial systems that have been employed. Inferences appropriate within one may not be appropriate within another. In Egyptian drawings where rectangular corners are "flattened out" onto the page,[21] the above-mentioned indicators of right-angular corners make no sense at all. This emphasizes the importance of relativizing discussion of picturing to particular systems of picturing, and opens the way for a final example where keeping systems straight is quite important: caricatures.[22]

A peculiarity of caricature is that two systems are at work at

20. D. Perkins, "Geometry and the Perception of Pictures: Three Studies," *Harvard Project Zero Technical Report*, no. 5, 1971.

21. R. Arnheim, *Art and Visual Perception* (Berkeley: University of California Press, 1954), p. 96.

22. D. Perkins, "A Definition of Caricatures" (Unpublished paper, 1973).

the same time. On the one hand, a caricature can be read as picturing a facelike spatial form with, for instance, a nose three inches long, an absurdly weak chin, and so on. On the other, that same caricature can be read as providing information about the person it stands for, a person whose nose is not *that* long, nor chin *that* weak. The correct inference would be something like: this person's chin is somewhat weak; this person's nose is longer than average. These features of the caricature specify directions of deviation from physiognomic norms, but not the exact magnitudes of deviation. Thus caricature both describes a metrically exact but nonexistent three-dimensional space form (which a sculptor could model from the picture) and the metric trends of its subject's face.

One may well question the value to any artist of knowing about such things as "imitations," "systems of picturing," and so on; that is a most difficult and subtle issue. But hard to dismiss is the value to the aesthetician, the art historian, the critic, and not least to the educator. Consider the consequences of his supposing that realism in art amounts to projective drawing styles, or that there is really only one basic system of pictorial representation, certain foreign or "primitive" arts being viewed as unsophisticated statements in that system rather than as statements in another language. Or consider the damage of supposing that the teaching of technique is stultifying. For what does stultify is constraining the student artist to acquaintance with only one system; some adequate technique to deal with a given system is a necessity that frees the student to work effectively in it. Or consider the cost of ignoring the alternative communicational advantages of different schemes of representation: information-rich photographs versus the selection and emphasis of caricature versus the circuit diagram, which only represents connectivity of components, variations in the layout of such diagrams serving solely to explain the connectivity.

SEARCH STRATEGIES IN DENSE SYMBOL SYSTEMS

One of several themes underlying the theory of symbols has been that the nature of a symbol system employed for some purpose constrains the sorts of skills and abilities necessary for interpreting or producing within that system. Of particular interest is the question of how properties of symbol systems employed in the arts might create special problems. We shall consider here the challenge to the artist posed by two "symptoms of the aesthetic": repleteness and density.

A central process in the artist's or scientist's functioning is search —the subconscious or conscious exploration of alternatives. In replete and dense symbol systems, search presents a special problem because the search space is multidimensional, with many different aspects of the art work counting as significant (repleteness), and these dimensions often consisting of a continuous range of alternatives (density). To meet this problem, the artist may adopt strategies to limit the number of dimensions he searches at one time and adopt strategies for searching a continuum of possibilities.

Some examples of search strategies will illustrate how these notions can be used. The collage medium shows overtly what are often internal procedures. An artist may rotate a fragment holding its position constant, and then change position, holding its orientation constant. Thereby he limits the dimensions searched at any one time. The artist might deal with the continuum of possibilities offered by orientation through a partial sampling strategy, placing the fragment at a few disparate alternate angles, finding one that seems most suitable, then attempting finer variations around that.

The linguistic arts, too, are an appropriate domain for the investigation of search strategies. Consider a poet seeking a rhyme; he may choose from whatever occurs to him; he may go through the alphabet—ache, bake, cake, drake; he may consult a rhyming dictionary. Here the symbols themselves (words being a symbol scheme) are not continuously variable. But the symbols find their referents in the semantically dense range of all possible meanings and connotations. When the poet designates the appropriate connotations, he has selected a "position" in this dense range and his problem is to find an appropriate symbol in the articulate and discontinuous range of words to render the desired connotation. Because the range of reference is richer that the symbol scheme, one will often not find the word one wants. One useful strategy here is metaphor, another is circumlocution.

There is no lack of general questions about heuristics of search: What is the full range of strategies in fact adopted for a particular art form? How do various artists acquire these and can these be usefully taught? Are some disabilities of would-be artists ascribable to inept searching practices? The examples offered here have dealt with the artist overtly and deliberately seeking to manipulate his channels of communication. Underlying this is the enormous substrate of unconscious routinized search processes that are always active in human cognition in any area. The necessities of processing that a symbol system or medium imposes by virtue of its properties offer one route into the analysis of these subtle phenomena.

A NOTATION FOR RHYTHM PERCEPTION

In addition to probing the properties of particular symbol systems, our investigations have been concerned with properties such as rhythm and style which cut across different symbol systems and play a pervasive role in the arts. Here the concept of notationality is brought to bear on the perceiver's cognition of the work. The lack of a clear notion of rhythm has stood in the way of analyzing its place in symbolic communication. The need is not for a means of prescribing performance, as does conventional music notation, but of describing the organization, structure, or orderliness that a listener perceives in a rhythmic stimulus. The difference becomes striking when it is recognized that a piece of music is often rhythmically ambiguous, lending itself to various nuances by the performer and also to different hearings even of the same recording by the listener.

As a partial solution, Perkins and Howard [23] have devised a notation for the perception of rhythm in music. Two aspects of rhythm, called "clustering" and "counting," are highlighted. "Counting" is a generalization of the conventional concept of meter. The listener hierarchically organizes the sequence of notes into cycles of equal time period; larger cycles are composed of smaller cycles and one level of cycling is the measure. "Clustering" extends the notions of upbeat and downbeat; short sequences of notes are heard as forming a group, with one note at either end or in the middle standing out as an accent. A listener may record the counting and clustering patterns he perceives on a score for the music, using a system of nested horizontal brackets. The cluster-

23. V. Howard and D. Perkins, "Toward a Notation for Rhythm Perception" (Unpublished paper, 1972).

ing notation is in some respects a revision of that proposed by
Cooper and Meyer,[24] a revision hopefully in the direction of testable psychological theory.

But how can such notations as these provide empirically testable models of perceptual phenomena? The hopeful answer is that
experiments in which subjects match, identify, tap back, or transform and tap back rhythms presented to them can be described and
analyzed by means of the notations. Just such experiments are now
underway. Critical to this effort is whether the rhythm notation is
a "notational notation" in Goodman's sense. The usefulness of the
notation as a psychological theory depends on the possibility of
always (finite differentiation) and consistently (semantic disjointness) being able to transcribe a hearing or to judge that a notated
passage "fits" a hearing. If these conditions are not met, the notation cannot fulfill its analytic function. It appears at present that
the other conditions are met trivially and these crucial two are in
fact met by the notation, though for some examples determination
has been difficult (owing to individual differences in perception,
the effects of multiple hearings, and so on).

Here Goodman's criteria are seen as relevant not just to the
study of overt symbols in communication but to the framing of
models which describe internal cognitive processes, such as those
involved in the perception of rhythm in various domains. The
processes may themselves be in part a consequence of efforts to
deal with symbolic and nonsymbolic aspects of the world. For another example of the mechanisms involved in dealing with aesthetic
(and nonaesthetic) products, we turn briefly to some studies of
style perception.

INVESTIGATIONS OF STYLE PERCEPTION

Like rhythm, style cuts across the various art forms, even as it
is a crucial component of each. A variety of studies by Gardner
of children's capacity to detect the styles of diverse artists have
uncovered a consistent pattern: younger children tend to focus on
the dominant subject matter or figure in a work of art and to assume that two works containing the same figure will be produced

24. G. Cooper and L. Meyer, *The Rhythmic Structure of Music* (Chicago:
University of Chicago Press, 1956).

by the same artist, irrespective of strong differences in other aspects of the work. These children bring a rigid "figural" or "subject-matter" approach to the task. It is only the older child, on the verge of adolescence, who shows some spontaneous awareness that subject matter is not a reliable guide to style, who attends to the dense aspects of the work, and who bases his judgment on less "linguistic" aspects of works, such as expressiveness, texture, overall composition.[25]

To determine whether younger children fail to perceive the denser aspects of a painting, or whether they do perceive these aspects but are overpowered by the more dominant figural aspects, a training task was carried out with young elementary school children, seven to ten years of age. This study provided clear evidence that young children are able to sort on the basis of style and, hence, do perceive at least some of those dense features of stimuli thought central for style detection.[26] Studies using literary and musical materials suggested,[27] in fact, that preadolescents may be especially sensitive to some of these subtle aspects of stimuli, while adolescents, who bring an abstract and categorical approach to these tasks, exhibit impoverished access to the richness and repleteness of artistic works. For example, sixth-graders surpassed older children in a task of musical-style detection. The older subjects appeared to make judgments based on their knowledge of the categories of musical analysis, while younger subjects tended to rely on their less linguistically mediated, noncategorical "feeling" or "sense" of the work.

Between the "subject-matter orientation" of the young child and the "abstracting" or "categorical" tendency of the adolescent, there seems to be a period of several years, during which children show a special openness to the subtleties of the dense symbol systems in-

25. H. Gardner, "Style Sensitivity in Children," *Human Development* 15 (1972): 325-38; H. Gardner, "Children's Sensitivity to Painting Styles," *Child Development* 41 (1970): 813-21; H. Gardner and J. Gardner, "Children's Literary Skills," *Journal of Experimental Education* 39 (1971): 42-46; H. Gardner, "Children's Sensitivity to Musical Styles," *Merrill-Palmer Quarterly* 19 (1973): 67-77.

26. H. Gardner, "The Development of Sensitivity to Figural and Stylistic Aspects of Paintings," *British Journal of Psychology* 63 (1972): 605-15.

27. Gardner, "Children's Sensitivity to Musical Styles," op. cit.; Gardner and Gardner, "Children's Literary Skills," op. cit.

volved in the arts. This sensitivity appears to emerge at an earlier
time with respect to art forms which do not employ linguistic
schemes. While the child contemplating a literary work has a tendency to treat it in a digital manner, focusing only on its manifest
"figures," the same child will find it easier to attend to the non-
figural aspects of a painting, given the greater number of percepti-
ble dimensions which do not lend themselves readily to notational
treatment.[28] The "notationlike" processes relevant to rhythm perception play a less clear (and perhaps less positive) role in style
perception. Such findings have implications for the time, sequence,
and materials appropriate for introducing the concept of style to
the student.

Educational Implications

Now that the theory of symbols and some research stimulated
by it has been reviewed, we may consider certain educational implications. Some follow directly from the research described above,
others from our general orientation. We shall begin by pointing to
a few of the conceptual clarifications it has yielded, then proceed
to more specific developmental and educational sequellae.

CONCEPTUAL CLARIFICATIONS

Goodman's classification of symbol systems, and particularly his
notion of notationality, has permitted a comparison of various symbols along a logically specifiable dimension. Though there is no
claim that symbol systems can be classified only along these lines,
at least one reliable basis for distinguishing between words and
pictures, scientific and aesthetic discourse, scores, scripts, and
sketches has been propounded. Untenable dichotomies, such as the
verbal and the visual, have been replaced by the more plausible
poles of notationality and nonnotationality. Vague terms like *information* and *imitation* have been given analytic power through a
clearly defined application to relevant domains.

It was initially thought that Goodman's distinctions might be
faithfully reflected in the nervous system (or vice versa) but so
simple an isomorphism no longer seems likely. Nonetheless, that

28. H. Gardner, "On Figure and Texture in Aesthetic Perception," *British
Journal of Aesthetics* 12 (1972): 40-59.

some distinction exists between the psychological processing of languagelike and nonlanguagelike symbols seems fairly reliably established.[29] Thus, in dealing with words, numbers, and other symbols of a notational ilk, the individual naturally and productively comes to make discrete replicable distinctions. In dealing with paintings and other artistic works, on the other hand, the individual must resist the tendency to categorize in a limited number of replicable ways, taking care instead to sample as much of the infinite density and repleteness of the symbol as practicable. Both the analyst and the practitioner are cautioned against assuming an easy translation between different symbols with different properties, though of course rough equivalences and similarities are not to be excluded. Yet caution is in order; similarity may be determined by the nature of the symbol systems involved rather than by being a product of direct judgment by a naïve (but "truth-knowing") sense system.[30] We favor allowing the nervous system to tell us, by its generalizations and sortings, which symbols and situations are "similar" to one another.

Regrettably, this discussion casts little light on the important question of whether specific sense systems (vision, audition) or specific media (film, lecture) are particularly suited or unsuited for particular symbol systems. These questions can and should be subjected to empirical investigation. The present theory contributes through suggesting one way in which symbol systems can be classified on an a priori basis.

NOTATIONS

One central concept of the theory of symbols—that of notationality—raises a number of provocative psychological and educational issues. The brain-damage evidence indicates that the human may not immediately treat notational (linguistic) systems in a distinctive way; rather, as the brain becomes sensitive to the linguistic elements implicit in a symbol system, it may gradually come to

29. Cf. L. R. Brooks, "Spatial and Verbal Components of the Act of Recall," *Canadian Journal of Psychology* 22 (1968): 349-68; P. Kolers, "Some Modes of Representation," in *Communication and Affect*, ed. P. Pliner et al. (New York: Academic Press, forthcoming).

30. Goodman, "Seven Strictures on Similarity," op. cit.

treat it in a manner different from denser, less differentiated systems. This points to the more general conclusion, emphasized by Kolers, that one must learn how to deal with, to "read," any symbol system,[31] even as one learns to read music, mathematics, maps, or models. The misconstruals and mistakes children make in dealing with symbols, and the deficits encountered in individuals suffering from focal brain damage, only serve to underscore the constructive processes involved in symbol use. Questions arise as to when formal instruction in reading a notational system should begin, how skill in reading dense symbol systems can be developed, and what form instruction should take.

Though there are no ready answers to these questions, our work with children has suggested some general principles. To take an example from music instruction, traditional practice has emphasized the importance of musical notation, a system which begins from the single note, and gradually builds up to larger units such as measures, phrases, and sections. Yet research on the child's initial encounter with a musical work provides convincing evidence that the child first experiences a piece as a relatively undifferentiated whole, only gradually becoming able to pick out themes and sections within this whole.[32] Though this "global" or "contextual" approach to the piece may cause him to miss detailed features, it often engenders a sensitivity to general affinities and differences among works which a more atomistic approach might miss. Indeed, younger children may have keener sensitivity to musical style than their older counterparts, and they appear to recognize an underlying rhythmic structure which is missed by subjects trained in traditional Western notation.[33]

Such evidence, supported by research with diverse art forms, indicates that, at the very least, caution should be exercised before the child is formally introduced to a notational system or asked to master traditional notational approaches to it. It may be preferable to embrace a procedure where considerable free exploration in a

31. P. Kolers, "Reading" (Invited address at the 1971 Meeting of the Canadian Psychological Association).

32. J. Bamberger, "Thinking about Time" (Unpublished paper, 1971).

33. J. Bamberger, unpublished research, 1972.

symbol system is encouraged, and the child's own categorical propensities can be realized; more structured traditional approaches should be introduced slowly and the child should have ample opportunity to devise his own (perhaps more appropriate) modes of analysis and notation. Indeed, the discovery and description of notational systems should not imply that these systems have a necessary place in the curriculum. It is debatable whether a good dancer or musician need know standard notations, except perhaps at a late stage of his career. Often these notations serve best as aids to the teacher or analyst, rather than as necessary features of the student's armament; however, they may well have a constructive use for creative artists, facilitating consideration and recording of alternatives by composers, choreographers, or directors.

DEVELOPMENT AND TRAINING

The literature on human development suggests appropriate and inappropriate methods of instruction in handling diverse symbol systems in the arts and the sciences. Knowledge of developmental norms and stages would seem essential to a determination of the optimal time to introduce concepts related to particular systems or groups of systems.[34] While a review of relevant literature cannot be undertaken here, the general trend with age toward adopting a "notational" or "linguistic" approach to experience should be noted. If it is true that very young children tend to treat symbols primarily in terms of their evident "subject matter" properties, it seems equally clear that adolescents and older persons in our society bring a strong categorical, analytical, and abstract approach to their activity with symbols. In view of this tendency, the teachers might take special care to bring out the denser, nonnotational aspects of diverse symbols, and to encourage their students to do likewise.

There may, indeed, be something to the adage that the artist is childlike, because he remains open to the subtler, noncodable aspects of experience and does not let a "linguistic" approach dominate his work. It is striking to note, in this context, that painters who have become aphasic do not lose their ability to draw; and, indeed,

34. J. Piaget and B. Inhelder, *The Psychology of the Child* (New York: Basic Books, 1968).

such individuals sometimes realize improvement in their work as a concomitant of speech loss.[35] In contrast, an exclusive concentration on a linguistic, categorical approach may result in a loss of aesthetic sensitivity, as noted by Darwin:

> My mind seems to have become a kind of machine for grinding general laws out of large collections of facts. . . . If I had to live my life again, I would make a rule to read some poetry and listen to some music at least once each week; for perhaps the parts of my brain now atrophied wold thus have been kept active through use.[36]

Accompanying appreciation of developmental milestones must be an assessment of the educational setting and situation. Here, regrettably, there has been little systematic research. Bearing in mind the disparate demands of specific symbol systems, we have attempted a preliminary taxonomy of modes of teaching and modes of learning. Efforts thus far have suggested that certain traditional modes of instruction such as informing, describing, or lecturing may be ill-suited to nonlinguistic systems, forcing finely grained patterns into unduly restrictive categories. However, a different set of instructional methods may well be appropriate for instruction in the use of nonlinguistic systems. Such pedagogical approaches as demonstrating, illustrating, encouraging, providing an enriched environment and a variety of models may result in more appropriate presentations of the desired material and in more flexible learning on the part of the student.

Naturally, in any educational setting, some consideration of standards of success is essential. If the setting of standards has become increasingly difficult in the sciences, it is notoriously elusive in the arts, and in the realms of nonnotational systems. Indeed, if the past history of the arts has taught us anything, it is that current criteria of excellence are likely to be totally rejected by succeeding generations. Faced with this situation, it seems preferable to suspend evaluation of the final symbolic product[37] and to concentrate instead on the skills and abilities which are considered pre-

35. T. Alajouanine, "Aphasia and Artistic Realization," *Brain* 71 (1948): 229-41.

36. C. Darwin, quoted in H. Read, *Education through Art* (New York: Pantheon Books, 1945), p. 255.

37. N. Goodman, "Merit as Means," in *Art and Philosophy*, ed. S. Hook (New York: New York University Press, 1966), pp. 43-44.

requisite to any artistic endeavor. Though having skills by no means insures an interesting and worthwhile product, the lack of skills would seem to prohibit its realization. Analogously, if evaluation of the final artistic product is not possible, the devising of simple problems and an observation of attempts to solve them would seem a less objectionable way of evaluating a student's progress.

This line of argument has fostered an investigation of the nature of skill development, the interaction between skills, the relationship between discipline and creativity, and the nature of the problem-solving processes. We have sought to determine whether particular skills are suited (or inappropriate) for particular symbol systems. Few firm conclusions have yet been reached but the general approach has proved productive, while remaining free of the more severe hazards accompanying traditional education and evaluation approaches. We shall mention only a few preliminary findings here.

While problem-solving has been seen as a crucial aspect of both scientific and artistic education, the emphasis in artistic problem-solving falls on the student's ability to work effectively with a medium.[38] In particular, the kinds of dense media with which artists typically work have peculiar problems associated with them, producing certain pathologies of problem-solving (failure to take into account the revisability of a medium) and favoring certain economical search strategies (such as varying a selected set of the infinite range of possibilities). Particularly productive are problems which direct the artist to focus his attention on an unexpected area and to use skills he has built up, without constraining the particular form of his solution. Thus metaphoric instructions (describe the father as a caged lion) or impossible ones (play this passage as if your elbow were attached to your hand) often suggest novel and appropriate uses for developing skills and lead to unexpected and appealing products. Here a linguistic system of instruction is extended in an effort to deal with a dense domain of influence. Similarly, use of materials where a standard of judgment is obvious, such as the recognizability of a caricature, is often an effective pedagogical ploy.[39]

A certain facility and access to one's developed skills seem a

38. H. Gardner, "Problem-Solving in the Arts," *Journal of Aesthetic Education* 5 (1971): 93-114.

39. Perkins, "Caricature and Recognition," op. cit.

prerequisite for accomplishing the intricate activities involved in artistic production. Yet, as skills become increasingly mastered and routinized, there is the danger that the individual will have difficulty breaking away from these routines and coming up with creative combinations of them. There may even be a tendency to treat non-linguistic systems in a linguistic way. How to train effective, yet flexible, skills remains a mystery, yet encouraging students to use their skills in novel ways clearly seems preferable to their repeated use of a skill in only one routine. Nonetheless, considerable drill, with the competence it produces, has its uses, for without it the student may become overly critical of his immature works and discontinue his activity with a symbolic system.

Concluding Remarks

Our contrast of artistic and scientific education should not be construed as an attempt totally to divorce these two educational realms. Indeed, a major contribution of the theory of symbols is a demonstration that certain arts have much in common with certain sciences. It is true, nonetheless, that the arts do highlight systems characterized by density and repleteness, and our pedagogical thinking has accordingly centered upon ways of utilizing symbols with such characteristics. Yet, certain practices in the sciences, for example, the reading of electron micrographs or the analysis of anatomical structure, involve considerable attention to nonnotational aspects; the techniques espoused in aesthetic education would transfer to these aspects of scientific education. Likewise our analysis of particular aesthetic components, such as rhythm, caricature, and style, should not be restricted to this domain; the processes involved in recognition, pattern differentiation, and organization of stimulation seem equally manifest in the recognition of faces, the identification of gait, and the organization of complex motor patterns.

Though we have presented our views about educational procedures, we should stress their preliminary nature. The theory of symbols offers no easy and foolproof guide to psychology and education. Indeed, some of our earliest hunches have been disconfirmed. What Goodman's orientation does provide is, first, a systematic way of talking about diverse kinds of symbols, second, a challenge to facile and ill-considered classifications of media and modalities, and finally, a series of testable hypotheses about the psychological implications of processing different kinds of symbols. Much of our work has merely involved the sorting out of these hypotheses, a tentative evaluation of their tenability, and the piloting out of a few paradigms. Though in this chapter we have stressed research on notationality, the larger part of our research has concerned other questions involved in symbol use; and many of our findings can be considered without reference to the theory of symbols outlined here.

In lieu of providing answers, we hope to have presented media, communication, and symbol systems in a light different from that in which they are currently viewed. In this effort we have been guided by an interdisciplinary approach, confronting such questions as these: If distinctions are logically valid, can we assume that the human organism will necessarily reflect this logic? Does an analysis of the skills involved in a task suggest how children can and should learn to perform it? Can an inventory of psychological capacities be mapped onto particular sets of symbols and specific educational settings? Some of our empirical investigations have redounded productively upon our conceptual framework, suggesting new ways of thinking about symbol systems. It is our feeling that, whatever may be known about the kinds of symbols involved in scientific practice, remarkably little has been determined about the way in which individuals work with these dense systems and the extent of transfer between these realms. We would call for systematic study of nonnotational systems and for the inclusion of dense and replete symbol systems in the curriculum. For our inquiry has suggested that both linguistic and nonlinguistic kinds of symbols contribute importantly to knowledge and no simple translation between them can be assumed.[40]

40. Much of the research undertaken by members of Project Zero and summarized here has been more fully outlined in various *Technical Reports* issued by Harvard Project Zero. For a relatively complete summary of research, see *Harvard Project Zero Summary Report*, 1972. We thank Professor Nelson Goodman for his comments and guidance throughout the preparation of this paper. Work on this paper was supported in part by Harvard Project Zero (through Office of Education Grant # OEG-0-9-310283-3721 [010], N. Goodman, Principal Investigator; by National Science Foundation Grant # GB-31064, D. Perkins, Principal Investigator; by the Canada Council [grant to Vernon Howard]; by the Social Science Research Council and the Veterans Administration [grants to Howard Gardner]).

CHAPTER III

Modes of Communication and the Acquisition of Symbolic Competence

LARRY GROSS

The Aims of Education

The aims of education include the transmission of knowledge, the instillation of values, and the development of intellectual, physical, social, and artistic skills and competencies. The present paper will concentrate on the nature of these skills and competencies and the conditions governing their acquisition.[1] This emphasis, shaped by certain normative assumptions, is specially conditioned by the way in which the concepts of intelligence and ability are formulated.

Symbolic thought and communication is a uniquely human attainment and can be thought of as the source and substance of culture and civilization. Only through competence in the modes of symbolic behavior does man transcend private experience and achieve even a modicum of creative mastery over his environment. Given the responsibility of contributing to the development of a citizenry which is capable of thinking and of realizing its creative potentialities, we must devise educational systems which permit and encourage the acquisition of the widest possible range of symbolic competence.

In the following it will be argued that thought and knowledge are always active processes and that they exist in a variety of distinct modes. These modes are systems of symbolic thought and ac-

This paper will also appear in G. Gerbner, L. Gross and W. Melody, eds., *Communications Technology and Social Policy*. (New York: Wiley–Interscience, 1973, in press), chap. 13.

1. I would like to thank Ray Birdwhistell, Charles Hoban, Susan Schwartz, and Sol Worth for their useful criticisms of earlier drafts of this paper.

tion which (dependent upon the nature of our biological structures and physical environment) determine the kinds of information we can perceive, manipulate, and communicate.

Meaning can be understood or purposively communicated only within a symbolic mode, and some minimal level of competence is the basic precondition for the creation or comprehension of symbolic meaning within such a mode. It follows that the central goal of education must be the acquisition of competence in the modes of symbolic behavior. This paper focuses on the early stages of education because it is there that the emergence of these competencies seems to be best facilitated or tragically discouraged.

That symbolic thought is created and communicated through more than one mode will be seen to have fundamental implications for the determination of educational techniques and priorities. Among these implications is an emphasis on direct experience and active exploration and manipulation. And, if we accept the importance of direct, immediate, and active participation as fundamental learning processes, we must view the growth of the technological media of communication with guarded enthusiasm.

The view of thinking basic to the arguments to be presented is derived largely from Piaget's formulations of intelligence and learning:

The essential functions of intelligence consist in understanding and inventing, in other words in building up structures by structuring reality. . . . The essential fact . . . which has revolutionized our concepts of intelligence, is that knowledge is derived from action. . . . To know an object is to act upon it and to transform it, in order to grasp the mechanisms of that transformation as they function in connection with the transformative actions themselves.[2]

Thinking is an *activity* embracing the perception and the cognitive processing, storage, and retrieval of structured information. Structured and meaningful information can be received, stored, transformed, and communicated through a variety of symbolic modes which are variously amenable to formulation in symbolic code systems. These modes are partially but not totally susceptible to translation into other modes. Thus, they are basically learned only through actions appropriate to the particular mode.

2. J. Piaget, *Science of Education and the Psychology of the Child* (New York: Viking Press, 1970), p. 27.

To comprehend a concept of "symbolic modes" as related to thinking demands that the common Western assumption (increasingly questioned but still powerful) that thinking is above all a verbal activity be rejected along with the attendant almost exclusive emphasis on verbal skills in education. The primary flaw in our educational system is a fixation on reading, writing, and arithmetic, which has resulted in a blindness to the richness of symbolic thought in other modes. A pioneer in the use of visual methods in education has recently testified that educators "have tended to narrow the spectrum of symbol systems to (a) the verbal and (b) the mathematical." [3]

Accepting the assumption that thinking is a multimodal process requires that we focus on a wide range of physical, perceptual, and cognitive skills that are appropriate and necessary for the full development of intellectual and social potentialities. These skills can and must be acquired fairly early in the educational process. Without them the child is largely dependent for encouragement and direction on the one primary symbolic system which we all attain —verbal language—and will be exposed to other modes almost entirely through impoverished and inherently limited translations into the verbal mode.

This is tragic for two reasons. It guarantees that the child will never attain the ability to be creative (or truly appreciative) in the nonverbal modes, for he will lack the generative ability to go beyond the given. To either produce or comprehend new forms requires skill in manipulating objects and/or symbols within the terms of these modes. Perhaps, more importantly, he will not be motivated to develop and extend his skill in these modes because he cannot experience or share the pleasures which derive only through the exercise and appreciation of these skills and competencies. While it is true that learning a symbolic system via translation may provide the child with many extrinsic rewards of social approval, mere translation does not offer the child (and his teacher) the more powerful and meaningful satisfactions of creative performance. And it is these satisfactions which potentiate his continued growth and development as a multimodal creator and thinker.

3. C. F. Hoban, "Communication in Education in a Revolutionary Age," *AV Communication Review* 18 (1970): 368.

The Multimodal Nature of Symbolic Thought
and Action

A mode of symbolic behavior is a system of potential actions and operations (external and internal) in terms of which objects and events can be perceived, coded cognitively for long-term storage and retrieval, subjected to transformations and orderings, and organized into forms which can elicit meaningful inferences (of whatever level of consciousness) by the creator and/or others who possess competence in the same mode.

Modes of symbolic behavior are not identified with specific sensory systems. The fundamental system of symbolic communication, the lexical mode, requires at the minimum both the auditory and the visual senses. Symbolic modes may be largely organized within a single sensory system, but they may also blend and overlap. Present evidence indicates that the same sensory system is capable of being utilized for performance in various distinct modes of perceptual organization and symbolic communication. Symbolic modes are primarily shaped by the culture; innately determined, universal communicational codes, while a possibility, are of little relevance to the comprehension of the vast range of culturally specific codes of symbolic knowledge and action.

CODES, SYMBOLS AND MEDIA

A code or symbol system may be defined as an organized subset of the total range of elements, operations, and ordering principles correlated with a field of reference that are possible in a given mode or family of symbol systems. In the simplest sense, then, any single language is a code existing within the verbal mode. We invariably encounter symbolic modes in terms of a particular "native" code which will shape our perceptions, memories, and cognitive processes in that mode. Most human beings (throughout history and even today) need never be aware that the code they know is not coextensive with the symbolic mode. Phenomenologically, then, the code—not the mode—is the primary level of analysis.

Most adult Americans, for example, are probably unaware that our base-ten number system is but one of many possible mathematical codes for the symbolic expression of quantities, one code within what we shall subsequently describe as the logical-mathematical mode. While there can be no doubt that we never really transcend our native codes, the precise extent to which knowledge of one code determines our ability to operate creatively in related codes is not known.

Many of our symbolic codes have been formalized through the development of notational systems, such as the alphabet, numerical and mathematical signs, and musical notation. These are remarkably powerful cultural tools for the storage and transmission of symbolic messages. Skill in decoding a notational system and retrieving the stored information in the code in which it was formulated frees one from dependence upon one's immediate experience and allows the widest possible access to the heritage of our culture.

The development of technological media for the storage and transmission of performances and messages also permits the simultaneous exposure of symbolic communications to vast and widely separated audiences. The role and importance of these systems should be neither underestimated nor overrated.

It is clear that our civilization would not exist in its present form had it not been for the development of technologies to record symbolic codes. Very likely, as McLuhan argues, these have operated as well to shape the very nature of the symbolic behavior which they were created to serve.[4] However, the modes of symbolic communication precede the development of whatever technological media may be used to store and transmit their coded products. Moreover, the fact that means exist to make available to the learner the performances of others more competent than he in a symbolic mode does not in any way obviate the necessity for active performance by the learner if he is to acquire such competence himself. Such performances, whether observed directly or via a technological medium, may provide inspiration and guidance, but they will substitute only to a limited extent for active learning.

MODES: PRIMARY, DERIVED, AND TECHNICAL

The *primary* modes of symbolic behavior that roughly characterize a culture are: (a) the linguistic, (b) the social-gestural, (c) the iconic, (d) the logico-mathematical, and (e) the musical. While each of these possesses the basic communicational character-

4. M. McLuhan, *Understanding Media: The Extensions of Man* (New York: Signet Books, 1964).

istics outlined above, it should be noted immediately that they are not all equally elaborated and formalized, that they have many areas of interpenetration, and that they do not exhaust the total range of human symbolic activity.

Hence it is necessary to recognize the existence of *derived* modes which seem to be built upon one or more of the primary modes. Among these I would include poetry, dance, and film as well as technical modes.

Modes of expression are not, of course, restricted to the symbolic. *Technical* modes of knowledge and action involve the application of competence in the primary modes to the understanding of physical and biological systems and structures which function as the basis for skills which are not primarily symbolic in nature. Such skills are involved in the production of material goods and the execution of complex nonsymbolic performances. These practical modes would include the various sciences, engineering and technologies, architecture, and so forth. All of these utilize verbal, social, logico-mathematical, and visual skills (at least) and are therefore dependent upon the prior acquisition of competence in the primary symbolic modes.

The criteria which determine whether a mode will be considered primary are those of independence and self-sufficiency. A primary mode is one which can be identified with (a) a range of objects and events or field of reference, (b) a distinctive memory-storage capacity, (c) a set of operations and transformations, and (d) specific principles of ordering which govern the formulation and communication of meaning, and (e) nontranslatability into other modes. This last point means that information which is coded within one mode will not be capable of being fully recoded in terms of another. The "essence" of a specific symbolic message will be appreciated only within the code in which it was created. There is no adequate verbal translation of an equation in differential calculus, or of an elaborate physical gesture, or a Bach fugue, or the smile of *La Gioconda*. All of these convey specific meanings with great precision, but only within the terms of the proper mode.

The derived modes, while not fully translatable into any one primary mode, are each dependent upon at least one of these for the formulation and communication of symbolic meaning. Scientific knowledge is verified by logico-mathematical operations as well as by empirical observation. Poetry is understood in the context of our verbal competence:

First of all, a poem cannot be regarded as totally independent of the poet's and reader's extrinsic experiences—not if we recognize that our experiences include *language itself*, and that it is upon our past linguistic experiences that poetry depends for its most characteristic effects. Moreover, a poem does not, like the proposition systems of mathematical logic, make its own rules; it adopts and adapts the rules (i.e., the conventions) of nonliterary discourse, so that the principles which generate and conclude the one are conspicuously reflected in those of the other.[5]

There may be a sense, however, in which symbolic communication is always an impoverished translation. It is not clear whether or not creative thought is ever carried on entirely within any symbolic mode. Possibly, the ultimate nature of thought is solipsistic and fluid to the extent that we can never fully communicate the nature of our internal thoughts and feelings. Jakobson, writing to Hadamard about the use of signs in thought, notes:

For socialized thought (the stage of communication) and for the thought which is being socialized (the stage of formulation), the most usual system of signs is language properly called; but internal thought, especially when creative, willingly uses other systems of signs which are more flexible, less standardized than language and leave more liberty, more dynamism to creative thought.[6]

But the most important educational implication of the non-translatability of the symbolic modes is that in the absence of sufficient competence in a mode, one will be unable to fully appreciate, much less be creative in that mode. The vast riches of our culture testify to the almost infinite range of creative and productive performance and the equally unlimited range of sophisticated appreciation and connoisseurship available to those who have achieved the necessary competencies.

THE TACITNESS OF SKILL AND COMPETENCE

Competence in a symbolic mode involves the ability to perceive and/or manipulate symbols. The basic skill is that of receiving and

5. B. H. Smith, *Poetic Closure: A Study of How Poems End* (Chicago: University of Chicago Press, 1968), p. 97.

6. J. Hadamard, *The Psychology of Invention in the Mathematical Field* (New York: Dover Publications, 1954), pp. 96-97.

comprehending an organized symbolic message. The process of reception and decoding is not passive and, it will be argued, the process of acquiring even a minimal level of skill cannot be passive.

Symbolic competence minimally involves (a) knowing the range of symbols and the range referents to which they apply; (b) some awareness of the operations and transformations involved in coding such messages and activities; (c) the ability to store and retrieve information coded in the proper mode; and often, if not always, (d) some awareness of the results of prior performances (by oneself or others) which may serve as the basis for evaluating the quality of the encoded behavior/message.

Beyond these requirements for the proper reception and comprehension (and, possibly, evaluation) of symbolic messages, one may see the development of two complex, distinct, but not mutually exclusive levels of skill in a symbolic mode. These are the levels of creative production and sophisticated appreciation.

Creative activity in a symbolic mode is deeply rooted in the process of reception and comprehension in that same mode. In the most fundamental sense, appreciation is a constant aspect of the exercise of any symbolic skill. One of the most important emphases of the generative grammarians has been that, in order to understand verbal behavior, one must deal with the fact that any member of a linguistic community is capable of, and constantly involved in, creating and comprehending sentences and sentence combinations which are completely novel to the individual.[7] In a higher and more complex sense of the term, we tend to call an individual creative if he can regularly produce organized symbolic objects, events, or messages which are novel (exactly in what sense is a very complicated question) and which satisfy certain criteria (rarely made consciously explicit) of beauty, scientific and/or practical utility, expressive meaning, and so forth. The sine qua non of creative performance is competence in the proper mode. The act of performing creatively is one in which appreciative skill (reception and comprehension) is constantly being exercised, however tacitly and unconsciously, at a high level of competence.

Sophisticated appreciation of organized symbolic events requires

7. N. Chomsky, *Aspects of the Theory of Syntax* (Cambridge: M.I.T. Press, 1965).

competence in perceiving and attending to skillful aspects of the performance, remembering previous performances and comparing them with present ones, understanding the levels of decision-making involved, and evolving and applying criteria for the evaluation of the beauty, utility, expressiveness, and integrity of performances.[8]

Symbolic competence, whether at the level of basic decoding or at more complex levels of appreciation and creativity, is characterized by a further set of psychological properties. The existence of competence is dependent upon extensive and continual action. Skillful action in a symbolic mode is intelligence and knowledge itself,[9] and at the same time it is the only way in which such knowledge can be acquired, maintained, extended, and utilized in creative and productive activity. "Intelligence is skill in a medium, or, more precisely, skill in a cultural medium."[10] All such skills are largely *tacit, transparent*, serve to *involuntarily structure* perception, memory, and cognition, and are *generative*.

In setting out to discuss the nature of science, Polanyi insists on the centrality of the notion of skill, and on its tacitness: "*The aim of a skillful performance is achieved by the observance of a set of rules which are not known as such to the person following them.*"[11]

Basic motor and perceptual-cognitive skills become increasingly less explicit and conscious as they become better "known" through practice. In this sense it seems that skillful activity can be carried on efficiently only when we need not (cannot) consciously and explicitly attend to the ongoing physical, perceptual, and cognitive operations.

At least one of the reasons for this often noted tacit property of skillful action is that, while we tend to conceive of conscious

8. L. Gross, "Art as the Communication of Competence" (Paper presented at the Symposium on Communication and the Individual in Contemporary Society, under the auspices of the International Social Science Council, the International Council for Philosophy and Humanistic Studies, and UNESCO, Rome, 1972), *Social Science Information*, in press.

9. Piaget, op. cit.; idem, *Biology and Knowledge* (Chicago: University of Chicago Press, 1971); D. Olson, *Cognitive Development: The Child's Acquisition of Diagonality* (New York: Academic Press, 1970).

10. Olson, op. cit., p. 193.

11. M. Polanyi, *Personal Knowledge* (Chicago: University of Chicago Press, 1958), p. 49.

and explicit attention in terms of verbally coded information and thought, in fact much if not most of the physical, perceptual, and cognitive elements of skillful performance are not amenable to being coded and comprehended verbally.

It is indeed true, as Polanyi claims, that "we know more than we can tell." [12] We know much that we cannot tell in words but which we tell in other symbolic forms which express and communicate that knowledge. This second sense of the tacit nature of skill is the crucial nontranslatability of knowledge in one symbolic mode into some assumed verbal *lingua franca* of individual consciousness and social communication. This fact is of utmost importance for the development of a method of instruction which would develop skill and competence in a symbolic mode.

Symbolic codes are also involuntary and transparent structurings of thought and action. In the sense defined by Piaget (and implied by Whorf and Sapir), symbolic codes govern our structuring of reality. We assimilate the world via perceptual-cognitive schemata which, although dependent upon innate structure, are developed, modified, and extended through interactions with and accommodations to our environment. Knowledge is acquired and expressed through performance in a medium and the use of that medium becomes automatic and transparent. As we become competent "native speakers," words and sentences in our native language become carriers of meanings and we no longer need pay (or, in fact, can pay) conscious attention to their actual auditory or visual characteristics. We come to hear meanings rather than sounds, and we do so involuntarily.

As evidence of this aspect of lexical transparency, think of the difficulty encountered in training students of linguistics to attend to the actual phonetic aspects of speech and to ignore the phonemically carried meaning. This kind of perceptual transparency involves an involuntary structuring and organization of symbolic information. One cannot voluntarily fail to understand words spoken or written in one's native tongue or voluntarily not hear musical dissonances in a style one has learned (or become familiar with). Beyond a certain level of competence in any symbolic mode, it is

12. M. Polanyi, *The Tacit Dimension* (New York: Doubleday & Co., 1966), p. 4.

only with great effort (actually, with the acquisition of a rather specialized secondary skill) that one is able to avoid structuring a symbolic message in terms of its organized meaning. While it is not at all clear what the "perceptual units" are in the various modes, it is certainly the case that most of us comprehend symbolic messages in organized chunks before we are able to deliberately attend to and evaluate their constitutent elements.

Only when one can perceive, select, store, recall, transform, and order objects, events, and information without constant recourse to nontacit levels of attention and consciousness is one capable of generating or comprehending novel and aesthetically pleasing symbolic performances. In our culture such competence is found almost exclusively in the lexical and social modes.

The acquisition of this fundamental level of appreciative-generative skill, however, requires learning and practice in performance *in the mode itself*. Although much of what we learn and what we hope to teach our children can only, or most efficiently, be learned through a linguistic code, skill and competence in the full range of symbolic modes cannot be acquired in translation.

Varieties of the Symbolic Experience

THE LEXICAL MODE

The fundamental mode of symbolic thought and communication is that of verbal language. This lexical mode is so dominant an element of our consciousness that we have tended to see it as *the* embodiment of thought and intelligence. While not minimizing the central role of the lexical mode in the formation, storage, and transmission of symbolic meaning, that mode must be seen in the context of the full variety of human symbolic experience.

THE SOCIAL-GESTURAL MODE

One of the major achievements of modern cultural anthropology has been the increasingly explicit insight that most human behavior, particularly in the presence of others, is determined by learned, culturally specific modes and patterns which communicate to fellow members of that culture a great deal of precise information about the stable characteristics and situational intentions of the actor.[13] Aside from verbal language, in fact, the social-gestural is the only mode of thought and action which every member of a culture will acquire. It is also, as with verbal language, one which is never really taught via formal instruction but acquired primarily through observation, imitation, and trial and error.

Usually, one will only become consciously aware of the fact that actions and gestures carry decodable information about one's background, intentions, etc., when one is (a) placed in a foreign culture, (b) being trained to deliberately observe such processes (e.g., in ethnographic or psychiatric training), or (c) attempting to consciously convey misleading information. In the latter instance, for example, one can avail oneself of books on etiquette if one wishes to "pass" successfully in social circles in which one was not originally acculturated. Such code-dictionaries are not written for "native speakers" of a culture, who often regard the use of such devices as a sign that the user "doesn't belong."

A child who cannot acquire the basic verbal and social codes of his culture will not be able to function as a normal human being:

A system exists in which (the child) must be assimilated if the society is to sustain itself. If his behavior cannot, after a period of time, become predictable to a degree expected in that society, he must be specially treated. . . . This special treatment can range from deification to incarceration. But ultimately the goal is the same: to make *that child's* behavior sufficiently predictable that the society can go about the rest of its business.[14]

It is an open question whether the other cultural modes have not attained this sort of priority in our culture because we do not yet know how to ensure the successful achievement of competence in them; or, conversely, we have not learned how to cultivate them universally because they are not crucial to the business of our society.

13. R. Birdwhistell, *Kinesics and Context* (Philadelphia: University of Pennsylvania Press, 1970); E. Hall, *The Silent Language* (New York: Doubleday & Co., 1959); idem, *The Hidden Dimension* (New York: Doubleday & Co., 1966); E. Goffman, *The Presentation of Self in Everyday Life* (New York: Doubleday & Co., 1959); idem, *Behavior in Public Places* (Glencoe, Ill.: Free Press, 1963).

14. Birdwhistell, op. cit., p. 6.

THE ICONIC MODE

Arnheim has recently discussed the relation of thought and visual perception.[15] He establishes in great detail the nature, extent, and importance of perceptual-cognitive symbolic behavior which is organized visually in the iconic mode. Minimally, it must be accepted that visual images and symbols are capable of communicating and expressing meaningful information that cannot be formulated in the lexical or, indeed, any other mode. Ivins points out that words, being in essence "conventional symbols for similarities," are incapable of communicating the unique and singular aspects of objects and events that can be depicted visually.[16]

Iconic symbols are highly suitable for the purpose of organizing and communicating information about the spatial, topological nature of objects, about relations between objects in space, and for expressing and evoking emotional responses. To see visual images as merely a peculiar way to tell a story is, as Ivins,[17] Gombrich,[18] Arnheim,[19] and many others have shown, to misunderstand totally the nature of the iconic mode.

A topical issue here is the status of film as a mode of communication. Increasingly we are being told that our children are becoming primarily oriented towards visually communicated information via film and television. A corollary argument has been that they are thus learning a (new?) "visual language" and that educators should accept the conclusion that the "language" used by these media be taught in schools.

Film is considerably more complex than "simple" visual communication in that it is organized in temporally sequential images which do, indeed, require the viewer to exercise skill in order to

15. R. Arnheim, *Visual Thinking* (Berkeley: University of California Press, 1969).

16. W. Ivins, *Prints and Visual Communication* (Cambridge: M.I.T. Press, 1953).

17. Ibid.

18. E. H. Gombrich, *Art and Illusion*, rev. ed. (New York: Bollinger Series, Pantheon Books, 1960); idem, "The Use of Art for the Study of Symbols," *American Psychologist* 20 (1965): 34-50; idem, "Visual Discovery through Art," *Arts Magazine* 40 (November 1965): 17-28.

19. Arnheim, op. cit.

comprehend and appreciate the intended meaning (cf. Panofsky).[20] However, it is not at all clear exactly to what extent this organization is culturally specific or, if so, whether it is a function of the linguistic code of the culture.[21]

Second, it does not seem to be the case that competence in appreciating the meaning conveyed in a film is dependent upon the same degree of performatory skill as has been claimed to be true for the primary modes. Finally, it is highly debatable whether there is any heuristic benefit to be gained in the understanding of how film communicates by starting from the assumption that film is a "language" (cf. Worth for a detailed discussion of this point).[22]

THE LOGICO-MATHEMATICAL MODE

The logico-mathematical mode may be of two rather distinct levels. In his recent book, Piaget describes logico-mathematical knowledge as "one of the three main categories of knowledge, coming between innate structures and knowledge based on physical or external experience." [23] He also notes, however, that it "takes on a differentiated form only in the higher ranges of human intelligence." This is an important distinction, for it allows us to see those aspects of action which are logical in nature, as well as the particular culturally elaborated mode of logical and mathematical thought. In describing the basic category of logico-mathematical knowledge, Piaget further clarifies the independence of knowledge from verbal language:

Logic . . . is not to be reduced, as some people would have it, to a system of notations inherent in speech or in any sort of language. It also consists of a system of operations (classifying, making series, making connections, making use of combinative or "transformation groups," etc.) and the source of these operations is to be found beyond language, in the general coordinations of action.[24]

20. E. Panofsky, "Style and Medium in the Motion Pictures," *Critique* (1947).

21. S. Worth and J. Adair, *Through Navajo Eyes: An Exploration in Film, Communication, and Anthropology* (Bloomington: Indiana University Press, forthcoming).

22. S. Worth, "The Development of a Semiotic of Film," *Semiotica* 1 (1969): 282-321.

23. Piaget, *Biology and Knowledge*, op. cit., p. 4.

24. Ibid., pp. 6-7.

In this sense, then, it would appear that all of the modes of symbolic thought are logical in nature. However, the higher, "differentiated" form of logico-mathematical thinking can most certainly be seen as an organized system of operations which permit those who have acquired the requisite competence to manipulate, store, retrieve, and organize symbolic information in this rather complex and specific code.

The French mathematician Jacques Hadamard obtained statements from many eminent mathematicians about their conceptions of the nature of logico-mathematical thought. The most consistent aspect of these reports was the claim that mathematical thought is not performed in the linguistic mode: "I insist that words are totally absent from my mind when I really think." [25]

THE MUSICAL MODE

In every known human culture there exists a musical code of formally organized communication. At the level of a culturally determined symbolic code, music, like mathematics, expresses and communicates specific but verbally ineffable meanings.

It seems to me quite clear that music, far from being in any sense vague or imprecise, is within its own sphere the most precise possible language. I have tried to imply this by saying that music embodies a certain type of movement rather than that it expresses it. All of the elements of this movement—rhythm, pitch, accent, dynamic shading, tone quality, and others sometimes even more subtle—are, in competent hands, kept under the most exquisite control, by composer and performer alike; the movement that is the stuff of music is given the most precise possible shape. It was for just this reason that both the ancients and the teachers of the Middle Ages accorded to music such high place in educational discipline. By these means, a musical gesture gains what we sometimes call "musical sense." It achieves a meaning which can be achieved in no other way.[26]

The creation or appreciation of musical meaning depends, as in the other symbolic modes, upon the same order of tacit fluency. As Meyer explains:

. . . we perceive and think in terms of a specific musical language just as we think in terms of a specific vocabulary and grammar; and the

25. Hadamard, op. cit., p. 75.

26. R. Sessions, *The Musical Experience* (New York: Atheneum, 1968), pp. 23-24.

possibilities presented to us by a particular musical vocabulary and grammar condition the operation of our mental processes and hence of the expectations which are entertained on the basis of those processes.[27]

Meyer shows that Western music is architectonic and hierarchic in nature and that music appreciation involves the continual arousal of expectations which are confirmed or modified as the listener "recreates" the structural organization of the piece. While this is not the only possible mode of musical organization (cf. Keil),[28] it does seem to be the primary mode of Western "classical" music. The ability to decode the structure of musical organization is dependent upon the competence of the listener in the particular cultural code or style in which a piece has been formed. Musical meaning exists only in the perceptions of those who have acquired specific culturally determined habits and dispositions:

These dispositions and habits are learned by constant practice in listening and performing, practice which should, and usually does, begin in early childhood. Objective knowledge and conceptual understanding [verbally coded information] do not provide the automatic, instinctive perceptions and responses which will enable the listener to understand the swift, subtle, changeable course of the musical stream.[29]

This is a point of crucial importance for the understanding of symbolic communication. Only upon the basis of the competence to appreciate meaning presented in a symbolic mode can one hope to achieve the realization of creative potential in that mode. Early learning, through action and performance in a cultural mode, is necessary for the achievement of appreciative skill, and creative skill can emerge only if the individual has already attained this fundamental competence. The process of creation in a symbolic communicational mode presupposes and constantly involves the process of appreciation. "It is because the composer is also a listener that he is able to control his inspiration with reference to the listener." [30]

27. L. B. Meyer, *Emotion and Meaning in Music* (Chicago: University of Chicago Press, 1956), pp. 43-44.

28. C. M. Keil, "Motion and Feeling through Music," *Journal of Aesthetics and Art Criticism* 34 (1966): 337-49.

29. Meyer, op. cit., p. 61.

30. Ibid., pp. 40-41.

The Acquisition of Skills and Competencies

COMPETENCE IS ITS OWN REWARD

The kinds of activities which lead to the acquisition of skill and competence in the modes of symbolic behavior seem to be intrinsically rewarding. This fact is implicit in the conclusions drawn by White on the basis of evidence from a wide range of research on animal learning, child development, and psychoanalytic processes. White describes a class of behaviors which seem to share a common biological and psychological significance:

> . . . they all form part of the process whereby the animal or child learns to interact effectively with his environment. The word *competence* is chosen as suitable to indicate this common property. Such activities in the ultimate service of competence must . . . be conceived to be motivated in their own right.[31]

Among the behaviors which White claims are motivated by their role in the development of competence are the activities which are crucial for the development of competence in interacting effectively with the symbolically organized aspects of the environment. The intrinsic satisfactions of such activities are related to the playful character of many of the basic experiences in symbolic communication.

> [Play] in its two essential forms of sensorimotor exercise and symbolism is an assimilation of reality into activity proper, providing the latter with its necessary sustenance and transforming reality in accordance with the self's complex of needs.[32]

The pleasures of effective interaction with the environment are not at all limited to the young child's development of competence. At all ages and at all levels the exercise of competence in the skillful manipulation of the physical and symbolic environment provides continual intrinsic satisfaction. In fact, I would claim that the most quintessentially human form of pleasure is that which derives from the exercise of creative and appreciative skills. Moreover, such skills are open-ended. One cannot speak of a point at which competence in a perceptual-performance skill has been completely achieved.

31. R. W. White, "Motivation Reconsidered: The Concept of Competence," *Psychological Review* 66 (1959): 329.

32. Piaget, *Science of Education*, op. cit., pp. 156-57.

Rather, competence is continually being acquired and extended through performance and therefore it is continually satisfying.

LEARNING THROUGH ACTION

All competence in a skillful mode is acquired on the basis of constant practice and repetition (as well as observation and appreciation). While at the higher levels of competence practice may get you to Carnegie Hall, at the initial stages of learning it is the only way to get anywhere. One achieves competence in a medium by slowly building on routines which have been performed over and over until they have become tacit and habitual. This basic repetitious activity can be easily seen in children who derive enormous satisfaction from performing over and over some action which results in a predictable effect. The feeling of efficacy, as White terms it, is the basic and initial form of satisfaction in competence. It is on the basis of a repertoire of often repeated actions that the child can begin to introduce and perceive slight variations and thus extend the range of his perceptual-intellectual competence to more complex forms of organized behavior.

The acquisition of competence in modes of symbolic communication entails the learning of the "vocabulary" for representing objects and events proper to a particular mode, and of the "grammatical" and "syntactical" operations, transformations, and organizational principles which are used to structure these into conveyers of meaning and intention. In our culture some of the basic modes of symbolic knowledge have been formalized in terms of notational systems and technological media. As a result, an important aspect of the acquisition of communicative competence in these modes is the development of skill in manipulating these notational and technological forms.

The most important of the notational systems is the visual recording of phonetic symbols in written language. It does not necessarily follow, however, that skill in reading and writing should be taken as a paradigm for learning and instruction in other modes which may have quite different formal properties.

THE VERBAL FALLACY

A basic corollary of the assumption that thinking is primarily linguistic is the view that skill in reading and writing is a precondition for all meaningful learning. The enormous cultural value of reading skill is undeniable, as it is largely through reading that one can come into contact with the vast realms of stored knowledge which are the key to our highly complex civilization. However, knowledge—in the sense of competence in the linguistic mode—is required in order to learn to read and write in the first place. In fact, based on the work of Piaget, Furth argues that "a school that in the earliest grades focuses primarily on reading cannot also focus on thinking." [33]

While I do not agree with Furth that reading cannot offer the intrinsic satisfactions of competence-extending activities, it does seem clear that an overemphasis on reading skills is detrimental to the fullest development of competence in the nonverbal modes of symbolic knowledge. This approach tends to commit the errors of introducing the child to the nonverbal modes almost exclusively via impoverished verbal translation (which largely consists of applying verbal labels to objects and events coded in these symbolic modes) and, hence, of not allowing the child to engage in active behavior within the modes themselves. Yet this activity is the only route to the acquisition of competence.

The mistaken identification of verbal assimilation of information with the acquisition of knowledge about the referential world is the source of many unfortunate educational practices. Once one has achieved a symbolic skill, it can be highly efficient to use verbally coded information in order to record or convey certain aspects of the knowledge embodied in that skill. But one would not have been able to acquire that skill, in most instances, on the basis of such verbal information. "Verbal description appears never to be equivalent to a motor performatory act." [34]

The realization that we cannot convey most information about the important aspects of reality to children via the linguistic mode is, unfortunately, still relatively rare. One of the most difficult intellectual tasks is that of being able to understand what it means not to know something which one has already assimilated at the level of tacit and transparent knowledge.

33. H. Furth, *Piaget for Teachers* (Englewood Cliffs: Prentice-Hall, 1970), p. 4.

34. Olson, op. cit., p. 200.

. . . whenever it is a question of speech or verbal instruction, we tend to start off from the implicit postulate that this educational transmission supplies the child with the instruments of assimilation as such simultaneously with the knowledge to be assimilated, forgetting that such instruments cannot be acquired except by means of internal activity, and that all assimilation is a restructuration or a reinvention.[35]

We also tend to mistakenly treat the child's ability to repeat verbally coded information as evidence that he has the ability to use that information constructively. The performatory ability of a child, for example, to recite the alphabet is not at all the same as competence in the verbal mode, let alone the same as being able to read. In fact, it is not at all clear whether this ability is a useful or necessary precondition for the development of skill in reading and writing (cf. Robin et al.,[36] Makita,[37] Smith[38]).

At the point at which they begin their "formal education," most children are already quite fluent in the linguistic and social-gestural codes of their culture. If they are to achieve even this not inconsiderable degree of competence in the modes of logico-mathematical, iconic, and musical communication (or in other derived modes), they must be given the same kind of ample opportunity for active exploration and the same kind of responsive and appropriately coded feedback which were necessary preconditions for the emergence of their verbal and social competence. It is only possible to attempt such "instruction" once the initial level of linguistic and social culturation has occurred, but it is impossible to achieve it if one relies primarily on verbally mediated communication and social approval.

THE SEDUCTIVENESS OF THE VISUAL

As psychological research and pedagogic experience have exposed the dangers of the "linguistic fallacy" in education, it has

35. Piaget, *Science of Education*, op. cit., pp. 39-40.

36. P. Rozin, S. Poritsky, and R. Sotsky, "American Children with Reading Problems Can Easily Learn to Read English Represented by Chinese Characters," *Science* 171 (1971): 1264-67.

37. K. Makita, "The Rarity of Reading Disability in Japanese Children," *American Journal of Orthopsychiatry* 38 (1968): 599-614.

38. F. Smith, *Understanding Reading* (New York: Holt, Rinehart & Winston, 1970).

become ever more tempting to turn to the increasingly available and pervasive technologies of visual communication. While it is true that still photography, film, and television are capable of yielding enormous educational benefits and offer valuable opportunities which could not otherwise be realized, they are a mixed blessing. These technologies of communication are not equally appropriate and useful at all levels of instruction and learning.

At the higher levels of education, when basic competence in symbolic modes of communication can be taken for granted, the availability of iconic images is a fundamental requirement for the attainment of skill and knowledge in a great number of specialized fields of intellectual activity. As Ivins has clearly demonstrated, the development of many scientific fields became possible only when it was technologically feasible to produce exactly repeatable pictorial images.[39] The later development of exactly repeatable moving visual images has further extended the range of such specialized intellectual activities through our ability to capture, store, and review movement and action and even permits us, by slowing down or speeding up the rate of viewing, to observe aspects of these events which could never be directly perceived.

Many of these potentials of visual communication are of value also in earlier stages of education. As McLuhan has most clearly indicated, it is more and more the case that we come to know the world as it exists beyond our immediate horizon primarily through the media of electronic telecommunications. We should avail ourselves of these technologies for the instructionally guided exposure of our children to the world they are living in. Several dangers and dysfunctions inevitably arise, however, if we fail to realize the important limitations of these methods and to take into account, once again, the nature of the audience.

One potential dysfunction of improperly conceptualized enthusiasm for the educational use of pictures and film results from the failure to realize that children may not perceive or interpret these images in the way we intend them to. Just as with the verbal transmission of information, we tend to forget that children often lack the assimilative structures necessary to comprehend properly the intended meaning.

39. Ivins, *Prints and Visual Communication*, op. cit.

There is a level of sophistication necessary for the proper understanding of visual images. Pictures and films often convey misleading impressions of scale, distance, time, and relationship. By overcoming the limitations of space and time they may also fail to communicate the reality and importance of these dimensions. More importantly, perhaps, the images conveyed via these media may be deliberately or inadvertently false. The potential for misleading and dissembling, for confusing fiction and reality, is at least as great with photographs and films as with words and actions, and quite possibly much greater.

On the one hand, this would imply that an important task for modern education is the development of a level of sophistication sufficient to permit our children to be aware of this potential danger of communications technologies. On the other hand, however, it is clearly incumbent upon those who utilize these media for instructional aims to themselves be aware of these problems and of the extent to which they themselves are susceptible to them.

There is, however, a more important dysfunction in the reliance upon these media of visual communications at the early stages of learning. It has been argued that verbally coded information is not sufficient for the acquisition of competence in the nonverbal modes of symbolic thought. Similarly, it is a mistake to think that showing the child visually presented images of the actions which constitute performance in a symbolic mode will instill competence in him. One will not learn to compose music or even to play the piano by watching a film of a virtuoso pianist performing.

The observation and imitation of sounds and actions are crucial to the development of verbal communicational competence. They are also a basic part of the process of acquiring any mode of symbolic skill. But the observation is important only insofar as it stimulates the child to perform on his own and insofar as it makes him perform the kind of actions which will evoke meaningful feedback.

. . . if we compare the memories that distinct groups of children retain of a grouping of cubes, according to whether the grouping has been (a) simply looked at or perceived, (b) reconstructed by the child itself, or (c) constructed by an adult while the child watches, we find that the memories produced by case (b) are clearly superior. The demonstration by an adult (c) produces no better results than simple perception (a), which shows once again that by carrying out experiments in the child's presence instead of making the child carry them out, one loses the entire informational value offered by action proper as such.[40]

It is quite possible that one might be able to avoid substituting passive observation for meaningful and instructive action, but there is no reason to assume that this is more easily achieved via pictures and films. Olson found that a particular kind of nonverbal modeling developed by the Montessori school seemed effective in evoking skillful performance in the viewer. The important aspect of this method was that, rather than simply performing the task correctly and smoothly, the model went through a simulated process of trial and error, committing and rectifying errors as well as making the right moves. Thus, Olson concludes, he "indicated to the child what the choice points were, what his alternatives were, and how he was to choose among them." [41]

The medium of live or animated film could quite possibly be used to present performance sequences organized in this fashion. While these would not be a substitute for actual performatory activities on the part of the child, they would be a useful way of introducing a wide range of learning behavior.

As new media emerge, they evoke new forms in which symbolic knowledge and action can be organized and communicated. What we must always keep in mind, however, is that the emergence of new forms of symbolic skill and knowledge at the higher levels of complexity and sophistication does not in any way reduce the vital importance of competence in the basic modes of cultural intelligence and communication. It is folly to assume that new media of technological communication will obviate the necessity for these competencies or provide shortcuts that permit their acquisition without the basic experiences of learning through active performance within the domains of the modes themselves.

Educational Policies and Technological Imperatives

The implications of the arguments presented are not entirely in accord with many of the current technological and economic

40. Piaget, *Science of Education*, op. cit., pp. 35-36.

41. Olson, op. cit., p. 201.

considerations which influence our educational institutions. The position taken with regard to the usefulness of the new forms of communications technology for early education in particular is fundamentally conservative and skeptical. Rather, the conditions necessary for the acquisition of the kinds of skill and competence described above would seem to be as indicated in the following:

1. That the child be exposed to physical and social settings which permit and encourage the initial exploratory behavior in the context of the symbolic modes which develop and extend his competence in effectively interacting with his environment
2. That this exploratory activity and the increasingly competent behavior which it leads to be carried on with the assistance of adults who are themselves skilled and competent in the various modes of symbolic communication, and who are also trained to provide appropriate feedback and reinforcement
3. That, as the child attains higher and more complex levels of competence, he be encouraged and guided in becoming familiar with the existing bodies of stored knowledge and meaning in these modes and thereby develop the ability to apply criteria for judging the aesthetic, scientific, and practical success of his own and others' performances

While this may be a somewhat utopian set of requirements, it is also the only way to evolve a society in which its members can appreciate the highest achievements of the culture and in which creative potential (in any mode) will be developed and expressed.

Even at a more modest level, however, these arguments suggest that the focal points for improvement in educational practice are the provision of proper learning environments and the training of teachers who are competent in the various modes of communication and also sensitive to the particular requirements of early education.

It is obvious, however, that the centralized production and mass distribution of television programs that are viewed by millions of children are faster, easier, and cheaper than the recruitment, training and distribution of teachers, or the accomplishment of fundamental changes in the prejudices and policies of those who already staff our educational institutions. Given the current economic limitations on our school systems, and given the need to improve the educational opportunities of children whose earliest learning environment has not allowed them to attain the level of initial performance skills we expect of children when they enter school, it seems inevitable that we will see more and more attention and resources devoted to centrally produced, mass media–carried education programs.

It will be necessary, therefore, to find means whereby these media can be utilized more successfully to evoke and direct activities which will facilitate the acquisition of skills and competencies in the fullest possible range of symbolic communication modes. At the same time, it is even more important that we work towards the provision of the kinds of settings and the kinds of teachers that are critical for the full acquisition of these skills.

If you want to gain knowledge you must participate in the practice of changing reality. If you want to know the taste of a pear you must change the pear by eating it. . . . All genuine knowledge originates in direct experience (Mao Tse-Tung, *On Practice*).

CHAPTER IV

The Beholder's Share and the Problem of Literacy

HARLEY PARKER

I grew up in a world where kids were allowed to discover everything for themselves, by personal observation rather than formal instruction. Nobody said to us "this is a desk," we learned that that was a desk by other people using the word, calling it "a desk." We began to use that word, too, but we related to that desk in our own way, not because somebody told us that was a desk and that's what you do with it, you write at it, or that is a table and this is a chair and you sit on a chair. We probably used chairs in many different ways, like most kids, but we also knew that you could sit on that chair. We made the same discoveries that other people had made centuries before us, but they belonged to us, they didn't belong to some despot or expert, someone who tells you, I've got the answers, so you quit being curious, quit exploring. That didn't happen to me until I went to school, from then on was a matter of suppression.[1]

Pelletier's account of "growing up Indian" delineates an important difference between an aural tribal culture and a visual literate one—a distinction that marks off our culture, as readers and writers of this book, not only from the Indian culture but also from the youth culture, which has been induced by the electric speed of communication.

The visual is the only sense we have which provides us with an apprehension of connected spaces. Probing space with the eye involves a number of recurring actions with the head in order to direct the eye to the next event. But this purposeful passing of the eye includes an awareness of the connecting space between, and this awareness gives the man of the eye the ability to anticipate an oncoming event. He can even look back into the past, as it were,

1. Wilfred Pelletier, *For Every North American Indian Who Begins to Disappear I Also Begin to Disappear* (Collection of essays compiled and published by Neewin Publishing Co., Toronto, 1971).

to perceive the links connecting the event with its cause. The man who regards visual signals as of primary importance easily moves into the world of logic—the world of lineal and sequential connections.

There is also orderly meaning in the world of the ear, which is perhaps best described as "paralogic," a word used by Bazin[2] to describe the rebus writing of the Aztecs. He used this word to describe a method of organization in which symbols can be read in any order. The "reader" chooses the order and "makes" the communication. While this method leaves a great deal of room for ambiguity, it certainly leaves less room in a tribal state of corporate existence than it would in our world of individualism and fragmented specialization. Because the symbols in a rebus do not have to be read in any particular order, they are not organized on the basis of connectedness, which is a dominant feature of the visual. Rebus or "cluster" writing comes from the world of the ear, where all directions coexist simultaneously and unconnectedly. It is this very lack of connections which moves us into the Oriental world of an awareness of the interval—the vacuum where all action occurs. Unfortunately, we, in our eye-biased society, have been constrained to ignore the paralogic of the ear. But if the Aristotelian *causae ad invicem, causae sunt* can be accepted, then we must accept the paralogic of mosaic all-at-onceness.

If space is to be our metaphorical bridge between the cultures of the eye and the ear, then we must conscientiously elaborate on the difference of effect when the eye is stressed, or contrarily, when the bias is toward the ear.

The eye as an instrument of perception is scalpellike in its incisiveness. It seems to demand a fragmentation so that small areas can be explored in depth. This, in the end, tends to build disciplines which make it almost impossible for an expert in one field to talk to an expert in another. The ear is a gestalt instrument, interpreting a totality of field in a manner aptly described by IBM as "pattern recognition." The eye dissects to fragment, the ear apprehends to unify. We are here, of course, dealing with impossible worlds of *simple* inputs via eye or ear. What actually exists is a sensory orientation which in one case gives more credence to the one-

2. Germain Bazin, *The Loom of Art* (New York: Simon & Shuster, 1962).

thing-at-a-time modality of the eye and, in the other case, to those modulated primarily by the all-at-once bias of the ear. Nevertheless, for the purpose of elucidation, we shall consider these worlds as separate and unaffected by the other senses, unless otherwise noted.

It is interesting to compare the uses of language in an aural and in a visual, literate culture. On one hand, the aural mode moves to multileveled exposition with its concomitant ambiguity. It revels in puns and aphorisms. The use of speech in an aural society is remarkably complex. On the other hand, the visual, literate world of categorization yields the familiar rules: "one thing at a time," "a place for everything," and the like. The unaccented typographic chatter of T. S. Eliot's Mrs. Equitone is a beautiful parody of the literate mode of speech. The literate man talks on a line of single, explicit meaning, abhorring the multileveled pun. Havelock, in his *Prologue to Greek Literacy*, uses this distinction in accounting for the clash between the oral Homeric tradition and the literate Socratic tradition:

The syntax of memorized rhythmic speech is therefore not friendly to that type of statement which says, "The angles of a triangle are equal to two right angles," or "Courage consists in a rational understanding of what is to be feared or not feared." It is not friendly precisely to that kind of statement which the Socratic dialectic was later to demand, a statement which prefers its subject to be a concept rather than a person, and its verb to be an "is" verb rather than a "doing" verb. Neither principles nor laws nor formulas are amenable to a syntax which is orally memorizable. . . . Orally memorized verse is couched in the contingent: it deals in a panorama of happenings, not a program of principles.[3]

These variations in the use of speech are, of course, intimately connected to the accepted organizing principles of the variant cultures.[4] The man of the eye, readily trained to the assimilation of book knowledge, will easily accept concepts based on written information about percepts of which he has no experiential knowledge. For written exposition follows the logic of connection that

3. Eric Havelock, *Prologue to Greek Literacy* (Oklahoma City: University of Oklahoma Press, 1972).

4. The literate tradition with its visual bias would involve a symbol system that Gardner, Perkins, and Howard (see chap. 2) call "notational." The oral poetic tradition would utilize a "nonnotational" or "dense" symbolic system.

is originally specified to the eye. For the ear man, the world of perceptions has no such connection. Therefore, for him, the world of the book cannot act as a basis for the formulation of concepts. For him, direct perception (or words organized in terms of aural paralogic) is necessary. The reason for equating these two forms, perception and aural paralogic, is that the book necessitates a form of organization that comes from the eye. It is possible, as many contemporary and ancient writers have shown, to organize with the logic of the ear. But the great and dominant tradition of the book is lineal and sequential. It appears (and this is said from the viewpoint of a practicing painter and designer) that the world outside the perceiver is much more related to the paralogic inherent in the all-at-onceness of the ear than to the logic inherent in the arbitrary imposition of linear organization by the eye. In fact, reality legislated by the eye virtually eliminates the aural, the tactile, and the kinesthetic as effective delineators of reality. The "real" world has become the world specified in our visual linear space.

When the visual logic replaces the aural paralogic—as it has in our culture—direct perception is hindered by a priori assumptions. In downgrading perception, we have too often packed students with knowledge but with too little ability to perceive or to meaningfully relate their knowledge to the world outside. Concepts are built upon concepts without either being built upon perception. This is a dangerous game. Sooner or later the cantilevered extension will become too long, and they will once more find themselves back in the game of perception but with inadequate skills to be successful.

Indeed, this is happening now. The gap between our institutions and the new generation growing up is ever more apparent. The ubiquity of nonverbal forms in our technological society has tended to downgrade the primacy of the eye and its corollary, the phonetic alphabet. Our media have created a generation different from preceding generations not so much in terms of what they think but of how they put their thoughts together. This situation has received scant attention. Following precedent, our educators tend to blame it on a lack of correspondence between the content of the curriculum and the content of the minds of our children—a simple lack of matching. What they don't realize is that our young are reintroducing us to the world to which the nonliterate, the non-industrialized, have easy access—to the world of direct perception.

While children throughout all ages have shown a tendency to depart in some way or another from the ways of their fathers, these differences are usually culturally progressive—that is, they are extensions and elaborations of the prevailing cultural patterns. Occasionally, however, there occur disruptive events which are disastrous to an older order. There have undoubtedly been hundreds of such events which have brought about changes in the nature and patterns of communication, but four stand out. The first outstanding event occurred with the shift from a paleolithic to a neolithic culture ten thousand or so years ago. This complete, or almost complete, change from a nomadic hunting, food-gathering existence to a relatively stable agricultural one undoubtedly led to a great development in oral communication. The second occurred some fifteen hundred years before Christ, when phonetic symbols were developed, probably in Mycenae or Knossus. These enabled man to translate the whole reverberating aural world into a system of static, abstract, visual symbols. The further development and wider dissemination of this ability, which came with the invention of movable type and the printing press in the fifteenth century, effectively ended the primacy of the ear. The fourth shattering event was the introduction of telegraphy in the middle of the nineteenth century and the development of electronic communication in the twentieth. This last event, which has led to a worldwide network of instantaneous communication, has effectively changed Western man from an "eye" man back to an "ear" man. The pervasive bias of the Western world is now that of the ear. This is not to suggest that the organizing principles of the eye are no longer with us. In historic fashion, they have become exaggerated as they approach the end.

If one thinks in terms of the preservation of the better aspects of literate culture, then television should be closely examined. Its low-definition image automatically calls for a high degree of involvement by means of memory fill-in. This, coupled with relatively high-definition sound and instantaneous global coverage, is inimical to the preservation of literate values. Low visual definition elicits from the viewer a participative "making" process as opposed to a "matching" one. In education proper since the time of the Greeks, the concern has been with the changing of behavior to match that of a given standard. However, as Gombrich [5] points out, "making comes before matching." Not only does it come before in all the arts; it is the most important. In fact, matching only has a function in the area of *categorization* and, as such, has but a peripheral value in the arts. When we feed in low-definition visual images, as in television, the audience is automatically constrained to complete the image. Of course, making occurs at both ends of the communication loop. The television director *makes* as he orders incidents to create a form which is conducive to further audience remaking on the basis of individual knowledge and cultural assumptions. Active participation or involvement in the communication process is, naturally, inimical to the dispassionate survey which is so necessary to the critical and analytical stance developed by two thousand years of literacy. If the education system is to retain for our culture this critical stance, which is, of course, one of the fine qualities of the literary heritage, then it must be aware of the ability of television, in fact of all media, to restructure the recipient mind.

The low-definition image of television, exaggerated by a relative inability to convey foreshortening and coupled with the necessary shallow depth staging, is also inimical to developing any awareness of perspective. Television image-makers could, to advantage, take a long appraising look at images of the High Renaissance, where depth is portrayed as a series of frontal parallel planes with few diagonal connections, or none. The High Renaissance rendering of space was an attempt to bridge the differences between the visual spaces of a developing literate culture and the multidimensional images of the medieval period. Television could effectively act as a bridge between the spaces of our literate culture and the multidimensional spaces of the electronic age. The illusion of three-dimensional space is a cul-de-sac. It limits the observer to a perception of one time and one place from a single point of view. Preliterate man, because of his aural bias, and our postliterate children, because of instantaneous global coverage by our media, survey their world from many points of view. A graphic illustration of the methods of perception of our children before literacy is contained in

5. E. H. Gombrich, *Art and Illusion* (New York: Pantheon Books, 1960).

cubism. The artists and the writers anticipated the current sensory stance at the beginning of the twentieth century. The British essayists applied to prose-writing techniques learned from the painters, namely, the examination of an issue from several, but fixed, points of view. It does not follow, however, that writing can easily be made into a communication instrument suitable to the electronic age. Joyce's *Finnegan's Wake* is a remarkable exegesis of the impact of media, but literary purists would like to regard it as nonliterature because it does not operate within the linear logic imposed by the medium of writing. However, all the arts are to some extent hybrids because they utilize the organizing principles of many sensory modalities. In addition, a fixed point of view is not necessarily a perspective. It can, for example, be a point of view related to what might be called "the significant profile," that is, a point of view chosen because it illuminates an object as it would be known in the world of touch. A recognition of the validity of Ezra Pound's phrase "the artists are the antennae of the race" and a close study of the effects of contemporary arts could provide educators with insights into a solution for our present educational quandary. Cubism at the end of the nineteenth century effectively demonstrated that the use of the two-dimensional plane placed the viewer in the position of surveying multidimensions. In fact, cubism was referred to as multilocationalism. A stress on the efficacy of the two-dimensional plane to convey the instantaneity of communication factors in the contemporary world may not appear at a casual glance to be important, yet it is central to an understanding of contemporary mental and emotional attitudes. For it is in the area between linear apprehension (of which the three-dimensional illusion is a concomitant) and mosaic apprehension (based on two-dimensional imagery) that a fruitful abrasion can occur. All creativity happens at the point of interface.

This is the factor which can permit educators today some degree of optimism. All that is necessary is to recognize and to capitalize on the fact that there exists a pregnant interval between the old methods of organizing and the new. The young today have been bludgeoned by media into a state of mind which, in terms of the old literate tradition, is chaotic. Because technologically we can do it, we proceed to play on the central nervous system such a cacophony that, without aid, the young fail to create a new order that will make experience meaningful. It is obvious that in such a world simple cause and effect relationships have little meaning.

The very antipathy of many of the young to the educational system is a part of our culture and must be understood as such. There are few who deny the need for change. But the salient problem is to decide the new direction. Herrigel [6] tells the story of a Zen archer who, after hitting the bull's-eye on a target once with his eyes open, could later hit the same spot while blindfolded. The story is an illustration of the ability to set the stance of the whole body by sense receptors other than the eye so that a performance can be duplicated. Perhaps there is a lesson here. Our problem is certainly one of educating children who no longer accept the primacy of the eye. Owing to the impact of our media, the stress is now much more audile-tactile-kinetic. Can it be that the old target of the visually oriented can be achieved through the other sense receptors? This is obviously too simple a parallel. To the Zen master, the target that he shot at blindfolded is not the same one that he shot at while sighted. To him, the senses involved and the target are an inseparable whole. If the sense orientation changes, then the total act must be different.

Many modern artists and poets have made statements relative to the changing sensibilities of man. Paul Klee commented that all his work was a dedication to his original childlike vision, while William Butler Yeats made the comment that in all his later work he attempted to rid his poetry of visual imagery.

The effects of our electronic media are in the direction of removing the bias of the eye and reorchestrating sensibility with the bias on the audile-tactile. The closest parallel to this state of being is the perceptual stance of children. Child art is always concerned with perception through all the senses; there is no overbearing stress on the eye. Now it must be understood that the perception of the child is only inferior to that of the adult in terms of content. The content of the adult mind is obviously much more rich and varied. But the *form* of preliterate perception is not inferior— it is simply different. (It is interesting to note here that Western

6. E. Herrigel, *Zen in der Kunst des Bogenschiessens* (Munich: O. W. Barth, 1959).

European civilization is the only one that has ever existed in which the father draws differently than the child. It is true that in China the mature artist-poet is much more sophisticated than his child, but his modes of perception are the same, that is, based on the primacy of the audile-tactile. Their outstanding facility with mathematics reinforces this statement for, as Danzig has made abundantly clear in *Number: The Language of Science*,[7] mathematics is based on the tactile). In the Western world we take the young child, who uses a style of imagery derived from direct perceptions through all his senses and, through teaching him the alphabet, effectively reduce the whole resounding world into a series of visual abstractions. This is not to be construed as an attack on the value of literacy, but as an appeal to reintegrate those organizing principles which are inherent in a sensitive use of the eye into a balanced sensorium. Much has been written about the fact that a very large proportion of our information comes to us through the eye. But such arguments fail to recognize that we do not see with the eye. We see with the whole sensorium.

The fragmentation of sensibility that results from living in a world of high specialization can and does have a deleterious effect on our emotional life; the primacy of the eye has been achieved, but only at the expense of the other senses. Our children joyfully start out to draw the world around them until they encounter the sophisticated world of literacy and the ubiquitous high-fidelity photographs in magazines and films. Then they cease to draw, because they don't have the requisite skills or the sensory set to achieve such images. In other words, for some years after becoming literate they are effectively separated from making any really meaningful contact with the world except through the eye.

When the child is taught to read and write, his other experiences in the world of touch and the ear need to be augmented. Certainly children do compensate for the visual bias in their play. The joy of the normal child in movement is almost an embarrassment to the stiff adult, and I suspect that the small child uses his eye to reinforce his sense of touch rather than the reverse.

If the school is to avoid being categorized by the child as an

7. Tobias Danzig, *Number: The Language of Science*, 4th ed. (Garden City, New York: Doubleday & Co., 1956).

activity separate from living, then equal training in the use of other sensory areas is vital. One way to preserve the other senses is through the multisensory images of much contemporary and all preliterate art. The child must not be allowed to grow up with one sensory antenna longer than all the others.

People who organize their lives on the basis of the primacy of the visual find it extremely difficult to understand the types of images which people construct in the mind when the primary sense is other than the visual. Take the gentleman from the Harvard Business School (which, like most schools, represents the final flowering of the old visual system of ordering) who asserted that the only order possible was lineal, sequential, and based on single causation. He assumed that the blind are always attempting to conceive the world in visual terms. On the contrary, how could the blind possibly have a sense of perspective? They can have no idea that, visually, objects diminish in size as they recede from the spectator. Nor is there any possibility that the blind could be told that this was the case in such a way that they would thereby perceive it as so. All their experience would deny the validity of such an argument; a concept cannot be understood without a perceptual ground.

The hang-up which the visually orientated encounter in attempting to understand the new ordering of the electronic world is their assumption that the end of all perception in the audile, tactile, kinetic world is to imaginatively structure a visual world. They completely fail to appreciate that there can be a re-membering which is aural or tactile. They fail to understand that visual input might be used to reinforce an aural image. When one thinks of individuals with this mind-set attempting to cope with the new world of instantaneity, one realizes the extent of their present and future ineptitude.

Today, the whole history of the bias of the eye and the concomitant developments of logical thought and the industrial revolution (a translation of our sinews into steel) must be placed within the context of the electronic revolution (a translation of our nervous system into copper, wavelengths, and lasers). The waning of the visual is not a catastrophe. It merely faces us with the necessity of formulating new methods of living and new aims in education. Education should create perceptive individuals who will act upon and transform the world, both individually and collectively.

Perceptive individuals know how to deal with experience, for they have been trained to see *effects*. It will be perceptive individuals who will bring pressure to bear on governments, private enterprise, and social agencies to create environments more conducive to a development of human dignity. Marshall McLuhan is very fond of quoting, "We don't know who discovered water but we're sure that it wasn't a fish." Environments are unperceived by most men. They are accepted as an act of God, just as, I presume, fish accept water. But the environment of man is increasingly modified by the acts of men. Man-made environments must not be accepted casually. Our children must be trained so that they will not tolerate environments, whether they be economic, educational, or whatever, which are inimical to human well-being. In other words, our children must be trained to be intelligent rebels—for rebel they will.

Here, then, is the heart of the educational problem. The sensory orchestration of the young has changed, and the educational system must change to accommodate this new sensory mix. It is necessary to make this new sensory orchestration and the educational feed-in compatible.

It should be noted that these sensibilities may not be mutually exclusive. The human psyche can live in a variety of modes, adopting one mode or attitude for one problem and another mode for a second. Such a situation already exists in science, where scientists can operate with both Newtonian and Einsteinian concepts. In relatively simple situations, a cause and effect orientation may produce effective understanding, but in other situations linear formulation may be misleading and a mosaic or the paralogic of instantaneity may be productive. One of the problems for educational theory to face is that of developing a multiplicity of necessary competencies through education in the arts.

In the educational system, as it currently exists, the arts are peripheral studies. This attitude is a nineteenth-century hangover from the time when the superficial knowledge of an art was necessary for genteel young women. Men were relegated to nonsentience and industrial production. If one wants to train individuals to be sensitive to sound, surely music is the best area for study. If we want to train people to be aware of color and shapes in the environment, then the study of the visual arts is applicable. If we want to educate people to their bodies, then the dance and athletics is obviously the answer. In other words, the arts (and I consider any action which changes the environment of man constructively an art form) should be central to any curriculum, for they constitute the best methods of training perception. Our computerized world will soon eliminate the necessity for uncreative thinkers. The automated society could offer an unprecedented opportunity for the full development of mankind. Released from our fragmentary modes of living, which were the result of the industrial revolution, man could conceivably move into the world of mankindness. This is no idealistic dream but a necessity if our global village is to evolve into an environment suitable for man. Well-informed sentience is the answer.

> God guard me from the thoughts men think
> In the mind alone;
> He that sings a lasting song
> Thinks in a marrow-bone. (W. B. Yeats)

or again:

> . . . Now that my ladder's gone,
> I must lie down where all ladders start,
> In the foul rag-and-bone shop of the heart.
> (W. B. Yeats)

Our society is moving into the world of unified sensory perception and away from two thousand years of fragmentation of the sense life. The futility of clinging to the old methods of organizing thoughts or actions is apparent when we are faced with the phenomenon of dropouts in so many areas of life. Students, executives, and university presidents have all manifested this urge to get away from it all. The very act of dropping out is a recognition of defeat, but it is an *effect*, and effects must be studied. There is no specific cause for dropoutism, but it is certainly indicative of a pervasive malaise. The malaise is, in part, caused by a recognition, in most cases subliminal, that the old methods of organization, whether they be in business, in education, or in life generally, are no longer effective in a milieu where:

> It is impossible to say just what I mean!
> But as if a magic lantern threw the nerves
> in patterns on a screen. (T. S. Eliot)

It appears that in education there are two general concerns with media. The first, which seems to attract most attention, is the question of how media should be used in the educational system. The second, which is much more important but receives much less attention, is the effect of media, inside and outside school buildings, on our children.

To take the first area of concern, too often the question being asked is, "How can the media be used to teach the old established curriculum, albeit with a few additional frills?" The answer is simple, but abrupt. They cannot. As in the story of the Zen archer, a change in sensibility will automatically change the target. The unique orchestration of the senses is the ground for the figure of shooting the bow and arrow. It is axiomatic that if one changes the ground, the figure will change. As Salvador Dali proved, a piano in a tree is not the same as a piano in a concert hall. It is no longer possible to dispute the idea that a change in method of communication changes the mind of the receiver. A change in the medium changes the message. Anthropologists have long ago shown that the patterns of living of preliterate peoples are largely the result of oral speech being the main method of communication. The very language a man thinks dictates the thoughts he can think. A German cannot think like a Frenchman. A German could no more have invented the style of rococo than the French could have originated the Bauhaus. All languages are molded to express the attitudes of a people. The language, in turn, molds what can be expressed.

It would seem almost unnecessary to defend such obvious truths were it not that attempts are still widespread in education to use new media to express old concepts. This is effective providing one recognizes that a subtle change will occur in the concept. There is a saying that the only thing history teaches us is that history teaches us nothing. But it should be understood that the remark was made about "book" history. At least, that is the only history that most of us in the Western world know. One wonders whether history via film will teach us nothing, or history by way of television. We don't know yet because we have consistently used these methods to teach only book history. TV is an all-at-once medium. Should it be teaching our children all-at-once history? As a matter of fact, that is the only kind of history it could teach effectively.

There is a wide area of ignorance of the effects of media. It would probably be more profitable, generally, to examine our ignorance of effects rather than our knowledge of them. Currently we move blindly forward on the assumption that all media are merely alternative forms for conveying logical, literate messages, with no awareness of the profound restructuring capacity of the media. As an aside, it is ironical that cars were first promoted on the basis that they would reduce the pollution of horses.

We turn now to the second point: the effects of various media upon our children. All methods of communication can be art forms, inasmuch as they do fulfill a primary obligation of art, that of re-structuring the environment. All art is an abstraction from life. All arts play variously upon the senses. Let us analyze these effects in terms of four prominent educational media:

Radio is a medium which depends entirely upon the dissemina-tion of sound. Thus it is an abstraction of one sense from the many we have. It is, of course, excellent for music, and audiences have long ago separated music from the visual performance. Whenever the voice is used in dramatic situations, the cultural bias of the visual comes into play. As a matter of fact, even speeches of the logical, precise sort come across this way on radio. Poetry of the visual kind, that of Milton or Wordsworth, seems to be success-ful; on the other hand, paratactic poetry—Ferlinghetti's *Coney Island of the Mind*, for example—is unsuccessful. Of course, we are discussing radio in a literate society of compulsive visualizers. Inas-much as radio in our society demands visual fill-in, much like the book, radio does not constitute a grave threat to literacy. It rein-forces the already existent visual bias. The effect of radio on non-literate peoples is very different. In a preliterate milieu, it has proven to be highly tribalizing and inflammatory. In such circum-stances it reinforces the aural modality. Preliterate people do not live very much in the world of the eye, therefore the need for mnemonic visual picturing does not occur to any great extent. The imaginative fill-in is much more in the area of touch, kinetics, and sound.

What, then, is the effect of radio on our own preliterates—pre-school children? It reinforces the aural stance and the quality of closely knit tribal unity. Much of the individualistic bickering among children is the result of the abrasion between their natural sense of organization and the organization imposed on them by the adult world. Our children at a very early age are forced into a rather schizophrenic position, trying to live with a bias of the ear and a bias of the eye simultaneously. When radio is encountered by the child who is struggling to achieve literacy, it will act as an aid to developing a visual bias.

The effects of print technology depend somewhat on the use to which it is put. One of the important qualities of the book is the single point of view, but other print forms, such as the magazine or newspaper, present a multitude of points of view on myriad subjects. The latter, therefore, are regarded as very important in the formulation of political attitudes. It is interesting to look at the difference in attitude toward political position in oral and literate societies. The mosaically organized newspaper leads to an awareness much akin to tribal awareness, inasmuch as it presents many points of view paralogically juxtaposed. On the other hand, political opinion is disseminated on the editorial page, the page which is essentially literate in character. The editorial page is a form eminently suited to the bolstering of the concept of majority rule. This form of government is based on bureaucratic principles and can be seen reflected in the organization of any large corporation. In contradistinction, tribes arrive at positions vis-à-vis their environment by consensus, based on lively discussion of any dissident opinion.

In our society we have not only the oral stance of the preliterate child but also that of the postliterate young who have closer affinity with preliterate modes of apprehension and organization than they do with methods of organization based on the book. These, despite the fact that they use the printed word, tend to undermine the dominant biases of literacy—a single point of view, perspective, and traditional logic. The telegraph also militates against these biases. In a newspaper one finds logical organization only on the editorial page, and often editorials run along the rails of logic to unreasonable ends.

Film as a medium tends to be more of a bolster to the visual, literate tradition than a threat. The viewing of films is done privately even though one goes to a public theatre. At most, we are really *with* one other person, but the discussion of responses to the film almost always is left until the film is over. This, of course, is very different from television, which is generally viewed within the family community and allows for repartee with the family or with the set. Film, like the book, tends to be private. The viewing of paintings, too, seems to be largely a private experience. Most educated viewers look upon guided tours of art galleries with scorn. The effect of the eye in reinforcing the individualism inherent in a single point of view appears to make those communication media which have an eye bias a private affair. Films are essentially a story-telling device. Locked as the film-maker is, within visual three-dimensional space, it is very difficult to work with the multitudinous simultaneous dimensions of the aural world. Film is an extremely powerful medium. If the viewer gets too involved with a movie, if he fails to constantly reassure himself that it is a vicarious experience, it can be most harrowing. Without question, film can be the medium par excellence to strengthen the literate tradition. Conventional film with its story line can tie an audience most effectively into the linear, connected spaces of the fifteenth, sixteenth, seventeenth, eighteenth, and nineteenth centuries. The spaces of the twentieth century belong to television, or conversely, television in its current form belongs to the spaces of the twentieth century.

The effects of television are, of course, a primary concern here. It has already been established that the lower the definition of the image, the more fill-in is required. All people call on remembered tactile, kinetic, and aural experiences to complete low-definition images, but they will tend to remake images in terms of their own cultural imagery. The child who is not yet imbued with literate values will complete the television image imaginatively by an image involving all the senses, but his completed image will be much more related to the feel of things—a tactile image. The aural man will remake the image in terms of his own cultural sensory bias toward the ear. Because of the high value placed on the visual by our society, literate man will replace the low-definition image of television with an image of higher visual definition. In fact, the book man will tend to re-create all images, whether aural, tactile, or visual, in a visual modality.

Of course, in feedback terms, the sensory bias of the medium will eventually move to reconstruct the sensory bias of the culture, so that the new medium's reinforcement of the prevailing cultural stance will only be initially true. Any image will be the result of the abrasion of the sense bias of the medium on the sense bias of the audience. In the area of media studies, therefore, no definitive answers can be given. All that can be done is to educate people to find creative opportunities where the waves of media batter the shores of social mores.

But television, like other media, is too often regarded by educators as a mere carrier of data. "Sesame Street" and "Electric Company," for example, use television in an attempt to teach children the patterns and values of the literate society. Aside from the fact that the organizational principles of phonetic literacy are relatively obsolete in the electric age, program designers do not realize that the cartoon form is inimical to literate values. The cartoon form comes from the aural world as medieval iconography illustrates. Purveyors of literacy on those programs are using a communication form which, because of its all-at-onceness, militates against phonetic literacy and they are using images which are in themselves antiliterate, coupled to a literate content. The form and content are polarized. Only low-grade literacy can be taught by this method, for the medium and its form impose organizational principles which are in opposition to the content. Lucidity in oral comment is very different from lucidity in written composition. Cartoons on television could do very well in teaching the first, but they cannot be truly effective in the second.

The Open University of Great Britain is, of course, merely adult "Sesame Street." The cartoons have been eliminated but the structuring capacity of the medium, its ability to militate against literate values, is present. The Open University, in terms of true cultural achievement, is as ineffectual as the American baby talk.

Parallel to our attempts to teach the logic of literacy to children through television are UNESCO's attempts to teach literacy to preliterate peoples in the undeveloped countries of the world, on the noble but misguided assumption that the literate mode is necessarily an advancement for all people. In the electric world this can be questioned. In addition, there is an inherent contradiction in the fact that another arm of the United Nations fights to reduce a concomitant of industrialization, world pollution, which itself comes out of phonetic literacy. That methods of communication structure cultures cannot be questioned. But can we assume that the methods of cultural organization which are imposed by literacy are automatically the best that can be devised?

These contrasts are perhaps overdrawn inasmuch as the sensory life of people is in a constant state of flux, with visual values dominant in one situation and aural values dominant in another. If one recognizes that it is the bias of *sense* in a culture which is important, it is possible to appraise the extent to which media are effective in perpetuating a sensory bias or repudiating it. Educators must take a position in relation to sensory bias and decide whether they want to perpetuate visual values as inviolate norms or whether they are prepared to incorporate the hard-won values of the visual into a new sensory orchestration. If they decide for the first, they are fighting a losing battle. Some, however, will decide that, losing the battle or no, it is better to defend every inch of ground before surrendering it, on the assumption that the more time gained, the more possibility of consolidating the defenses. In this case, however, we are not attempting, as in the past, to fight opinions contrary to the accepted norm. We are attempting to cope with a changed sensibility. The efforts of educators must be directed towards finding the human values inherent in the new sensory stance and doing everything possible to organize these values in ways that will be meaningful to the new emergent man. Perhaps it is a matter of preserving visual bias as one among a set of options for dealing with our experience of events.

The arts, because of the fact that they utilize various sensory modalities, offer the best opportunity for education today. In our world, the bias of a literate, visual culture, with its linear and logical forms of organization—what we have called the bias of the eye— is losing its monopoly on perception and on social organization. It is losing its monopoly on education, too, as schoolmen come to realize that their task is not simply to preserve an obsolete, exclusively literate culture, but to develop intelligence—a balanced sensitivity to all forms of experience, a sensitivity that may be cultivated through the arts.

CHAPTER V

Powers and Limits of Signs

I. A. RICHARDS

Special Uses of Language

Our starting point can be Roman Jakobson's admirably forth-right formulation:

> For us, both as linguists and as ordinary word-users, the meaning of any linguistic sign is its translation into some further, alternative sign, especially a sign "in which it is more fully developed," as Peirce, the deepest inquirer into the essence of signs, insistently stated.[1]

Jakobson's opening qualification here is highly significant—both as distinguishing linguists [2] from ordinary word-users and as indicating that there are also other than ordinary, or special, *uses* of language.

EDUCATORS, TEACHERS, LEARNERS

Among these—and there may be many—some are of particular importance to educators, to teachers, and, above all, to learners. They concern the educator as being the overall student of the acquisition, development, and degeneration of meanings, their transmission, cultivation, upkeep—all the "agronomic" aspects.[3] These include the pathology of meanings and the principles of remedial

---

1. Roman Jakobson, "On Linguistic Aspects of Translation," in *On Translation*, ed. Reuben A. Brower (Cambridge, Mass.: Harvard University Press, 1959), pp. 232-33.

2. In the sense here, "students of how languages work" rather than "speakers of more than one language." It is well to avoid the awkward and somehow slighting term *linguisticians*. It would be interesting to inquire into how this disparaging tinge arises. Is it from the word's rime group: beauticians, dialecticians, metaphysicians?

3. See subheading "Nonverbal Sign Systems . . ." under heading "Translations into Alternative Signs" and, especially, third and fourth paragraph headings under subheading "Principles of Useful Depiction" (under heading "Exploratory Activity").

treatment, not to mention the problems of conservation and pollution. In view of the growth patterns of our present de-traditionalized urban agglomerations (the megalopolitan trend), these last may well be thought to be of utmost consequence. These special uses concern the teacher, particularly in his capacity as the conveyer, the authority, the exponent, and representative of what he teaches—the deputy, moreover, increasingly called on to replace traditional sources of values as these are, sources and values progressively disabled and destroyed. Qua teacher his particular use of language must be, or should be, peculiar. He is not fulfilling his special functions if it is not. And the learner's use of language, that too (if he is really a learner) is correspondingly or reciprocally peculiar—he is (or should be) a recipient, an inverse to the teacher as conveyer.

It is easy, I well know, to misrepresent the points I have been trying to make and to mistake necessities in the process of communication for mere accidentals of manner: tricks of pontification and affected docility that are no more than maladies—most incident to the classroom, I admit. The essentials of this communicative situation are that the teacher speaks as an addresser possessing knowledge to an addressee who does not possess that knowledge. It is these essentials that unavoidably make their uses of language peculiar or extraordinary. These are not matters of postures which may be put on or dropped: pomposity on one side, submissiveness on the other. They are inherent and inescapable factors in the structure of the operation taking place.

What the teacher conveys may, of course, be doubt. To have called it knowledge, as I have just done, may be misleading; but what he has to convey is a knowledge of doubt, of a degree of uncertainty. And in a further way—equally to be guarded against—to talk here of knowledge may occasion or invite misconceivings. What is conveyed in teaching must not be supposed to be purely, or even primarily, cognitive; it may be and often is primarily conative or affective. Commonly, what has to be communicated is a *position* in which cognitive, affective, and volitional components are distinguishable with difficulty, if at all. One of the teacher's chief tasks, then, is to present the position in a fashion which will enable the learner both to reproduce it and to begin that exploration

of it which is the reason why it was offered. The point, the very
heart, of that exploration may well be to make out how these components are related in the message: how feeling, will, and thought
combine to do its work. It would be a gross misunderstanding of
communication theory which would equate its information with
data or factual content.

In thus *theoretically* distinguishing the educator's, the teacher's,
and the learner's special, other than ordinary uses of language from
ordinary use, it is no less necessary to insist that to distinguish is
not to separate. Any user of language—from moment to moment—
may find himself in a situation imposing upon him some special use.
The educator's duties constantly require in him a clinical, evaluative
attitude towards meanings and the transactions they mediate. But
we may, most of us, find ourselves at any moment in a situation in
which we have to be educators. So, too, we may, almost all of us,
have to teach. And certainly we do, all of us, have to learn. What
special use is requisite is determined by the character of the situation governing the communication.

OTHER SPECIAL USES

We may widen and confirm our reflections upon *uses* of
language at this point by asking what may be some of the other
special uses of language. (We are trying, clearly, to find a sense
for "use" which will be serviceable, and further examples may
help.) Among those that may be suggested, the following seem to
merit particular notice.

Playwright's special use. The playwright has two sets of addressees. Each sentence he pens has one or more of the *dramatis
personae* as its addressee(s). And yet, the play, as a whole, has an
audience, to which, in a necessarily somewhat changed sense, it is
addressed. Again, in a somewhat changed sense, much of this applies to the actors. With these two distinctly special uses of language we can put some diplomatic and political utterances. The
speaker may have his constituents, his party, his own nation as addressees in the ordinary sense; he is talking to them. But, in addition, what he says and how he says it, his utterance, may be being
shaped by how he supposes other audiences (at the highest level,
say, the foreign offices of the world) will take his remarks. The

skill shown by so many in handling such situations is indeed nota-
ble. It is a skill which is being threatened by contemporary trends,
by the de-traditioning mentioned above, since it is dependent to
no slight degree on the influence of good models, and that influence
is being increasingly cut off.

Advertiser's special use. To some extent, the place of good
models is being taken by another category of special uses of language: uses that in our day have enjoyed a probably unexampled
sophistication and expansion, those of *advertisement.* That the use
of language—and its cooperating media, to which we shall return—
in advertising is truly a special use (in the sense of *use* we are
trying to clarify in these paragraphs) will, I believe, be little questioned. In the script, layout, or video employed, whether on the
page or on the air, the controlling motive is generally both acknowledged and recognized. It is sales. On the other hand, a main
or key principle of successful design (in no very Machiavellian
sense, but in the ordinary honest sense of direction of selected
means to conscious ends) is that the controlling motive should be
hidden behind one or other of a number of motives and devices
more likely to be influential with the addressees. Need I detail
them? The desire to propagate "truth," benevolent eagerness to
help, neighbourly impulses to convey good news to especially
esteemed recipients, pardonable vainglory in unbelievable accom-
plishments and in heaven-inspired breakthroughs toward the relief
of human ills, offerings of sympathetic understanding to the neglected, arousal of generous indignation against mishandlings, and
innumerable diverse wheedlings and cajoleries of every sort of
velleity: appeal to all the status fears as well as to all the easily
detected anxieties of those inferiority complexes. But why go on?
My reader will have many other such attention-getting gimmicks
within his recollection. My point is simply that such dressing up,
such disguisal of the prime motive of utterances, does constitute a
special *use* (in our sought-for sense) of language. It is true that an
advertisement may openly confess its prime aim—sales. But it will
be using this confession in the hope of persuading its addressees to
become purchasers. The distinctive feature of advertisement in the
above sense of the term, I suggest, is disguise of the essential aim.
Here again, the situation in which the communication is occurring
is what is determinative of the special use.

Probably, indeed all but certainly, considering what media are now available, never before have such vast proportions of the human race had their attention, their feelings, their wishes, hopes, fears, etc., solicited or played upon by such percentages of disguised appeals, by such cunningly masterful efforts to persuade them. No doubt, many of the ablest advertisers have the best intentions. There is a famous and frequented road that is so paved. And perhaps the ability levels maintained in the advertising business as a whole would be found (if reliable measures were devisable and available) alarmingly higher than those evidenced in the literary professions, both creative and critical. But such remarks will rightly be thought invidious. I refrain here from pointed reference to the teaching profession, though recent attempts to enlist advertisers to help out with the literacy crisis may be recalled by some.

Pornographer's special use. With these sad thoughts in mind it is appropriate to consider the adjacent territories in which this same use of language marked by disguisal of the prime purpose by other ostensible aims can be observed to rule. They include evidently much political discourse, all sorts of personal seductions, much social ritual—"Thank-yous," and so forth—and not a little that is somehow still being called "literature" in one of the old high senses of the word. Until very recently, the courts and the police were still able to defend the market from what its upholders like to talk about as "porn." People have often believed that it is society that is threatened. This is probably a misestimation of the mind's self-defensive and recuperative powers. What does need protection is *shelf space* in bookstores and outlets, and, above all, literary standards, sanity, and sagacity in the conduct of meanings. These degradations have not yet, I believe, had any adequate semiotic study. Perhaps George Steiner alone, among literary critics and semioticians, has shown the acumen, independence, and courage to remark on how much and what sorts of damage they can do.[4]

As a sewage inflow can distort the ecology of a river (or an antibiotic wreck the enzyme system in the mouth, on which the

---

4. George Steiner, "Night Words, High Pornography and Human Privacy," in *Language and Silence*, pp. 68-77 (New York: Atheneum Publishers, 1970). For example, "The present danger to the freedom of literature . . . is not censorship or verbal reticence. The danger lies in the facile contempt which the erotic novelist exhibits for his readers, for his personages, and for the language."

powers of taste depend), so the flood (it has been that) of pornography into the display shelves and the cinemas has not only displaced invitations more needed by the growing mind, but, analogously, the contents of this bedizened pulp and film have narrowed,
crudified, and blunted a public percipience which was too under-
cultivated already.

To balance such losses, such deteriorations in meanings against
any possible gains in freedom (in some worthy sense), in improvement of people's potentials and securities of control is, as I said
earlier, the educator's business; essentially, to be able to weigh just
such things is his professional qualification, though not a few of the
ʼeducatorsʼ I have known would be much surprised to hear it. To
develop his own powers and those of his charges in such discriminations should be his prime endeavor. He and his advisers—
critics, linguists, moralists—are ignorant of their tasks if they do
not acknowledge this. They need not (nor should they) often
openly claim such awesome duties; but if they are to know what
they are doing they must in their hearts admit that it is so.

That most of what they have to judge does indeed border on
the adman's province in its disguisal of designs cannot be doubted.
The banners the march-by carries may bear fine words: Honesty,
Frankness, Truth, Exposure, Openness, Down with Hypocrisy,
Down with Taboo, Down with Modesty, and so on. Those who
finance and run the racket know better. There may still be a very
few among the products which do not deserve the accusation that
quest for sales is being camouflaged as love of nature, frankness in
confession, or something of that sort, but, if there are such, they
are lost, buried beneath the rest. It should be added that the other
than verbal signs—from the pictures in the ads to the covers of
the pulps—deserve study by semioticians and educators almost as
much as the verbiage. But to *depiction* I will be returning.

Special use in poetry. A fourth special use of language that may
be suggested is that of poetry. I use this word here in Jakobson's
sense:

In poetry, verbal equations become a constructive principle of the text.
Syntactic and morphological categories, roots, and affixes, phonemes and
their components (distinctive features)—in short, any constituents of
the verbal code—are confronted, juxtaposed, brought into contiguous

relation according to the principle of similarity and contrast and carry
their own autonomous signification. Phonemic similarity is sensed as
semantic relationship. The pun, or to use a more erudite, and perhaps
more precise term—paronomasia, reigns over poetic art, and whether
its rule is absolute or limited, poetry by definition is untranslatable. Only
creative transposition is possible: either intralingual transposition—from
one poetic shape into another, or interlingual transposition—from one
language into another, or finally intersemiotic transposition—from one
system of signs into another, e.g., from verbal art into music, dance,
cinema, or painting.[5]

This distinctive use of language flickers in and out of most
verbal communication, of course. It occurs in varying degrees and
in various relations to the other functions of language—as it serves
them and/or calls on them to serve it. How much of advertising,
of political sloganry (I Like Ike), etc., is applied poetry—poetic
means diverted to other than poetic ends—will hardly need pointing out. It cannot be a healthy society in which the majority of
susceptible people meet poetic language not in the service of the
high aims of poetry—Shelley's unacknowledged legislation of mankind [6]—but in the pursuit of gain of one kind or another. Such bar-
rages of suspectable messages are propitious neither to poetry nor
to sane living.

Translation into Alternative Signs

These attempts to discriminate special uses—another one might
be the mathematician's and others, those of liturgists and of some
metaphysicians—send us back to the ordinary use of language. One
somewhat hopeful way of clarifying this may be to consider more
strictly and seriously what Jakobson states in the quoted passage
in the first paragraph of this chapter. Taking "ordinary word-users"
as the linguistic sign it there is can approach meaning nearer by
"translation into some further, alternative sign" through which the
meaning in question can be "more fully developed." The first
problem in so doing turns on the phrase "is its translation." The

5. Jakobson, op. cit., p. 238.

6. See the last sentence of Shelley's *A Defense of Poetry*, edited with
introduction by A. S. Cook (Boston: Ginn & Co., 1890) and, for a comment,
see my *So Much Nearer* (New York: Harcourt, Brace & World, 1968), pp.
151-52.

word *is* here marks, I take it, an ellipsis, itself calling for expansion, calling for a sign in which its own meaning is more fully developed. What should our expansion be? When we have settled that, we will be readier to answer questions about "its translation." The most helpful "further, alternative sign" among those that occur to me is, I think, "can be clarified by." I find myself loath, through a resistance which hardens as I experiment, to accept a reading that takes *is* more literally, e.g., "is nothing other than," "is, in fact, actually," and such. Perhaps this resistance reflects possibilities in the reading of "its translation"—to which we may now turn.

In common with very many other words ending in *tion*, *translation* may represent either a process of translating or the product that is the outcome of the process.[7] I take it to be the process which is being talked of here, not the product. This probably is the cause of my difficulty in taking *is* more literally. With *translation* as product, I seem to see less clearly how any one such outcome could be said to be the "meaning of a linguistic sign." But with *translation* as a process of weighing, comparing, amending, adjusting possibilities of interpretation, selecting, testing, etc., I seem to find myself much nearer to a viable view. As process, *translation* allows for the flexibility, the adaptability, the manifold resources of most of the meanings I have had dealings with. Figuratively, the process view offers us cells cooperating; the product view, merely bricks in a wall.

THREE KINDS OF TRANSLATION

A related set (system, rather) of ambiguities with *translation* seems worth exploring here. Jakobson neatly presents (p. 233) "three kinds of translation . . . to be differently labeled:

1. Intralingual translation or *rewording* . . .
2. Interlingual translation or *translation proper* . . .
3. Intersemiotic translation or *transmutation* . . . an interpretation of verbal signs by means of signs of nonverbal sign systems"

His essay in *On Translation* is largely devoted to bringing his extraordinary range of knowledge to bear on (2). I confine myself to (1) and (3).

7. I. A. Richards, *How to Read a Page* (New York: W. W. Norton & Co., 1942), pp. 135-37.

Relatively little explicit analytic discussion of the organization of nonverbal sign systems has, until recent times, been available. Those numbered (1) and (2), being more accessible, have pre-empted attention. It is easier to talk about our words than about the other than verbal signs which may very likely be our necessary means of comparing and controlling what our words are doing.

We must recognize that Peirce's doctrine, along with its encouraging positive aspects, has a negative interpretation which can be grimly forbidding. Many have taken it as denying that we can do more in exploring our meanings than switch from one phrasing to another and again to yet others. Positivists, behaviorists, and their nominalist allies, who make it a point of conscience to enact and obey self-denying ordinances in matters such as the occurrence and use of concepts and of images—visual, mobile, tactile, kinesthetic, gustatory, olfactory, and the rest—have seemed to wish to empty the mind of all but verbal equivalences and to substitute wordplay for thinking. But *substitutable* and *equivalence*, along with *compare* and *control*, are terms whose meanings are as explorable as they are important. Human education indeed might well be described as learning how to explore them.

The key question is: How do we decide whether an expression is or is not equivalent to, substitutable for, able to replace (and so on) another? If we answer, "By comparing," we then have to try to say what we are comparing with what, and how we do it. And, as we do so, we have again to decide whether or not our account is ⸢satisfactory⸣, ⸢sufficient⸣, ⸢able to explain the facts⸣, ⸢intelligible⸣, and so on. These expressions again we have to compare (bearing in mind our account of comparing). We see why Peirce held that interpretation is a conversation without an ending.

NONVERBAL SIGN SYSTEMS: PUBLIC AND PRIVATE

What are we comparing? Not the expressions alone, apart from their meanings. But meanings they have. What is our mode of access to them? Must we not have other means than just our phrasings through which to focus our attention on them and, as we say, make them out? Here is where our nonverbal sign systems come in, supplying us with (theoretically illimitable) cultivatable resources for noting within ourselves, to ourselves, how the meanings we are comparing are alike or unlike, require, preclude, supplement, etc.; in general, how they are related to one another. The meanings compared are relations within the overall fabric of sign systems.

The nonverbal sign systems are of two orders: public and private. If we ask ourselves what corresponds to a nod or shake of the head or to a face we would like to pull on occasions when we must give no sign of what we think, we will have these two orders conveniently present for comparison. There are batteries of such questions we may ask ourselves (without necessarily putting them into words) that similarly can destroy any contention that thinking is nothing but internal speech. What is a forgotten name which you know is none of those suggested? How do you know what you have to say before you know how you will say it? What is a plan before it is begun to be worked out? Or any movement before it is made? When we recall, moreover, modern accounts of the signaling systems which control cell growth and cooperation in the body, to try to substitute subvocal speech for thinking appears to be absurd. The point is that we are beginning to have better ideas about how we think, about what thinking must be like.

Nonetheless, if we are ready to let parapsychology go on crying in the wilderness, we only communicate with others through public signs, verbal and nonverbal. With ourselves we have too many modes of communing. We do talk to ourselves and more than a little; but guiding and controlling these internal colloquies too is thought: a capacity to compare meanings.

Along with a reconception of thought should go a more developed idea of meanings. It is not surprising that meanings— through the last fifty years—have been variously out of favor in psychology and in linguistics. Doctrinaire dogmatisms apart, much of the recurrent headshaking and shoulder-shrugging over 'meaning' has sprung from a fair recognition of its enigmatic status. The forbidding side of Peirce's view represents a wish to replace meanings by more examinable fabrics, unduly limiting them to "further alternative verbal signs" and overlooking the indispensable cooperations and constant support of the nonverbal sign-system components. However, his fundamental insight that the meaning of any sign consists in its relationship to other signs retains all its value. This relationship may extend very far. As any word may be conceived as related, via the words most immediately connected with it, to all the other words in the language, so at least some of the nonverbal sign systems have, span by span, an analogous though less extensive and inclusive connexity.[8] Consider what the composer is doing in the auditory field and what relationships his phrases may have to other possible phrases. For each phrase, its relationships, at that point within the setting of the composition, are its musical meaning. Compare too what the tennis player is doing in the optical-motor-kinesthetic-tactual field. His strokes, too, can be thought of as having meanings—their relationship, rich and subtle or poor and crude, to his other possible strokes.

TWO KINDS OF ASSOCIATION

These relationships are highly complex. If we think of them as associations, we risk making them seem too mechanical and we must remember that all activity is purposive. Throughout there is selection and control of means by ends. Jakobson performed a fine service to theory of meanings when he reminded linguists[9] that there are traditionally two kinds of association: (a) by *similarity-opposition* and (b) by *contiguity*. These operate in collaborative rivalry. A meaning is what it is through (a) what it is like and unlike and (b) where it is in its setting. A term with no opposite or a term by itself alone would be meaningless. X is *here* through not being *there*. And it is *there* through not being *here*. But without an X to be here or there, no meaning arises. (It may be worth adding that a number of what look like very important but, unhappily, insoluble problems seem to arise through forgetting this. But that does not make them less painful or important. The theological troubles of omniscience and omnipotence are the prime examples, linked as they are with the nature of defect. Evil seems a very high price to pay for the possibility of good.)

Depiction

Our most variously powerful nonverbal sign system is depiction: our iconic use of visual signs. Many of its aspects naturally

8. See my *Interpretation in Teaching* (London: Kegan Paul, 1937, and New York: Humanities Press, 1973), chap. 18, "The Interpretation of *IS*," and chap. 19, "Some Senses of *IS*." See also my *How to Read a Page*, op. cit., pp. 162-73.

9. R. Jakobson and M. Halle, *Fundamentals of Language* (Gravenhage: Mouton & Co., 1956), pp. 60, 80, 81.

parallel those of other signs. Thus a depiction, e.g., a visual image, may occur in degrees of vividness and presence varying from hallucinatory strength to the faintest, minimal, rudimentary sketch or indication—*without*, in some respects at least, loss of efficacy. So a sentence, heard in the mind's ear, can be reduced to a mere fragment, to barely a syllable, without losing meaning adequate to the occasion. Depiction too has, very evidently, its private and its public sectors. Consider how we decide whether a portrait is or is not "a good likeness" or whether any drawing is or is not "right." We have our internal means (not necessarily confined to more or less veridical visual images) by which to check (control: etymon, *contra*—"over against" what is on a *roll*) the meanings that public signs may offer us. Depiction has not as yet received anything like the attention and study it deserves, either in semiotic or in theory and practice of education. In semiotic, to consider how depictions work can serve as valuable *control* over accounts of how verbal language works. The metaphor by which we call depiction a "visual language" is deeply instructive. In education, both what depictions can do and how they do it are among the largest relatively untapped resources the educator might command.

THE TYPE-token DISTINCTION

It is fitting that the semiotic of depiction should itself use depictions: with which to distinguish and hold clear for study the cooperative factors in depictive communication. Let us begin with a $\frac{SITUATION\ (SIT)}{situation\ (sit)}$ and a $\frac{PICTURING\ (PIC)}{picturing\ (pic)}$. Here the *capitals* vs. *lower case* contrast represents Peirce's TYPE vs. token distinction.[10]

GRAPHIC AND DEPICTIVE NOTATIONS

In the last two sentences (*SENTENCES, SENs*) the graphic contrast between capitals and lower case (between C and c represents the semiotic distinction (between an instance, c, and that of which it is an instance, C). In these *SENs* both verbal and non-

10. *Collected Papers of Charles Sanders Peirce*, ed. Charles Hartshorne and Paul Weiss (Cambridge, Mass., 1933) IV, par. 527. Also see C. K. Ogden and I. A. Richards, *The Meaning of Meaning* (New York: Harcourt, Brace & Co., 1923), pp. 280-81.

verbal signs are cooperating in a way which deserves fuller exploration than can be attempted here. What I have called a *graphic* contrast is not *depictive*, for it will not do to describe *C* and *c* as picturings of *C* and *c*. (Otherwise, the indispensable distinction between a picture and that of which it is a picture would lapse.) On the other hand, in $\dfrac{SEN,\ PIC,\ SIT}{sen,\ pic,\ sit}$ . . . the line under *SEN* . . . and over *sen* . . . can properly be regarded as a depictive sign of the relationship between TYPE and token, between what is instanced and instances of it. As with all signs, it can be read in various ways (varying with the setting and purpose: the *sit*). Thus it may be indicating just this token status, or it may be going further and telling us that our dealings with TYPES (Ts) are mediated only through ts (TYPES being known to us and dealt with by us only through tokens, no TYPE being seen or smelled or touched or even thought of except through tokens of it). In other words, TYPES have to be carried by tokens: what occurs, being timeless and placeless, must be represented by datable, locatable occurrings. And this division line may be read (in yet another sense): *verbalized,* worded as "over," or as "is conveyed by," and so on.

Inevitably, in using such a line we are inviting an immensely powerful system of meanings: those deriving from the $\dfrac{\text{numerator}}{\text{denominator}}$ relationship, to intervene if and when they can. I mention this to illustrate the point made above that any meaning has to defend itself from interpretations not relevant. Indeed, its resistances to these usually define what it is. There are exceptions to this. One is exemplified by the fact that a depiction, say, of the relation of a point to a line, if taken strictly as concerned only with their positions on a plane, is definite in ways in which no verbal transmutation of it normally can be. All we can do, in words, is to indicate and approximate. That is why architectural depictions are so useful. No verbal description can take their place. And any builder's performances based on them will depart, less or more, from what they depict. But this definiteness attends only while they are being regarded as visual statements of relations between items on a plane. Let them be taken as *pictorial* representations of objects in space and they become as open to misinterpretation as any verbal description could be.

Such a notational device and the semiotic reflections it prompts can help to protect us (a) from confusions between TYPES and tokens and (b) from confusions between "what is said" and "our ways of saying it." Both must—as far as possible—be avoided if we are to trace successfully the powers and limits of depiction and of its cooperations with verbal signs.

THREE MODES OF EXPLORING SITUATIONS

As Jerome Bruner has usefully reminded us, we have three modes of exploring situations:

1. By performances: fingerings, trials, searchings, etc.—*enactions* (*en*s)
2. Imagery: iconics, simulations—*depictions* (*pic*s)
3. Verbalizations: *sentences* (*sen*s)

Relationships between these three are endlessly neglected in actual classroom practice. For example, a teacher who has not thought about and is not thinking about what may be happening in the learners' minds can invite very persistent confusions through careless handling of her enactions and depictions of such very important verbal distinctions as that between *on* and *off*. With a ball and a table and a floor, the prime physical relationship from which all the manifold metaphysical meanings derive (and on which they depend) can in a few minutes be planted, germinated, and developed. In as little a time endless unclarities can be created by careless handling and disregard of timing and pausing. *To* and *from*, *up* and *over*, *in*, *on*, and *at* (*at* a point, *on* a wall, *in* a room, *at* eight, *on* the first Monday *in* 1973)—all our fundamental means of control over space relations and motions, as we represent them in language, can be blurred, and an immense additional burden imposed by an unaware and stupid teacher. This is one of the reasons why well-designed films, sufficiently tested and criticized, are so valuable in the teaching of such keys to a command of English. Probably only through the alerted attention their design requires can better cooperations between *en*s, *pic*s, *sen*s, and *sit*s be developed and set to work.

An example here will clarify the terms in the discussion. Let the *SITUATION* be that in which a child is attempting to find out how writing works by comparing the following two *SENTENCES*:

This is a man.
This is a hat.

Each *sen* is accompanied by a maximally simplified undistractive *pic*, placed in contiguous relationship with the *sen*. The *sens* themselves are contiguous. They are so placed, on the page facing the child, that the parts of them that are similar and the parts that are dissimilar are as manifest as can be. On the blackboard and on the walls of the room the two *sens* appear again in different writing and print. In some of these, sameness and difference are indicated by difference in script:

This is a man.
This is a hat.

The accompanying depictions are also varied.

Before the child is a typewriter with all but the following keys covered with blank paper disks: *a hi mn st.* (On an electric typewriter all but these seven keys can be inoperable.) It will be noticed that these letters are minimally confusable: the differences between them overpower the sameness. Not one of them is a reversed form of another (as *n* and *u*, *b* and *d*, *p* and *q*) or is an incomplete form of another (as *c* and *e* may be of *o*).

If the keyboard is in capitals, the child is shown how to depress and lock the shift. He then experiments with the seven lettered keys, noting that each yields on paper a replica of what is on the key. In this he is comparing an enaction with its outcome. He goes on to compare two or more *ens* with their outcomes. In these comparings the joint operation of similarity-difference and contiguity is at its clearest.

He now passes to attempting to reproduce the two *sens*. They will have been said *to* him (and *by* him and others) in a variety of voices (sen_1, sen_2, sen_n): all tokens, differing one from another, of the same *SEN*. Thus continually, one aspect of the overall *SITUATION* being explored is kept active—the relation of graphic forms to speech sounds—but *not* in such a way as to occult the more important relation of the seen word to its enactable and depictable meanings.

The first word here to be tackled will be *This*, followed immediately by what may be perceived as a part of *This*, namely, *is*. The exercise in comparings continues as *a* appears again within *man* but surrounded by differents: *m* and *n*, between which the difference is one which is uncommonly visible and significant— that between 2 and 3 (II and III), two lollipops and three.

From letter to word to $\dfrac{sen}{pic}$, thence to $\dfrac{SEN}{PIC}$ (via the other scripts and depictions on the walls), so the sequence of comparings should proceed; but it will do so (if, as we should, we let it) in a seesaw or pendulum fashion. The letters on paper at the very start of the enaction (at *en*) are being compared with the letters on the keys. But, after that, typed letter on paper is compared with letter in the model word (on the blackboard) as, later, the typed word, as enaction product, is compared with the word in the model *sen*. In almost all learning, the control of part by whole and of whole by part is, or should be, reciprocal. In advancing from our initial pair of *SEN*s to such pairs as

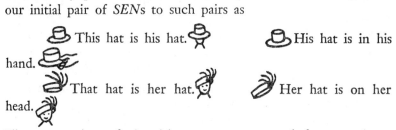

This hat is his hat.   His hat is in his hand.

That hat is her hat.   Her hat is on her head.

The cooperations of *pic* with *sen* may go as much from *sen* (now being read) to *pic* as from *pic* to *sen*. In general, we may note that *SIT*s form enclosure series. An overall problem, How does writing work? is approached via a series of smaller problems whose solving contributes towards its apprehension.[11]

11. For the detail of the design of the instructional sequences this example has been referring to, see 1972 edition of I. A. Richards and C. M. Gibson, *English through Pictures*, Books I, II, III (New York: Pocket Books, 1972) and *First Steps in Reading English* (New York: Pocket Books, 1957). Information on cassettes, filmstrips, sound motion-pictures, television programs, and other teaching aids for use with these texts is available from Educational Services, 1730 Eye St., N.W., Washington, D.C. 20006, and from Language Research, Inc., 134 Mt. Auburn Street, Cambridge, Mass. 02138.

For a fuller discussion of the rationale of these recommendations see my "Instructional Engineering" in S. Baker, J. Barzun, and I. A. Richards, *The Written Word* (Rowley, Mass.: Newbury House Publishers, 1971).

Exploratory Activity

In passing now to a general account of exploratory activity, the relationship between the *sit* and the *en*s, *pic*s, *sen*s has first to be described. Normally, the *sit*, which is an event in which the percipient is taking part, an occurrence to him, is in large measure re-cognized. It is being taken as an instance of a *SIT* whose character is predominantly familiar, though it may, of course, be much mistaken. How to deal with it is accordingly more or less grasped, though there will also be fringes of uncertainty, and it is as attempts to adjust these that exploratory activity via *en, pic, sen* develops. What *en*s occur (handlings, pokings, turnings, approachings, and so on) take place as representatives of *EN*s by which they are guided and controlled. Similarly, *pic*s that assist (images, say, of what something may look like if turned) derive from *PIC*s. And the *SIT*, as it is being apprehended, has been represented by other *sit*s before. While this sort of *en, pic* exploration proceeds, it may be accompanied by verbalization (subvocal or not). The explorer may be talking to himself or to a companion: "Let's see how it looks this way," "Try the key upside down," "Don't push it quite so far in," and so on. Through all this, influences from unimaginably many and various former *en*s, *pic*s, *sen*s, ordered through the relations between their *EN*s, *PIC*s, *SEN*s, are attempting to bring the *sit* home under its appropriate *SIT*.

All this, as the formation, growth, and control of concepts, has for millenia been familiar ground to educators, though perhaps in recent times the consequences of it for communication have been somewhat neglected. We are too ready to think of a concept as existing merely in the mind of the conceiver. But any one person's concept is properly to be regarded as itself a representative: depictable in our notation as $\frac{CONCEPT}{con_1 \; con_2 \; con_n}$. Learning can thus be conceived as the taking over in the individual of an order towards the apprehension of which he is progressing. (There is a pathological side, of course, on which I must not dilate here.)

We have not yet entered upon the major complexities, however. We have to recall that these cooperating items, from the *SIT* down through all the *en*s, *pic*s, *sen*s that are joining in its exploration, are, each and all of them, what they are through their relationships of similarity-difference and contiguity to their neighbors and rivals—those that may be competing for a hand in the job. It is this interplay which gives signs their power and makes the wholeness and sanity of acts of clear, self-controlled, and just discernment so impressive.

This saving connexity—this consistency—is maintained, we have suggested, through the relationships among the TYPE systems. For every lower-case item that takes part there is a capital, by virtue of which it acts and to which it appeals. Its relations to its fellow lower-case components in the comprehending of the situation are governed, in short, by the order that has been attained among the types. All growth in cognitive abilities comes about through improvement in that. We may cite Coleridge: "I call that *genuine* knowledge only which returns again as power." The prime difference between a mind which "knows what it is doing" (in the laudatory sense) and one which doesn't is in the organization of its type-systems.

PRINCIPLES OF USEFUL DEPICTION

Against some such background as has been sketched let us now consider a few of the principles that govern reasonable use of depiction for instruction.

Mutual dependence of signs. Since similarity-difference and contiguity are jointly ruling throughout, what any depictive sign can do depends on other signs: those like and unlike it in the percipient's experience *and* cooperative with it in the situation. No depictive sign (any more than any verbal sign) carries its meaning inevitably within it. What it can mean for the addressee turns on what other signs have meant for him and on what other present coactive signs can mean.

Due sequence in design. Reverse or displace the order of the steps and relatively little of significance can develop. Sequence in depiction can therefore be of decisive importance. The designer of a course of instruction can do far more than use illustrations as attention-getters, cues, and incidental entertainment. By sequencing them aright he can construct series of invitations to intelligent exploration, in which depictions stand in opposition and in contiguity relationships to one another and in which earlier *SITUATIONS* intelligibly *prepare* for instructive *comparison* with those that follow. Such designing is, of course, most desirable and most feasible in the beginning phases of learning in a new field: in "beginning reading" and in the entering and early stages of a second language. In these it is possible to use depiction to conduct a learner's insight through the fundamental discriminations upon which his grasp of how the scriptal notation and the new language work. There is a reasonable order to be shown him here (as there is for early stages in geometry) and pictures are the ideal means through which to do so. Unfortunately, at present it is in these very fields that current use of depiction can be seen at its least enlightened. It is primarily *distractive*, which is worse than putting powdered glass in the sugar.

Cultivation of insight. The prime aim in depiction is to invite and guide *insight* into how representation *varies with* the situation represented. What the learner is attempting to acquire is increased command over a system of representation. In this, the last thing he needs and the thing he should most be spared is being dragged away to attend to something else, something allegedly *amusing* or *diverting*. (Educators could find in the derivations of these two words the strongest reasons against current practice.) It is the growth of this insight, not any product of the drilling in of stimulus-response routines or habit formation, that leads to advances in skill and power. In all this the role of controlled depiction is, as yet, only in its initial phase of development. The most familiar example is the graph and it is worth noting that *graph*, in this sense, "a line or system of lines symbolizing variations of occurrence or intensity," is a word still less than a hundred years old. Educators should acquaint themselves with what has in the present decade been made possible in the field of computer graphics and how compact, forceful, and illuminating can be its representations of data otherwise complex beyond any imagining. That the most striking applications so far have been to urban and megalopolitan problems is not surprising. If we add what seems likely to happen in three-dimensional photography, for example, the new powers for the cultivation of insight that are becoming available in teaching—from elementary levels up—are truly astounding. It is hard not to be hopeful. They may make the triumphs of antibiotics, say, look like a minor advance. But they will require, of course, judicious handling.

Elimination of distraction. Simplification and the strict elimination of irrelevances and potentially distracting elaborations are conditions for efficiency in depictions. Their styling should be under the control of the designer of the instruction sequences, not left to publisher's art editor or to the artist, who are in this field very much at the mercy of fashion. It should be remembered that a depiction is a sign calling for interpretation of a situation. Normally it will be (notably in "beginning reading" or a second language) predominantly cognitive. Variations in its components that are not *significant*—that do not contribute to the interpretation of a situation—are to be avoided as overlikely to be distractive. The learner is learning, above all, to discern what is significant, what varies with what; and he should, in early stages of his task, be protected from accidental occasions to go astray. He should certainly not be Pied Piper'd away into nonsense. It should be remembered too that these early steps are his best, perhaps his only, introduction to method of inquiry. They can establish in him his standards as to what to expect; they can and should plant, in fact, the very seeds of his conceptions of order and of reasonable procedure. Ought we not indeed do our best to put before him good models? What he is learning is the essential technique of science, how to look for *what varies with what* in a given setting, how to observe this under the joint control of similarity-difference and contiguity.

This principle of cooperation between likeness-unlikeness and neighborhood operates universally. I began by taking the phrase "ordinary word-users" and looking for "special users of language" to put into opposition with it. Very likely, Jakobson as he wrote was simply opposing ordinary word-users to linguists, and it will be useful to consider some of the relevant contrasts here more closely. They bear very directly on what educators, teachers, and learners should and should not be trying to do—especially in their directives, in their instruction, and in their work with language.

The linguist knows (in the sense of being able to state, discuss, support or refute) innumerable things about languages which the ordinary word-user does not in that sense know. The ordinary user may be an admirable word-user (even a Shakespeare) without any of that knowledge. He has another sort of knowledge of the language, a know-how with it, which serves him in its place. Furthermore, there is little or no evidence that the linguist's knowledge would necessarily help the ordinary word-user, if he had it. People can have a great deal of linguistic knowledge and yet be inferior word-users.

The Art of Conscious Comparing

There is, however, one branch of special linguistic knowledge which can help everyone, though it is not enough just to have it; we must learn to use it. This branch has no safe and handy name, but it can be readily described. It is the art of conscious comparings of meanings and of the explicit description of them through linguistic signs.

The lack of a safe name for this art is not hard to explain. In part it is due to the enigmatic status of meanings: they were felt to be such dubious entities that few could be sure what was being done when they were discussed. In part, it is due to people giving to the art names much used for other things, for example, *rhetoric, exegesis*, and, worst of all, *semantics*, including Korzybsky's "general semantics." Two good names exist covering parts of this study. *Lexicology*: the knowledge and skill and judgment required for good work in preparing articles in a dictionary. But the art of comparing meanings requires ability to see what the setting of a meaning is as well as discernment as to which parts of a dictionary article may be relevant. Study of *synonymy* suffers from similar drawbacks.

SOME PRINCIPLES

Indication of a few principles of this fundamental art, strangely neglected in schools, eminently useful though it is, will help to show what it should try to do.

Cooperation and interference. One principle has just been mentioned: the dependence of meanings on the meanings of other words surrounding them in the setting as well as upon other factors in the ambience. What should be brought out is how what a word does is changed by a change made elsewhere in a passage. In this, words behave very like people engaged in what should be a cooperative undertaking.

This principle emerges from comparisons between alternative phrases. To risk overstating it: any change in the phrasing entails some change in the meaning of a sentence. Sometimes it is a change that matters, sometimes not. To question *why* is continually a penetrating thrust of inquiry.

Tenor and vehicle. A long while ago, some forty or more years, I tried to further inquiry into metaphor by introducing two new terms (to be technicalized, if possible) to replace the appalling welter of ambiguous phrasings that labored to distinguish (a) what was being said (offered, presented) from (b) the way in which it was being said (offered, presented).[12] They were: (a) *tenor*, (b) *vehicle*, to stand respectively for the what (the tenor) and the way (the vehicle). I did not then, I think, so generalize, being too close to the problems of metaphor. Nor did I write the distinction down depictively as $\frac{T}{V}$, making V into *signans* and T into *signatum*. I did, however, realize then, as much earlier, that what T, the tenor, would represent could not normally be unaffected by changes in V.

Notations have strange powers, as has been frequently shown in the history of mathematics. They can simplify and make routine what otherwise might call for an effort of thought, a recalling of principles. Korzybsky (the Apostle of General Semantics and not averse to being introduced to gatherings as Count Korzybsky, the Time Binder) tried in his *Science and Sanity*, in its day a gospel for a cult, to introduce various useful notations to serve as reminders of what we all know but frequently forget. Typical was the sign *etc.*—to remind us of the rest that should be in our awareness more often than it is. He proposed to abbreviate it to..or..as it was placed in the midst or at the end of a sentence. This doubtless would be a salutary procedure, though so inconspicuous a sign would be likely to be overlooked or treated as a misprint. I have tried out, myself, a set of specialized inverted commas with various intents. One of these is concerned with the tenor-vehicle terminological innovation mentioned above. It is the affixing, as superscripts, of ˢʷ_____ˢʷ in place of ˢʷquotation marks ˢʷ, to distinguish words and phrases which the writer knows may very possibly be taken by the addressee in senses seriously different from that in which he hopes to have them understood. ˢʷ_____ˢʷ is short for *said with*, which is again an abbreviation

12. See my *Interpretation of Teaching*, op. cit.

of ᔆᵂsomething that may be said withˢʷ. The implication is that
language at that point, as it can be used for the particular purpose being pursued, is deficient (at least, as the writer can use it)
and that, failing a perfectly fit term, something known to be less
than fully efficient is being used. The indulgence of the reader
is being begged and his guessing capacity being alerted by the little
alphabetic fleas perched at both ends of the word or phrase.

This notational device, neither complex nor exacting, can serve,
I believe, several compatible purposes. It can warn the reader to
ˢʷstep warilyˢʷ and to ˢʷselect wiselyˢʷ. It can, furthermore, help
to defend us from an error into which we far too frequently fall:
the mistake of supposing that our statements are doing more than
they possibly can do, that they are indeed putting the very truth
down on the paper. One of Korzybsky's most famous metaphoric
slogans is useful here: "The map is not the territory." In a cool
moment we may perhaps suppose we couldn't think it is. And
a moment later we find ourselves so doing and realize once more
how great is the power of signs and at the same time how strict
their limits.

Object language and metalanguage. A third principle of this
art of comparing meanings will seem from one point of view to
be the same thing said in another way. It can be put as an injunc-
tion: Do not confuse statements about things with statements about
the language used in the statements. In other words: Distinguish
between object language and metalanguage. Object language is
talk about "the context referred to"; metalanguage is about the
code being used in the communication. But, here again, we must
distinguish without separating and remember that a sentence can
very well be both referential—tell us about something—and metalingual—tell us about the code. If I say, "That is a quail," I may
be telling someone something about a bird. How much I tell him
will obviously depend upon how much he knows about quails already. Or I may be telling him something about the word *quail*:
that it is the name for a certain sort of bird. What is referential for
one addressee may be metalingual for another. Into all comparisons
of meanings, all attempts to assess and describe the powers and
limits of signs in their actual operation, the inevitable differences
enter. Occasions differ, speakers differ, recipients differ. In spite
of which, human communication is somehow maintained.

SECTION II

THE EDUCATIONAL POTENTIAL OF VARIOUS MEDIA: HOW MEDIA INFORM, INSTRUCT, AND INFLUENCE

CHAPTER VI

Learning through Experience and Learning through Media

DAVID R. OLSON

and

JEROME S. BRUNER

This paper is concerned broadly with the consequences of two types of experience which may be designated as direct experience and mediated experience, their partial equivalence and substitutability, and their differing potential roles in the intellectual development and acculturation of children. Our analysis will begin with the problem of the nature of direct experience and its effect on development. A clearer conception of the processes involved in direct experience will permit us to better examine the manner and extent to which mediate experience may complement, elaborate, and substitute for that direct experience.

Much of a child's experience is formalized through schooling. Whether for reasons of economy or effectiveness, schools have settled upon learning out of context through media which are primarily symbolic. Schooling generally reflects the naïve psychology which has been made explicit by Fritz Heider.[1] The general assumption of such a naïve psychology is that the effects of experience can be considered as knowledge, that knowledge is conscious, and that knowledge can be translated into words. Symmetrically, words can be translated into knowledge; hence, one can learn, that is, one can acquire knowledge, from being told.

Congruent with this is the belief that what differentiates child from adult is also knowledge and that the chief mission of school is to impart it by the formal mode of pedagogy. Concern for "character" or "virtue" centers not upon the school, but upon the

---

1. A. L. Baldwin, *Theories of Child Development* (New York: John Wiley & Sons, 1967).

home and the child's more intimate surroundings, the sources that provide models.

The assumptions that knowledge was central to the educational enterprise and that it was independent of both the form of experience from which it derived and the goals for which it was used had several important and persisting effects on educational thought. First, it led to a certain blindness to the effects of the *medium* of instruction as opposed to the content, a blindness that McLuhan has diagnosed[2] well; and, secondly, it led to a deemphasis of and a restricted conception of the nature and development of *ability*. As the effects of experience were increasingly equated to the accumulation of knowledge, experience was considered less and less often the source of ability. Since knowledge was all, ability could be taken for granted—simply, one *had* abilities that could be used to acquire knowledge. Abilities were, then, projected rather directly into the mind in the form of genetic traits. Culture and experience were both ignored as possible candidates to account for the development of abilities. The effect of this strange turn has been to downgrade the task of cultivating abilities in students, often thereby making schooling a poor instrument for the performance of this important task.

Education critics have, of course, long attacked educational goals formulated in terms of the simple acquisition of knowledge. Dewey's[3] concern with the relationship between knowledge and experience has much in common with contemporary reanalysis. In his view, genuine experience involved the initiation of some activity and a recognition of the consequences that ensued. Experiences of this sort would result, Dewey argued, in the natural and integrated development of knowledge, skills, and thinking. Schooling, on the other hand, attempted to develop the three independently of each other and with little regard for the experience of which they were products. No surprise, then, that schools frequently failed to achieve any of them. Dewey's revised conception of the relation between experience and knowledge reappears in the current attempts at educational reform which emphasize the

2. M. McLuhan, *Understanding Media, the Extensions of Man* (New York: McGraw-Hill Book Co., 1964).

3. J. Dewey, *Democracy and Education* (New York: MacMillan Co., 1916).

role of process rather than content, or, more specifically, emphasize activity, participation, and experience rather than the acquisition of factual information.[4] The contemporary critic and Dewey alike would attack the assumption that knowledge is acquired independently of the means of instruction and independently of the intended uses to which knowledge is to be put.

That knowledge is dependent on or is limited by the purpose for which it was acquired has been illustrated in experiments by Duncker,[5] by Maier,[6] and by many other students of thinking and problem-solving. The conventional use of a pliers as a gripping instrument makes them difficult to perceive as a pendulum bob. Knowledge per se does not make it possible to solve problems. The same appears to be true of verbally coded information. Maier, Thurber, and Janzen[7] showed that information which was coded appropriately for purposes of recall was, as a consequence, coded inappropriately for purposes of solving a problem. Information picked up from experience is limited in important ways to the purpose for which it is acquired—unless special means are arranged to free it from its context. But this conclusion is at odds with the naïve view that one can substitute "instruction" for "learning through experience."

We must, then, reexamine the nature of direct experience and its relation to both knowledge and skills or abilities. Of course, the term "direct" experience is somewhat misleading in that all knowledge is mediated through activity, and the resulting knowledge is not independent of the nature of those activities. But, if we consider both the knowledge of objects and events that results from experience and the structure of activities involved in experiencing,

4. J. S. Bruner, *The Process of Education* (Cambridge, Mass.: Harvard University Press, 1960); *Living and Learning*, Report of the Ontario Provincial Committee on Aims and Objectives of Education in the Schools of Ontario, Cochairmen, E. M. Hall and L. A. Dennis (Toronto: Ontario Department of Education, 1968).

5. K. Duncker, "On Problem Solving," *Psychological Monographs* 58 (1945): 270.

6. N. R. F. Maier, "Reasoning and Learning," *Psychological Review* 38 (1931): 332-46.

7. N. R. F. Maier, J. A. Thurber, and J. C. Janzen, "Studies in Creativity: The Selection Process in Recall and in Problem Solving Situations," *Psychological Reports* 23 (1968): 1003-22.

we may come closer to an adequate conception of "direct experience." We will then be in a better position to contrast it with mediated or, more accurately, the symbolically encoded and vicarious experience that is so important in acculturation.

Direct Experience

Psychology, mirroring an earlier physics, often begins an account of the nature of experience with the concept of the "stimulus." What occurs in behavior is thought to be a reflection of the stimulus acting upon the organism. At a more abstract level of analysis, the shape of the effective stimulus is seen as the result of certain physical filterings or transformation of the input given by the nature of the nervous system and its transducers. This conception is much too passive and nonselective with respect to what affects organisms. Living systems have an integrity of their own; they have commerce with the environment on their own terms, selecting from the environment and building representations of this environment as required for the survival and fulfillment of the individual and the species. It follows that our conception of physical reality is itself achieved by selective mediation.[8] The search for a psychological account of behavior must begin with the organism's activities and then determine the nature of the "reality" sustained by that type of activity. It is a point that is explicit and central to Piaget's conception of adaptive behavior in general and intelligence in particular: objects and events are not passively recorded or copied, but, rather, acted upon and perceived in terms of action performed.[9]

What does this view imply about the nature and consequence of experience? As we have said, we have a picture of reality that is biased by or coded in terms of our actions upon it; knowledge is

8. This central point appears in several related disciplines, including psychology, psychophysiology, and biology. See E. C. Tolman, *Purposive Behavior in Animals and Man* (New York: D. Appleton-Century Co., 1932); K. H. Pribram, *Languages of the Brain: Experimental Paradoxes and Principles in Neuropsychology* (Englewood Cliffs, N.J.: Prentice-Hall, 1971); E. N. Sokolov, "The Modeling Properties of the Nervous System," in *A Handbook of Contemporary Soviet Psychology*, ed. I. Maltzman and M. Cole (New York: Basic Books, 1969); E. von Holst, "Vom Wesen der Ordnung im Zentral Nerven System," *Die Naturwissenschaften* 25 (1937): 625-31, 641-47.

9. J. Piaget, *Biology and Knowledge* (University of Chicago Press, 1971).

always mediated or specified through some form of human activity. But note that any knowledge acquired through any such activity has two facets: information about the *world* and information about the *activity* used in gaining knowledge. In an aphorism: from sitting on chairs one learns both about "chairs" and about "sitting." This distinction is reflected in ordinary language in the terms *knowledge* and *skill* or *ability*. There are, therefore, two types of invariants that are specified through experience. The set of features that are more or less invariant across different activities may be considered as the structural or invariant features of objects and events that constitute our *knowledge* about those objects and events. Similarly, the set of operations or constituent acts that are invariant when performed across different objects and events may be considered as the structural basis of the activities themselves—that which we call *skills and abilities*. It is our hypothesis that "knowledge" reflects the invariants in the natural and social environment while "skills or abilities" reflect the structure of the medium or performatory domain in which various activities are carried out (see figure 1). Obviously, major significance must be attributed to *both* facets of experience.

Consider more specifically how both facets are realized in practice. The performance of any act may be considered a sequence of decision points, each involving a set of alternatives. These decision points are specified jointly by the intention motivating the act, the goal or end point, and the structure of the medium or environment in which the act occurs. A skilled performance requires that the actor have information available that permits him to choose between these alternatives. Problem-solving is a matter of trying out various means and assessing their contribution to the achievement of the end state. He must assess the means while keeping the end criteria in mind. It is a universal routine—in love, in war, in writing a paragraph or solving an equation, or, indeed, in managing to get hold of objects during the initial phases of the infant's mastery of reaching.

From this point of view, mastery depends upon the acquisition of information required for choosing between alternative courses of action that could lead to a sought-after end. The most obvious way to acquire such information is through active attempts to

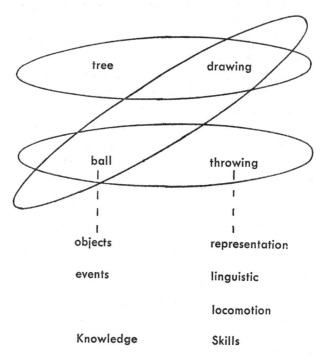

Activities
or
Experiences

Fig. 1. The relation of knowledge and skills to physical activity

achieve various goals in a variety of performatory domains. The most obvious way to learn about a country is to walk its streets, read its poets, eat its foods, work in its fields, and so on. In so doing, one will learn both about the country (*that* the country is poor or hilly, etc.) and how to proceed in the activities required to be of that country (*how to* mend a net or tell a story). This is surely what is meant by learning through one's own direct contingent experience.

Mediate Experience

But there are other ways to acquire information. From seeing a man struggle with his load, one can make some estimate of its weight. That is, one can experience vicariously or mediately. Psychological studies have repeatedly shown that learning can occur when neither of the primary conditions for learning through contingent experience—self-initiated action or direct knowledge of its results—is fulfilled. Bandura[10] has summarized a wide range of data showing how behavior can be modified and new behavior patterns acquired by exposing the learner to modeling stimuli even in rather artificial laboratory situations. An illustrative experiment was performed long ago by Herbert and Harsh.[11] Two groups of cats learned to pull strings and open doors by observing other cats. One group of cats saw only the final errorless performances of cat models while the other group saw the early error-filled performances as well as the correct performances. Both groups of cats learned to solve the problems more quickly than the control cats, who learned only from their own contingent experience. But the cats that saw the error-filled performances learned more readily than those who saw only the error-free performances.

Another alternative to learning directly is through symbolically coded information, that is, the information that is transmitted through the media—the spoken or printed word, film, diagram, and so on. It is learning through these symbolic systems that most readily substitutes for direct experience in formal schooling. Vygotsky[12] and Bruner[13] have emphasized the extent to which language provides the means par excellence for teaching and learning out of context, out of a situation in which action is in process and contingent consequences are most direct. Language, as we shall see, provides an opportunity for acquiring knowledge which, while it is less useful for any particular line of action, has the advantage of ordering knowledge in a form compatible with the rules of abstract thought.

We have, therefore, three modes of experience which map

10. A. Bandura, *Principles of Behavior Modification* (New York: Holt, Rinehart & Winston, 1969).

11. J. J. Herbert and C. M. Harsh, "Observational Learning by Cat," *Journal of Comparative Psychology* 37 (1944): 81-95.

12. L. S. Vygotsky, *Thought and Language* (Cambridge, Mass.: M.I.T. Press, 1962).

13. J. S. Bruner, R. Olver, and P. M. Greenfield, *Studies in Cognitive Growth* (New York: John Wiley & Sons, 1966).

roughly onto the three forms of representation discussed else-where [14] as enactive, iconic, and symbolic: the first is related to direct action, the second to models, and the third to symbolic systems.

More important to our purpose is the fact that these three modes of experience map onto evolutionary development.[15] While all animals learn from contingent experience, primates are distinctive in their capacity for learning by observation—there is an enormous amount of observation of adult behavior by the young, with incorporation of what has been learned into a pattern of play. The human species is, of course, marked by its reliance on symbolically coded experience—so much so that the development of language is taken as the distinctive characteristic of the human species and the development of literacy in various symbolic codes is the primary concern of formalized schooling. It follows that these three forms of experience differ greatly in the assumptions they make about the organism; that is, they differ primarily in terms of the skills they assume and develop in the learner.

On the Acquisition of Knowledge

To this point, the burden of our argument has been to show that one can learn from three very different forms of experience and that these forms of experience, whether mediate or direct, qualify what is learned. This section of the paper is directed to an examination of what is common to different forms of experience; the next section is concerned with what is distinctive about them. Our conclusion will be that different forms of experience converge as to the knowledge they specify, but they diverge as to the skills they develop.

The assertion to be examined here is that different forms of experiencing an object or an event can be mapped onto a common underlying structure—a coherent and generalized conception of reality. Information about a particular event, regardless of the activity or medium through which it is obtained, has in common the property that it permits the differentiation of that event from the

14. Ibid.

15. J. S. Bruner, "Nature and Uses of Immaturity," *American Psychologist* 27 (1972): 687-708.

alternatives with which it is in danger of being confused. Consider the experience of actually seeing a zebra with that of hearing the instructional statement "A zebra is a striped, horse-like animal." The same features detected in the act of discrimination are specified in the statement; hence, they are informationally equivalent and they can both be mapped onto an underlying conception of zebras, horses, animals, and so on. This is not to deny that each mode has a residual uniqueness, but only to point out that they share a common structure as well. The range of topographically dissimilar forms of experience, including various forms of instruction, may be considered as various "surface structures" which relate in their special ways to a common underlying structure of knowledge. Indeed, it is the very fact that information relevant to action can be acquired through means *other* than direct action itself that makes instruction possible. Thus, one can learn to sail, perhaps only to a limited extent, through watching films and reading books. There is considerable evidence from controlled laboratory experiments to show that common learning results from different types of experience. A child can learn to construct a diagonal either through activity coupled with reinforcement, through an appropriate demonstration, or through verbal instruction. Others have shown that children can learn difficult-to-teach Piagetian conservation tasks through quite different training techniques.[16] And it is well known that there is almost an infinite number of ways to teach reading.[17] The problem is to specify as far as possible the structure of information in these various instructional forms or surface structures and to see how they each relate to the underlying structure described above. Once these forms of instruction have been specified, it may be possible to indicate how each of them relates to the various technologies involved in their production and distribution. These relationships are set out in a preliminary way in figure 2. This figure indicates

16. P. E. Bryant, "Cognitive Development," *British Medical Bulletin* 27 (1971): 200-5; G. S. Halford, "A Theory of the Acquisition of Conservation," *Psychological Review* 77 (1970): 302-16; R. Gelman, "Conservation Acquisition: A Problem of Learning to Attend to Relevant Attributes," *Journal of Experimental Child Psychology* 8 (1969): 314-27.

17. J. S. Chall, *Learning to Read: The Great Debate* (New York: Carnegie Corp., 1965).

Cognitive Development			Categories of Behavior from Which Information May Be Extracted	Technological Realizations
Knowledge	Skills			
chair | | | objects events space time causality	sitting drawing describing | locomotive prehensive linguistic mathematical iconological	Information Extraction Processes	Contingent experience ⟨ Direct / Directed (instructional) Observational learning ⟨ Observation / Modeling (instruction) Symbolic systems ⟨ Communication / Instruction	–Structured environments –Laboratory experiments –Simulations –Educational toys –Automatizing devices –Films and animations –Demonstrations –Modeling –Print –Drawings –Diagrams –Models –Graphs –Maps

FIG. 2. The acquisition of knowledge and skills and the forms of experience from which they are derived

that there are three basic forms of instruction: through arranged contingent experience, observational learning, and symbolic systems, all of which have their effect by providing information relevant to the acquisition of both knowledge and skills.

All three forms of *instruction* can only be extensions of basic forms of interaction with the world and its symbols. They may be characterized as "instructional" only when their use is marked by the intent of another person who for some reason, usually institutionally derived, accepts responsibility for the learner. *Learning from one's own contingent experience* can be regarded as instruction only in special circumstances, such as when the environment is intentionally prearranged by another person. The learner's role in this process is readily described as "learning by doing," and the instructor's role is primarily that of selecting, simplifying, or otherwise ordering the environment so as to make the consequences of the action, the reinforcement, both obvious and safe. The second form of instruction may be designated *observational learning.* The learner's role may be described as "learning by matching," and the instructor's role is primarily that of providing a demonstration or model and perhaps some feedback. The third form of instruction involves the *use of various symbolic systems,* including a natural language. The learner's role is primarily that of "learning by being told" and the instructor's role is that of telling—providing facts, descriptions, and explanations.

The three categories of instruction depend (as do the modes of learning on which they are based) upon the three modes of representing experience, namely, enactive, iconic, and symbolic.[18] In our view, these forms of instruction and the related modes of representation reflect different surface structures of experience that share an underlying informational or *knowledge* structure. To see how each of these surface structures relates to the common underlying knowledge structure, we must determine what information is invariant to all instruction and how information is coded in the instructional programs we have considered to this point. We shall accordingly examine reinforcement, modeling, and verbal instruction.

Reinforcement

Firstly, consider the instructional effects or contingent experience that is of reinforcement. Reinforcement broadly conceived is knowledge of the consequences of an act.[19] Reinforcement assures a means of determining when an appropriate choice among alternatives has been made. Reinforcement, by its universality across species, provides a medium of information exchange whereby a Skinner can communicate with a pigeon, and vice versa, for organisms are potent sources of consequence for the actions of other organisms. This assumes that organisms respond systematically to the responses of others—though not necessarily by a simple calculus of good and bad outcomes. And, obviously, reinforcement mediates much interacting with the inanimate environment. But while the discovery of new knowledge may be dependent on our direct contingent experiences with nature and with other organisms, reinforcement has the limitation of being ambiguous in outcome. When a teacher reinforces a child for asking a question, the child may not know if it was the question-asking that she approved or the merits of that specific question. Reinforcement can rarely indicate the critical alternatives but can indicate the consequences of the final performance. Guthrie's [20] cats, for example, did not know

18. Bruner et al., op. cit.

19. R. Glaser, *The Nature of Reinforcement* (New York: Academic Press, 1971).

20. E. R. Guthrie, "Conditioning: A Theory of Learning in Terms of Stimulus, Response and Association," in *The Psychology of Learning*, Forty-first Yearbook of the National Society for the Study of Education, Part II, pp. 17-60 (Chicago: Distributed by the University of Chicago Press, 1942).

what aspect of their action in the puzzle box was critical for obtaining their release; hence they preserved many irrelevant ones. And given the fact that other human beings—with their obvious variability—are often the principal source of reinforcement, the ambiguity is confounded. It is surprising how uncritically many people accept the idea of control of behavior by reinforcement, in view of the constrained circumstances necessary for it to be effective at all. And more important for instruction, a child obtains no relevant information from a reinforcement if he happens not to be considering the critical alternatives. Modern theories of discrimination learning move increasingly in the direction of distinguishing between feature selection (attention) and reinforcement to deal with this point.[21] Given such considerations, one can account not only for the effects of this type of instruction but also for some of the anomalies in reinforcement theory.[22]

Three devices are widely used to render reinforcement less ambiguous. One is by immediacy: tagging the reinforcement directly to the act. The second is by disambiguating the feature of the stimulus to be attended to by placing it in a context that differentiates it from an alternative.[23] The third is through "scientific method," by unambiguously assigning certain sequelae to certain prior events so that the necessity of the conceptual link cannot be overlooked. This is typically the way of "guided discovery" which, as with the other two techniques, relies on control of attention. In time, one who must learn by direct encounter comes to control his own attention in one of the three ways suggested: by keeping an eye "peeled" for immediate results, by being selective in his scanning of features, and by attending to necessity and regularity of relationship. Obviously, there is a technology and a form of materials that must go with the learning of such "discovery or

21. N. S. Sutherland, "Visual Discrimination in Animals," *British Medical Bulletin* 20 (1964): 54-59; N. J. Mackintosh, "Selective Attention in Animal Discrimination Learning," *Psychological Bulletin* 64 (1965): 64, 124-50.

22. Glaser, op. cit.; M. Levine, "Hypothesis Theory and Nonlearning Despite Ideal S-R Reinforcement Contingencies," *Psychological Review* 78 (1971): 130-40.

23. W. R. Garner, "To Perceive Is to Know," *American Psychologist* 21 (1966): 11-19; P. E. Bryant and T. Trabasso, "Transitive Inferences and Memory in Young Children," *Nature* 232 (1971): 456-58.

reinforcement skills." It would be foolish to assume that such learning is not crucially dependent on education. If such were not the case, there would be far more learning from direct experience than there seems to be.

Modeling

One of the more transparent instructional approaches is that of modeling or providing demonstrations, an approach that makes up an important part of Montessori programs. How is information conveyed through modeling? Complex acts cannot be imitated unless the performer already knows how to carry out the act. That is, modeling may initiate or instigate known behavior but not, in any simple manner, produce learning. Yet, learning does occur in some situations.

How can information be conveyed appropriately through modeling? In line with the general theory advanced above, information permits a choice between alternatives. That is, consciousness of the alternatives is a necessary prerequisite for the pickup or acquisition of new information. In another context it was reported that a Montessori teacher successfully modeled, for a three-year-old child, the process of reconstructing a diagonal pattern, a task that is normally solved only by four- or five-year-olds.[24] The demonstration consisted of showing the child each of the choice points, that is, the critical alternatives, and then indicating how to choose between them. The demonstration of *where not to go* or *what not to do* is important to the extent that those alternatives are likely to mislead the child. In this light, it is possible to understand the finding of Herbert and Harsh,[25] mentioned earlier, that the cats who saw the error-filled performance learned more than those who saw the error-free performance. The latter performance deleted what the critical choice points or critical alternatives were. A final skilled performance does not render observable the critical alternatives; hence, the observer does not detect the information required to choose between them.

Good instruction through modeling depends upon the sensitivity

24. D. R. Olson, *Cognitive Development: The Child's Acquisition of Diagonality* (New York: Academic Press, 1970).

25. Herbert and Harsh, op. cit.

of the instructor to the alternatives likely to be entertained by the child. Modeling or providing demonstrations is, therefore a skill to which most pedagogic theories are blind. I. A. Richards[26] provides an illustration of the pedagogic implications of such a theory:

A teacher should know how to demonstrate the meanings of sentences and other things in ways which are at once unambiguous, memorable, and easily imitated. . . . For instance, with a ball and a table, a skilled teacher can in two minutes make the primal opposition of *on-off* evident. . . . A careless teacher in the same minutes can generate potential confusions with other distinctions to be handled with *to* and *from* and *up* and *over*, confusions which may later on make the learner's tasks far harder than they need be.

Just as providing clear demonstrations involves skill, it seems possible *that learning from demonstrations itself demands a skill*; depending upon its generality and utility, it may be a skill worth including in our educational aims (aside from the knowledge conveyed by that means). Elsewhere it has been argued that learning through modeling depends precisely on the capacity not so much to imitate directly as to construct behavior from already mastered constituent acts in order to match selected features of the model— a procedure more like paraphrasing than imitating.[27]

To summarize, any skilled performance, be it doing, saying, or making something, requires perceptual information for the guidance of each component of the act, that is, for selecting between all possible alternatives at each choice point in the performance. Modeling as an instructional technique is successful to the extent that it creates an awareness both of the critical alternatives and of how to choose between them. To this extent a good demonstration is different from skilled performance.

Verbal Instruction

Finally, consider language as an instructional medium. It is an instructional device par excellence by virtue of the fact that a word indicates not only a perceived referent but also an excluded set of alternatives. Words function contrastively—they differen-

26. I. A. Richards, *Design for Escape: World Education through Modern Media* (New York: Harcourt, Brace & World, 1968).

27. D. J. Wood, J. S. Bruner, and Gail Ross, "A Study of Tutorial Modeling," in preparation.

tiate alternatives. The ordinary claim that "words name things" overlooks the fact that words indicate or point to objects or events *in the implied context of the excluded alternatives.*[28] This point may be grasped by noting that the name or the description of an event is determined by the contrasting alternatives. Thus, a large white block in the context of a small white block is called "the large one," while the same block in the context of a large black block is called "the white one." Reciprocally, hearing such a sentence, or any other instructional sentence, the listener knows about both the intended referent *and the likely alternatives.* That is, language is structured precisely in the way that is required for instructional purposes in general. For this reason, the instruction of literate subjects almost always involves language; when experimentally tested, such instruction competes favorably with that making use of reinforcement and ordinary demonstrations; language coding is less ambiguous, that is, it conveys more information than those other media of instruction. (This, too, accords with the results obtained by Masters and Branch[29] and with those of many of the discovery-expository studies reported in the literature.)[30]

But there are many ways in which language can specify an intended referent, and these ways provide a microcosm for examining the major premises of the instructional model presented in this paper. The point is that certain very different sentences convey the same information and hence are generally called paraphrases of each other, or synonymous sentences. Consider these simple examples:

    1. (a) George is here.
       (b) My father's brother is here.
       (c) My uncle is here.
    2. (a) The stick is too short.
       (b) The stick is not long enough.

28. D. R. Olson, "Language and Thought: Aspects of a Cognitive Theory of Semantics," *Psychological Review* 77 (1970): 257-73.

29. J. C. Masters and M. N. Branch, "A Comparison of the Relative Effectiveness of Instructions, Modeling, and Reinforcement Procedures for Inducing Behavior Change," *Journal of Experimental Psychology* 80 (1969): 364-68.

30. R. Glaser and L. B. Resnick, "Instructional Psychology," *Annual Review of Psychology* 23 (1972): 207-76.

The sentences in (1) all designate the same intended referent and in some contexts are informationally equivalent. The specific sentences in each case differ, however, in the way the information is coded and in the specific mental processes involved in arriving at their meaning. They also differ in the assumptions they make about the listener; the first could be used only if the listener already knew who George was, and so on. This picture is complicated by the fact that different sentences frequently appear to arrive at a common effect without having a common meaning. Thus, Sheila Jones[31] gave subjects sheets of paper filled with the randomly ordered digits *1* through *8*. Some subjects were given the instruction in (3a) while others were given that in (3b).

3a. Mark the numbers 3, 4, 7, and 8.
3b. Mark all the numbers except 1, 2, 5, and 6.

Subjects found the latter more difficult, a result implying that information is more easily processed when coded one way than when coded another way. This example raises the question of the nature of the equivalence of sentences which are superficially different. It may be noted that in the context in which they were given, both of these sentences convey the same information: it is the *3, 4, 7,* and *8* that are to be marked. Hence, in this specific context they are paraphrases of each other, as may be a very dissimilar sentence such as (3c).

3c. Beginning at the right side of the sheet, mark the first, third, seventh . . . numbers.

These sentences are paraphrases of each other only in this immediate context, however. A new context would render them nonequivalent. Given the choice between two equivalent instructional sentences, one would choose between them on the same basis as between two instructional forms in general, that is, in terms of the complexity of the demands they make upon the learner and their generalizability to new but related problems.

The last point warrants an additional comment. In teaching children to find the perimeter of a particular rectangle, two in-

31. S. Jones, "The Effect of a Negative Qualifier in an Instruction," *Journal of Verbal Learning and Verbal Behaviour* 5 (1966): 495-501.

structional sentences which would convey the same information are the following:

4a. Add the 7 to the 5 and multiply by 2.
4b. Add the length to the width and multiply by 2.

Yet these two statements differ radically in their demands upon the listener, the latter statement being more complex than the former, and, in terms of their generality, the latter being more generalizable than the former. Generalizability refers to the fact that the second statement could apply to many different rectangles while the first could apply only to the particular given rectangle. It is interesting to note that the greater the generalizability of an instructional sentence (roughly, its instructional value), the greater the intellectual demand it makes (roughly, its difficulty of comprehension).

The teaching of rules and strategies falls into a similar position; they are difficult to comprehend but they have wide generality. There is always a trade-off between these two factors, a trade-off that is reflected in an instructional rule of thumb formulated by Carl Bereiter (personal communication) to the effect that if the rules are easily stated and have few exceptions, teach the rule and let the learners practice applying it to various problems; if the rules are not easily stated or have many exceptions, simply give practice on the problems and let the learners extract what rules they can for themselves.

The major limitation of language as an instructional medium, along with all cultural media such as graphs, diagrams, numbers, mime, and so on, is that the information is conveyed through a symbolic system that places high demands upon literacy in that medium. Further, the meaning extracted from those symbolic systems will be limited to the meaning acquired by the use of that symbol in the referential or experiential world.[32] Stated generally, this limitation of language implies an ancient point that no new information can be conveyed through language. If the information intended by the speaker falls outside the listener's "competence," the listener will interpret that sentence in terms of the knowledge

32. J. Carroll, "Words, Meaning and Concepts," *Harvard Educational Review* 34 (1964): 178-202; Olson, *Language and Thought*, op. cit.

he already possesses. It follows that instruction through language is limited to rearranging, ordering, and differentiating knowledge or information that the listener already has available from other sources, such as modeling, or through his own direct experiences. Parker (see chapter 4) has illustrated this point by showing the impossibility of verbally explaining perspective to the blind. In spite of this dependence of language upon perception, perception does come to be shaped in a way to permit easier comment, for reasons examined in the remainder of this essay.

On the Acquisition of Skills and Abilities

Having said that knowledge from different forms of experience can map onto a common deep structure, we must now make plain that there are also differences. The most important non-equivalence among experiences of events in the three forms is manifest not so much in the knowledge acquired, but in the skills involved in extracting or utilizing that knowledge. It is true that common knowledge of zebras may be obtained from actual experience and from appropriate sentences, but the skills involved in the two cases are entirely different; it is obviously a skill to extract symbolically coded knowledge from a sentence, but it is no less a skill to discriminate zebras from horses, albeit a skill so over-learned that we fail to recognize it as such until we are faced with a subtler but equally "obvious" discrimination such as that between Grant's gazelle and an impala. However combinable the outcomes, the skill of obtaining information by perceptual discrimination is a radically different skill from that of extracting the same information from language. The crucial issue for instruction, then, becomes one of deciding which skill one wishes to cultivate.

What of these skills? As we pointed out earlier, they are frequently rendered invisible by our habitual focus on the knowledge specified through the activity. As we examine a rock by turning it over in our hand we are aware of the fact that we acquire knowledge about the rock, but the skilled manipulation that gave rise to the knowledge of the rock is transparent to us. Our earlier example suggested that in carrying out any activity, such as kicking a ball, we are learning not only about the ball, but about the act of kicking. Carrying out that act across widely divergent ob-

jects or events would be responsible for the development of a
skill of wide applicability. But if we look at the general skills that
make up our cognitive or intellectual ability, we see that they are
marked by the same property. Verbal, numerical, and spatial abilities reflect skills in such cultural activities as speaking and writing,
counting, and manipulating Euclidean space.

Consider these skills in more detail. It is enormously to Piaget's
credit to have insisted and demonstrated that the structure of any
ability must be conceptualized in some major part in terms of
"internalized activity." Activities one carries out in the physical
world—rotating an object in space, lining up objects to form a
straight line, ordering objects serially—come to be internalized or
carried out mentally. There is not only an internalization of operations, but an increasingly economical representation of diverse
events operated upon. A face looked at from various angles comes
to be represented as a single face. Even more important are the
temporal ordering operations, which permit an appreciation first
of physical order and then of logical relations. Once we can convert back from a changed state to our original one, we come to
appreciate that such reversibility is a logical possibility or property of events and not simply an act one performs. In turn, such
operations make it possible to transform a novel event into a standard or base event or to convert some base event into a new
structure more appropriate to novel contexts.

The operations specified by Piaget were largely those appropriate to the manipulation of real objects in the physical environment. His basic premise is that their internalization not only produces the groundwork for logic, but assures that logic will be
appropriate to the state of the world one experiences. Such operations, consequently, have a wide range of applicability and appear
to be almost universally relevant to problem-solving.

But internalized activity related to the physical environment
does not begin to describe the range of activities of the human
mind. Specifically, it leaves out of account how we learn to cope
with the cultural or symbolic environment. "Learning from the
culture," like learning from physical activities, involves the act of
picking up information to decide among alternatives; it also involves skills, and it also results, finally, in a biased knowledge of

reality. Sentences, for example, to the extent that they are about something, carry information common to the other forms of experiencing and are comprehended and spoken in terms of those general underlying structures of knowledge we discussed earlier. But the skills involved in using sentences are unique to the particular mode of expression and communication. The skillful use of a symbolic system involves the mastery of both its structure and its rules for transformation. Once mastered, these skills may be considered to be "intelligence," primarily because the range of their applicability is virtually open.

This wide and expanding range of applicability is further indicated in the arts, which may be viewed in part as creative attempts to expand the limitations of a particular medium or symbolic system. These expanded symbolic systems may then be applied to nature, if appropriate, much as the binomial distribution was found to be an appropriate description of the range of human variability. In this way, our use of symbolic systems, like our practical activities, results in a version of "reality" appropriate to the activity. There is no objective reality to "copy" or to "imitate," but only a selection from that reality, expressed in terms of the kinds of practical and symbolic activities in which we engage. Thus, Nelson Goodman is led to say that "the world is as many ways as there are correct descriptions of it." [33] Similarly, Cezanne pointed out that the artist does not copy the world in his medium but, rather, re-creates it in terms of the structure of that medium. So too with the ordinary man operating in the various symbolic systems of his culture. Whorf was among the first to argue that we "dissect nature along lines laid down by our native language." But the process probably goes even beyond that, to something comparable to Gide's advising young poets to follow the rhymes and not their thoughts.[34] For the child, as for the creative artist, the uses of the culture involve processes of expanding and refining the code, of defining "lawful" or "comprehensible" or "possible" options as he goes. This is the heart of skill in the use of symbolic codes.

33. N. Goodman, *Languages of Art* (Indianapolis: Bobbs Merrill Co., 1968).

34. P. Goodman, *Speaking and Language: A Defense of Poetry* (New York: Random House, 1971).

Even our failures in understanding new media, as McLuhan [35] has pointed out, come from a failure to recognize that they require different skills than does the medium they replace— as in going from an oral to a written code, or in going from print to television.

Man in culture, like the artist, is in continual search for ways of applying symbolic systems to his ordinary experience. Translation into a symbolic code such as logic or mathematics is even taken as the criterion for "understanding" a phenomenon; to express the relation between temperature, pressure, and volume in the form of an equation is to explain that relation. Hansen [36] goes so far as to say that scientific knowledge consists of statements known to be true.

But can one affirm that translation of experience into any one medium has more validity than translation into any other? A historical account of the intellectual roots of the industrial revolution may be of a different symbolic system but not necessarily of greater validity than Yeats's famous epigram:

> Locke sank into a swoon;
> The garden died;
> God took the spinning jenny
> Out of his side.

Yet a scientific and technological culture like our own has put a premium on translation into a few symbolic systems—written language as in literature and explanations, in logical and mathematical statements, and in spatial systems such as maps, models, graphs, and geometry.

We would argue that it is not only scholars, poets, and scientists who seek constantly to cast experience into symbolic codes. Our conjecture is that there is a form of metaprocessing that involves the constant reorganization of what we know so that it may be translated into symbolic systems. It is a matter of "going over one's past experiences to see what they yield" [37] both for the

35. McLuhan, op. cit.

36. N. R. Hansen, *Patterns of Discovery* (Cambridge, Eng.: Cambridge University Press, 1958).

37. Dewey, op. cit.

purpose of facilitating the communication that is required for the survival of the culture and for the purposes of rendering one's own personal experience comprehensible. We may label this form of activity as "deuteropraxis," or second-order information processing. Deuteropraxis is elicited not only by failed communication but also by conflict and difficulties in attempting to carry out an action or solve a problem. It occurs whenever there is information-processing capacity available not demanded by the task in hand. Deuteropraxis is involved in all translations of specific experience into general accounts. It can occur in any mode but it is clearly represented both by the poet's or essayist's search for the appropriate phrase or the summarizing aphorism and by the scientist's search for the most general mathematical statement. Merleau-Ponty [38] has this in mind when he suggests that all intention wants to complete itself in saying. It is deuteropraxis that is responsible for the radical economization of the experience of the tribe or nation in a few great myths and, more generally, for the world view implicit in one's native language. It should not, however, be assumed that this process is simply one of translation. It more generally requires that the creator have more information available than was required for the ordinary experience of the event. This can easily be seen in the difficulties one encounters in an attempt to draw a map of a well-known territory or to give a description of a friend's appearance. New requirements, new purposes, or new activities alter our perceptions of events; this is no less true when these activities involve those that have been shaped or evolved by the culture, as in the arts, than when they involve various practical or physical acts. It follows that such symbolic activities as drawing an object, describing an object, or photographing an object require somewhat different information about that object than does the manipulation of that object. To the extent that these new forms of cultural or symbolic activity require previously undetected information about the world, the media of expression and communication are *exploratory devices*—a point of immense importance to an understanding of the child's acquisition of knowledge.

38. M. Merleau-Ponty, *Phenomenology of Perception* (London: Routledge & Kegan Paul, 1962).

Finally, deuteropraxis makes possible the organization of information into a form that is particularly appropriate for cultural transmission to the young. Since it is often difficult for the child (or an adult for that matter) to link an action with the consequences that follow, he is greatly aided by the deuteropraxis account of the event. Such accounts, whether in the form of an abstract equation, a principle, a noiseless exemplar, or an appropriate model, have the effect of "time-binding" or virtually simultanizing temporal events and thereby surpassing ordinary experience.[39]

It is such deuteropraxis accounts that are examined in more detail in other chapters of this volume in terms of their instructional potential. The very accounts that render experience comprehensible render it instructible. But there are limits in the degree to which such representations, whether in language or other symbolic systems, can substitute for or extend ordinary experience. As a summary of experience they are indeed powerful; as an alternative to experience they are sometimes woefully inadequate. One can learn or memorize the summary without having a grasp of the information summarized. In *Portrait of the Artist as a Young Man*, Joyce tells how his teachers taught the young the aphorism "Zeal without prudence is like a ship adrift" to show how instruction often falls wide of the mark. To some adult no doubt such a statement has meaning; it summarizes his own experience in a simple code. To the young it summarizes nothing. In large measure, the same is true of the great myths; to the extent that they summarize no experience, they convey little or no information. On the other hand, it is also true that aphorisms, like new vocabulary items, may serve as pointers from which experience is progressively assimilated. At an appropriate level, such instruction may be successful in aiding the assimilation of experience. Experience in this case instantiates the categories created through the symbolic code. Frye[40] makes a parallel point in regard to literature: "criticism . . .

39. C. H. Judd, "Practice and Its Effects on the Perception of Illusions," *Psychological Review* 9 (1902): 27-39.

40. N. Frye, *The Critical Path* (Bloomington: Indiana University Press, 1971).

is designed to reconstruct the kind of experience we could and should have had, and thereby *to bring us into line with that experience*" (p. 27).

Technological Realizations

We return for the last time to the scheme offered in figure 2. The column headed "Technological Realizations" indicates, in a rough manner, the media appropriate to each of the modes of experiencing the world. Learning through contingent experience may be facilitated through rearranging the environment to render the consequences of activity more obvious. Laboratory experiments are prototypic attempts to simplify direct experience. Structured environments, simulations, toys, and automatizing devices of various sorts have the advantages of both extending the range of a child's experience and making the relations between events observable or otherwise comprehensible.

Observational learning is realized through the provision of a model—"This is how you break out a spinnaker." As we pointed out earlier, carrying out a performance for its own sake and carrying it out so as to instruct another are not identical. A good demonstration makes explicit the decisions made in the course of the activity—thus a good demonstration shows the student what not to do as well as what to do; a skilled performance makes these same decisions invisible. Technological media can greatly facilitate these processes by highlighting in various ways the critical points in the performance; slow motion or stopped action as well as descriptions and drawings (including caricatures) may have this effect. Such instruction, while it may convey some of the same information that would be apprehended through direct contingent experience (by virtue of its shared deep structure), is never complete in itself but, rather, specifies some of the major features to be looked for when actual performances are attempted. That is, these forms of instruction rely heavily on prior or subsequent experience to instantiate the information.

The instructional effects of a model are greatly increased by tying that demonstration to an appropriate symbolic representation as in the provision of a few mnemonic rules. The words "keep your weight on the downhill ski" coupled with a demonstration will render the demonstration more comprehensible—the observer knows what to look for. But even this will not perfect the novice's performance; direct contingent experience is required to "instantiate" the instruction. Indeed, it is probably not until such instantiation occurs that the proposition is fully comprehended. One says (after the first fall), "So that's what he meant." Hence, all modes of instructing are in some sense incomplete or inadequate for achieving full performatory power or efficiency, and knowledge in the last analysis is tied to one's own experience.

Learning through the various symbolic systems, including language, graphs, mathematics, and the various systems of visual representation, is realized through books, graphs, maps, models, and so on. These media make strong assumptions about the literacy of the learner. The properties of a "good" explanation, description, or portrayal are complex subjects worthy of study in their own right. But to untangle the educational effects of these symbolic systems we again have to differentiate the knowledge of the world conveyed through the system from the skills involved in the mastery of the structure of the medium itself. Recall our aphorism: instructional means converge as to the knowledge conveyed but they diverge as to the skills they assume and develop. As to the knowledge conveyed, different systems are useful for the partitioning of alternatives or the conveying of information in a way that is fundamentally compatible with the information picked up from other types of experiences. You may learn that the stove is hot by touching it, by seeing someone recoil from touching it, and by being told that it is hot. Granted some level of literacy and granted that the learner has had some experience to instantiate the experience, the three forms are essentially equivalent, as we pointed out in the first part of this essay.

However, as to the skills they develop, each form of experience, including the various symbolic systems tied to the media, produces a unique pattern of skills for dealing with or thinking about the world. It is the skills in these systems that we call intelligence. The choice of a means of instruction, then, must not depend solely upon the effectiveness of the means for conveying and developing knowledge; it must depend as well upon its effects on the mental skills that are developed in the course of acquiring that knowledge.

We return, then, to our point of departure. The acquisition of knowledge as the primary goal of education can be seriously questioned. The analysis we have developed points to the contingent relationship between the knowledge acquired and the intellectual skills developed. To neglect the skills is to forget that they are the primary tools for acquiring and using knowledge—tools that are critical for the child's further self-education.

CHAPTER VII

The Potentials and Limitations of Print as a Medium of Instruction

JOHN B. CARROLL

Introduction

The task of this paper is and must be to defend print as a medium of instruction. This task is paradoxical in the extreme, if only for the reason that all the "papers" for this yearbook were initially circulated in "print" (if one can use that term for mimeograph), now formally appear in print, and, if they are attended to at all, will be nearly always read rather than listened to. It is also paradoxical because I am very sure that, whatever I might say in this paper, instruction will continue to occur in the print medium—if anything, increasingly so. It does not appear necessary to defend print as a medium of instruction, yet it is. Voices have been raised to the effect that print is a plague upon us. After having devoted a considerable amount of effort to reviewing the research literature on learning from verbal discourse—primarily *printed* discourse[1]—I find myself confronted with the coy question: why should anyone want to learn from printed discourse?

Some would say that the premise of this paper—that it is important to talk about a particular medium (in this case print)—is erroneous. They will argue that since print is only a medium for conveying something—we will not commit ourselves to what that something may be—the medium is not as important as what is communicated in the medium. I will not go so far as to grant that the "medium is the message,"[2] for the message is "where the action

1. John B. Carroll, *Learning from Verbal Discourse in Educational Media: A Review of the Literature*, Research Bulletin 71-61 (Princeton, N.J.: Educational Testing Service, 1971). (ERIC Document ED 058771)

2. Marshall McLuhan, *Understanding Media* (New York: McGraw-Hill Book Co., 1964).

is," as I see it. Nevertheless, I believe that each medium has certain inherent characteristics that tend to determine what kinds of messages are transmitted by that medium and how those messages are attended to, understood, and acted upon overtly or covertly. I hope to demonstrate that this belief is valid in the case of print.

There is ambiguity in the term *print*. If it is defined as "anything that can be produced by a printing press" (and this is indeed suggested by the etymon of the term), then we need not limit the content to language, for a printing press can produce "prints" of visual forms, charts, diagrams, musical scores, mathematical tables, and strikingly faithful reproductions of works of visual art. But doubtless what the organizers of the yearbook hoped I would address myself to is "print" as meaning strings of characters representing verbal discourse. If so, we have to point out that many educational media use "print" in this sense—not only books, pamphlets, workbooks, programmed instruction courses, and the like, but also films and televised courses with their captions and with their frequent views of scenes containing printed characters.

Since problems of visual representation are considered in other chapters, I will focus on "print" as frozen language.

Ideological Objections to Print

And there's the rub. Print is frozen language. Starkly cold, deadened, unrelated to reality, cut from context, "irrelevant," print is the last thing any lively-minded educator would want to concern himself with. Such is the thrust of current rhetoric.

Any defender of print as a medium of instruction now confronts multiple ideological obstacles. The hidden agenda of some present-day educational trends might sound (I almost said *read*) like this:

Language is an inadequate substitute for direct experience.
Language is something to mistrust because it can mislead.
We live in an "oral culture"; thus, learning through print, even learning to read, is unnecessary and undesirable.
Solving the practical problems of society, which can be done only by direct action, is more important than learning to appreciate the literature of our own and other cultures.

These propositions are, in a way, witnesses to their own seeming validity. For they do not state the whole truth; they fail to convey the complete context, situation, or matrix in which they might, indeed, have a certain measure of sanction. They are ambiguous and deceptive. They lead to paradoxes which make us uncomfortable.

Let us, therefore, consider these propositions and try to explicate them—literally, unfold them to reveal the many levels at which they have partial truth, partial falsehood. It will be a bootstrap operation because we must use language, yes, printed language, with its pitfalls; but we must do this in order to clear away some of the misconceptions with which language and printed language are surrounded. We will also find ourselves defending language itself, as well as language in print.

LANGUAGE VS. DIRECT EXPERIENCE

The simplest kinds of opposition between language and direct experience are evoked when we set out contrasts like:

Reading books about travel vs. traveling.

Reading or talking about problem-solving vs. practicing the solution of problems.

Reading about the grammar of a foreign language vs. learning to speak it in the foreign country.

Reading or talking about skiing vs. skiing.

Talking about love vs. making it.

It is obvious, but never painfully or embarrassingly so, that language (in the form of descriptions, narrations, explanations, prescriptions, or whatever) cannot be a complete substitute for direct experiences such as those mentioned here. But neither can other forms of representation, such as travel films, television shows, or tape recordings. The fact is that there are limits to the kinds and amounts of "direct experience" than can be supplied in educational settings. A good deal of educational media technology is addressed, in fact, to the problem of providing suitable vicarious experiences; thus our concern should be with the degree to which such vicarious experiences offer a context in which desirable learnings can take place.

Actually, the mature reader will credit printed matter with the capability of providing vicarious experiences that are nearly as good as the "real thing" and sometimes even better. Surely most of us can remember reading adventure stories, historical narratives, and the like, that have aroused our interest and emotions to a degree that the corresponding direct experience, if we could have had it, might not have done. Even in technical fields like psychology, it has been found possible to stimulate students' interest by recommending certain books, like Skinner's *Walden Two* or Lorenz's *King Solomon's Ring*, that capture the imagination with vicarious experiences or novel conceptions.[3]

The ability of printed matter to provide vicarious experience is partly a matter of its inherent style and content and partly a matter of the reader's set. One of the dimensions of prose style that I identified in a factor-analytic study[4] was its concreteness (as opposed to its abstractness). This dimension seems to correspond to the dimension of "imagery evocation" identified by Paivio and his collaborators,[5] whereby words and even sentences can be measured for their power of evoking images. Anderson[6] found that subjects instructed to use imagery in remembering sentences retained them better than a group not so instructed, and Anderson and Kulhavy[7] found that although high school seniors who were asked to form mental images while reading a two-thousand-word passage performed no better, on the average, than a comparable group that was merely asked to read the passage carefully, their

3. Ivan N. McCollum, "Psychological Thrillers: Psychology Books Students Read When Given Freedom of Choice," *American Psychologist* 26 (1971): 921-27.

4. John B. Carroll, "Vectors of Prose Style," in *Style in Language*, ed. T. A. Sebeok (Cambridge, Mass.: Technology Press, and New York: John Wiley & Sons, 1960).

5. Ian Begg and Allan Paivio, "Concreteness and Imagery in Sentence Meaning," *Journal of Verbal Learning and Verbal Behavior* 8 (1969): 821-27. Also see Sydney J. Segal, ed., *Imagery: Current Cognitive Approaches* (New York: Academic Press, 1971).

6. Richard C. Anderson, "Encoding Processes in the Storage and Retrieval of Sentences," *Journal of Experimental Psychology* 91 (1971): 338-40.

7. Richard C. Anderson and Raymond W. Kulhavy, "Imagery and Prose Learning," *Journal of Educational Psychology* 63 (1972): 242-43.

performance on a posttest was an increasing function of the amount of time that the subjects reported using imagery during the reading.

Another dimension of prose style identified both in factor-analytic studies [8] and in studies of "readability" [9] is the "human interest" factor whereby the use of personal pronouns prompts the reader to draw himself into the action, so to speak, and even to empathize with the characters in a plot. The use of personal pronouns may not make prose any easier to read, understand, or remember, but it does tend to arouse a kind of vicarious experience.

But the attempt to contrast language experiences with direct experience seems to stem from deeper, subtler concerns. One of these is the fact that a linguistic statement can never be completely veridical. A description or narration cannot encompass *all* the aspects of the scene or event it purports to describe; it must necessarily be selective. A proposition can never completely delimit the possibilities of its interpretation (unless, perhaps, it is one that has been formulated within some carefully developed axiomatic framework). Legal phraseology is as complex as it is because it attempts to provide within itself the limits of its interpretation. The ordinary mismatch between language and reality (and the elusiveness of even an approximate match) seems to be a reason for preferring "direct experience" of reality as a context of learning.

Certainly there are many situations in which direct experience is possible and feasible—the child can have direct experience of shapes, colors, weights, sounds, motions, etc.; one can take him on trips to factories, ponds, concert halls, and scientific laboratories; one can have him practice making things, doing things, observing things, hearing things. But as we have said, there are limits to direct observation and experience in education. There are even limits to the amount of time that can be spent in providing vicarious visual and auditory experiences through pictures, recordings, films, television, and the like, despite the fact that (as we are told) the average child now spends more time in front of a television set than he does in school. Not everything can be taught through direct experience, or even vicarious experience. Whether through his-

8. Carroll, "Vectors of Prose Style," op. cit.

9. Rudolph F. Flesch, "A New Readability Yardstick," *Journal of Applied Psychology* 32 (1948): 221-33.

torical accident or because of their abstract nature, most of the world's resources of knowledge are given through language—for the most part, printed language.

Part of the discontent with language can be alleviated by pointing out that direct experience and various forms of vicarious iconic experience are almost always accompanied by language and often require language to make them intelligible. A picture usually requires a caption; a sound-recording requires a label to indicate what it is a recording of. Teaching through "direct experience" is normally guided by at least *oral* instructions and explanations. Printed language, in the form of instruction books, manuals, and the like, is found to facilitate this kind of teaching in an essential and critical way. In fact, the use of instructional manuals in connection with "direct experience" courses (as in teaching, say, radio repair or auto mechanics) has seldom been questioned; the issue that has been rather thoroughly studied, however, is whether the instructional manuals are written at a level that can be comprehended by the learner.[10] Only in recent years has there been much research on other questions concerning instructional materials that accompany "direct experience" teaching, such as whether the explanations are clear and concrete, properly sequenced, and so on.[11]

We must remember also that most direct experience is interpreted either immediately or mediately in some kind of symbolic form. At an immediate level the difference between raw sensation and perception is a matter of what kind of symbolic interpretation is made.[12] A certain envelope of sound is interpreted as the sound of a bell; another envelope of sound is interpreted as an instance of a certain phoneme, and so forth. A certain pattern of light is perceived as coming from a "drinking glass"; another is interpreted as coming from the person known as "mother," and so on. I am

10. George R. Klare, J. E. Mabry, and L. M. Gustafson, "The Relationship of Style Difficulty to Immediate Retention and to Acceptability of Technical Material," *Journal of Educational Psychology* 46 (1955): 287-95; Richard P. Kern, Thomas G. Sticht, and Lynn C. Fox, *Readability, Reading Ability, and Readership* (Alexandria, Va.: Human Resources Research Corporation, 1970).

11. Leslie J. Briggs, *Sequencing of Instruction in Relation to Hierarchies of Competence* (Pittsburgh, Pa.: American Institutes for Research, 1968).

12. Ulric Neisser, *Cognitive Psychology* (New York: Meredith Publishing Co., 1967).

not sure whether it is legitimate, in the terminology adopted by the authors of other chapters, to refer to this kind of perception in terms of "symbols," and undoubtedly some perceptions are of a "prelinguistic" character, particularly in the young child. As the child develops linguistic competence, his perceptions take on a more linguistic character. (We recognize, of course, that other symbolic systems, such as those of music or visual form, may become involved, depending on the source of the stimulation, but verbal symbolism seems to be the predominant type in normal experience.) At a less immediate level our direct experience is mediated by the linguistically formulated knowledge we have of it. For example, we come to know the meanings of certain kinds of bell sounds as identified with churches, telephones, alarm systems, etc., and it is only in verbal terms that we can formulate this knowledge, perhaps by the process of "deuteropraxis" of which Bruner and Olson speak in their chapter.

It is said, nevertheless, that language is inadequate and often ambiguous and/or misleading. This stems partly from the nature of language. Language is a finite system of symbols that is based on classifications of experiences, not upon the raw experiences themselves. Language is selective: a given sentence brings to attention only certain aspects of the situation that evokes it. Actually, we would not want it otherwise, for if language were not selective and classificatory in nature, it would take us infinite time to express the simplest idea, like "that table is round." At the same time, the well-known "creativeness" of language implies that language operates only under the constraints of its *own* grammatical and semantic rules; for all practical purposes, an infinite number of sentences can be generated within these rules; they may be true or false; in many instances they may be ambiguous in the sense that identical "surface structures" can be generated by different sets of rules.

This means that people can use language to persuade us of notions or ideas that are not true (in some sense of "truth"), to draw our attention to things we would prefer not to attend to, or to evoke emotions and desires in us that no amount of direct experience, of itself, would necessarily lead to.

The remedy that has been repeatedly urged but seldom effectively applied is to alert students, by teaching, to the dangers and misuses of language. The general inadequacy of educational programs that are undertaken to this end (and the lack of easy ways to evaluate their effectiveness) is perhaps one of the reasons language is still so much mistrusted. (The returns are not yet fully in from two promising curriculum projects that have attempted to meet this need—those of Oliver and Newmann[13] and Allen and Rott.[14]) It is small consolation that perverted uses of language have become so brutal and obvious—in television commercials, for example—that (as we are told) children no longer believe advertising of any kind. The danger is that they will no longer attend to *any* verbal message.

TEMPORAL PROBLEMS WITH LANGUAGE

Language takes time if it is to be effective and at the same time as precise and communicative as it needs to be. Conversationalists and lecturers need time to make their points, even if they are not rambling on; libraries contain endless stacks of books that would take several lifetimes to peruse. This temporal characteristic of language is epitomized by the fact that linguists sometimes speak of language as composed of "strings." The speed of spoken language is governed by parameters either in the speaker or in the listener that cannot be varied much even by means of electromechanical "compression" of speech. In printed language the laying out of characters in horizontal or vertical lines is a physical representation of the temporal nature of language, and, although marvels can be accomplished in the photographic compression of print, there are again parameters that control the bringing of print to the eye. Careful reading is time-consuming.

In contrast, we have the illusion that direct experience is immediate and not time-bound. We can, presumably, absorb the con-

13. Donald W. Oliver and Fred M. Newmann, *Cases and Controversy: Guide to Teaching the Public Issues Series: Harvard Social Studies Project, and Supplement* (Columbus, Ohio: American Education Publications, Education Center, 1967).

14. R. R. Allen and Robert K. Rott, *The Nature of Critical Thinking. Report from the Concepts in Verbal Argument Project. Theoretical Paper No. 20* (Madison: University of Wisconsin Research and Development Center for Cognitive Learning, 1969).

tent of a visual experience in the flickering of an eye, or at least, we are told, in a few dozen milliseconds. There is an instantaneous character of insight—the "aha" experience seems to come to us suddenly. There is also an instantaneous character in our awareness of knowledge and skill; we recognize instantly that we know whatever we know about a certain person, place, or subject matter; we are aware instantly that we have achieved a certain level of skill in some activity like violin-playing, chess-playing, automobile-driving, or whatever.

This apparent instantaneity of direct experience and of our awareness of our competence makes us impatient with language, impatient with learning from language. We want to learn in no time at all, thus we turn to experiences that we believe will give us instantaneous learning. The notion of "one-trial learning" is deceptively appealing. And where we realize that we must learn from language, we turn to methods of speeding up language comprehension (by listening to "compressed speech" or taking courses in speed-reading).

Of course it is not true that direct experience is always instantaneous and it is rarely true that learning is instantaneous. Even when an experience is essentially a repetition of similar experiences, like a ride on a roller coaster, we enjoy its temporal character and willingly pay for it by the minute or hour. Films depict direct experiences at a governed speed: we normally object to speeded-up films, just as we would object to speeded-up music. We require variety in experience and this requirement seems even to have a basis in our physiological makeup.[15] And almost any psychologist will tell you that the primary variable in all learning is time.

In its partial relaxation of time requirements, print has an advantage over spoken language. We can normally read a passage faster than we can listen to the same passage in spoken form. While the research evidence is by no means conclusive,[16] it appears that

15. Karl H. Pribram, "Neurological Notes on the Art of Educating," in *Theories of Learning and Instruction,* Sixty-third Yearbook of the National Society for the Study of Education, Part I, pp. 78-110 (Chicago: Distributed by the University of Chicago Press, 1964).

16. Carroll, *Learning from Verbal Discourse,* op. cit.; Robert M. W. Travers, *Man's Information System: A Primer for Media Specialists and Educational Technologists* (Scranton, Pa.: Chandler Publishing Co., 1970), pp. 84-94.

we can learn more (in a given amount of time) from reading something than we can from listening to it being read. (The reverse is true, mainly for persons who have not learned to read efficiently.) Print gives us more options for selecting a strategy for comprehension: we can read carefully if we so desire, or we can scan or skim. We can control, to a considerable extent, our rate of reading even in the case of word-for-word reading. We can read in a strict left-to-right manner, or we can search for subjects and verbs, independent and dependent clauses, and the like, in case we wish to understand sentences better through analysis. I find myself doing this in the case of difficult technical materials, legal documents, and the like. Bever and Bower [17] seem to have found that children trained to read this way comprehend more than children reading in the usual left-to-right manner. One would hope, however, that careful writers would compose their sentences so that such mental acrobatics would be unnecessary.

To the extent that language can provide a running account of experience and can parallel the course of learning, we should take advantage of its temporal dimension. And, in fact, writers often do this instinctively: Narrations and histories are normally laid out chronologically, and textbook authors make a conscious effort to organize their materials in a physical sequence (translatable into a temporal sequence) that makes some kind of pedagogical sense. The beneficial effect of making the temporal order of language parallel normal experience can be seen even when applied in the case of single sentences.[18]

But more can be done to make the laying out of print parallel the course of learning. The work of Rothkopf and of others [19] sug-

17. Thomas G. Bever and T. G. Bower, "How to Read Without Listening," in *Readings in Applied Transformational Grammar*, ed. Mark Lester, pp. 305-14 (New York: Holt, Rinehart & Winston, 1970).

18. Herbert H. Clark and Eve V. Clark, "Semantic Distinctions and Memory for Complex Sentences," *Quarterly Journal of Experimental Psychology* 20 (1968): 129-38.

19. Richard C. Anderson, "Control of Student Mediating Processes during Verbal Learning and Instruction," *Review of Educational Research* 40 (1970): 349-69; Lawrence T. Frase, "Boundary Conditions for Mathemagenic Behaviors," *Review of Educational Research* 40 (1970): 337-47; Ernst Z. Rothkopf, "The Concept of Mathemagenic Activities," *Review of Educational Research* 40 (1970): 325-36.

gests that the temporal relations between elements of the text and placements of questions that prompt more careful inspection of the text is critical. Two major findings are that (a) a question on an element of the text should not follow that element by too short or too long a time period and (b) that questions placed *after* a text are more effective in maintaining learning behavior (or "mathemagenic" behavior, as Rothkopf calls it) than questions preceding a text. There is also the whole matter of laying out material in terms of the prerequisiteness relationships that obtain among the items to be learned:[20] even though some types of materials are just as effectively learned when their elements are presented in any random order, other types of materials require close attention to their ordering.

The temporal aspect of language makes for an inherent difficulty that is less of a problem in visual presentations, namely, that contrasts and conflicting ideas must be presented sequentially in language. For example, two shapes or colors, or two contrasting representations of a face, can be presented simultaneously and viewed almost simultaneously, but two conflicting arguments concerning a proposition (e.g., one "pro," the other "con") can be arrayed side by side in print only awkwardly. It is more usual to present them separately and discretely, with a spatial separation that corresponds to a temporal separation in the reading process. In the rapid give and take of oral argumentation, the difficulty of presenting balanced views containing judicious considerations of apparently conflicting ideas often makes for misunderstanding when the speaker is not allowed to expound his full views. The problem is not so severe in print, for the writer can assume that the reader will bear with him; he can even alert the reader to the subsequent structure of his discourse, i.e., to the fact that he will consider contrasting views, for example.

Somewhat related to this, but not necessarily a limitation caused by the temporal nature of language, is the fact that any statement seems to preclude its alternatives, or to feature what is said over what is unsaid. If a politician states that he is going to fight pollution, there is a temptation to infer from this that he will not also support population control, merely because he has not mentioned

20. Briggs, op. cit.

his views on population control. Actually, of course, no inference in either direction is legitimate. So it is with many statements in textbooks—to say that a cause of the Civil War was the issue of slavery is not to say that there were not other causes. This fallacy of misplaced emphasis is only one of numerous fallacies to which language is subject, but perhaps it is more critical in print than in oral communication because of the authoritative character that people (especially children) are inclined to ascribe to print.

LANGUAGE AND THOUGHT

Further sources of stress and strain concerning language generally, and printed language in particular, are the notions that language controls thought and that thinking in verbal terms is not necessarily the proper way to think. One of our conferees (see chapter 3) has referred to Hadamard and to Piaget in pointing out that thought in a "lexico-mathematical" mode is not clothed in words. Scattered throughout our discussions are also references to the Whorfian idea that the structure of language channels thought. This issue of the relation between language and thought is an extremely complex one, on which much has been written.[21] I, myself, after energetic attempts to investigate the relation empirically, came to the conclusion that if language has any influence on thought, the influence is small and sporadic.[22]

There is very little evidence to support the view that major trends in thought are affected by the structure of one's language, or by the structure of any language. Even if one restricts "thought" to those activities that can be carried on and formulated in linguistic symbols—and this is by no means all that there is to "thought"—one can be quite sure that thought is independent of language in the sense that its operations can occur independently of the particular language symbols and structures that are avail-

21. Franklin Fearing, "An Examination of the Conceptions of Benjamin Whorf in the Light of Theories of Perception and Cognition," in *Language and Culture*, ed. H. Hoijer, pp. 47-81 (Chicago: University of Chicago Press, 1954); Joshua A. Fishman, "A Systematization of the Whorfian Hypotheses," *Behavioral Science* 5 (1960): 323-39.

22. John B. Carroll, "Linguistic Relativity, Contrastive Linguistics, and Language Learning," *International Review of Applied Linguistics* 1 (No. 1, 1963): 1-20.

able in which to formulate it. Clothing thought in language is an operation that, as it were, takes place posteriorly to the act of thought. Certain phenomena related to this point can be appreciated by simple introspection. For example, one can often recognize a picture of an object or person before being able to retrieve an appropriate name; one can notice a difference between two pictures before one can formulate the nature of the difference; and so on. The point I would make, however, is that language is not as dangerous and misleading as the prevailing opinion would have it—or to be more precise: language structure and its coding system does not necessarily mislead in the way one associates with the notion that "language channels thought." Only if indeed one's basic concepts are awry can one be misled by them—but the concepts are prelinguistic in any case. If a child thinks a whale is a fish, he is being misled, but he is being misled by his concept of a whale, not by anything in the linguistic code. One can doubt that one ever truly thinks in linguistic symbols. Even though the putting of thought into words seems to be an automatic and instantaneous affair, timing of such responses in microseconds shows that it is not at all instantaneous.[23]

Despite all this, we should point out that there are different modes of thought—visual, auditory, musical, kinesthetic, and so on—including the logico-mathematical type of thought alluded to by Gross.[24] Each mode permits a particular type of thought and each mode has its appropriate mode of expression. There is a range of "thoughts" that seem to have their proper mode of expression in language, just as there is a range of "thoughts" whose proper expression is in musical notation, or mathematical notation, or whatnot.[25] Although it may be that educational institutions have overemphasized the linguistic system to the partial neglect of other systems, it still remains true that the linguistic system is a domi-

23. John B. Carroll and Margaret N. White, "Word Frequency and Age Determiners of Picture-Naming Latency," *Quarterly Journal of Experimental Psychology* 25 (1973): 88-95; Tom Trabasso, H. Rollins, and E. Shaughnessy, "Storage and Verification Stages in Processing Concepts," *Cognitive Psychology* 2 (1971): 239-89.

24. Gross, see chap. 3.

25. On systems of notation for symbolic systems, see Gardner, Howard, and Perkins, chap. 2.

nant and precious one. While not every child can be an artist, a musician, or a mathematician, every normal child can be a speaker, a listener, a reader, and a writer. The creativeness of language endows him automatically with at least a minimum of creativeness in expression.

THE FALLACY OF THE ORAL AND VISUAL CULTURE

Some educational romantics have attempted to construct a view of our present-day culture that depicts it as no longer critically dependent on the communication of ideas by printed language. Such media as television, they claim, provide the kind of communication medium through which the individual can learn from direct or vicarious experience and from oral transmission. This notion seems to derive from a kind of nostalgia for the presumed idyllic state of primitive cultures where knowledge was transmitted from generation to generation by demonstration, imitation, and an oral tradition.[26] People cite with glee the fact that traffic signs in Europe no longer use printed language, forgetting that the symbolism was invented to overcome language barriers, not to do away with print. I have known even university professors to boast that they seldom read anything, but derive all their professional information and knowledge from listening to their colleagues talk.

Against such views, what can we say? They seem so absurd as to require no answer. Yet these views prevail in some quarters and must be countered. If we cite the obvious fact that the knowledge and literature of our culture is stored in books and other printed matter, we are told that all that information is gradually becoming available in spoken form. (If this is so, the process is extremely slow.) If we try to say that our cultural ecology is based on printed language, we are told that this is undesirable and unnecessary. It is almost as if Ray Bradbury's fantasy *Fahrenheit 429* has arrived— the fantasy, you will remember, of a society where it was illegal

26. I do not doubt that oral traditions are transmitted in these cultures, often extensively and accurately. For a startling example see an account (*New York Times Magazine Section*, July 16, 1972) by Alex Haley of how he located in Gambia a venerable Mandinka tribesman who told him a tradition about the strange disappearance of a certain chieftain's son two hundred years before—a story that matched an oral tradition in Haley's own family about how his great-great-great-great-grandfather was captured as a slave.

to possess a book and where all mass intercommunication among the citizenry was carried on through super-sized television screens. What the proponents of these romantic and possibly fascist ideas seem to forget is that the capacity to read and use print must still exist *somewhere* in the population—perhaps in some anonymous class of scribes or priests, as in ancient Egypt—in order to make the system work in any civilization as advanced as ours. My professorial friends who claimed not to do much reading were depending upon the reading abilities of their colleagues.

There are sound psychological reasons for valuing print and writing as a mode of expression. Except possibly for a few who are extremely gifted in oral discourse, certain kinds of thinking seem to make the use of written expression mandatory. The elaboration of a complex sequence of reasoning, with the setting forth of necessary definitions, qualifications, and logical constraints, is one example. It is commonly accepted that Socrates's dialogues could not have had quite the elegance and force that was imparted to them by Plato's consummate skill in writing. One doubts that Cicero's orations were delivered without the help of a written text. The development of the essay, the novel, and certain other forms of belles-lettres would probably have been impossible in a purely oral culture. The elaboration of scientific thought would be unimaginable in such a culture.[27]

Let us come to terms with reality. Given the widespread use of print in our culture in all its forms, given the fact that the complex ideas that our citizens must be able to handle can hardly be stated in language of a lower level of difficulty than what is recognized as "twelfth-grade reading difficulty," and given the ideal of universal education through at least the twelfth grade, there can be no reasonable alternative to a goal of twelfth-grade level of literacy for all, or nearly all, our citizens.

One hears from various quarters the view that this ideal is unrealistic, that substantial portions of the populace do not have the capacity to attain twelfth-grade literacy, that even in the best-run schools half of the students in the twelfth grade are below twelfth-grade literacy. If the goal is unrealistic, that fact has yet to be

27. Eric Havelock, *Prologue to Greek Literacy*, Lectures in memory of Louise Taft Semple (Cincinnati: University of Cincinnati, 1971).

demonstrated. Possibly the view that this goal is unrealistic is influenced by notions such as that a certain (substantial) amount of "dyslexia" or reading disability is inevitable (because of constitutional or genetic factors). Although reading retardation is a serious problem, the view of the experts is that it can be surmounted in nearly all cases—at least to the point at which the adult is able to read anything he can understand in spoken form. The point that half of the twelfth grade does not attain twelfth-grade literacy is a more serious one, however. Here we must take account of developmental facts: there is no assurance that the bottom half of the twelfth grade cannot *eventually* attain twelfth-grade literacy, even though this might occur several years after leaving the twelfth grade. Twelfth-grade literacy is indeed a fairly high standard—even nations that claim nearly 100 percent "literacy" (such as Japan or Iceland) may not be able to claim literacy at this high level. But this is no reason for not stating it as a reachable goal.

With so much stirring on the educational scene today—"Sesame Street" and "The Electric Company" programs on television and a host of innovative instructional programs operating at the elementary school level—we cannot assume that universal twelfth-grade literacy will *not* be attained some years hence. One basis for optimism is that average reading performances on standardized reading tests have improved substantially over the past decade or so. Of course, making it possible for nearly all to attain twelfth-grade literacy will not guarantee that they will read or otherwise enjoy the benefits of their skill, but at least we would be giving them their rightful opportunity, their "right to read." We know that people who have learned to read prefer generally to acquire information by reading.[28] Moreover, we should remark that any "right to read" program should include the "right to write." If, as Francis Bacon observed, "reading maketh a full man," writing makes him an exact man.

Although we have tried to suggest that the capacity to comprehend printed language at a fairly high level of complexity in

28. Thomas G. Sticht, "Learning by Listening," in *Language Comprehension and the Acquisition of Knowledge*, eds. R. Freedle and J. B. Carroll, pp. 285-314 (Washington, D.C.: V. H. Winston & Sons, 1972).

CARROLL 167

vocabulary, syntax, and ideation is a proper, desirable, and feasible goal for the citizens of an advanced society, we have thus far ignored the question of whether print has any limitations, as compared with oral communication, in the degree to which it can communicate all the nuances that are possible in oral communication. Is there any "information added" when the full range of intonational ("suprasegmental"), gestural, and other "paralinguistic" communication in oral speech is taken advantage of? We cannot now give a definite answer to this question. It is only in recent years that we have begun to analyze and document such paralinguistic information,[29] and I am not aware of any thoroughgoing studies on the subject. There are intuitive and á priori reasons for thinking that something is added when we learn from viva voce communications, but—and here is a paradox—that little is *lost* in printed communication because the receiver can fill in, through the redundancy of language and the élan of his imagination, the needed information. We prefer to see the live or filmic presentation of a play rather than to read it (a fact to which high school teachers of Shakespeare might give more heed) for many reasons —we enjoy the artistry of the players, this is the intended medium of presentation, and we need not exert ourselves to infer the paralinguistic features of the lines and actions from their printed form. Yet, if we are forced to do so, we can get almost as much out of a play by reading it as we can from seeing it. Note also that college students have become disenchanted with the lecture medium of instruction; many claim that they can learn as much from the assigned readings as they can from the lectures. The information added by the histrionics of the professor is for them superfluous. From the professor they expect, rather, sensible commentaries on readings and a willing and responsive ear in discussion sessions. At least, this is what I am told about present-day college students in the humanities and social sciences; the case is somewhat different, we hear, among students of mathematics, physics, and the pure and applied sciences generally, who are more likely to require and demand oral presentations, explanations, and demonstrations.

29. Ray L. Birdwhistell, *Kinesics and Context: Essays on Body Motion Communication* (Philadelphia: University of Pennsylvania Press, 1970).

PRINT IN DIRECT SOCIAL ACTION

It seems superfluous to mention that print has had and will undoubtedly continue to have a large role in effecting social changes
—through the operation of mass print media, the publication of
records, the amassing of statistics, the formulation of written plans,
and so forth. Students oriented toward social action have in fact
shown themselves keenly aware of this, for example, through their
often very effective use of the "underground press." The ideologies
underlying social change are certainly not in conflict with literary
appreciation—it is only that the standards of what is "relevant"
in literature may be influenced by one's ideology.

The Potentials of Print

Print, to be sure, is not the only effective means of mass communication.
It is probably not even the most important means of reaching the population directly. . . . But print still remains the only vehicle of communication which is not restricted to particular times and places, which can
present all sorts of ideas to anyone who can read, and which can develop a subject to any desired fullness of detail. . . .[30]

This statement is no less true now than it was in 1940, even
in the presence of a wealth of tape recordings, television receivers,
films, and other means for the transmission of information in audiovisual forms. It is possible that since 1940, more has appeared in
print than had ever appeared in print before that time in the history of the human race. But has print achieved its full potential?

Certainly we cannot fault print as a technology. The arts of
the typographer, the platemaker, the pressman, the bookbinder
seem to have reached their peak. The maker of a book can produce it in almost any form or special arrangement that one might
desire. Neither quality nor quantity presents any special problems
other than financial.

Possibly one of the reasons for the current disenchantment with
print is that we are flooded with it. Pollution from print seems
almost as threatening as pollution in the atmosphere. Perhaps ZPG
should stand not only for Zero Population Growth but also for

30. D. Waples et al., *What Reading Does to People* (Chicago: University
of Chicago Press, 1940).

Zero Print Growth. But we cannot stop or retard the explosion of knowledge, nor can we abridge the freedom of the press or, more specifically, the freedom of authors to write and publish. I have not seen any sensible proposal for limiting the amount of material that is put into print, although letters continue to appear in scholarly journals decrying the "publish or perish" policies of universities or urging that there be more selectivity in what is written or published. As far as a solution for this problem is concerned, we can take some comfort in the fact that simple laws of supply and demand will continue to provide checks and balances.

How does this affect the use of print in the schools? Above all, it means that the schools must renew efforts to teach discrimination between what is worthy and what is less worthy, in literature, in science, in history, and in other categories of printed material. It also means, however, that the student needs to be taught about tools for searching, finding, and selecting materials. Library science has been developing many new tools and devices, but the future will probably see further advances in information retrieval systems, techniques for evaluating instructional materials, and means of disseminating information about the range and quality of printed material available.

What goes into a book, pamphlet, journal, or handbill is one quarter of the problem. Another quarter of the problem is what the reader brings to the process of absorbing and reflecting upon the contents. The remaining half has to do with adapting the contents to the reader and bringing the right books to the right readers. But it is difficult to discuss any of these elements without consideration of the others.

In the context of education, the problems of deciding upon the contents of books, selecting books, and presenting books to students have always been anxiety-ridden. The problems seem particularly fearsome today when other media press themselves upon us. What seems to be needed is some kind of theoretical analysis of what kinds of learning experiences can be transmitted best by books and other printed material. By using the word *best*, we necessarily involve ourselves in a consideration of what criteria are to guide our discussion: do we mean "best" in terms of efficiency, economy, learner achievement, learner satisfaction, or what? Obviously we cannot opt for any one of these criteria; they must be balanced against each other.

A theoretical analysis ought to start, one should think, with an examination of what kinds of learning experiences we want to give. Yes, there is "direct" experience: actual, immediate contact with some aspect of reality. Note, however, that some kinds of desirable "direct" experience are *of* books and printed matter: we want students to have contact with books, libraries, reference works, magazines of all sorts because all these are aspects of our present culture. Literature itself—both the classic writers and the moderns —is something that constitutes an important part of our culture; thus we can talk about exposure to literature as a kind of direct experience.

There are, of course, many kinds of direct experiences that cannot be had through print. Immediate experience that comes to us through visual, auditory, tactile, kinesthetic, olfactory, and gustatory sensations that can only be described in language is not for books and printed matter to give us, although I must confess that sometimes I can relish the smell or feel of a book! But many of these experiences are acquired just through the process of living; unless a child has been shut up in a closet all his life it seems rather pointless to worry about giving the total range of immediate experience in a school context. Only if immediate experience is directly *required* to achieve some educational aim, or to open the mind of a child, is this an important consideration. The learning of many kinds of active skills does indeed require immediate experience. But I have pointed out that there may be limits to the kinds of direct experience one can offer in an educational setting. We would object, for example, if direct experience of physical danger were proposed as a part of normal schooling.

Earlier, I discussed "vicarious experience" without defining the term. Vicarious experience is the mental modeling or representation of the immediate experiences that one could have, given circumstances appropriate for such immediate experience. By watching a film or television program about hunting tigers, I can to some degree have the experiences that are had by tiger hunters. But, then, it is probable that such a film would be accompanied

by a verbal narration. Given a basis for visual and other kinds of
imagery in my previous experience, I could probably get the flavor
of tiger-hunting just as well, or even better, by reading about it,
perhaps in some of Ernest Hemingway's short stories—with active
arousal of the emotions surrounding danger. A question may be
posed: is one's ability to appreciate vicarious experience through
print enhanced by having had samples of the corresponding immediate experience? Is my ability to appreciate Ernest Hemingway's stories about tiger-hunting enhanced if I have been in a
jungle, or seen a tiger in a zoo, or done some target practice with
a rifle? I doubt it, and the question seems too trivial to propose
for any kind of systematic research. Vicarious experience doubtless depends upon *some* degree or kind of prior immediate experience. A blind child would have difficulty fully appreciating a
description of visual art; a deaf child would have difficulty understanding a piece of musical criticism. But, for the normal person,
the possibilities of appreciating vicarious experience and learning
from it are usually not limited by lack of any prerequisite immediate experience, simply because such a person has already
sampled at a basic level the kinds of sensory experience from which
more complex and special experiences derive their meaning.

This is not to say that nonverbal aids to the formation of appropriate vicarious experiences are not helpful and often necessary. This is the function of pictures, diagrams, illustrations, and
other accompaniments of print. They are useful to the extent that
they help the learner form correct or plausible representations of
potential immediate experience. In a textbook of physics or biology such representations are practically indispensable; in works
of fiction they are still regarded as useful in children's literature,
short-story magazines, and the like, although for various reasons
they rarely appear in serious fiction written for adults (as they
frequently did in the nineteenth century).

Thus far we have been speaking of prose that in some way relates to concrete experiences, actual or potential, as if we were to
assume that all learning must likewise relate to concrete experience. Such an assumption would be very unwise. In contrast to
immediate experience (and to vicarious experience as well) lies abstract thinking, which necessarily involves symbolic systems. At

least some of our educational objectives are predicated on our hope that the student can grasp abstract concepts such as the notion of truth, or justice, or the credibility of a source of information. In Piagetian terms this is the realm of formal operations, where the concreteness of the referents falls away. Assume for the sake of argument that there is such a realm—maybe of Platonic ideas—in which all association with concrete experience evaporates. Certainly we have such a realm in higher mathematics, where we are dealing with a language of specialized symbols. But in every branch of science or scholarship, even those dealing initially with concrete substances, groups or events, as we mount some kind of abstraction ladder there is a point at which discourse ceases to make reference to these concrete entities. It is in this realm that the use of language becomes of paramount importance and in which print reigns supreme because of its many advantages over oral language: the care and leisure with which it can be formulated and recorded, its constant availability, and the attention with which it can be studied. It is difficult to imagine a truly advanced culture without a notational system for manipulation in this realm of thought. In the educational setting, print makes possible a realm of abstraction that could hardly be provided by any other means.

To summarize at this point: learning experiences may be classified as either immediate, vicarious, or abstract.[31] Insofar as the object of study *is* a printed work, print provides direct experience; otherwise, print rarely substitutes for direct experience. But print can provide a wide variety of vicarious experiences, which are often more effective and usually less expensive than direct experience, and it can often serve as a guide to and annotator of direct experience. There appear to be many kinds of abstract learning experiences for which print (i.e., printed language and printed

---

31. In this paper I have assumed that experience can be classified as either immediate, vicarious, or abstract. The classification is not quite the same as Bruner's classification as either enactive, iconic, or symbolic (see references in Olson and Bruner, chap. 6); it cuts across that classification. I am emphasizing here the degree of contact the learner has with the actual referents of learning—these referents may in fact be symbolic or iconic, but the learner may have immediate, vicarious, or purely abstract contact with them. Thus, I talk about *immediate* experience with great literature—the actual reading of great literature, as opposed to reading *about* literature.

symbols, whether in a book or other medium) is the only possible mode of representation. After all this is said, let it be noted that wherever some "nonprint" medium can teach more effectively or economically, it should be the medium of choice. I say this on the assumption that the proportion of the curriculum for which non-print media would be more effective is not so great as to cause serious reduction in the amount of exposure to print that students would receive and that most nonprint media (film, television, etc.) actually involve considerable use of printed expression.

Many are the ills of the publishing field. For reasoned discussion of some of them, I recommend the Winter 1963 issue of *Daedalus*, entitled *The American Reading Public*. For horror stories, I recommend Hillel Black's popular survey *The American Schoolbook*.[32] The frightening impression that these sources leave is that the publishing of textbooks, trade books, and of literature in general is—and has been for at least a century—endemically rife with commercialism, catering to base tastes, and compromising with standards. One wrings one's hands in despair, and there is no comprehensive solution in sight. Perhaps we need a Ralph Nader of the publishing world! The realities of the economics and politics of publishing have been severe detriments to the development of the full potential of print.

Yet the publishing world is in many respects only responding to trends and realities in the educational field. The textbook publisher's dilemmas reflect the lack of consensus concerning educational content and objectives. The publisher's efforts to grade reading materials in difficulty by readability formulas and limited vocabulary lists are an attempt to adapt the book to the pupil. The commercialism of publishing practices only panders to the chaotic and often mindless standards, regulations, and prejudices by which textbooks are selected and adopted in different regions of the country. The mistrust of print which now appears in the educational scene must be in part a reaction to the difficulties posed by publishing practices, on the one hand, and book selection and adoption practices on the other. The liberal-minded educator must feel frustrated at every turn in his effort to use print wisely, and

32. Hillel Black, *The American Schoolbook* (New York: William Morrow & Co., 1967).

students can hardly be blamed if they get "turned off" by the pap with which they are presented in the guise of educational material.

Despite all this, many excellent books continue to become available for the educational market. At least some curriculum areas are well served; one thinks of English, mathematics, and biology, for example.

It is noteworthy that almost all the new curriculum projects have placed their emphasis on producing more adequate *materials*, and printed materials have figured very heavily in such ventures, whether as basic texts or as guides to the additional items that take the form of science kits, films, tape recordings, and so on. It would be hard to evaluate the contribution of printed materials as such in these curriculum projects, however, because they are integral, nonseparable parts of "packages." Insofar as we can judge the effects of these new curricula, it would appear that their success is in large measure traceable to the care and attention that has been devoted to the preparation of printed materials to be used in instruction.

It could be argued, of course, that the decisions made in the new curriculum projects to concentrate on the preparation of printed materials were based on false premises—that the Harvard Project Physics curriculum, for example,[33] should have put all its efforts into producing laboratory equipment, science kits, videotapes, and the like, that would minimize the use of printed language, even of oral language. It could be further argued that the evaluations of such programs were misleading in that they were based largely on students' performance on printed tests. I have no easy way of dismissing such arguments because I know of no curriculum evaluations that have focused on the assessment of students' behavioral performances with concrete materials as opposed to their abilities in applying knowledge in written tests. But I would think that a curriculum that consisted only of gadgets and paraphernalia would be no curriculum at all.

What the experience of the new curriculum projects does seem to demonstrate, however, is that printed materials *alone* are not sufficient to enable students to achieve the aims of these curricula

33. Gerald Holton, F. James Rutherford, and Fletcher G. Watson, *About the Project Physics Course* (New York: Holt, Rinehart & Winston, 1971).

readily. The almost unprecedented efforts on the part of these curriculum projects to provide concrete materials and procedures for
learning—often drawing on both direct and vicarious experiences
—seem to have supplied the critical elements that were needed for
their success. Activity is not confined to the major curriculum
projects: as I write this, I have just received a pamphlet from the
McGill University Centre for Learning and Development giving
some examples of "experiential learning in higher education." [34] In
a physics course a professor has his students not only learning the
equations of classical mechanics, but also trying to measure the
acceleration of objects and vehicles such as subway trains. A psychology professor sends his students to hospitals to do supervised
work in the application of operant conditioning principles in the
treatment of patients with maladaptive behavior; an architecture
professor gets his students working in the community, consulting
on problems of urban design, housing codes, zoning changes, and
the like. All this is in marked contrast to traditional forms of
education that have depended solely on lectures and reading assignments.

For all we may admire these ventures in "experiential education," it would be difficult to appraise their exact effects. For example, the experiences associated with the courses at McGill must
involve a good deal of social facilitation; in field experiences it is
usually true that students learn from each other. Of course this is
well and good, but it compounds the difficulties of appraising the
relative amount of learning that is caused by the books and lectures
on the one hand and the field experiences on the other.

Let me cite, however, one illustration of an attempt to disen-
tangle the effects of different aspects of instruction. This comes
from recent research of Rothkopf and Bloom.[35] Rothkopf had previously found in a number of studies that when "adjunct questions"
are inserted into a text at regular intervals, students learn more
from the text than when these questions are omitted. But what

34. Charles E. Pascal and Lynda Kaplan, "Some Examples of Experiential
Learning in Higher Education," *Learning and Development* (Centre for
Learning and Development, McGill University) 3 (March 1972): 1-4.

35. Ernst Z. Rothkopf and Richard D. Bloom, "Effects of Interpersonal
Interaction on the Instructional Value of Adjunct Questions in Learning from
Written Material," *Journal of Educational Psychology* 61 (1970): 417-22.

would happen, Rothkopf and Bloom asked, if these questions were presented not by the text itself but by a live teacher while the text was being read? To answer this question they had to employ a rather unusual setup: the text was presented on a screen, projected from slides. For one group a question relevant to the immediately preceding material was presented on every sixth slide; the student answered in writing. For another group the question was presented not by a slide but orally by a teacher-assistant who was standing by to do this, and the student gave the answer orally. In a third group there were no questions, no live teacher-assistant. On a post-test covering all the material, a passage on earth science, the results clearly favored the second group, the one that had questions asked by a live teacher. This group was significantly better than the first group, which had written questions on slides, and the first group was in turn significantly better than the control group which had no questions at all. Apparently the social facilitation of a question from a live teacher was the critical factor. If one were permitted to generalize from such a finding, one could speculate that printed material is best used in situations in which there is active social involvement.

LEARNING FROM PRINT

Beyond any doubt, students can and do learn from print. The interesting questions about learning from print have to do with how print is to be used and in what proportions and relative emphases, together with other media of instruction. I have already indicated that there are no hard and fast answers from research. We can make only the most limited generalizations having to do with the relative efficiency of learning from print as opposed to oral language, and there is little information about the relative efficacy of print (or oral language) as opposed to concrete experience. Although I would be last to disparage research, I think we must realize that research is unlikely to yield any simple or quick answers to these questions, for the answers would depend upon many variables: what is being learned, the conditions under which it is presented, the motivation and ability of the learner, the time allowed for learning, and so forth. Even the most energetic and optimistic investigators in this area feel they are still only breaking ground.

I would suggest, instead, that both students and teachers have their own responsibilities with respect to selecting modes of learning. As they move through their educational careers, students must find out through experience what kinds of learnings come most easily and profitably to them by various media—that is, through print, through oral discussion, or through direct or vicarious experiences. Similarly, it is up to teachers to learn to make judgments about what media are more appropriate for a given subject matter, a given curriculum objective, a given student, a given time and place. Beyond this, teachers must give students a wide range of experiences with a variety of media so that students can arrive at their own judgments. Modern life requires us to view education as a lifelong process and the years of formal schooling as nothing more than a foundation for learning in later years. In formal schooling the student can acquire the basis for decisions about how he can best meet the demands of the learning he will accomplish later in his career.

Some provisional thoughts about factors to be considered, however, may be set down:

1. Facts and information that have already been amassed and, perhaps, well analyzed by others are most efficiently learned from print, to the extent that it is at all necessary to learn them. What the learner needs most, usually, is direct experience in finding and locating information so that he will know where to find new information.

2. For learning that involves understanding of complex concepts and relationships the print mode is often to be favored, for it lends itself to the careful study that may be necessary to acquire understanding. But text should be supplemented by illustrations, diagrams, schematics, etc., wherever appropriate, and the theoretical learning should be alternated with practical experience.

3. If the learning objective entails primarily skill in dealing with persons or things, then demonstrations, concrete experience with the activity, and oral coaching and guidance would seem to be more effective media than print. It would be practically impossible, for example, to learn to play the piano just by reading a textbook.

4. If the learning objective involves acquiring some kind of direct

experience with concrete reality, one should consider how difficult, time-consuming, or expensive it would be to acquire such experience. One should consider the possibilities of giving this experience vicariously through films or other audiovisual aids, or even through print. For example, in training teachers of remedial reading, a good casebook can give the student the equivalent of quite a few months of direct experience and might present types of cases that, though rarely occurring in practice, are of sufficient importance for the student to know about. Similar remarks could be made about casebooks in medicine, law, business administration, and many other fields. Although certain kinds of cases might best be presented on film, the limited amount of time for viewing such films and their limited availability would militate against any extensive reliance on the film medium.

5. Many kinds of learning—in particular those that involve the learning of algorithms and procedures, the understanding of hierarchically structured conceptual systems, and practice in applying these algorithms and systems—require active guidance of the learner and reinforcement of and feedback from his responses. Reinforcement and feedback may be required also to prompt rehearsal strategies in the rote learning of factual materials. Ordinarily, printed materials have limited capability of providing such feedback. Most audiovisual media, in fact, share these limitations with print. It is a rare educational film that attempts to prompt by asking questions, and the learner most often remains quite passive in viewing a television set. Nevertheless, print offers considerable possibilities for providing guidance and feedback. Various programmed instruction formats require active response from the learner and give knowledge of results only after the response has been made. The "adjunct questions" used by Rothkopf and his colleagues to prompt better "mathemagenic activity" on the part of the learner constitute another way in which printed materials can provide active guidance. Further, it is with textbooks and workbooks that we can most fully exploit the need for repetition, practice, and review.

Unfortunately, printed materials are not always organized in such a way as to provide for feedback and review. A high school mathematics teacher pointed out to me that some of the early versions of the School Mathematics Study Group textbooks made no provision for review periods, and he found that by interpolating his own review periods he could produce a marked improvement in student accomplishment at the end of the course. The end-of-chapter review questions given in many textbooks are too often mere probes for factual information. Davis and Hunkins [36] found that such questions appearing in social studies textbooks rarely challenge the student to think about the content and apply his knowledge.

If active structuring of learning by the medium of instruction is a chief requirement, I suspect that the medium of choice would be CAI (computer-aided instruction), in which it is possible to make the development and pacing of the program depend upon the students' responses. Of course, printed material, either in the form of accompanying workbooks and guides, or in the form of verbal messages displayed by teletype or a CRT (cathode-ray tube), can be an integral part of computer-aided instruction. But CAI is still more of a promise than a reality, as far as its widespread implementation is concerned. I propose that we make as much use as we can of that teaching machine that someone has aptly labeled with the acronym BOOK (Built-Out Organized Knowledge).

36. O. L. Davis and Francis P. Hunkins, "Textbook Questions: What Thinking Processes Do They Foster?" *Peabody Journal of Education* 43 (1966): 285-92.

CHAPTER VIII

Virtues and Vices of the Visual Media

RUDOLF ARNHEIM

Introduction

Today's educator is faced with an embarrassment of riches. He has come to realize that in teaching and learning, more often than not, mere talking and listening or writing and reading do not convey their message sufficiently. The sensory presence of the objects and events to which language refers is indispensable if the words are to exert their impact and be grasped in their full meaning. This sensory presence concerns all perceptual modalities; but even if limited to visual images, the abundance and variety of "visual aids" must bewilder the teacher and the student.

Hardly any of the traditional procedures of picture-making have become useless, although their functions may have changed and become more limited. The prehistoric methods of drawing a likeness on a surface or shaping a figure in clay are still with us; they are still profoundly useful and will always remain so. At the same time, mechanical, photographic, and electronic techniques have given us new ways of creating, preserving, and distributing images. More or less clearly, we sense that some of the old and the new media serve certain purposes better than others. But our attempts to use them wisely still rely too much on trial and error.

So influential have been the technological innovations of our time that one is tempted to declare a fundamental difference between the media of today and the media of yesterday. And so pervasive is this influence that it may seem to shape our lives totally and thereby distinguish the mentality of twentieth-century man in principle from that of his forefathers. Such dichotomizing is more dazzling than useful. The basic capacities and reactions of the human mind remain what they always were; and, if one examines the visual media somewhat less passionately, one finds that they all rely on the same limited number of perceptual dimensions. Remote though the wall paintings of the ice age may be from the television screen, the eye looks at pictures in both instances; and with all the differences between writing hieroglyphs on papyrus and setting type by computer, the psychology of reading has not changed substantially. By examining the media in the light of their dimensions, one can begin to clarify some of their similarities and differences, and these comparisons of their character lead almost automatically to practical guidelines for the producer and user of visual material.

This seems all the more necessary since anybody who has set his heart, not to mention his money, on a particular medium tends to consider its capacities in isolation from what other media can do and perhaps do better. He will entrust his favorite contraption with as many functions as possible, whether it is suited for them or not. A glaring example of misuse is the kind of television program that is based entirely or predominantly on talking and presents to the eyes of the viewer the embarrassing presence of newscasters reciting the latest bulletins or of groups of discussants uncomfortably perched on their seats. This goes on even though radio, ideally suited for the intelligent presentation of disembodied voices, is available to everybody.

The visual media differ from each other in certain fundamental ways. Some use two-dimensional surfaces, e.g., drawing, painting, photography, printing, and television. Others produce three-dimensional shapes, e.g., sculpture or the models of chemistry or biology. Some use immobile images, such as book illustrations, slides, maps, or writing and printing; others show things in motion, such as film or video. Some reproduce mechanically, some manually. These and other differences reflect profoundly on the best use to be made of the media.

Throughout this brief survey we shall have to keep in mind the active as well as the passive use of the various media. Passive use serves the dispensing of knowledge. Pictures carry images of the world into the classroom. They offer the raw material for factual information. However, the pictures or models have been made by experts somewhere else. They arrive ready-made. Student and teacher act as consumers. Their acts are responses.

Active use of the media is furthered or hampered by technical and economical factors. Some material is readily available: a pad of cheap sketch paper, a box of crayons, a technique that can be mastered by a child without instruction. More forbidding is the equipment of the cameraman, the technical knowledge needed to make a simple film turn out as intended, the cost of material, development, and so on. However, even the more intricate and expensive media have become accessible to common use beyond all expectation, and the educator needs to find out what equipment to put in the hands of his students for what purpose.

Before I go into specifics, one point should be stressed. There is no automatic correspondence between active and passive use of material and active and passive use of mind. Mere looking can be a very active occupation, which strains all the cognitive powers of the mind. Learning material can be cunningly presented in such a way that it not only transmits data but raises questions and reveals problems. In such an intellectually active climate no apology is needed for the passive presentation of pictures, slides, films.

Drawing, carving, model-building, and film-making favor an active concern with the subject matter. It takes a dull mind to make a drawing of the skeleton of a lizard without any curiosity about how and why all those little bones are put together in just that way, or to film the goings-on at a bus stop without asking who are the people who are waiting, where they are going, how they relate to each other. But it can be done. Mental inertia, if encouraged by the teacher, can use the gadgetry of picture-making as an easy substitute for the intelligent exploration of the things painted, collected, photographed. Under such conditions, "active" teaching puts the mind to sleep.

These considerations will concern us more tangibly as we look at the properties of various visual media. The survey cannot be exhaustive, and perhaps all that is needed here is to define and illustrate some of the relevant dimensions and to suggest by a few examples what to look for in the use of instructional media.

Physical Presence vs. Recording

Man, as distinguished from animals, can represent the things of nature by making images. The urge to do so arises early and the advantages accruing from images are obvious. However, since there are irreplaceable virtues also in experiencing "the real thing," the educator must never assume without question that recorded images are a suitable substitute for direct experience.

The "real thing" is tied to its time and place. The local post office, the aquarium, the United Nations building must be traveled to in order to be seen, and a solar eclipse occurs rarely. This anchoring in time and place is not merely a limitation. Positively, it provides the observer with a context that may be indispensable for understanding. Post offices are strategically located in town, the aquarium is remote from the natural habitat of its prisoners, the United Nations have entrusted their headquarters to New York City; and it is essential for the understanding of eclipses to realize that they occur rarely. There are ways of pointing at these contexts of space and time when images are used instead of the real thing. But we do well to keep in mind that we pay for the comfort of using substitutes by uprooting and isolating the objects and happenings we show.

Images store the visual appearances of physical things. Some such replicas can not only be seen but can also be explored by touch. Some can be heard. Even so, the replication is always partial. This has certain advantages. The limitations of what is shown make the mind concentrate on some of the aspects of a particular subject matter. An Audubon print lets the student look at the shape and plumage of a bird from a convenient distance, in clear sight, unhurried, undisturbed by motion. If the picture is well made, it carves a valid likeness into the student's memory—an accomplishment not easily matched by the fleeting appearances of reality.

In the presence of a "real" situation we are free to look at what is before us in an attitude of contemplation, unless it entices or assails us too strongly. But reality also invites active participation. We feel impelled to explore what we see, to handle it, to walk around it and into it. If we notice something wrong, incomplete, unjust, we are challenged to remedy the situation. The image, on the other hand, lets and makes the viewer see what he would not see otherwise, but it also transforms the events of reality into objects of contemplation. It suggests the attitude of the detached observer, the philosopher, the pure scientist.

Visual aids are meant to alleviate the indirectness of much modern experience. The primitive hunter or farmer is in direct interaction with all that matters to him. The city dweller, on the other hand, rarely deals directly with the things that concern him. The businessman replaces products with papers; the student reads about distant things, sees their pictures.

Ironically enough, although pictures are intended to remedy the blindness resulting from indirectness, they serve at the same time to replace real things by their images. The world becomes something to look at. The effect of the enormous amount of information poured upon the citizen by television and illustrated papers every day is notoriously ambiguous. It provides a direct look at violence, poverty, and injustice, but it confirms the status of these atrocities as things happening beyond reach. It risks confounding them with the figments of story films, which are exciting but, as every grown-up person knows, untrue. Hence the enormously important task of the teacher to counteract the sense of unreality that comes with all pictorial representation. He must keep alive the awareness that the world he shows is a challenge: something to be dealt with, acted upon, explored, improved.

The impressive popularity of photography and film among young people today may exemplify the problem. A generation suffering from a sense of remoteness and isolation seizes upon a medium that records the appearances of human existence with great immediacy. This closeness to the facts may express and activate a deep concern with social, political, and natural events, as demonstrated by the work of our best photographers and film-makers. But the photographic medium can also provide the illusion of engagement, obtained simply by pressing a button. It allows the picture-taker to be present without having to participate. He can remain a detached observer with a good conscience because, after all, he is "reacting."

In the schoolroom the pictures must be prevented from fortifying the notion that the learning material is like a show to be consumed passively. Recorded or transmitted lectures have the obvious value of supplying excellent teachers and facilities not otherwise available. But these opportunities must be used in the light of the educator's conviction that without active response there is no true learning. And since the televised lecturer, even more clearly than the "real" orator at the academic lectern, is a person to whom one cannot talk back, it is again the task of the live teacher to transform the object of passive assimilation into an instrument of active learning.

The "real world," although a challenge to active participation, is at the same time much less easily manipulated than its image. The real world is given. The image is created. The subject matter of the image is selected from the array of existing things, and the various formal devices offered by the medium shape the image to suit the picture-maker's purpose. The power of determining what the image shall look like is greatest for drawing and painting, smallest for the photographic media. But even the photographic technique adapts itself to a variety of approaches. Recently this has become evident by certain basic differences that exist between the media of film and television. Offhand, it is not obvious that there should be such differences, if we ignore for the moment the social and perceptual factors that distinguish viewing at home or in the schoolroom from attending a performance in a movie theater. In fact, the offerings of the two media largely overlap, e.g., when films are shown on television.

Yet, a very different relation to reality is suggested by the fact that television allows for direct transmission without recording. It is in the nature of such transmission that it eliminates much of the shaping, characteristic of film work. Direct transmission leaves the continuity of time unbroken. The switch from one viewpoint (camera) to another is possible but improvised. Good shots and bad shots, relevant and irrelevant sights reach the viewer somewhat indiscriminately. This lifelike messiness, so different from the careful control at all stages of typical film work, can also be obtained with the film camera. In fact, some of the younger film-makers, impressed by the style of television reportage, have adopted it. The new video-tape equipment favors this development. The reason for this preference is of interest here. It suggests that good visual material should strike the right ratio between carefully controlled form and the authenticity of good reporting. How much of the one and how much of the other is appropriate in each particular case must be considered by the maker and the user of visual material.

On the whole, it is advisable, of course, to see to it that visual aids make their point as clearly as possible. For instruction in chemistry one is not likely to use a film in which an experiment goes wrong or even lacks polish and efficient execution. Yet, the very perfection of a successful performance can cast a chill upon the viewer. He knows in advance that the demonstration will work. The suspenseful uncertainty as to whether an enterprise will be successful is one of the great thrills of the scientist's and the explorer's endeavor. A cooking lesson, transmitted live over television, gains rather than loses by small mishaps: ingredients missing, tools pushed off the table, the cake sticking to the pan. The sense of adventure is a great asset in learning, and the realization that the teacher is not perfect provides legitimate encouragement. Recorded demonstrations tend to lack this incentive. We pay a price for the great virtues of prepared imagery. Here again, a shrewd compromise between immaculate presentation and the lures of lifelikeness will often be in the interest of successful education.

Active and Passive

By its very nature the image excludes active exchange in the usual sense of debate, examination, or conversation. The viewer cannot respond, retort, ask questions—in the tangible manner of a discussion. Another factor that makes it difficult for the recipient to work up an effort of his own is that he knows it to be a "canned" performance; he knows that the effort needed to formulate the lecture, conduct the experiment, address the audience is not being made right now but was exerted in the past. Right now, nobody is exerting himself on the platform, This eliminates the incentive of responding to the teacher's effort with an effort of one's own. It is difficult to react genuinely to a mere wraith.

The educator should be aware of these drawbacks. But he should also realize that weighty counterarguments can be summoned in defense of the image. It is true that one cannot talk back, e.g., to a painting, but the silent response of some viewers is most powerful and active. This happens when two conditions are fulfilled. The image itself must be strong, relevant, interesting enough to deserve the response, and the mind of the viewer must be prepared for what the image has to offer.

These two conditions hold for the use of all visual material. An effective image must be able to arouse a sense of wonder, it must capture the mind by its novelty. To understand it should require a mental exertion. However, the material should also convey the reassuring impression that it is within the range of the viewer's capacities. Otherwise it will discourage him from the outset. It should offer a soluble problem, a challenge that looks as though it can be met. To decipher the map of one's hometown for the first time is such a challenge. To figure out how a cable car works is a discovery. To watch an astronaut walk under conditions of reduced gravity raises questions.

The image must not be too eager to explain. It is good practice to present the puzzle first, let the facts pose the questions, give the mind a chance to come up with an answer, and supply the solution in due time. Mere exposition of all the pertinent facts is not good teaching, because mere information does not educate. At the same time, the visual material must not be expected to do all the work of putting the student in the right frame of mind. Basically, the image is a tool, not a teacher. Since the older child and the adolescent are no longer as prone as the preschool youngster to be puzzled by the basic miracles of nature and technology and to demand explanations, it is the teacher's task to rekindle this native intelligence—to warn the student when he is taking things for granted that are not obvious. After all, the capacity to puzzle about the obvious stimulates the most productive thinking.

Ideally, the first move should not be up to the image. The visual material should not turn up for some purely extrinsic reason and demand attention, but the student should take the initiative to call for such material when he needs it in order to answer his questions. What does the skeleton of a dolphin look like? How do crystals multiply? What happens when a person lies down on his back in the middle of a busy street? The image is the answer to the request: Let's find out! There is now concrete experimental evidence to suggest that even animals learn much less from being passively exposed to an environment in which they are carried around than they do by actively exploring it under the guidance of their own initiative.

More technically, visual material varies as to the extent to which it can be actively manipulated. The photographs in a book illustrating, say, life in an African town can be consulted in any order, whereas it is quite laborious to pick out particular sections of a film without running through the whole in its established sequence. Furthermore, our view of an object depicted in a drawing or painting is limited to the particular aspect presented by the artist whereas the film camera can explore complex shapes, such as those of a building, from all sides. With the coming of holography it will be possible not only to see photographed objects stereoscopically on the screen, but also to receive a different view by changing one's point of observation, just as in physical reality. This will make the exploration of projected images physically more active. If we wish to go beyond mere looking, we can employ three-dimensional models of biological or technological structures, which can be touched, turned around, and taken apart.

Always or Rarely

The mechanical mass production of images, which began with the graphic techniques in the fifteenth century, has made visual material readily available. The advantages of this progress are too obvious to warrant discussion. One need only mention the most recent facilities for the instant duplication of documents, drawings, or scientific articles—inventions we are not yet taking for granted and are still actively thankful for. What does require discussion is the cheapening of effect that results from mass reproduction under certain conditions.

A moment's reflection shows that it is not merely the frequent exposure as such that creates the problem. To be sure, everybody knows how pictures on the wall tend to disappear. They are no longer looked at; they are not missed when they are taken away. On the other hand, there are images that require permanent presence: the altar statues in a church, the family photographs on the desk, the subway map in the station, the eye chart in the oculist's office, the trademark on the product. Clearly, the problem is not permanence as such, but its relation to function. Consider a beautiful painting hanging in a room through which students pass every day on their way to the auditorium. The painting not only disappears from sight, but it also loses value. The piece of sculpture in the living room vanishes from what psychologists call the life space of the inhabitants if it does not serve a continuing need. When Rembrandt's *Syndics* are used for the decoration of a cigar box or when the *Mona Lisa* or Van Gogh's *Sunflowers* are exploited in advertisements, magazines, and dime-store art, it is obviously the cheapening and falsification of function, not the multiplication of the object, that is to blame.

Shoddy reproduction techniques help to debase a valuable work of visual art in the eyes of the viewer. Such techniques put it in the company of pictures that deserve no better treatment. Here again it is up to the educator to take advantage of modern technology without letting its faulty use defeat his purpose. Bad prints that falsify color and brightness values should be banned from instruction. Also, it is good practice to vary the pictorial equipment of the schoolroom, just as in the traditional Japanese home one honors one's art treasures by showing them only at special occasions and for a limited time. Whatever is on display should be referred to as often as the occasion arises. A geographic map paling and peeling on the wall from years of neglect like an old window shade, acts as a symbol of disrespect for the instruments of human knowledge.

Exposure to visual material should not be overdone. The showing of a film should be made an occasion to be looked forward to, not the tired routine of running perfunctory material through the projector. It is bad education to screen substandard documentaries offered free of charge by the public relations departments of industry, only because something is needed for scheduled assembly meetings. Just as a reading of poetry can be made a festive occasion even though the poem is available in thousands of inexpensive copies, a useful or beautiful image will create a heightened experience even though it is available in millions of prints. Inversely, the visit to a rare original can be a tedious duty performed by an exhausted tourist. It is the attitude of the viewer, not the availability or the price of visual material, that makes the difference between gain and loss.

Movement and Immobility

Until less than a century ago, movement could be produced only by live performance or by automata. Immobile pictures, known since prehistoric times, represented things in action as well as things at rest; and even though they could not show locomotion, good artists never had any trouble in conveying a sense of "life."

The main perceptual principle to be observed here is that a successful immobile image is rarely a slice of a temporal action. If one stops a film or enlarges single frames, one observes more often than not that the momentary phases of an action look absurdly paralyzed and unnatural. The same is true for many snapshots of sports scenes or animals in motion. A picture is not a segment of time; rather, it represents its subject outside of time. The sense of "life" is not guaranteed by the mere correctness of the representation but is conveyed by the visual nature of the shapes, their interrelations, and their orientation in pictorial space. A detailed treatment of these visual properties cannot be provided here.

Immobile images have the great virtue of permitting careful perusal without time limit. One particular aspect of the object or action is chosen to represent innumerable possible ones. The selection requires great skill, not only in order to do justice to the object "as such," but also to serve the particular purpose intended. The image may be meant to show the anatomy or the beauty or natural habitat of an animal; it may focus on the style, the aerodynamics, or the functional design of an airplane. In each case a different choice of aspect, distance, lighting, setting, etc., may be appropriate.

The recording of motion, as it has become available through film and television, serves first of all to make the vital distinction between motion and immobility. To the child this distinction coincides with that between the animate and the inanimate. Motion also introduces the essential element of causality into the picture. The interaction between things is presented as an actual occurrence, not just through its results. In a film one actually sees the thermometer rise when it is immersed in warm water.

The conception and experience of nature as process is greatly enhanced by the presentation of change through movement. Change, however, must be understood in relation to what persists unchanged, and here it is the visible difference between a static setting and the action taking place within it that makes the particular dynamics of natural, technical, or social processes visible.

Also, apparent immobility can be shown to be due to the limitation of our visual sense, which registers change only within a definite range of speed and size. By now everybody is familiar with the spectacular enrichment of our world of visual experience obtained by accelerating or slowing down the speed of recording natural processes. Such adjustments of speed enable the viewer to study the characteristics of plant growth, muscular behavior, splashes, or explosions by direct inspection.

Movement is a prime means of increasing attention and facilitating identification. It is the most elementary and effective stimulus to the sense of sight. Even a small change in the visual environment will attract attention automatically. This means that in any demonstration the objects that move should be the ones on which the viewer is supposed to concentrate. Actors know from their experience on the stage that any slight action in the background will easily distract the audience from the principal happening.

The movement of a snake will detach the animal from the surrounding complex environment of underbrush, scattered leaves, branches, and rocks. Any change of place or shape creates a helpful distinction between figure and ground, the moving object being generally the figure, the immobile setting being the ground. Thus the principal object is effectively isolated from the rest of the scene, and the spatial relation between object and environment is revealed as being liable to change. The snake moving across the screen is not permanently connected with the objects surrounding it, as it is in a photograph or drawing in the textbook. It displays its independence from any particular location.

Identification is facilitated more specifically by the character of the movement. A butterfly, a goldfinch, a mosquito, an airplane are clearly distinguished by the shape and speed pattern of their flight path, even when the object is seen as a mere shapeless dot in the distance. This quality of behavior also characterizes an object as energetic or weary, controlled or disturbed, quick-minded or slow, liquid or viscous. The changing shape of clouds reveals them to the eye as being vaporous rather than solid.

Thus the visual dimension of motion in time enriches the learning experience if it is deliberately employed and controlled by the picture maker. The virtues of visual motion are well worth the greater effort it demands of the viewer. Being fleeting and changing, the mobile image requires quick apprehension and a good visual memory if the viewer is to extract from it the lasting, invariant qualities of the subject matter.

It is necessary, finally, to distinguish between the effects of two kinds of movement, namely, that of the object and that of the observer. If the object turns, bends, or changes place, it will display different shape and different relations with its environment. By handling a small polyhedron the viewer can obtain an integrated image of the complex total form. The range of different partial aspects revealed by the turning supplies visual raw material for the mental acquisition of a form that cannot be covered fully by any one view. The mobile images of film and television can duplicate this sort of display by recording the object in rotation or locomotion. The effect will be particularly complete if the mobility of the image can be supplemented by stereoscopic vision.

Visual change is also obtained when the observer moves across, around, or through an object or setting. Movements of the eyes, the head, the body are used for such exploration in visual space, and the film camera can imitate the displacements. However, the effect of the moving image is strongly counteracted by the lack of the corresponding muscular sensations in the body of the viewer. Since his body tells him that he is sitting motionless in his chair, the displacements on the screen are perceived as motions of the image. This illusion of locomotion is fairly easily accounted for by the viewer, e.g., when he sees a scene taken from a moving airplane or by a camera traveling along the facade of a building. Much more serious is the change of the visual angle, carried out by the camera but not identified by the viewer. This interferes with spatial orientation, especially when the camera explores an interior by rotation. The three-dimensional room looks flattened out and the spatial relation between the walls is almost impossible to discern. A single screen offers no efficient substitute for looking around in a building or scanning the panorama of a mountainscape that surrounds the viewer from all sides.

Linear Sequence

All locomotion is linear in the sense that objects travel along a one-dimensional path. But there exists also two- or three-dimensional movement. The surface of an expanding inkblot changes two-dimensionally, that of an expanding ballon, three-dimensionally.

The movement of the glance is always a linear sequence. In order to see at all, the eye must constantly move or be moved, and if one records the path of the fixation movement, one obtains a linear trace. To look at a picture means, therefore, to scan its parts. In most cases, the order of the scanning sequence is not prescribed by the picture and, in fact, does not matter. The resulting complete image is independent of the order in which its details were explored.

The process of perceptual integration is influenced, however, by the relative size of the image, i.e., by the visual angle resulting from the objective size of the physical object and the distance from the observer. If the picture occupies too much of the visual field, it is difficult to apprehend as a whole. The viewer will be induced to pick out details in isolation. This happens when students sit too close to the projection screen or a large wall map.

The compositional structure of the picture also influences perceptual integration. The more orderly the structure and the simpler the order, the more easily does the scanning lead to an image perceived as an organized whole. If the composition organizes around one central theme, it is more easily read than if there are two or more such centers. The distance between the centers also matters. If, e.g., a marksman taking aim is seen at the right margin of a photograph and his target at the left, the picture may read badly.

Naturally, the time needed to explore a picture adequately varies. A single shape on an empty ground is apprehended in a fraction of a second; a microscopic slide or a painting may require an hour. On the screen of film or television the scanning time available for perceiving any one phase of the action is inevitably short, and it is necessary, therefore, to allot sufficient length to each scene, depending on its importance and difficulty.

Certain types of images prescribe the overall sequence in which they are to be seen. A Japanese picture scroll that has to be unrolled laterally establishes the direction in which the picture sequence should be viewed, but not the speed at which this has to be done. Film and television are also linear media since they impose a sequence of viewing.

Depending on whether the principal dimension of a medium is

space or time, it serves certain purposes well, others less well. It also conveys a particular conception of reality and promotes certain attitudes of the viewer over others. The immobile image on the wall or in the textbook shows each thing and, by implication, the world as a whole in permanent existence. It says: This is the way things *are*! Even actions are correspondingly transformed. A chart indicating the sales curve of a business surely depicts a process, but the emphasis is on the persistent being of the firm, as distinguished from the dramatic happening in time one would see if the rise and fall of fortune were presented in animation as a growing curve. Similarly, a painting showing Washington crossing the Delaware represents a milestone rather than the course of history.

To what extent an immobile picture is read as an active event rather than a mere state of affairs depends not only on the picture itself but also on the mental attitude of the viewer. It would be important to know whether children react more to the dynamic or the static elements of immobile pictures and whether these reactions are related to age, intelligence, experience, and so on. It is quite possible that a picture which tells an adult a dramatic story is read essentially as an inventory of things and characters by certain types of children—e.g., those who are constantly exposed to television—and that therefore pictorial material prepared for them must stress action more conspicuously or must even be replaced by films or television.

In the contemplation of immobile images it is the viewer who must introduce sequential action. He scans the picture, looks for essentials, traces relations. The process of understanding a picture runs along a linear track, even though the outcome of the effort is the integration of the immobile image in the simultaneity of all its parts. Similarly, in order to understand the three-dimensional model of a molecule in chemistry or in order to "see" a piece of sculpture, one must continuously walk around the object or turn it back and forth. From the sequence of the sights emerges a nonsequential entity, the Being of the immobile object.

Film and television can initiate and control such a process of exploration, e.g., when the weatherman explains the maps with a pointer. It is he who imposes the sequence of apprehension upon the viewer. An essentially static situation can also be explored by action of the camera. The initiative is clearly with the explorer, the interpreter, the guide. In the lecture series *Civilization*, Sir Kenneth Clark often assumed the role of the museum guide or teacher of art history by directing the glance of the viewer to the relevant items.

This sort of procedure is at its best when it transforms a state of being into an event and animates it thereby. In one of the *Civilization* films, the camera traveled upward along the female figure of Bernini's marble group *Apollo and Daphne*, thus showing in dramatic sequence how the woman is gradually transformed into a tree. For another example, one may think of an anatomical model, say, of the human body, which allows the removal of layer after layer, thereby creating a suspenseful sequence that leads from the epidermis to the sanctum of the inner organs. Another example is a film by Charles Eames which shows the changes of sight from the scale of the human range to that of the galaxies and inversely to that of the electrons. Here the stepwise leaps along the size and speed scales present the static architecture of the universe as an exciting journey to the infinitely great and the infinitely small.

Such dynamization of static structure is a step toward the kind of effect obtained when film or television portrays actions, changes, events. The initiative is taken on by the movement and change of the subject matter itself, and the viewer plays the more receptive role of the witness. Things are presented as happenings and, in the larger sense, the world as a whole appears as a process, as Becoming rather than Being. The most typical example is the "story" narrated by the feature film. But the growth of the embryo, the conquest of a mountain, and the progress of a surgical operation are also subjects of this nature. The particular appeal of such a performance derives from the fact that the viewer is carried by the dynamics of the story rather than having to supply the impulse and leadership himself.

This means that the viewer himself is allowed to assume the role of the consumer. In any consumer society, which thrives on the passivity of the customer, communication is based on the principle of supplied action. The work of the public media is concerned with "news value," i.e., with what changes rather than what is. The risk of this one-sided approach is that it tends to create an unnatural resistance to anything that fails to take the viewer on a trip of action, but requires action initiated by the viewer. The result can be a distorted image of the world, in which nothing counts or even exists except what changes, what "is going on." By the time a child becomes addicted to his daily television program he leaves behind him the age at which he could explore an old clock with the endless patience of a scientist. Here, then, the educator faces a problem of attitude, largely created by a special use of the media but remediable, in part, with the help of the media themselves.

Written or printed language as a visual medium is neither linear nor nonlinear in itself. Posters, advertisements, inscriptions, charts, and tables can use arrangements of words not intended to be read in sequential order, and the so-called concrete poetry distributes letters, words, or sentences on the page in the form of two-dimensional images to be perceived as nonsequential compositions like paintings. Dictionaries, calendars, time schedules are to be consulted, not read. In all these instances it is important to design the arrangement of verbal material in such a way that linear perusal is discouraged and, instead, a different and freer order is suggested. To this end, sequences are broken up, items are separated by clear subdivision, dominant and subordinate elements are distinguished by size, color, and location, and crossconnections in space are established by visual means, such as similarity of appearance.

In the special case of consecutive reading, which develops gradually during the history of written language, the visual presentation of words is used in order to record the sequence of logical thinking. Here the writing provides linear channels, but since the medium in itself is immobile, action and sequence must be supplied by the reader, somewhat as in the Japanese picture scrolls. Reading, in other words, is a visual activity in which the initiative rests largely with the recipient. This demand, together with the indirectness of any verbal medium, calls for a mental discipline more stringent than that required for the intake of visual action. In this respect, the character of the verbal medium remains unchanged when writing is supplemented by printing.

It follows from the linear nature of speech that when written or spoken captions or comments are used to interpret pictures, they introduce a temporal sequence into the order by which the picture is apprehended. Obviously it makes a difference whether the verbal description proceeds mechanically, say, from the left to the right, indicating objects in the arrangement in which they appear during the lineup, or whether the description starts with the most conspicuous element of the picture or—and this is by no means always the same thing—with the most revealing item, which holds the key to the whole story. Also the verbal description will pick out and make explicit certain relations between parts which the picture itself may not isolate or stress so clearly.

Simultaneity

All visual media have some aspect of spatial simultaneity. Even Morse code, the most linear of them all, requires that the dots and dashes be apprehended in bunches rather than one by one. In normal reading, not only every single letter must be perceived as a whole, but entire words and indeed phrases are grasped as units. The momentary images of film or television must be followed not only in their succession but also scanned spatially, to the extent to which a rapid change permits it. I have already referred to the task of apprehending a complex image, e.g., a painting or the sky of a planetarium, as a whole by integrating the details scanned in succession.

Simultaneity becomes most explicit when several images are presented together. The projection of two or more slides at the same time has become so de rigueur among educators that to limit oneself to one picture seems almost old-fashioned. The method is indeed attractive in that it permits explicit comparisons between scenes taken at different places. There are precedents in the history of painting: triptychs and altars, combining a variety of scenes; series of paintings to be displayed in the same room; photomontages, which combine shots of different origin. The first experiment with three film scenes projected on three screens was contained in Abel Gance's *Napoleon* of 1925, and projections on the backdrop of the stage and on the walls around the audience were used in the political theatre, e.g., by Erwin Piscator, to supplement the principal action. During the last few years batteries of carousel projectors synchronized by programming tape have led to multiple-slide shows as a matter of routine in teaching.

It is necessary to emphasize that such simultaneity of several visual wholes strains considerably the apprehensive capacity of the sense of sight and the mind. Therefore, unless there are clear relations between the units, the effect will be an amorphous bombardment, leaving the viewer with nothing better than a vague overall impression of what it is all about. Incapacity to understand encourages a defeatist attitude of mere indulgence in sensory stimulation.

Therefore, the presentation as a whole must be organized with sufficient lucidity. The organization concerns not only the subject matter of the pictures, but also their purely visual appearance. For a simple example, various aspects of the same object can be shown in multiple presentation: the back and front sides of a coin, different shots of the same building, and so on. The two sides of a coin are easily related by their common roundness, but the façade and the north wall of a church may display no such obvious visual kinship. Different views may be derived from the same object, and yet the eyes may be unable to relate them properly. How they belong together may not be evident. It is not enough to rely simply on what the viewer knows about the subject matter. Images will not do their work unless the eyes are persuaded, and the eyes require a sufficient common denominator as the visual base for any comparison.

If, for example, several pictures are meant to show objects possessing the same property, say, various minerals of crystalline structure, this key property must be clearly emphasized by visual means; and if crystals are to be compared with sedimentary rocks, the geologist must have the eye of an artist to make the confrontation convincing. Confrontation is effective in showing contrasts. However, if the student is to compare two pictures—a city or landscape before and after the destruction of war—the views must be sufficiently similar to make the contrast dramatic. If everything is different, comparison does not come easily.

Simultaneity requires even greater skill when two different media, notably, image and sound, are to be combined. Little needs to be said here about the benefits of recorded noises, which help in identifying animate and inanimate things, introduce them by their sounds even when they are not visible, emphasize the rhythm of machines, and complement the mood of the scene. Music prevents the ears from straying from the performance, defines the dynamic nature of a setting as quiet, gay, or foreboding, and promotes a general sense of action and liveliness. Music can be disturbingly hyperactive. It should not emulate the reckless appeals of television commercials by trying to "jazz up" the sobriety of an instructional picture. Music can legitimately enhance the action inherent in a film without resorting to false dramatics or romantic gloss. Quiet pursuits deserve quiet sounds.

By far the most delicate problem is posed by the combination of picture and speech. Pictures and spoken commentary, when properly used, complement each other quite naturally. In particular, photographs, films, and other realistic images can be helped by language because they show human beings, animals, plants, minerals in all their individuality. They make the viewer remain aware of the endless variety of actual existence and stay away from schematization. At the same time, however, learning aims at general concepts, and language helps to nail down the general in the particular. By naming a part of the picture an Irish setter, a colonial mansion, or a spinning machine, the commentary defines the species, class, and function of that particular image. Language also helps in singling out defined items from the continuum of the visual world. When we are told in so many words that next to the cottage there stand an oak and a birch, it is as though someone were cutting out each tree with scissors and setting it apart for special examination.

The combination of picture and speech can be achieved successfully in two fundamentally different ways: the first is epitomized by the slide lecture, in which a coherent speech presentation dominates while the illustrations accompany it as subordinate aids; in the second, a coherent visual performance plays the leading part and is merely supported by the commentary. The decisive difference between dominant and subordinate medium is not one of quantity, i.e., the subordinate medium does not have to be limited to occasional entrances while the dominant one holds the stage all the time. It is rather a matter of content.

The slide lecture, as just mentioned, may be a coherent train of thought, presenting verbally some principle, e.g., of visual perception or social behavior, and illustrating it by as many examples on the screen as needed. However, a lecturer can also function as a mere commentator. He may present a dominant and coherent series of slides, let us say, the sketches for Picasso's painting *Guernica*, in chronological order. In such a case, the words should limit themselves to what can be seen in the screen image or directly deduced from it. The lecturer must make up his mind which attitude he wants to create in the viewer. If he wants him to be absorbed by the procession of pictures on the screen, he cannot hope for attention when, in the midst of the show, he takes off on some historical or theoretical consideration.

Experience seems to indicate that the dominance of speech is almost negligible for the purposes of film and television, unless the speaker himself constitutes the visual spectacle, made more rewarding perhaps by interesting demonstrations during the talk. The nature of the two media requires that the picture be dominant. In the aforementioned lecture series, *Civilization*, the presentation was successful when the lecturer underscored and explained in words the art objects he was showing, but the unity of image and speech came apart when he introduced historical or philosophical expositions, thus forcing the pictures into a background role, for which they could only be much too dominant.

The spoken commentary has always been the bane of travelogues, documentaries, and instructional films. It has been much ridiculed ("and as the sun descends in the west . . .") but hardly improved. The principal trouble is that when the picture, a non-discursive medium, predominates, the spoken commentary cannot fit as long as it is discursive in thought and syntax. The film-maker, like any other artist, conveys general statements through concrete sensory experiences. The freshness, directness, and originality of the images are sabotaged when the spoken commentary reduces the objects, actions, and qualities to their conceptual names. This deadening of the picture by words is hard to avoid since the commentary has precisely the task of spelling out the message of the picture. It should not duplicate in dry or, worse, falsely poetic words what the picture tells more attractively but, rather, amplify and explain, always within the range of the visible subject matter.

The very form of logical discourse adapts itself badly to the free flow of film images. One should experiment more boldly with commentaries made up of questions, dialogue, exclamations—anything that breaks the flow of discursive reasoning. Instruction can be equally well served—perhaps better—by such freer linguistic expression. Granted that in order to produce a good sound track of this nature one needs an expert practitioner of theatrical speech, the kind of person not often employed by the makers of educational films.

Size and Distance

All images have two sizes: that of the physical carrier of the image itself and that of the objects represented by it. A picture of an elephant may be only an inch high; a plastic model showing the anatomy of a flower may be twenty times the size of the real flower. There are obviously good reasons for making an image small enough to fit the page of a book and large enough to show the needed detail, but the educator must be wary of the misleading effects of what is, after all, the "wrong" size.

The older student is not likely to be fooled by the giant size of an ant on the screen. However, in the teaching and learning of art history it is hard to protect oneself against the distorting effects of a miniature painting appearing as large as Michelangelo's *David*. On the screen all things, from the microscopic to the astronomical, are the same size. It is well known also that children have trouble realizing that maps differ in scale, so that Belgium, although it fills the page of the atlas just as does Africa, is nevertheless much smaller.

Correct comparison is a particularly critical matter when intimately related objects are shown at different scale. Machines or organisms consist of parts in all sizes, from the tiniest detail to the whole mechanism or body. Any such part, in order to be shown, has to be adapted to the optimal visual angle of the viewer, who nevertheless has to be made to understand how all these contraptions fit together in their correct sizes. Here the teacher may have to resort to additional resources, preferably to the inspection of the original object itself.

Size has other, less tangible but educationally important, connotations. An insect enlarged to giant size is put in the company of prehistoric monsters. A highway viewed from a helicopter produces an image that makes the traffic artery look like an artery of the human body, through which blood corpuscles run their course. Such comparisons can be poetical and they can also be enlightening by pointing to unexpected similarities. But the difference of character obtained by a change of size must be intended and controlled. The peaceful order of the landscape seen from the air hides the noisy struggle of human existence—an effect that may or may not serve the educational purpose.

The relativity of size inherent in all visual representation can make the student realize that man's view of the world, dependent on the accidental size of the human body, has no absolute validity, but there are as many realities as there are size levels, and only the synthesis of all of them provides us with an intelligent sense of the world, whose measure we are not.

The human size in relation to the size of an object affects our attitude toward it. A small artifact or living creature seems powerless, graceful, remote, miraculous in its functioning. A monumental statue is equally remote from our own kind, but awe-inspiring, threatening, overpowering. The room-filling size of Renaissance murals, abstract-expressionist paintings, or giant screen projections is designed to surround and overwhelm the viewer, whereas today's small television screen remains something of a toy, never quite an arena for the sort of power that can assail us from the movie screen. The television set is a piece of furniture, like the blackboard or the desk, subject to our handling; therefore its images also seem to lack the strength to subdue us. This can make for more detached judgment. *Ceteris paribus*, it reduces the sense of real presence.

Both kinds of experience, the one that sucks us in and the other that keeps its distance, are educationally productive, as long as the teacher exploits the character of each medium with sensitive awareness.

The Range of the Image

Every image is carved out of the continuity of time and space. It represents a selection, whose range must fit the purpose. By picking the correct range of a problem one goes a long way toward solving it. In photographic terms, the range of the image, determined by the distance of the camera from the subject and the focal length of the lens, presupposes a judgment as to what "belongs." Depending on the correctness of the picture range, the viewer may or may not understand what he is supposed to see. The facial expression and posture of a disturbed child may be sufficient to suggest his state of mind, and therefore the sight of things and persons around him may be merely distracting for the viewer. If, however, the attitude of the child has to be understood as a reaction to his direct environment, this environment must be shown, either in the same picture or before or afterwards.

A part extracted from its whole becomes a different thing, and therefore extirpation must be performed with caution. It was probably André Malraux who in his *Psychology of Art* initiated a whole new way of reproducing works of art when he showed the astonishing revelations obtained simply by enlarging details of paintings. The surprisingly modern-looking sketchiness of background landscapes in a Venetian painting or in a Poussin discloses a variability of style easily overlooked under the impact of the picture as a whole. Yet, when the relatively small background landscape is looked at in the context of the whole work, it does not really possess the impressionist boldness it expresses in isolation. In other words, the practice of presenting parts as wholes offers revelation at the risk of falsification.

The sort of tunnel vision provided by any portrayal of reality has its pros and cons. The picture frame can clarify and intensify the subject, not only by limiting the quantity of what is shown, but also by cutting many of the relations the subject has to its surroundings. Such simplification may produce a one-sided impression. Just as the publicity folder of a resort hotel shows it surrounded by woods and topped by snowcapped mountains, but hides the other hotels and the highway nearby, so the limitation of the picture range may leave out relevant aspects of the subject.

The film medium can remedy this restriction more easily because the borders of the image are not permanent as are those of a photograph or painting; they change as soon as the camera turns or travels. From the continuum of the changing view the spectator can synthesize a more complete whole.

In the exploration of the visual world, time and space are inseparable. Objectively, every human being, just as any other thing, goes through its existence in an uninterrupted continuum of time and space. Conscious experience, however, is not continuous. Anesthesia interrupts experience without leaving as much as a sense of time lost. Sleep hides large portions of our day, and in a less predictable manner an hour's or a lifetime's image is patched together from separate moments of more or less complete awareness. This possibility of creating a coherent whole from separate samples of time and space is also used by film and television. The art of film editing consists precisely in combining scenes in such a way that the viewer receives a meaningful continuity while noticing, at the same time, the seams needed to tell him that objective time and space have been sampled rather than recorded completely.

The extent to which time and space can be skipped depends not only on the content of the happening, but also on the visual sophistication of the viewer. The director of a television reportage can switch cameras from the close-up of a single face to a long-range shot of a crowd and from one visual angle to a countershot in the opposite direction only because his free handling of space is matched by the visual literacy of his audience. Evidently, this capacity to "skip" develops gradually during childhood. Therefore, the material for the early years requires more continuity of time and space than is needed later.

To the educator, the elegance of economical editing means that topics can be presented with an intelligent grasp of essentials and a neglect of irrelevant and redundant detail. But the skipping of continuity may also favor superficial thinking. For example, our industrial age has trained the mind to skip the continuity between input and output. In the natural state, people obtain firewood by cutting trees they may have grown themselves. The urban child of today turns the switch on the radiator or electric stove to get heat energy. This reduces the chain of causality between input and output to the one instant connecting the turning of the switch with the delivery of heat, leaving out the entire process of how electricity is generated and how it is paid for by the consumer. The shortcut from need to supply, characteristic of the child's experiences at home, in school, in stores, and in the street, is surely justified for the purposes of practical behavior, but it cripples a thoughtful understanding of our way of life. Here, a film showing, e.g., how water gets from its original source to the faucet, refuses to imitate the shortcut of practical thinking and thereby contributes to insightful living.

Articulate Form

The optical mechanism of the eyes uses light energy to produce amazingly faithful images of the physical world; but, strictly speaking, it is not the recording of the object's visual appearance as such that provides information. It takes appropriate formal characteristics of shape and color to make the object visible. What is it we need to know about an object? We want to be informed about some of its properties, and these properties are transmitted exclusively through articulate form.

If we have to find out whether an object is round or angular, in motion or at rest, green or blue, only the precise form qualities of color and shape can give us the answer. Most drawings and paintings are geared to this basic demand. They endow the object with defined shapes and colors and thereby make it visible. Photography and film cannot be expected to do this to the same extent. The person handling the camera can, by the choice of his subject and the clever use of lighting, do his best to shape the image as clearly as possible, but the result can be successful only within limits. Photographs abound in visually ambiguous or undefined detail. This heightens their realistic quality and can be advantageous artistically, but when precise information is needed, photographic images easily let us down. The adult observer is often unaware of these deficiencies because he is accustomed to supplying by inference what the picture is supposed to show but does not. The child, however, must rely on the concrete visible presence of the facts and qualities he is to gather from the picture. If an illustration shows a Tyrolese playing the zither, the grown-up viewer, sufficiently informed about the instrument, may not notice that the photo fails to show the strings and to explain clearly what the man's fingers are doing. The child may possess no such knowledge and is let down by the picture.

Therefore, one fundamental rule for the use of visual material is this: Never take for granted that a picture which records a certain fact does actually convey the desired information! Especially when television transmits photographic material under unfavorable viewing conditions, the student, who is expetced to see a beaver dam, may see instead nothing but an unsightly smudge.

The formal difference between handmade and photographic images can be exemplified by the use of the contour line in drawing and painting. Nature contains no contour lines, but the shape of most physical objects is perceived only when their borders are clearly visible and when they are characteristic of that shape. The round shape of an apple is characterized by its round borders. If I look at the apple through a keyhole so that only a part of it is seen I will not recognize its shape because its true borders are hidden and the outline of the keyhole does not correspond sufficiently to that of the apple. Similarly, if the apple lies on a table-cloth of the same color, its outlines will be invisible by lack of contrast, and again I will not see the apple. The contour lines used by the draftsman, although "unnatural," resemble the border of the object structurally and thereby make identification possible. It is an invention of the human hand and eye, designed to show clear distinctions between objects. Photographs contain no more contour lines than the objects they depict. Similarly, such informative qualities as the bulging surface of an egg or a sail, the textures of metal or rock, the spatial relations of overlap, surrounding, containing, matching, etc., must be explicitly conveyed by formal means.

This is not to say that drawing and painting techniques guarantee the needed validity of shape and color. The old-fashioned style of mechanically realistic copying, for example, makes things easy to recognize but "invisible" as to their various structural qualities. If the viewer's eye tries to "pin down" the shapes of a tree sketched in the manner of a nineteenth-century drawing teacher, the tree vanishes. Also, the draftsmen employed for the illustration of textbooks and similar educational material do not always concentrate on the rendition of the features that are crucial for learning. Being artists rather than educators, they easily give in to fashionable style, originality of invention, flings of caprice, pleasant enough to look at but often fatal to the educational purpose. Not that the illustrator should "leave out the art." On the contrary, in order to produce images best suited for learning by seeing, a good draftsman employs the means of artistic expression to depict the objects he is called upon to interpret. Outstanding examples of this selfless devotion to the nature of the object are the anatomical and technical drawings of Leonardo da Vinci.

Leonardo teaches us that to draw something means to interpret it and that one can interpret it only if one understands it. Therefore, students will profit greatly from drawing, painting, or photographing objects, provided the teacher guides and judges their work with the proper criteria. For example, meticulous exactness in the rendering of detail may not be a virtue when a student draws what he sees under the microscope. On the contrary, such mechanical faithfulness may obstruct the purpose and promote an attitude of thoughtless copying and an incapacity to tell essentials from irrelevancies—a lack of intelligent abstraction. This leads us to our final and perhaps most important topic.

Abstraction as a Teacher

We have asked: What are the principal criteria a visual image has to meet in order to fulfill its educational purpose? The notion of *authenticity* presented itself soon enough, and we had no trouble realizing to what extent the mechanical faithfulness of the photographic media has increased the reliability of images, be they recordings of natural phenomena, reports of political or social events, or the reproduction of objects or works of art. No hand-drawn image can replace the authentic presence of a desert landscape, the Dead Sea Scrolls, or a medical syndrome shown in a good photograph or film.

At the same time, we realized that mere authenticity in the sense of unadulterated reproduction of the original is not sufficient to qualify a photographic or man-made image for its educational purpose. We remembered that learning means grasping relevant properties of a situation. To this end, the least realistic images are often the best.

Take as an example a series of drawings, developed by means of a computer, which illustrate some geological hypotheses on how the Grand Canyon may have arrived at its present shape. Each drawing is limited to a single contour line, showing the profile of the canyon at a particular phase of its development. The drawings are most instructive. When combined in an animated sequence, they actually let us witness the dramatic geological event in live action. And yet, the picture could not be less realistic. It leaves out almost everything. The story of thousands of years is reduced to a few seconds. The huge canyon is scaled down to a few inches. The masses of rock and sand and the sky above them are totally absent. There is nothing but a greatly simplified outline, which represents a section—and this section is unobtainable in the real world. You cannot slice through the Grand Canyon. Even so, the lesson to be learned is presented with supreme clarity.

Of course, the simple diagram has to be supplemented by realistic pictures of the real landscape. Otherwise, the lesson will perhaps be learned but may relate, in the student's mind, to the wrong kind of reality or to no reality at all. However, it is remarkable how naturally this sort of completely unrealistic presentation is accepted even by a person of little education. In fact, it closely resembles the style of drawing spontaneously invented by young children all over the world. In those drawings also, the ground on which we walk appears as a mere horizontal line, and nothing could look more convincing and appropriate. In other words, a highly abstract and unnaturalistic style of representation is the earliest, most widespread, and universally understood style of visual imagery.

Abstraction, in the simplest meaning of the word, refers to the leaving out of properties. The least we require of such omissions is that they should not interfere with the desired information. For example, pictures in black and white abstract drastically from colorful reality. However, they suffice for surprisingly many purposes, even though the usefulness of a guidebook for bird watchers is severely limited if the illustrations are not in color. Many art historians, repelled by the bad quality of most color reproductions, prefer to illustrate their lectures with black-and-white slides. These are indeed sufficient for discussions of subject matter; but to evaluate pictorial composition by looking only at the shapes can be quite misleading since shapes and colors tend to interact. The shape and size of a certain area of the picture may be incomprehensible and indeed may look wrong unless one sees that it is colored a strong red. A principal condition for the use of subtractive abstraction, therefore, demands that omissions should not alter any characteristics of the whole that are pertinent to the desired information.

Perhaps it is permissible, under the heading *abstraction*, also to refer to certain other liberties taken with the realistic image. Normal vision is limited to the outer surface of objects and indeed to those portions of the object that can be reached by a straight line from the eye or camera. We cannot see the back side of the moon; at the same time, this back side can be a relevant part of the information we require. An image showing the whole object, e.g., the polyhedrons of the mathematician, is best represented pictorially by what looks like a transparent image but is better described as a complete projection of all the edges, including those hidden from ordinary eyesight. Characteristically enough, when with the technique of computer graphics, the various aspects of a three-dimensional solid are to be shown on the face of a cathode-ray tube, a main difficulty consists in eliminating the edges hidden by the frontal surfaces because these are accidental subtractions from the total shape.

Ordinary vision cannot penetrate beneath the outer skin of objects. This is a severe limitation since the inside may be what matters most. Image-making can overcome this deficiency to some extent. Architects and engineers use sections and so-called exploded views showing outside and inside of a building or machine together in their spatial interrelation. In the pictorial arts, it has been quite admissible to omit the roofs or frontal walls of buildings in order to show what is going on inside, and the Bushmen represent the inner organs of an animal as a legitimate part of its image.

Images can be made at any level of abstraction, from the simplest form to the most complex. The correct choice of the appropriate level depends on the nature of what is to be shown and on the intellectual maturity of the viewer. Of a geographical map, for example, only a few global features can be apprehended in the early school years, and the complications of the actual shapes, crowded with detail of crooked rivers and coastlines, are likely to distract from the grasp of the basic facts. Or, to use another example, once the arrangement of the endocrine glands within the human body has been understood as an abstract system, a more faithful and therefore more complicated picture of the anatomical facts can be introduced with profit. This principle holds for any sort of instruction at any level of development. It is an application of the commonsense rule that learning must proceed from the simple to the complex.

Our examples will have made clear what we mean when we say in conclusion that what anybody needs to learn about anything is never the thing "itself" but only an organized whole of selected abstract character traits. It is the task of the visual media to put these traits in evidence. A good example is the learning about numbers. If the student is to see with his own eyes how many legs a fly has, those six visual items must be presented with all the clarity that shape, brightness, and color can muster. The same is true for the number of chromosomes, the number of jurors, the number of spots on a die. These quantities are an abstract trait of certain objects. Equally abstract are other traits of objects, such as their colors, their sizes, their movements, and they can be singled out for the purpose of learning.

A final step will remind us that the visual media serve not only to demonstrate the properties of physical objects. They also translate nonvisual facts into visual ones and thereby give them sensory concreteness. Curves showing the cost of living over time, barometric pressure or temperature changes display quantitative aspects of properties that are not visual in themselves. Similarly, flow charts, diagrams in books on logic or economics, and the like, suggest that there is no branch of human learning that cannot be helpfully displayed in some of its aspects by visual means.

The most appropriate level of abstraction for such a display may be the kind of highly realistic image that only photography can create or it may be as rarified as a geometrical outline figure. In each case the image helps to supply the human mind with the sensory vehicle that it needs for its travels.

CHAPTER IX

Icons and Information

JOHN M. KENNEDY

Introduction

An icon is an image or statue. Icons have often been the centers of cults and the treasures of collectors. In some ages icons were vilified and destroyed. More recently, the term *icon* has become technical and has come to mean a physical event or object which represents another event or object, in part because the two have some significant properties in common. As a technical term referring to a kind of representation, icons are members of a large family of representational displays.

Our age neither worships nor dismisses icons. It studies and exploits them for educational purposes. We use iconic displays to intrigue our students (the motivational function), to show things (the informative function), to serve as memory aids (the mnemonic function), and to arouse evocative or helpful associations (a generative function). But the attempt to understand icons and their relatives has barely begun. The significant properties icons share with the objects they represent are a matter of debate, and we still need to outline orderly steps that should be taken in any systematic study of icons and their family.

In this spirit, this chapter is intended as a kind of model for an attempt to understand icons and like displays. It will try to suggest some ways to study icons, give examples appropriate even for children, and provide a practical theoretical viewpoint for the instructor. The viewpoint is that only some displays rely on cultural canons; other displays (icons) rely heavily on perceptual skills that usually develop spontaneously, without tutoring.

Many displays, icons included, have the utilitarian but vital function of giving information to their users. It is this prosaic function that is the focus of this chapter. Icons represent things, allowing us to see things that are not present, to become familiar with things too bulky to bring into direct view; they acquaint us with imaginable possibilities and they display things that are impossible but can be imagined. How should we proceed to study these functions of icons?

The first task is to attend to the enormous variety of representational displays. If this first task were omitted, the risk would be that one casually chosen instance would be thoughtlessly adopted as the supposed prototype of all the others.

The second task is to tackle at least one kind of display in some detail, not with the aim of asserting that findings in one area will apply to all areas—that remains to be seen—but, rather, simply to become cognizant of some of the subtle and intriguing ways in which characteristics and functions can interrelate. So we will look for some of the roles played by various characteristics.

The third task is to present some viable concepts and explanations of the functions and capacities of various kinds of displays, concepts relevant to learning, and cross-cultural and developmental data.

In attempting all three tasks this chapter will begin by casting a wide net. Gradually the net will be drawn tighter, bringing together the essential ideas and demonstrations. Along the way I will try to show that many researchers have failed to attend to the variety of the phenomena being considered and so have tended to mislead us. And when tackling one area in detail I will try to show how clear and detailed description defends us from misleading implications.

Further, I will try to show that there are at least two important concepts—namely, information and fidelity—that can help us understand the power of informative displays. Investigators, stimulated by J. J. Gibson of Cornell, stirred by his thinking, and often arguing with his conclusions, have produced a network of studies and demonstrations that are fundamental to an understanding of iconic representation, from outline drawing to caricature and trompe l'oeil. In the discussion of Gibson's concepts, the problem of picturing and representation will be shown to pervade basic capacities of human perception.

The goals of this chapter having been outlined, it is now time to tackle the first task, that of inspecting the luxurious range and diversity of displays that possess significant representational characteristics. Then, later, we can come cautiously to basic concepts and studies that may anchor us in the flood of phenomena.

The Variety of Informative Displays

What kinds of displays do we make? What kinds of displays do we use to obtain information? Some objects are displays which can be seen as either themselves or, attendantly, as representations of other things. In the most common case, the observer sees both a representation and something represented. Such displays are enormously different in variety and the status of the matter represented is equally varied. To demonstrate the variety of displays, it is only necessary to list some types. Let me suggest that the list of kinds of displays be read with a query in mind. Ask, in reading the list, how many of the kinds of objects listed have been studied by psychologists or education researchers. The learning theory once so popular in psychology took as its paradigm case an arbitrary "association," arranged by the experimenter at his convenience, between events as disparate as a light and a morsel of food. Are associations representative of the kinds of informative displays listed in the following paragraphs?

Among the range of things informative about things other than themselves must be included: samples, signals, and symbols; badges, mascots, and emblems; indices, markers, maps, graphs, charts, and heiroglyphics; spoor, trophies, and fossils; expressive gestures, representatives, and actors; symptoms, statues, and descriptions; pictures and prototypes.

It was usual in the heyday of associationistic learning theory to speak of learning some particular association, and then "generalizing" it to other cases. Informative displays *cannot* be understood by generalization from known cases. For it is the differences between kinds of displays that enable a fossil to be informative in ways unlike a statue. To take a fossil *by generalization* to be a case of a statue would be to miss the key facts that fossils are not man-made and are residues, not artifacts. Generalization will not suffice as an explanatory mechanism, for differences, not merely similarities, are significant. Instead, the initiate must learn which dimensions of a display are relevant. Are colors relevant? Are absolute sizes? He must learn which poles of the various dimensions are important—fossils are residues, not precursors, in time. On the time dimension he must also distinguish which displays are "simultaneous" with their referent but also spatially separate from their referent, like notices.

The initiate must also learn how to evaluate a display—for example, for reliability and accuracy. An editor might have to evaluate an illustration in terms of its generative function (that of suggesting related ideas and relevant contexts). There are many types of displays and many uses for displays.

Some displays are as natural as tracks in the snow, some are as artificial and many-leveled as the *performance* of an actor, perhaps in a *play* within a *play*, perhaps shown on *television* as an *instance* of the art of another country. We adults have no trouble distinguishing these levels of cognition and confront many examples daily.

Young children, too, are offered many-level representation. On "Sesame Street" I once saw a puppet, appearing as a character in a play, protest that he had no desire to be in the play and then reluctantly repeat his lines. If three-year-olds understood this scene, their cognition is of a standard not mentioned in psychology texts. Not only was the variety of informative displays ignored in favor of concepts of association and generalization, but level of representation, as a systematic problem, remained almost untouched. A formal model of the "Sesame Street" scene must include:

Level One	Reality	A Television (TV)
Level Two	Representation (1)	A show is on the TV
Level Three	Representation (2)	A puppet is on the show
Level Four	Representation (3)	A play is put on by the puppet

Event: Level Three denies Level Four, then (reluctantly) accepts Level Four.

The "Sesame Street" example is more striking than most. We are more familiar with instances of, say, a picture of a room containing pictures—i.e., a picture of pictures—or words that apply to events that symbolize other events, as *Christmas* is a *word* applying to an *event* that *marks* someone's birth.

By and large, we have little evidence that bears on the critical principles I have used in the discussion so far. So I can only highlight them and move on to the task of describing one kind of display in some detail. To summarize, it seems that the variety of informative displays must be characterized (and understood by the growing child) as much in terms of differences as in terms of commonalities. Further, understanding displays requires an understanding of levels of representation, including interrelated levels of representation.

Characteristics of a Display

It would be impractical if not impossible to pin down here the significant characteristics of many kinds of displays. I propose instead to take at least one important kind of display and show some illustrative interesting facts about its obvious material characteristics. The lesson will be that it is not easy to say how displays function; intelligent ideas about the roles played by material characteristics have been sadly wrong.

Since the primary audience for this chapter is educators, it seems appropriate to analyze line displays in some detail. Line drawings are as common as words in our schools. But, while they are widely used, they are not widely understood. Let us examine their material characteristics and then some types.

CHARACTERISTICS OF LINE DISPLAYS

A line (usually a deposit of pigment) is an inhomogeneity on a surface between two boundaries (called contours) enclosing the width. The width between the two contours is slight compared to the line's length. The line may have two terminations demarking its length, like a dash (—), or it may have one termination, like a 6, or even no terminations, like an O. An O figure encloses an area, separating the area from other parts of the surface so that to go from the enclosed area to another area one must cross the two contours of the line. Line figures may also enclose more than one area and not have any terminations, like an 8, but to do so requires that the line figure includes "junctions" where there are at least three contours, as at each of the two junctions in Θ, or more than three contours, as in the four contours around the midpoint of an 8. The presence of junctions does not mean that the line must enclose an area; a Y has one junction but does not enclose areas.

The basic terms for describing lines seem to be contours (and related junctions) and terminations. The functions of even these basic properties of lines have been disputed. Consider contours first.

It has been said that single contours and also the two-contoured figures we call lines have the odd property that the shapes of both areas adjoining the contour or line cannot be seen at once. Lines and contours are "one-sided" in perception, it is said. The view that lines and contours are one-sided has grown popular, but it is simply a misunderstanding of the work of Edgar Rubin,[1] who was interested in one-sided impressions of lines and contours but never claimed that one-sidedness was necessary. Two-sided impressions are quite common.[2] Figure 1 shows two figures, the first a contour figure and the second a line figure. Either figure can be seen as "like beach balls," on which the triangular portions seem like eight adjacent panels. The lines and contours shape or demarcate both adjacent panels.

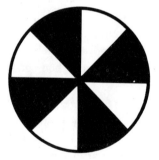

FIG. 1. Contour and line "beach-balls"

There are indeed figures where it is difficult to see the shapes of both sides of the line figure at one time. The interior line of

1. Edgar Rubin, *Synsoplevede Figurer* (Copenhagen: Gyldendals, 1915).

2. John M. Kennedy, "Lines in Pictures—Are They One-Sided?" (Eastern Psychological Association Conference, Philadelphia, 1968).

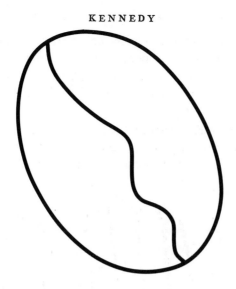

FIG. 2. Faces or a clam?

figure 2 can be seen as like a leftward-facing profile or as like a rightward-facing profile. It is very difficult to see both profiles at the same time. But it must be noted that the problem only arises when trying to see figure 2 as a certain kind of representational display. It is perfectly easy to see the shape of the line itself. Or, if the display is given another referent—say, a clam on its edge with its two sides clasped tight—difficulties disappear again. Apparently the incongruous referent (two faces jammed together, one slightly displaced compared to the other) is the difficulty in the first description of figure 2.

Even the simplest scribbles and crosses are capable of being representational. This lesson, lost to experimental psychology until 1951 [3] and only now being affirmed at length,[4] is inextricably bound

3. James J. Gibson, "What Is a Form?" *Psychological Review* 58 (1951): 403-12.

4. James J. Gibson, *The Senses Considered as Perceptual Systems* (Boston: Houghton Mifflin Co., 1966); Eleanor J. Gibson, *Principles of Perceptual Learning and Development* (New York: Appleton-Century-Crofts, 1969); John M. Kennedy, "Line Representation and Pictorial Perception" (Ph.D. diss., Cornell University, 1971); Margaret A. Hagen, "The Perception of Surface Layout as Pictured in Art" (Unpublished paper, Institute of Child Development, University of Minnesota, 1972).

up with perception of the fundamental characteristics of line figures. Consider yet more properties of the contours of lines.

The two contours of a line are of different shapes unless the
line is straight. One contour of a 9 is shaped like **9** and the other

like ▪▪▪. Note that special problems can arise when the two contours have different shapes and each depicts different things. For
example, consider figure 3, a line drawing of a glove. Look care-

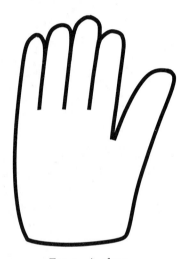

Fig. 3. A glove

fully and you will see that the exterior contour has the shape of
a mitten (like figure 4), while the interior contour has the shape
of a glove with its fingers separated, like figure 5. Now, figure 3
contains the contours of figure 4 and figure 5, combined. Yet, figure
3 depicts a glove with its fingers pressed together. Figure 3 does
not depict a mitten like figure 4, nor does it depict a glove with its
fingers separated like figure 5. In sum, a line figure does not simply
depict the sum of the things depicted by its contours!

Now let us consider the terminations of lines. Line figures are
defined as much by their terminations as by the deposits of pigment
between the terminations. Oddly enough, it has sometimes been
claimed that if one extends the lines of a figure, the figure remains
"geometrically the same" but becomes psychologically hidden. This

FIG. 4. A mitten

FIG. 5. A glove, fingers slightly separated

is surely wrong. Consider figure 6a. Extending lines from the terminations to yield, say, figure 6b does not leave figure 6a geometrically the same. The terminations have been removed, even if the pigment deposits of figure 6a are complete. Let only a little of the

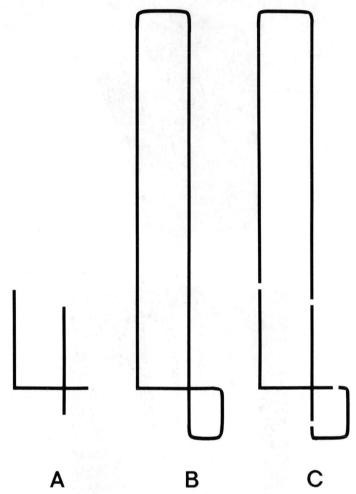

A   B   C

Fɪɢ. 6. Visible 4 and effects of loss of terminations

extra line length added in figure 6b be removed, returning the terminations, and the original figure 6a is now quite evident as in figure 6c. Figure 6a in its entirety was not hidden in figure 6b; it was
not completely present. Terminations are defining characteristics
of figures.

Skill in perception of line displays involves picking out relevant
terminations and noticing either individual contours or the shape
of the product of both contours.

Line displays have contours and terminations. What displays have in common is important, but differences between kinds of displays are equally important. So let us turn to a list of different kinds of displays and note some difficulties in developing a coherent list. Let us especially note what happens when perceivers look at a display, seeing it as one kind of display rather than another.

TYPES OF LINE DISPLAYS

Lines (made up of deposits of pigment between contours) having length between terminations make up different kinds of patterns or configurations.[5] Any attempt to list types of line configurations runs into problems. It is not clear how to keep the categories distinct, and neither is it clear how many categories are needed. Forewarned and forearmed, consider the following list of informative line displays.

Line pictures. These allow observers to see the layout of objects and scenes that are not in fact present. For outlines there are continuous lines with no areas of shading, i.e., there are no large areas whose width is several times larger than the lines in the drawing which have been covered or "filled in" with pigment or crosshatching. In outline figures, the length, direction, and shape of every line are significant. In cross-hatching, the lines are arranged in dense groups, and the direction and shape of individual lines are not significant; only their distribution and density are significant. Outline drawings will be discussed in more detail shortly.

Writing. Line configurations can be written or printed characters, forming letters, words, sentences, and higher-order units of text. Learning to read involves learning patterns that are letters, patterns that are words, higher-order patterns, and also skill in attention to "white space" between patterns. Subcategories of writing include:

1. Alphabetic writing. This may be block capitals or typewritten letters or cursive script. This kind of writing includes marks called punctuation marks. A subclass called shorthand has marks representing whole words or parts of words, and forms an intermediary with logograms.
2. Logograms. These are characters which are to be read as words,

5. Rubin, op. cit., especially pt. 2, "Plane Figures, Contours and Lines."

as 3 is read as *three* and + is read as *plus*. Included here can be some kinds of musical notation, dance notation, cattle brands, and brand labels.

3. Pictographs. These are a kind of writing in which some properties of the marks are pictorial. A pictograph of a tree might, by sensible guesswork, be selected as a referent for a tree rather than a bird, if the two possibilities were mentioned to a subject.

4. Ideograms. These are like pictographs in that they have pictorial properties. But, unlike pictographs, ideograms represent not just the object suggested by the pictorial properties but an idea for which the object is an emblem. A line-drawn cross is an ideogram which refers to a religion rather than only to a cruciform object. Compared to a pictograph there are more levels of comprehension needed to understand an ideogram.

Even within writing it is noteworthy that problems of iconic, pictorial qualities arise. And also there are different levels of representation, sometimes precisely because of pictorial qualities. Interestingly, pictorial problems arise again with geometrical figures.

Geometrical figures. Many texts contain line illustrations of geometrical figures, including (a) flat geometrical figures, like ovals, circles, squares, hyperboles, etc., and (b) geometrical figures "in depth." The status of these illustrations requires discussion. Consider only the geometrical figures that allow observers to say they see a "pattern in three dimensions" (e.g., figure 7).

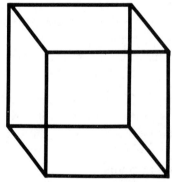

Fig. 7. A cube: A geometrical figure "in depth"

Researchers like Kopfermann,[6] Hochberg[7] and Attneave[8] have been intrigued by the fact that often line configurations do not seem as flat as the marks on the page which comprise the line configuration. They have tried to derive formulas to predict what instances of configurations made of straight lines, with each line forming junctions with other straight lines, would be seen as three-dimensional rather than flat on the page. Success has been limited. For example, the Hochberg formula cannot say what three-dimensional configuration will be seen, only that whatever configuration is seen will probably be three-dimensional. Perhaps the most promising lead has been taken up by Perkins,[9] who has restricted his attention to three-line junctions and shown which of them depict corners of cubes.

It must be noted that it is not enough to say that a line configuration seems three-dimensional. It has to be said, too, that observers are not fooled into thinking the displays are truly three-dimensional. The configuration is always definitely a flat deposit of pigment on a surface, not a wire form resting on a surface. In other words, geometrical illustrations are clearly functioning as "pictures" when they seem three-dimensional. Perhaps flat geometrical figures are *exemplified* by line configurations on paper, but figures for solid, three-dimensional geometry are *pictured* on paper. Students must take a *pictorial* attitude to these "three-dimensional," physically flat displays, and the pictorial view is ancillary to the realistic impression of flatness. In sum, it seems that even some geometrical figures are iconic depictions.

Diagrams. The essential feature of a member of this class of display is that the spatial arrangement of some of its components bears an orderly significant relation to some other domain of events.

6. Hertha Kopfermann, "Psychologische Untersuchungen über die Wirkung zweidimensionaler darstellungen Korperlicher gebilde," *Psychologische Forschung* 13 (1930): 292-364.

7. Julian E. Hochberg, *Perception* (Englewood Cliffs, N.J.: Prentice-Hall, 1964).

8. Fred Attneave, "Multistability in Perception," *Scientific American* 225 (December 1971): 62-71.

9. David Perkins, "Geometry and the Perception of Pictures: Three Studies," *Harvard Project Zero Technical Reports*, no. 5, 1971.

In other words, some of the spatial configuration is informative about something. Diagrams can be as close to pictorial displays as the plan of a building, where scaling down and parallel projection are involved in the relation between the plan and the building. They can also be very far from pictorial, as in graphs or flow charts. Not all of the components of a diagram are representational. The thickness of lines, or their color, may or may not be significant. Usually any diagram comes provided with labels or keys which inform the viewer which aspects of the diagram are significant, as a map comes with its code for roads, rivers, and heights. Training in understanding diagrams involves training in comprehension of codes or keys and in the special skill of adopting some particular key for the diagram immediately before one, rejecting any prior habits in favor of the convention of the moment.

It has been pointed out several times that many line displays seem to belong in several overlapping categories. One might wonder whether a helpful distinction could be made between *seeing* lines and *understanding* their representational status. A sharp distinction between perception and cognition might allow us to consign most problems to cognition and keep a simple process, called perception, unaffected by issues of representation. But it has been shown that many perceptual problems of shape and sidedness are involved with representation. And it can readily be shown by figure 8 that the problem of overlapping categories affects such a basic perceptual process as recognition.

Some line configurations can be seen as either meaningless writing or as profiles; some patterns can be seen as scribbles or numerals (figure 8). The displays are more recognizable on second showing if they are seen as profiles or numerals. Seeing writing or scribbles seems to exclude seeing alternative categories of line configuration (just as in figure 2, seeing the leftward profile excluded the rightward profile).

One class of informative displays has been described in some detail. It is important to note the often unsuspected role of pictorial properties in many kinds of displays. While some displays are entirely nonpictorial, like alphabetic script or logograms, some, like pictographs and ideograms, are partly pictorial, and others, like il-

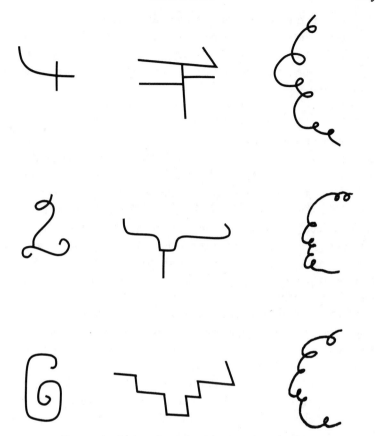

FIG. 8. Scribbles? Or faces, boats, and numerals?

lustrations of three-dimensional geometrical forms, rely completely on the pictorial mode of representation.

Gibson proposes [10] that we treat informative displays along the lines of the pictorial or nonpictorial distinction, as follows: Some displays, those with pictorial properties, rely on our perceptual skills developed in the everyday real environment in our commerce with the objects that can be pictured by displays. Other displays, the nonpictorial ones, capitalize on our capacities to understand conventions, for they represent only by arbitrary convention. The pictorial displays do not require training in any convention because

10. Gibson, *The Senses Considered as Perceptual Systems*, op. cit., chap. 11.

they canvas our procedures for gaining information about the solid (nonpictorial) environment. To understand Gibson's proposal, emerging as it does from a theory about light from the environment, it is necessary to review his conceptions of perception and information.

Information and Ecological Optics

Over the past two decades J. J. Gibson has attempted to define and describe an "ecological optics," aimed at understanding the relation between terrestrial light and the human environment. To Gibson, visual perception is the activity involved in getting to know the environment by making use of the optic arrays arising from objects and events. The key to his thought is his criterion for saying there is useful information in the light that meets our eye. If the light contains patterns that could only have originated from one particular kind of source in the environment, then the light is informative about that source, Gibson would have us say.

To understand Gibson's view of information, consider an analogy. The problem in general terms is to know the origins of the effects that reach one's perceptual systems. As a comparison, suppose some transistors were removed from their sockets in a circuit. If each transistor is marked differently—socket A, socket B, and so on—it will be possible to decide unambiguously what their original sockets were. If some of the transistors are marked identically, the job of finding the original sockets is complicated by ambiguities. If each transistor is marked in a way that is specific to its origin, it is possible to know the correct origin. Similarly, if the light patterns from various origins in the environment are all different and specific to their origins, it is possible to know what the origins are and perceivers can accurately register their environments without ambiguities.

To follow the analogy with examples, suppose we ask a perceiver to tell us whether there are two or more surfaces in his field of view. Are there properties of light that allow him to distinguish surfaces accurately? To answer this question we must ask what the surfaces of the environment are like and what optical results occur because of the characteristics of the surfaces. To distinguish surfaces from one another we should ask what makes one surface different from another in ways relevant to optics. One relevant property is texture. To the extent that surfaces are regions of texture, with each surface having different texture, surfaces will yield different "optic textures" in the light to our eye. So there is an optical basis for perceivers to distinguish different surfaces. Optic texture can be informative about the presence of surfaces and the differences between surfaces.

For another example, suppose a perceiver is asked which of two surfaces is more distant. The two surfaces might be arranged so one partly obscures the other, from the observer's point of observation. What properties of the light from the environment inform perceivers which surface is more distant? If the observer moves from one observation point to another, he may find that parts of one surface are obscured from one of the points of view and not from the other. In moving continuously from one point of observation to another, the originally obscured surface area comes into view, texture element by texture element. And, of course, the surface that gradually comes into view is the further of the two surfaces.[11]

To repeat: Gibson's proposal is that some properties of the light to points of view are specific to properties of the environment, and these optic properties can be said to constitute information for the layout of the environment. On this proposal Gibson founds an entire discipline, which he terms *ecological optics*. The aim of the discipline is to describe the relation between the environment and the light from the environment.

How can artificial displays be fitted into an ecological optics? Most especially, how can pictorial artificial displays, said to be independent of convention, be part of an ecological optics? Gibson began treating this question in 1951 in a paper in which he noted that studies of form perception can involve moments when the subject responds to pictorial qualities of a display rather than to the flat configuration of the display. And he stated, "The form of a surface with its edges . . . may be very different from the outlines representing the edges of such a surface, as a square carpet, for example, might be depicted by a trapezoid." [12]

Ecological optics attempts to find properties of light that are

11. George Kaplan, "Kinetic Disruption of Optical Texture: The Perception of Depth at an Edge," *Perception and Psychophysics* 6 (1971): 193-98.

12. Gibson, "What Is a Form?" op. cit., p. 409.

specifically related to one kind of environmental layout. How should optic properties that can come from not *one* but *two* kinds of origins—pictures of objects and the real objects—fit into a discipline that attempts to find *single* origins for specific properties? To begin to answer, consider again the texture of surfaces.

It was suggested above that naturally occurring surfaces have different textures. At this point it is important to realize that natural surfaces can be effaced by man's agency and that any natural texture can be radically changed. Natural pigmentation can be covered over with different pigments. And so a surface may be treated to artificially give optical structure that would not naturally come from such surfaces. (One of the commonsense strengths of this point is that painters do, in fact, *paint* pictures and do not *find representational* pictures in nature. To give a friend a picture of himself, one must "make" or "take" his picture; one cannot "find" it!)

After presenting the paper on form, Gibson in 1954 [13] took the step of classifying pictures as "artificial" displays. Consequently, two origins for the same optic structure are permissible if we first classify origins as either natural or artificial and then examine only the natural cases for optic specificities. Only after this will we return to artificial displays to see which of them repeat significant optic patterns. This resolution of Gibson's problems with two origins for one optic structure is conceptually neat and, as we shall see later, practical. For the moment let us note another step Gibson took in the 1954 paper—a step into a tradition traceable to Alberti and DaVinci, a step which Gibson recently rejected as unwise.[14]

In 1954 Gibson argued that pictures were "processed" or were artificial surfaces and went on to define a faithful picture. The underlying idea, as I noted in a thesis written under Gibson, was that "some pictures are schematic, obviously revealing only a limited part of their subject. In others the details may be so complete that a magnifying glass must be used to discover the finer work of the artist. So a concept of the extent to which the light

13. James J. Gibson, "A Theory of Pictorial Perception," *Audio-Visual Communication Review* 1 (1954): 3-23.

14. James J. Gibson, "The Information Available in Pictures," *Leonardo* 4 (1971): 27-35.

from the picture is more completely a presentation of the light from its object would be useful." Such a concept was offered by Gibson as the *fidelity* of a picture.[15] Gibson wrote: "a faithful picture is a delimited surface processed in such a way that it reflects (or transmits) a sheaf of light rays to a given point which is the same as would be the sheaf of rays from the original to that point."[16] Gibson added that "a sheaf of rays is 'the same as' another when the adjacent order of the points of color in the cross-section of one is the same as the adjacent order in the cross-section of the other."

In that thesis I argued that Gibson's definition of fidelity could be very misleading. If one uses this definition, "a careful line drawing (which need not share one point of color with the original) and an improperly colored and proportioned painting will both be considered *unfaithful*. Yet while the poor painting may be vague, the line drawing may provide very exact information about the distribution of the object's surfaces." I noted that "one could amend the concept of fidelity to cope with the outline drawing. The test for fidelity could be applied separately to each feature . . . of the object as opposed to each point of the object. So one could argue that the lines in a line drawing, being perspective projections of the edges of a chair, were faithful to the edges of the chair. Fidelity to the object as a whole would be checked by verifying that each feature of the chair that was of interest was represented faithfully in the optic array from the picture."[17]

Do pictures of objects in fact make available optic arrays comparable to optic arrays from the real objects? If so, one would expect that neither a particularly high level of intelligence nor schooling in canons of representation would be necessary to deal with pictures.

The first relevant study was made by Hochberg,[18] a close colleague of Gibson for many years. One way to examine Gibson's

15. Kennedy, "Line Representation," op. cit., p. 20.

16. Gibson, "A Theory of Pictorial Perception," op. cit., p. 14.

17. Kennedy, "Line Representation," op. cit., p. 24.

18. Julian E. Hochberg and Virginia Brooks, "Pictorial Perception as an Unlearned Ability: A Study of One Child's Performance," *American Journal of Psychology* 85 (1962): 624-28.

claim is to show that young children understand pictures without being trained in a convention of representation. Hochberg and his wife reared their child with restricted exposure to any kind of pictures. As far as possible, pictures were removed from the house. A few decals, advertisements, and the like were the only pictorial displays available to the child. More important than the limited exposure was the fact that the child was never trained in labeling pictures, never told that they represented anything, and was never read a story with attendant illustrations. Just before the child was two years old, at a time when he had a reasonable vocabulary, a test was given. Line drawings and black-and-white photographs of objects were put on view and the child was asked to label them. No photograph of an object was shown before a line drawing of the object was offered, and the child's responses were not corrected. *The child labeled the pictures correctly*, whether they were photographs or complex line drawings with interior detail (like a doll) or simple outline drawings with minimal interior detail (like a key in outline with only one interior line—a circle for the hole for a key ring). Evidently, pictures, whether line drawings or photographs, can depict layout without need of the associations of an arbitrary convention.

The significance of intellectual level as measured by IQ was tested in a study by O'Connor and Hermelin.[19] They tested seventy-two subjects with a mean IQ of less than 50. The subjects indicated which words from a list of nouns spoken by the experimenters went with which picture in a set of line drawings. Most of the subjects performed accurately. It seems that no specially high level of intelligence is necessary to pick up information from line drawings.

The effect of becoming accustomed to a nonprojective convention of representation was tested by Deregowski in a Zambian culture in which nonperspectival pictures are the norm. Some of the subjects were asked which drawings depicted a model better— the "preferred" drawings—while other subjects were asked to pick the model represented in a drawing. "The preferred drawings are

19. N. O'Connor and B. Hermelin, "Like and Cross-Modality Recognition in Subnormal Children," *Quarterly Journal of Experimental Psychology* 11 (1961): 48-52.

in fact worse than (perspective) drawings in conveying to the
subjects what the depicted object actually looks like . . . the results support the contention of Gibson that perspective is not a
mere convention." [20]

Cross-cultural studies and work with young and low-IQ subjects support Gibson's view that pictures rely on replication of
optical structure from the environment. If his definition of fidelity
is phrased in terms of features rather than points of color, then the
definition is applicable to line drawings and the evidence is that
line pictures are no more conventional than photographs.

What sorts of features can be represented by lines? Gibson's
analysis of the sources of optical structure can be used to define
features of an object. He mentions uneven surface, uneven pigment, and uneven illumination, to which can be added uneven
texturing. Let us consider these sources of optical structure, one
by one.

UNEVEN SURFACE

Various ways that surfaces can be arranged are depicted in figure 9, taken from my 1971 thesis.[21] This figure contains outline
representation of all the basic categories of surface layout. One seg-

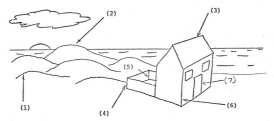

(1) Rounded edge ("occluding bound") with a background surface
(2) Rounded edge with background air
(3) Sharp edge ("occluding edge") with background air
(4) Sharp edge with background surface
(5) Corner facing away from the observer ("concave corner")
(6) Corner facing towards the observer ("convex corner")
(7) A crack

FIG. 9. Seven meanings of lines, depicting surface layout

20. Jan B. Deregowski, "Determinants of Split-Representation as an Artistic
Style," *International Journal of Psychology* 5 (1970): 21-26. (Quoted from
p. 24.)

21. Kennedy, "Line Representation," op. cit., p. 78a.

ment of line depicts a convex corner and another segment depicts a concave corner. Yet another segment depicts a convex corner acting as an "occluding edge," i.e., a convex corner only one face of which is visible. Another segment represents occlusion by a smoothly rounded surface, i.e., an "occluding bound." Some of the layout has background surface and some of it has only air or sky as background. And some line segments represent cracks; cracks (like wires) belong in a special category where several features of surface layout are close together and parallel, like the two occluding edges provided by the margins of a crack. In figure 3, discussed previously, line segments depict cracks (between fingers) and occluding bounds (formed by the ends of fingers).

UNEVEN PIGMENTATION

A pure case of uneven pigment is provided by the coloration of animals. The hide is uniformly textured, the surface of the hide is quite planar, but there is differential coloring of different areas. Can change of pigment be depicted by lines? Figure 10 depicts a

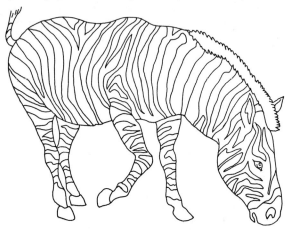

Fig. 10. A zebra—line depiction of pigment-change

zebra, in which change of pigmentation from dark to light is depicted by lines. In informal testing I found this figure is readily recognized by children, which suggests that line representations of change of pigmentation are meaningful without special training in a convention.

UNEVEN ILLUMINATION

A pure case of line depiction of shadows is provided by figure 11. Depiction of shadows by lines was quite rare in graphic art up

FIG. 11. Line depiction of shadows—change of illumination on a surface

until 1969. To my knowledge no schooling is given in line depiction of shadows. Yet, in testing adults (prior to 1969) I found they readily identified lines in figure 11 as representations of shadows of men.[22]

UNEVEN TEXTURE

Pure cases of uneven texture are provided by knitted garments with hems and cuffs. When this was pointed out to me I made a line drawing of a sweater, figure 12, in which there is a narrow band across the waist region. Adults described the line as representing change of pattern or change of weave, i.e., as change of texture.

All the sources of optic structure mentioned above seem to be capable of line depiction if the unevenness is *abrupt*, as it is in all

22. John M. Kennedy, "Outlines and Shadows" (American Psychological Society Conference, Miami, Florida, 1970).

FIG. 12. Line depiction of a sweater, including depiction of change of texture

the figures. A rule that follows is: Lines can depict discontinuities that are sources of optic structure. A rule that lines can depict discontinuities would have considerable power in iconography if it could be shown to apply to new cases of depiction, including subject's first encounters with new forms of depiction. I have been testing this rule with displays made of raised lines that subjects explore with touch only. It is exciting to find that blindfolded subjects recognize raised-line depictions of common objects [23] and that blind subjects, too, in their first encounter with raised-line depictions of common objects are also able to recognize the depicted object.[24] The theoretical and practical importance of the discontinuity hypothesis is evident. The hypothesis summarizes the "language" of lines—the language discovered centuries ago—and describes it in a way that is general enough to apply to more than one sensory modality.

It seems, then, that all the basic sources of optical structure in the environment are amenable to line depiction. These sources are the features to which to apply the concept of fidelity of depiction. The features are combined in the environment to form objects and scenes. In pictures, features are also depicted in combinations. Usually the features combine to form realistic objects, i.e., they follow

23. John M. Kennedy and Nathan Fox, "Haptic Pictures" (in preparation).

24. John M. Kennedy, Nathan Fox, and Kathy O'Grady, "Can 'Haptic Pictures' Help the Blind See? A Study of Drawings To Be Touched," *Harvard Education Association Bulletin* 16 (Spring 1972): 22-23.

the ecological rules of combination evident in the environment. But in depiction the ecological rules may be broken to form "impossible objects," as in figure 13.

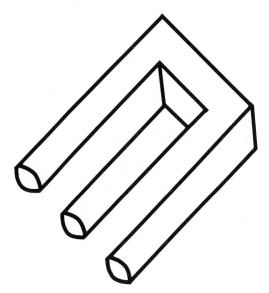

FIG. 13. The Devil's tuning fork—an impossible object

Impossible objects (like imaginary objects) are not conventions any more than are depictions of ordinary objects. Their existence does not disconfirm Gibson's position that pictures use the naturalistic patterns of light. It is ecological features that are depicted in impossible pictures and simply the combination of features that is unecological or impossible. For example, in figure 13 an impossible change of surface layout is depicted. What is impossible is that a boundary between air and surface should reverse so that air is now on the side where surface was and surface on the side where air was, without intervening surface edges. That is, the direction of occlusion cannot reverse in nature as it does in the innermost pair of lines of the fork. So, too, a crack (air between surfaces) cannot turn into a wire (air on either side) nor can cracks and wires turn into occluding edges or bounds (figure 14).[25]

One final support for Gibson's 1954 position rewritten in terms

25. Kennedy, "Line Representation," op. cit., p. 82a.

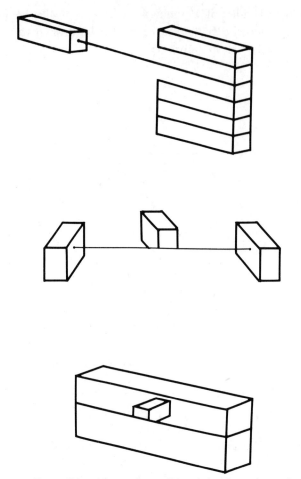

FIG. 14. Impossible objects—impossible air/surface alternations

of optical structure and environmental features deserves to be described before problems with the position are raised.

The tradition of trompe l'oeil art is testimony to the fact that pictures can be effective representations. Gibson [26] attempted a contemporary version of the experiments of trompe l'oeil art. He made a large photomural from a photograph of a long and dimly lit corridor. The photograph was arranged behind a peephole and another screen and peephole were arranged at the near end of the

26. James J. Gibson, "Pictures, Perspective and Perception," *Daedalus* 89 (1960): 210-27.

real corridor. Both the photograph and the corridor subtended the same angle to the eye, and the edges of the photograph were not visible. Subjects looked monocularly into each peephole and had to judge which peephole opened onto the corridor. Some subjects, about a third, guessed wrong! Trompe l'oeil can be effective even when the pictorial scene is arranged side by side with the original.

Two conceptions of a picture have been mentioned so far. Some pictures might repeat the optical energy (colored rays of light) from a scene. But most pictures, like line sketches, can be best thought of as repeating optical forms or structures and are thus faithful to features of the environment.

Gibson has recently begun to believe that the information in light is not in the light rays and energies nor even in the forms of form, but, instead, is often in the arrangements of forms. And with this thought in mind an experiment by Ryan and Schwartz,[27] his colleagues at Cornell, has become central to ecological optics.

Ryan and Schwartz tested pickup of information from a black-and-white photograph, an ink-and-wash (shaded) drawing, a line drawing, and a cartoon drawing (a line-drawn caricature). These were shown tachistoscopically to subjects who had to report, for example, the posture of the hands or the position of an electrical switch in a picture. That is, the subject had to detect the relative layout of parts. In the line drawing, the lines represented all the edges and corners of the objects. In the cartoon or caricature only some of the edges were represented and many of the outlines of objects were simplified, e.g., only a thumb and three fingers were shown on a hand, the digits were drawn with smooth curves, and details like the grooves in the skin at the knuckles were omitted (cartoon conventions, so-called). The results were that layout was detected with least difficulty from the cartoon or caricature, while photographs and shaded drawings were about equal in difficulty, and line drawings of high fidelity to the edges of objects were the most difficult.

So, a high degree of fidelity to a scene or an object as a whole may even be counterproductive to detection of a limited property of the scene. Caricatures can be appreciated with less exposure time

27. Thomas A. Ryan and Carol Schwartz, "Speed of Perception as a Function of Mode of Representation," *American Journal of Psychology* 69 (1956): 60-69.

than precise projective depiction. Recent work by Perkins supports this view—subjects make a more recognizable drawing of a person when told to exaggerate features than when asked to use tracing paper and make a faithful tracing of a photograph of the person.[28]

With the work of Ryan and Schwartz as background Gibson has redefined pictures, in terms of his newer views of the nature of informative structure in light. Gibson finds caricatures a compelling objection to the whole theory that pictorial information can be reduced to light rays. He now defines a picture as "a surface so treated that a delimited optic array to a point of observation is made available that contains the same kind of information that is found in the ambient optic arrays of an ordinary environment."[29]

The emphasis is still on artificiality and on optics and ecological informative light. However, the definition now applies not merely to pictures that replicate colored rays or repeat an optic structure with projective fidelity, but also to the yet more general category of optic information. And optic information, he suggests, is found in arrangements of forms, in the kinds of optic variables invariant over movement of the observer, or in the objects in the environment. "Change of type of optic texture" is one such invariant. (With moving pictures also there is "progressive emergence of texture from behind occluding edges.") The implication is that invariants are present in a sketch, though one cannot test that they are invariant, for the sketch is static. One has to know (through exposure to the environment presumably) what kinds of optic structures are invariant across motion and thus know what to look for when the invariants are presented, frozen, in a still picture. In theory, the environment tunes one's perceptual systems to such invariants and perception responds to such invariants even when presented with a static case.

Invariants, form, and forms of form. These are the terms on which Gibson's theory is based. There is a frustrating vagueness in these terms. Just what exactly is the form of a man, we might ask, if we wanted to depict a man. What are the invariants that

28. David Perkins, personal communication, 1971.

29. Gibson, "Information Available in Pictures," op. cit., p. 31.

should be present in a picture of a man if children are to recognize what is represented? At this point, it has to be admitted that we do not yet know. The geometry of form is not yet very far advanced. Gibson cannot yet be very explicit. How should we make the important aspects of form more evident, easier for children to notice? Gibson cannot yet say. (Arnheim's chapter in this volume points out some of the directions Gibson might consider useful, and some of the difficulties are examined in Kennedy's research on incomplete puzzle pictures [30] and in his book on obtaining information from pictures.)[31] Gibson can only say that if the child can see the form of the object, he can understand the pictured form, and vice versa.

Gibson's latest definition of a picture makes use of the studies that support the view that pictures are not simply conventions and the definition extends to caricatures (which were excluded as conventional symbols in his 1954 paper). His earlier definition spurred research on children and other cultures, on trompe l'oeil, and impossibles. The new definition will require as much research if it is to be substantiated. Are caricatures relying on informative arrangements of form shown in impressive exaggeration, or are they easy to follow because of simplifications and omissions of irrelevant details? These are questions for the future. And that is a reflection on the state of ecological optics. There are important studies and some well-defined concepts maintaining a solid platform. Around the platform is a scaffold of promising but vaguer concepts and new definitions, calling for an extension of the foundations. Perhaps the new definitions of pictures will be a scaffold on which to build, and some directions are clear. Or, perhaps, in another sense of scaffold, the definition will hang the theory of invariants as the basis for ecological information. Time and research will tell.

Conclusion

The nature of static, informative, flat displays has been discussed. This chapter has explained the view that there are two

30. John M. Kennedy, "Incomplete Pictures and Detection of Features," *Journal of Structural Learning* 2 (1971): 71-73.

31. John M. Kennedy, *Images and Information* (San Francisco: Jossey-Bass, forthcoming).

kinds—those that inform and represent, based on arbitrary conventions, and those that in the tradition of icons have pictorial properties. Conventions have to be taught; pictures portray the forms of objects in ways that are spontaneously meaningful, as shown by studies on children, caricatures, and the functions of lines.

The resulting theory suggests that educators can expect to make use of pictures with the very youngest school children to show objects and scenes. Even schematic outlines should be recognized without training. However hard is the process of learning to make pictures, learning to see by means of pictures is a process resting on the full foundation of everyday perception. Given pictures with a reasonable fidelity to their referent, children should have no difficulty. Pictures inform because light is informative in our everyday environment.[32]

32. Support from the Department of Psychology, Cornell University (James J. Gibson in particular) and Project Zero, Harvard University, operating under a grant from the National Science Foundation, was important in the preparation of this paper. The assistance of Elizabeth M. Kennedy; the Department of Psychology, Copenhagen University; and Harvard's Milton Fund was important in the preparation of materials, notably Edgar Rubin's papers, which were formative in the writing of sections of this paper.

CHAPTER X

The Visual Image

What a picture means to the viewer is strongly dependent on his past experience and knowledge. In this respect the visual image is not a mere representation of "reality" but a symbolic system.

E. H. GOMBRICH

Ours is a visual age. We are bombarded with pictures from morning till night. Opening our newspaper at breakfast, we see photographs of men and women in the news, and raising our eyes from the paper, we encounter the picture on the cereal package. The mail arrives and one envelope after the other discloses glossy folders with pictures of alluring landscapes and sunbathing girls to entice us to take a holiday cruise, or of elegant menswear to tempt us to have a suit made to measure. Leaving our house, we pass billboards along the road that try to catch our eye and play on our desire to smoke, drink or eat. At work it is more than likely that we have to deal with some kind of pictorial information: photographs, sketches, catalogues, blueprints, maps or at least graphs. Relaxing in the evening, we sit in front of the television set, the new window on the world, and watch moving images of pleasures and horrors flit by. Even the images created in times gone by or in distant lands are more easily accessible to us than they ever were to the public for which they were created. Picture books, picture postcards and color slides accumulate in our homes as souvenirs of travel, as do the private mementos of our family snapshots.

No wonder it has been asserted that we are entering a historical epoch in which the image will take over from the written word. In view of this claim it is all the more important to clarify the

First published in *Scientific American* 227 (September 1972): 82-96. Reprinted by permission of W. H. Freeman & Co.

potentialities of the image in communication, to ask what it can and what it cannot do better than spoken or written language. In comparison with the importance of the question the amount of attention devoted to it is disappointingly small.

Students of language have been at work for a long time analyzing the various functions of the prime instrument of human communication. Without going into details we can accept for our purpose the divisions of language proposed by Karl Bühler, who distinguished between the functions of expression, arousal and description. (We may also call them symptom, signal and symbol.) We describe a speech act as expressive if it informs us of the speaker's state of mind. Its very tone may be symptomatic of anger or amusement; alternatively it may be designed to arouse a state of mind in the person addressed, as a signal triggering anger or amusement. It is important to distinguish the expression of an emotion from its arousal, the symptom from the signal, particularly since common parlance fails to do this when speaking of the "communication" of feeling. It is true that the two functions can be in unison and that the audible symptoms of a speaker's anger may arouse anger in me, but they may also cause me to be amused. On the other hand, someone may contrive in cold blood to move me to anger. These two functions of communication are shared by human beings with their fellow creatures lower down on the evolutionary scale. Animal communications may be symptomatic or emotive states or they may function as signals to release certain reactions. Human language can do no more: it has developed the descriptive function (which is only rudimentary in animal signals). A speaker can inform his partner of a state of affairs past, present or future, observable or distant, actual or conditional. He can say it rains, it rained, it will rain, it may rain, or "If it rains, I shall stay here." Language performs this miraculous function largely through such little particles as "if," "when," "not," "therefore," "all" and "some," which have been called logical words because they account for the ability of language to formulate logical inferences (also known as syllogisms).

Looking at communication from the vantage point of language, we must ask first which of these functions the visual image can perform. We shall see that the visual image is supreme in its ca-

pacity for arousal, that its use for expressive purposes is prob-
lematic, and that unaided it altogether lacks the possibility of
matching the statement function of language.

The assertion that statements cannot be translated into images
often meets with incredulity, but the simplest demonstration of
its truth is to challenge the doubters to illustrate the proposition
they doubt. You cannot make a picture of the concept of statement any more than you can illustrate the impossibility of translation. It is not only the degree of abstraction of language that
eludes the visual medium; the sentence from the primer "The cat
sits on the mat" is certainly not abstract, but although the primer
may show a picture of a cat sitting on a mat, a moment's reflection
will show that the picture is not the equivalent of the statement.
We cannot express pictorially whether we mean "the" cat (an individual) or "a cat" (a member of a class); moreover, although the
sentence may be one possible description of the picture, there are
an infinite number of other true descriptive statements you could
make such as "There is a cat seen from behind," or for that matter
"There is no elephant on the mat." When the primer continues
with "The cat sat on the mat," "The cat will sit on the mat," "The
cat sits rarely on the mat," "If the cat sits on the mat . . ." and so
on ad infinitum, we see the word soaring away and leaving the
picture behind.

Try to say the sentence to a child and then show him the picture and your respect for the image will soon be restored. The
sentence will leave the child unmoved; the image may delight him
almost as much as the real cat. Exchange the picture for a toy cat
and the child may be ready to hug the toy and take it to bed. The
toy cat arouses the same reactions as a real cat—possibly even
stronger ones, since it is more docile and easier to cuddle.

This power of dummies or substitutes to trigger behavior has
been much explored by students of animal behavior, and there is
no doubt that organisms are "programmed" to respond to certain
visual signals in a way that facilitates survival. The crudest models
of a predator or a mate need only exhibit certain distinctive features to elicit the appropriate pattern of action, and if these features
are intensified, the dummy (like the toy) may be more effective
than the natural stimulus. Caution is needed in comparing these

automatisms to human reactions, but Konrad Z. Lorenz, the pioneer of ethology, has surmised that certain preferred forms of
nursery art that are described as "cute" or "sweet" (including
many of Walt Disney's creations) generate parental feelings by
their structural similarity to babies.

Be that as it may, the power of visual impressions to arouse
our emotions has been observed since ancient times. "The mind
is more slowly stirred by the ear than by the eye," said Horace
in his *Art of Poetry*, when he compared the impact of the stage
with that of the verbal narrative. Preachers and teachers preceded modern advertisers in the knowledge of the ways in which
the visual image can affect us, whether we want it to or not. The
succulent fruit, the seductive nude, the repellent caricature, the
hair-raising horror can all play on our emotions and engage our
attention. Nor is this arousal function of sights confined to definite
images. Configurations of lines and colors have the potential to
influence our emotions. We need only keep our eyes open to see
how these potentialities of the visual media are used all around us,
from the red danger signal to the way the décor of a restaurant
may be calculated to create a certain "atmosphere." These very
examples show that the power of arousal of visual impressions extends far beyond the scope of this article. What is usually described as communication is concerned with matter rather than
with mood.

A mosaic found at the entrance of a house in Pompeii shows a
dog on a chain with the inscription *Cave Canem*, Beware of the
Dog. It is not hard to see the link between such a picture and
its arousal function. We are to react to the picture as we might
to a real dog that barks at us. Thus the picture effectively reinforces the caption that warns the potential intruder of the risk he
is running. Would the image alone perform this function of communication? It would, if we came to it with a knowledge of social
customs and conventions. Why if not as a communication to those
who may be unable to read should there be this picture at the
entrance hall? But if we could forget what we know and imagine
a member of an alien culture coming on such an image, we could
think of many other possible interpretations of the image. Could
not the man have wanted to advertise a dog he wished to sell? Was

MOSAIC OF A DOG found at the entrance of a house in Pompeii has the inscription *Cave Canem* (Beware of the Dog). Without the inscription the message intended to be communicated by the mosaic is less certain. The mosaic is now in the National Museum in Naples.

he perhaps a veterinarian? Or could the mosaic have functioned as a sign for a public house called "The Black Dog"? The purpose of this exercise is to remind ourselves how much we take for granted when we look at a picture for its message. It always depends on our prior knowledge of possibilities. After all, when we see the Pompeiian mosaic in the museum in Naples we do not conclude that there is a dog chained somewhere. It is different with the arousal function of the image. Even in the museum the image might give us a shadow of a fright, and I recently heard a child of five say when turning the pages of a book on natural history that she did not want to touch the pictures of nasty creatures.

Naturally we cannot adequately respond to the message of the mosaic unless we have read the image correctly. The medium of the mosaic is well suited to formulate the problem in terms of the theory of information. Its modern equivalent would be an advertising display composed of an array of light bulbs in which each bulb can be turned either on or off to form an image. A mosaic might consist of standardized cubes (*tesserae*) that are either dark or light. The amount of visual information such a medium can transmit will depend on the size of the cubes in relation to the scale of the image. In our case the cubes are small enough for the artist to indicate the tufts of hair on the dog's legs and tail, and the individual links of the chain. The artist might confine himself to a code in which black signifies a solid form seen against a light ground. Such a silhouette could easily be endowed with sufficiently distinctive features to be recognized as a dog. But the Pompeiian master was trained in a tradition that had gone beyond the conceptual method of representation and he included in the image information about the effects of light on form. He conveys the white and the glint of the eye and the muzzle, shows us the teeth and outlines the ears; he also indicates the shadows of the forelegs on the patterned background. The meaning so far is easy to decode, but the white patches on the body and, most of all, the outline of the hind leg set us a puzzle. It was the convention in his time to model the shape of an animal's body by indicating the sheen of the fur, and this must be the origin of these features. Whether their actual shape is due to clumsy execution or to inept restoration could only be decided by viewing the original.

The difficulty of interpreting the meaning of the dog mosaic is instructive because it too can be expressed in terms of communication theory. Like verbal messages, images are vulnerable to the random interference engineers call "noise." They need the device of redundancy to overcome this hazard. It is this built-in safeguard of the verbal code that enables us to read the inscription *Cave Canem* without hesitation even though the first *e* is incomplete. As far as image recognition is concerned it is the enclosing contour that carries most of the information. We could not guess the length of the tail if the black cubes were missing. The individual cubes of the patterned ground and inside the outline are relatively more redundant, but those indicating the sheen occupy a middle position; they stand for a feature that is elusive even in reality, although the configuration we now see could never occur.

However automatic our first response to an image may be, therefore, its actual reading can never be a passive affair. Without a prior knowledge of possibilities we could not even guess at the relative position of the dog's two hind legs. Although we have this knowledge, other possibilities are likely to escape us. Perhaps the picture was intended to represent a particular breed that Romans would recognize as being vicious. We cannot tell by the picture.

The chance of a correct reading of the image is governed by three variables: the code, the caption and the context. It might be thought that the caption alone would make the other two redundant, but our cultural conventions are too flexible for that. In an art book the picture of a dog with the caption E. Landseer is understood to refer to the maker of the image, not to the species represented. In the context of a primer, on the other hand, the caption and the picture would be expected to support each other. Even if the pages were torn so that we could only read "og," the fragment of the drawing above would suffice to indicate whether the missing letter was a *d* or an *h*. Jointly the media of the word and image increase the probability of a correct reconstruction.

We shall see that this mutual support of language and image facilitates memorizing. The use of two independent channels, as it were, guarantees the ease of reconstruction. This is the basis of the ancient "art of memory" (brilliantly explored in a book by Frances Yates) that advises the practitioner to translate any verbal message into visual form, the more bizarre and unlikely the better. If you want to remember the name of the painter Hogarth, picture to yourself a *hog* practicing his *art* by painting an *h*. You may dislike the association, but you may find it hard to get rid of.

There are cases where the context alone can make the visual message unambiguous even without the use of words. It is a possibility that has much attracted organizers of international events where the Babylonian confusion of tongues rules out the use of language. The set of images designed for the Olympic Games in Mexico in 1968 appears to be self-explanatory; indeed it is, given the limited number of expected messages and the restriction of the choice that is exemplified best by the first two signs of the array. We can observe how the purpose and context dictate a simplification of the code by concentrating on a few distinctive features. The principle is brilliantly exemplified by the pictorial signs for the various sports and games designed for the same event.

SIGNS FOR THE 1968 OLYMPIC GAMES in Mexico are self-explanatory because the number of possible meanings is restricted. The use of pictorial images in international events overcomes the problem of communicating to people who speak diverse languages.

We should never be tempted to forget, however, that even in such usages context must be supported by prior expectations based on tradition. Where these links break, communication also breaks down. Some years ago there was a story in the papers to the effect that riots had broken out in an underdeveloped country because of rumors that human flesh was being sold in a store. The rumor was traced to food cans with a grinning boy on the label. Here it was the switch of context that caused the confusion. As a rule the picture of fruit, vegetable or meat on a food container does indicate its contents; if we do not draw the conclusion that the same applies to a picture of a human being on the container, it is because we rule out the possibility from the start.

In the above examples the image was expected to work in conjunction with other factors to convey a clear-cut message that
could be translated into words. The real value of the image, however, is its capacity to convey information that cannot be coded
in any other way. In his important book *Prints and Visual Communication* William M. Ivins, Jr., argued that the Greeks and the
Romans failed to make progress in science because they lacked
the idea of multiplying images by some form of printing. Some of
his philosophical points can hardly be sustained (the ancient world
knew of the multiplication of images through the seal impression
and the cast), but it is certainly true that printed herbals, costume
books, newssheets and topographical views were a vital source of
visual information about plants, fashions, topical events and foreign
lands. But study of this material also brings home to us that printed
information depends in part on words. The most lifelike portrait
of a king will mislead us if it is incorrectly labeled as being somebody else, and publishers of other times sometimes supplied on old
woodcut with a new caption on the principle that if you have seen
one earthquake, you have seen them all. Even today it is only our
confidence in certain informants or institutions that allays our
doubts that a picture in a book, a newspaper or on the screen
really shows what it purports to show. There was the notorious
case of the German scientist Ernest Haeckel, who was accused of
having tried to prove the identity of human and animal development by labeling a photograph of a pig's fetus as that of a human
embryo. It is in fact fatally easy to mix up pictures and captions,
as almost any publisher knows to his cost.

The information extracted from an image can be quite independent of the intention of its maker. A holiday snapshot of a
group on a beach may be scrutinized by an intelligence officer preparing for a landing, and the Pompeiian mosaic might provide new
information to a historian of dog breeding.

It may be convenient here to range the information value of
such images according to the amount of information about the
prototype that they can encode. Where the information is virtually
complete we speak of a facsimile or replica. These may be produced for deception rather than information, fraudulently in the
case of a forged banknote, benevolently in the case of a glass eye

or an artificial tooth. But the facsimile of a note in a history book is intended for instruction, and so is the cast or copy of on organ in medical teaching.

Even facsimile duplication would not be classed as an image if it shared with its prototype all characteristics including the material of which it is made. A flower sample used in a botany class is not an image, but an artificial flower used for demonstration purposes must be described as an image. Even here the border line is somewhat fluid. A stuffed animal in a showcase is not an image, but the taxidermist is likely to have made his personal contribution through selecting and modifying the carcass. However faithful an image that serves to convey visual information may be, the process of selection will always reveal the maker's interpretation of what he considers relevant. Even the wax effigy of a celebrity must show the sitter in one particular attitude and role; the photographer of people or events will carefully sift his material to find the "telltale" picture.

Interpretation on the part of the image maker must always be matched by the interpretation of the viewer. No image tells its own story. I remember an exhibit in a museum in Lincoln, Neb., showing skeletons and reconstructions of the ancestor of the horse. By present equine standards these creatures were diminutive, but they resembled our horse in everything but the scale. It was this encounter that brought home to me how inevitably we interpret even a didactic model and how hard it is to discard certain assumptions. Being used to looking at works of sculpture, including small bronze statuettes of horses, I had slipped into the mental habit of discounting scale when interpreting the code. In other words, I "saw" the scale model of a normal horse. It was the verbal description and information that corrected my reading of the code.

Here as always we need a jolt to remind us of what I have called the "beholder's share," the contribution we make to any representations from the stock of images stored in our mind. Once more it is only when this process cannot take place because we lack memories that we become aware of their role. Looking at a picture of a house, we do not normally fret about the many things the picture does not show us unless we are looking for a particular aspect that was hidden from the camera. We have seen many similar houses and can supplement the information from our memory, or we think we can. It is only when we are confronted with a totally unfamiliar kind of structure that we are aware of the puzzle element in any representation. The new opera house in Sydney, Australia, is a structure of a novel kind, and a person who sees only a photograph of it will feel compelled to ask a number of questions the photograph cannot answer. What is the inclination of the roof? Which parts go inward, which outward? What, indeed, is the scale of the entire structure?

OPERA HOUSE in Sydney, Australia, is so unfamiliar a structure that it is difficult to tell from a single photograph what the inclinations and relations of the various components are.

The hidden assumptions with which we generally approach a photograph are most easily demonstrated by the limited information value of shadows on flat images. They only yield the correct impression if we assume that the light is falling from above and generally from the left; reverse the picture and what was concave looks convex and vice versa. That we read the code of the black-and-white photograph without assuming that it is a rendering of a

colorless world may be a triviality, but behind this triviality lurk
other problems. What colors or tones could be represented by
certain grays in the photograph? What difference will it make to,
say, the American flag whether it is photographed with an ortho-
chromatic or panchromatic film?

DEPTH REVERSAL occurs when some pictures are viewed upside down
because the eye assumes that light is coming from the top. The valleys and
ridges in the picture on the left (an aerial side-looking-radar view turn into
ridges and valleys (right.)

Interpreting photographs is an important skill that must be
learned by all who have to deal with this medium of communication: the intelligence officer, the surveyor or archaeologist who
studies aerial photographs, the sports photographer who wishes to
record and to judge athletic events and the physician who reads
X-ray plates. Each of these must know the capacities and the limitations of his instruments. Thus the rapid movement of a slit shutter
down the photographic plate may be too slow to show the correct
sequence of events it is meant to capture, or the grain of a film may
be too coarse to register the desired detail in a photograph. It was
shown by the late Gottfried Spiegler that the demand for an easily
legible X-ray plate may conflict with its informative function.
Strong contrast and definite outlines may obscure valuable clues.
Needless to say, there is the further possibility of retouching a
photographic record in the interest of either truth or falsehood.
All these intervening variables make their appearance again on the
way from the negative to the print, from the print to the photo-
engraving and then to the printed illustration. The most familiar of
these is the density of the halftone screen. As in the case of the
mosaic, the information transmitted by the normal illustration pro-

cess is granular, smooth transitions are transformed into discrete steps and these steps can either be so few that they are obtrusively visible or so small that they can hardly be detected by the unaided eye.

Paradoxically it is the limited power of vision that has made television possible: the changing intensities of one luminous dot sweeping across the screen build up the image in our eye. Long before this technique was conceived the French artist Claude Mellan displayed his virtuosity by engraving the image of Christ with

STRIKING IMAGE OF CHRIST is created by a single spiraling line that thickens and thins to form features, shapes, shadings and background. The illustration is a detail from "The Napkin of St. Veronica," engraved in 1649 by the French artist Claude Mellan. Warburg Institute, University of London.

one spiraling line swelling and contracting to indicate shape and shading.

The very eccentricity of this caprice shows how readily we learn to fall in with the code and to accept its conventions. We do not think for a moment that the artist imagined Christ's face to have been lined with a spiral. Contrary to the famous slogan, we easily distinguish the medium from the message.

From the point of view of information this ease of distinction can be more vital than fidelity of reproduction. Many students of art regret the increased use of color reproductions for that reason. A black-and-white photograph is seen to be an incomplete coding. A color photograph always leaves us with some uncertainty about its information value. We cannot separate the code from the content.

The easier it is to separate the code from the content, the more we can rely on the image to communicate a particular kind of information. A selective code that is understood to be a code enables the maker of the image to filter out certain kinds of information and to encode only those features that are of interest to the recipient. Hence a selective representation that indicates its own principles of selection will be more informative than the replica. Anatomical drawings are a case in point. A realistic picture of a dissection not only would arouse aversion but also might easily fail to show the aspects that are to be demonstrated. Even today surgeons sometimes employ "medical artists" to record selective information that color photographs might fail to communicate. Leonardo da Vinci's anatomical studies are early examples of deliberate suppression of certain features for the sake of conceptual clarity. Many of them are not so much portrayals as functional models, illustrations of the artist's views about the structure of the body. Leonardo's drawings of water and whirlpools are likewise intended as visualizations of the forces at work.

Such a rendering may be described as a transition from a representation to diagrammatic mapping, and the value of the latter process for the communication of information needs no emphasis. What is characteristic of the map is the addition of a key to the standardized code. We are told which particular heights are represented by the contour lines and what particular shade of green stands for fields or forests. Whereas these are examples of visible features, standardized for the sake of clarity, there is no difficulty in entering on the map other kinds of features, such as political frontiers, population density or any other desired information. The only element of genuine representation (also called iconicity) in such a case is the actual shape of the geographical features, although even these are normalized according to given rules of transformation to allow a part of the globe to be shown on a flat map.

It is only a small step from the abstraction of the map to a chart or diagram showing relations that are originally not visual but temporal or logical. One of the oldest of these relational maps is the family tree. The kinship table was often shown in medieval manuscripts of canon law because the legitimacy of marriages and the laws of inheritance were in part based on the degree of kinship. Genealogists also seized on this convenient means of visual demonstration. Indeed, the family tree demonstrates the advantages of the visual diagram to perfection. A relation that would take so long to explain in words we might lose the thread ("She is the wife of a second cousin of my stepmother") could be seen on a family tree at a glance. Whatever the type of connection, whether it is a chain of command, the organization of a corporation, a classification system for a library or a network of logical dependencies, the diagram will always spread out before our eyes what a verbal description could only present in a string of statements.

Moreover, diagrams can easily be combined with other pictorial devices in charts to show pictures of things in logical rather than spatial relationships. Attempts have also been made to standardize the codes of such charts for the purpose of visual education (particularly by Otto and Marie Neurath of Vienna, who sought to vivify statistics by such a visual code). It is not necessary to discuss at length the mutual support of text and image in illustration.

Whether the developed practice of such visual aids is as yet matched by an adequate theory is another matter. According to press releases, the National Aeronautics and Space Administration has equipped a deep-space probe with a pictorial message "on the off chance that somewhere on the way it is intercepted by intelligent scientifically educated beings." It is unlikely that their effort

TREE OF AFFINITIES was used in medieval times to determine the relation that a husband and a wife each bears to the kin of the other. The illustration, a woodcut made in 1473 by Johannes Andrei, is reproduced with the permission of the Pierpont Morgan Library.

was meant to be taken quite seriously, but what if we try? These beings would first of all have to be equipped with "receivers" among their sense organs that respond to the same band of electromagnetic waves as our eyes do. Even in that unlikely case they could not possibly get the message. We have seen that reading an image, like the reception of any other message, is dependent on prior knowledge of possibilities; we can only recognize what we know. Even the sight of the awkward naked figures in the illustration cannot be separated in our mind from our knowledge. We know that feet are for standing and eyes are for looking and we project this knowledge onto these configurations, which would look "like nothing on earth" without this prior information. It is this information alone that enables us to separate the code from the message; we see which of the lines are intended as contours

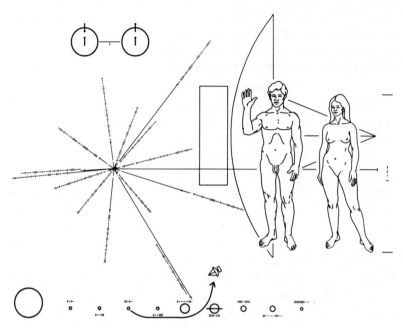

PICTORIAL PLAQUE on the *Pioneer* spacecraft is designed to tell "scientifically educated inhabitants of some other star system" who launched the craft. Without prior knowledge of our use of symbols, however, the inhabitants would not be able to decipher the message.

and which are intended as conventional modeling. Our "scientifically educated" fellow creatures in space might be forgiven if they saw the figures as wire constructs with loose bits and pieces hovering weightlessly in between. Even if they deciphered this aspect of the code, what would they make of the woman's right arm that tapers off like a flamingo's neck and beak? The creatures are "drawn to scale against the outline of the spacecraft," but if the recipients are supposed to understand foreshortening, they might also expect to see perspective and conceive the craft as being farther back, which would make the scale of the manikins minute. As for the fact that "the man has his right hand raised in greeting" (the female of the species presumably being less outgoing), not even an earthly Chinese or Indian would be able to correctly interpret this gesture from his own repertory.

The representation of humans is accompanied by a chart: a pattern of lines beside the figures standing for the 14 pulsars of the Milky Way, the whole being designed to locate the sun of our universe. A second drawing (how are they to know it is not part of the same chart?) "shows the earth and the other planets in relation to the sun and the path of Pioneer from earth and swinging past Jupiter." The trajectory, it will be noticed, is endowed with a directional arrowhead; it seems to have escaped the designers that this is a conventional symbol unknown to a race that never had the equivalent of bows and arrows.

The arrow is one of a large group of graphic symbols that occupy the zone between the visual image and the written sign. Any comic strip offers examples of these conventions, the history of which is still largely unexplored. They range from the pseudo-naturalistic streaking lines indicating speed to the conventional dotted track indicating the direction of the gaze, and from the hallucinatory medley of stars before the eyes after a blow to the head to the "balloon" that contains a picture of what the person has in mind or perhaps only a question mark to suggest puzzlement. This transition from image to symbol reminds us of the fact that writing itself evolved from the pictograph, although it became writing only when it was used to transform the fleeting spoken word into a permanent record.

It is well known that a number of ancient scripts for this purpose drew on both the resources of illustration and the principle of the rebus: the use of homophones for the rendering of abstract words. Both in ancient Egypt and in China these methods were ingeniously combined to signify sounds and facilitate reading by classifying them according to conceptual categories. Thus the name of the god Osiris was written in hieroglyphics as a rebus with a picture of a throne (*'usr*) and a picture of an eye (*'iri*) to which was adjoined a picture of the divine scepter to indicate the name of a god. But in all ancient civilizations writing represents only one of several forms of conventional symbolism the meaning of which has to be learned if the sign is to be understood.

Not that this learning need be an intellectual exercise. We can easily be conditioned to respond to signs as we respond to sights. The symbols of religion such as the cross or the lotus, the signs of good luck or danger such as the horseshoe or the skull and cross-bones, the national flags or heraldic signs such as the stars and stripes and the eagle, the party badges such as the red flag or the swastika for arousing loyalty or hostility—all these and many more show that the conventional sign can absorb the arousal potential of the visual image.

It may be an open question how far the arousal potential of symbols taps the unconscious significance of certain configurations that Freud explored and Jung was to link with the esoteric tradi-tions of symbolism in mysticism and alchemy. What is open to the observation of the historian is the way the visual symbol has so often appealed to seekers after revelation. To such seekers the symbol is felt to both convey and conceal more than the medium of rational discourse. One of the reasons for this persistent feeling was no doubt the diagrammatic aspect of the symbol, its ability to convey relations more quickly and more effectively than a

YIN AND YANG symbol in Chinese cosmology represents the dynamic bal-ance of the female principle (yin) and the male (yang).

GREAT SEAL of the United States has the ancient symbol of the eye of Providence.

OSIRIS in Egyptian hieroglyphics is a rebus with an eye, a throne and a divine scepter. Oriental Institute, University of Chicago.

string of words. The ancient symbol of yin and yang illustrates this potential and also suggests how such a symbol can become the focus of meditation. Moreover, if familiarity breeds contempt, unfamiliarity breeds awe. A strange symbol suggests a hidden mystery, and if it is known to be ancient, it is felt to embody some esoteric lore too sacred to be revealed to the multitudes. The awe surrounding the ancient Egyptian hieroglyphs in later centuries exemplifies this reaction. Most of the meanings of the hieroglyphs had been forgotten but it was remembered that the name of the god Osiris was written as an eye and a scepter, a fact interpreted to signify that the god symbolized the sun. The reader need not look further than a U.S. dollar bill to see how this association was tapped by the founding fathers in the design of the Great Seal. Following the advice of the English antiquarian Sir John Prestwich, the design expresses in words and image the hopes and aspirations of the New World for the dawn of a new era. *Novus ordo seclorum* alludes to Virgil's prophecy of a return of the Golden Age, and so does the other Latin tag, *Annuit coeptis*, "He [God] favored the beginning." But it is the image of the unfinished pyramid rising toward heaven and the ancient symbol of the eye suggesting the eye of Providence that gives the entire design the character of an ancient oracle close to fulfillment.

Interesting as the historian must find the continuity of a symbol, such as the eye on the Great Seal, reaching back over more than 4,000 years, the case is somewhat exceptional. More frequently the past influences symbolism through the stories and lore in the language. Cupid's darts, Herculean labors, the sword of Damocles and Achilles' heel come to us from classical antiquity, the olive branch and the widow's mite from the Bible, sour grapes and the lion's share from the Aesop's fables, a paper tiger and losing face from the Far East. Such allusions or clichés enable us to "cut a long story short" because we do not have to spell out the meaning. Almost any story or event that becomes the common property of a community enriches language with new possibilities of condensing a situation into a word, whether it is the political term "Quisling" or the scientific term "fallout." Moreover, language carries old and new figures of speech that are rightly described as images: "The sands are running out," "The pump must be primed," "Wages should be pegged," "The dollar should be allowed to float." The literal illustration of these metaphors offers untold possibilities for that special branch of symbolic imagery, the art of the cartoonist.

POLITICAL CARTOONS are a special branch of symbolic imagery. They often lose their impact as the circumstances that engendered them are forgotten. The wit of Vicky's 1942 cartoon "Achilles' Heel" is lost on those who do not know the situation to which it refers.

He too can condense a comment into a few pregnant images by the use of the language's stock figures and symbols. Vicky's cartoon showing Italy as Hitler's "Achilles' heel" is a case in point.

Like the successful pun that finds an unexpected but compelling meaning in the sound of a word, Vicky's cartoon reminds us that Italy has a "heel," and what else could it be but an Achilles' heel? But even if we can count on some familiarity with the shape of Italy and the story of Achilles, the aptness of the cartoon might need a good deal of spelling out 30 years after its initial appearance. If there is one type of image that remains mute without the aid of context, caption and code, it is the political cartoon. Its wit must inevitably be lost on those who do not know the situation on which it comments.

A glance at the imagery that surrounds us does not bear out the claim that our civilization lacks inventiveness in this field. Whether we approve or disapprove of the role advertising has come to play in our society, we can enjoy the ingenuity and wit used by commercial artists in the use of old symbols and the invention of fresh ones. The trademark adopted for North Sea gas in Britain cleverly combines the trident, that old symbol of Neptune, with the picture of a gas burner. It is interesting to watch how this idea was first coded as a realistic representation and then reduced to essentials, the increase in distinctiveness making both more memorable and easier to reproduce.

TRIDENT TRADEMARK adopted for North Sea Gas in Britain combines a symbol of the sea, Neptune's trident, with burning gas. Initially the idea was done realistically (*illustration* at left). Later it was encoded in an abstract form, making it easier to remember.

Freud's analysis of the kinship between verbal wit and dream-work could easily be applied, as Ernst Kris has shown, to the condensation of visual symbols in advertising and cartoons. Where the aim is first and foremost to arrest the attention, condensation and selective emphasis are used both for their power of arousal and for their surprise effects. The incomplete image and the unexpected image set the mind a puzzle that makes us linger, enjoy and re-

UNEXPECTED IMAGES are frequently used in advertisements to arouse and hold attention. An excellent example is the offset lithograph poster "Astral Peinture Émail," by Raymond Savignac, reproduced here with the permission of the Museum of Modern Art.

member the solution, where the prose of purely informational images would remain unnoticed or unremembered. (See Unexpected Images)

It might be tempting to equate the poetry of images with the artistic use of visual media, but it is well to remember that what we call art was not invariably produced for purely aesthetic effects. Even in the sphere of art the dimensions of communication are observable, although in more complex interaction. Here too it is the arousal function of the image that determines the use of the medium. The cult image in its shrine mobilizes the emotions that belong to the prototype, the Divine being. In vain did the Hebrew prophets remind the faithful that the heathen idols were only sticks and stones. The power of such images is stronger than any rational consideration. There are few who can escape the spell of a great cult image in its setting.

The strength of the visual image posed a dilemma for the Chris-

MARTYRDOM OF ST. LAWRENCE is depicted in the central portal of the cathedral of Genoa. Below the traditional image of Christ enthroned is the saint, marked with a halo, on a grid. The ruler on the left prompts executioners to fan flames with bellows.

tian church. The church feared idolatry but hesitated to renounce
the image as a means of communication. The decisive papal pro-
nouncement on this vital issue was that of Pope Gregory the Great,
who wrote that "pictures are for the illiterates what letters are
for those who can read." Not that religious images could function without the aid of context, caption and code, but given such
aid the value of the medium was easily apparent. Take the main
porch of the cathedral of Genoa, with its traditional rendering of
Christ enthroned between the four symbols of the Evangelists (derived from the prophet Ezekiel's vision of the throne of the Lord
as it is described in the Bible). The relief underneath will tell the
faithful from afar to which saint the church is dedicated. It represents the martyrdom of St. Lawrence. For all its impressive lucidity
the image could not be read by anyone unfamiliar with the code,
that is, with the style of medieval sculpture. That style disregards
the relative size of figures for the sake of emphasizing importance
through scale, and it represents every object from the most telling
angle. Hence the naked man is not a giant hovering sideways in
front of a grid. We must understand that he is stretched out on an
instrument of torture while the ruler commands an executioner to
fan the flames with his bellows. The truly illiterate, of course,
could not know that the sufferer is not a malefactor but a saint
who is marked by the symbol of the halo, or that the gestures
made by the onlookers indicate compassion.

But if the image could not tell the worshiper a story he had
never heard of, it was admirably suited to remind him of the stories
he had been told in sermons or lessons. Once he had become familiar with the legend of St. Lawrence even the picture of a man
with a gridiron would remind him of the saint. It only needed a
change in the means and aims of art to enable a great master to
make us feel the heroism and the suffering of the martyr in images
of great emotional appeal. In this way pictures could indeed keep
the memory of sacred and legendary stories alive among the laity,
whether or not they were able to read. Pictures still serve the purpose. There must be many whose acquaintance with these legends
started from images.

We have touched briefly on the mnemonic power of the image,
which is certainly relevant to many forms of religious and secular

art. The windows of Chartres show the power of symbolism to transform a metaphor into a memorable image with their vivid portrayal of the doctrine that the apostles stand on the shoulders of the Old Testament prophets. The whole vast genre of allegorical images testifies to this possibility of turning an abstract thought into a picture. Michelangelo's famous statue of Night, with her symbolic attributes of the star, the owl and the sleep-inducing poppies, is not only a pictograph of a concept but also a poetic evocation of nocturnal feelings.

ALLEGORICAL IMAGES can communicate abstract thought, as Michelangelo demonstrated in his famous sculpture "Night," with its symbolic star, owl and sleep-inducing poppies.

The capacity of the image to purvey a maximum of visual information could be exploited only in periods where the styles of art were sufficiently flexible and rich for such a task. Some great artists met the demands of naturalistic portraiture and faithful views with consummate mastery, but the aesthetic needs for selective emphasis could also clash with these more prosaic tasks. The idealized portrait or the revealing caricature was felt to be closer to art than the wax facsimile could ever be, and the romantic landscape that evoked a mood was similarly exalted over the topographic painting.

The contrast between the prose and the poetry of image making often led to conflicts between artists and patrons. The conflict increased in acerbity when the autonomy of art became an issue. It was the Romantic conception of genius in particular that stressed the function of art as self-expression (even though the catchword is of later date). It is precisely this issue that remains to be discussed here, since it will be remembered that the expressive symptom of emotions was distinguished in the theory of communication from the dimension of arousal or description. Popular critics who speak of art as communication often imply that the same emotions that give rise to the work of art are transmitted to the beholder, who feels them in his turn. This naïve idea has been criticized by several philosophers and artists, but to my knowledge the most succinct criticism was a drawing that appeared some years ago in

NONVERBAL COMMUNICATION of ideas and emotions is unlikely to take place unless there are some prior hints about what the possibilities are. This skeptical view is portrayed in a cartoon by CEM, which appeared in *The New Yorker*, copyright 1961.

The New Yorker. Its target is the very setting in which the term self-expression has had the greatest vogue. A little dancer fondly believes she is communicating her idea of a flower, but observe what arises instead in the minds of the various onlookers. A series of experiments made by Reinhard Krauss in Germany some decades ago confirms the skeptical view portrayed in the cartoon. Subjects were asked to convey through drawn abstract configurations some emotion or idea for others to guess at. Not surprisingly it was found that such guessing was quite random. When people were given a list of various possible meanings, their guesses became better, and they improved progressively with a reduction in the number of alternatives with which they were confronted. It is easy to guess whether a given line is intended to convey grief or joy, or stone or water.

Many readers will know the painting by van Gogh of his humble bedroom painted in Arles in 1888. It happens to be one of the very few works of art where we know the expressive significance the work held for the artist. In van Gogh's wonderful correspondence there are three letters dealing with this work that firmly establish the meaning it held for him. Writing to Gauguin in October, 1888, he says:

"Still for the decoration (of my house) I have done . . . my bedroom with its furniture of whitewood which you know. Well, it amused me enormously to do that interior with nothing in it, with a simplicity à la Seurat: with flat paint but coarsely put on, the neat pigment, the walls a pale violet. . . .

"I wanted to express an absolute calm with these very different tones, you see, where there is no white except in the mirror with its black frame. . . ."

A letter to his brother Theo confirms his intention and explains it further:

"My eyes are still strained, but at last I have a new idea in my head. . . . This time it is quite simply my bedroom, color alone must carry it off, by imparting through simplification a grander style to things, it should be suggestive of rest and sleep in general. In other words, the sight of the picture should rest the head, or rather the imagination. . . . The walls are pale violet, the floor tiles red . . . the doors are green, that is all. There is nothing in the room with the shutters closed. The squareness of the furniture should also express the undisturbed rest. . . . The shadows and modeling are suppressed, it is colored with flat tints like the Japanese prints. This will contrast, for instance, with the *diligence* of Tarascon and the Night Café."

Here we have an important clue. Van Gogh had written of "The Night Café" that he wanted to show that it was a place where one could go mad. To him, in other words, his little room was a haven after the strain of work, and it was this contrast that made him stress its tranquillity. The manner of simplification he adopted from Seurat and from the Japanese print stood for him in clear opposition to the expressive graphological brushwork that had become so characteristic of his style. This is what he stresses in still another letter to his brother. "No stippling, no hatching, nothing, flat areas, but in harmony." It is this modification of the code that van Gogh experiences as being expressive of calm and restfulness. Does the painting of the bedroom communicate this feeling? None of the naïve subjects I have asked hit on this meaning; although they knew the caption (van Gogh's bedroom), they lacked the context and the code. Not that this failure of getting the message speaks against the artist or his work. It only speaks against the equation of art with communication.

CHAPTER XI

The Uses of Film in Education and Communication

SOL WORTH

All too often debate about the place, purpose, and usefulness of film as a means of instruction and communication is clouded by confusion, defensiveness, and ignorance. Knowledge about how film works, how it affects people in or out of the classroom, how it should be described, and how it should be analyzed is extremely difficult to ascertain and is more or less primitive. Research in the uses of film in education has, in the opinion of one of the leading researchers in this area, remained almost at a standstill since 1950.[1]

Current writing and discussion about film in the classroom has assumed at times the aura of a Marx Brothers movie, in which many people are scurrying about, bumping into each other, muttering dark accusations at nonexistent opponents, and, as in *Duck Soup*, challenging visitors to a duel at the very moment that co-operation and friendship are offered.

This state of affairs is not unique for those who are interested in film. Jean Piaget, in his survey "Education and Teaching since 1935," notes under the subheading "Ignorance of Results" that "the first observation—a surprising one—that comes to mind after the passage of thirty years is the ignorance in which we still remain."[2] It seems to me that knowledge about the use of film in education cannot be developed in a vacuum—without reference to the socio-cultural context in which research about film in education and film as communication takes place.

1. Charles F. Hoban, Jr., "The State of the Art of Instructional Films," (ERIC Clearinghouse on Media and Technology, Stanford, California, September 1971).

2. Jean Piaget, *Science of Education and the Psychology of the Child* (New York: Grossman Publishers, 1970).

The situation I outlined in my opening paragraph refers to the current social context in which film is taught and in which film and film research is thought about. Piaget suggests that the social context (in relation to education) is crucial to an understanding of the problems facing educational research. It seems just as reasonable to consider as part of the social context the body of ideas current among spokesmen for, and researchers into, the use of film in education.

The purpose of this paper will be an attempt, first, to clarify some of the causes of the current confusion, which is characterized by seemingly irreconcilable goals, theories, and statements of purpose as to what film is and what it should be in education; second, to present a description of film as a process of communication that can be used in subsequent discussion; third, to discuss how film is used in the classroom; fourth, to present some evidence supporting several new directions in the use of film as a means of instruction related to the notion that film is a means of communication; and fifth, to suggest lines for future research in education relating to such uses of film.

Current Goals of and Theories and Statements about Film in Education

Before one can assess the role that film can play in education, it is necessary to examine its uses in sociocultural, artistic, political, and scientific endeavors. For the views developed about the role of film in education are necessarily colored by the views taken of film as art, film as propaganda, film as communication, and the views upon the effects of film on society in general. It must be further recognized that the arguments and theories involving film in general are in large part based on notions—on the one hand about "art" and "language" and, on the other, about "television," "mass media," "pictures," and vision itself.

Consider some of the general assumptions that are made about film. First, there are those who argue the primacy of film on social and psychological grounds. This argument is based somewhat loosely (but adhered to firmly) upon the notion of "visual thinking," and leads to the conclusion that film or television is psychologically primary to words. Another form of this argument is expressed in assertions that "film is a language," that it is *the* language of the "now" generation, and that it is becoming primary, sociologically and culturally.

A second view asserts the universality and potentialities of film as a medium. This position is reflected in statements that film is the newest art form, with the unexplored potential to do what words have failed to do—film is multimodal, multisensual, sensual (in its allied sense), and universal. Everyone, it is said, of all ages and across all cultures, likes and understands film. Most of the current discussion and justification for the use of film and television in schools can be traced to the above assumptions—psychological primacy, sociocultural primacy, communicative primacy (particularly as compared to words), and sensual primacy.

Research in the uses of film within a wide range of educational contexts—schools, churches, labor unions, the armed forces—and in the mass media in general has been going on since 1918. For the most part this body of research was not designed to determine the truth of the previously mentioned assumptions, not because of unawareness of the assumptions, but because of a conviction that they were not central to understanding how film works in the classroom. These assumptions have seemed so powerful and so implicitly true as to require only their assertion.

It is not the purpose of this paper to review the extensive research on film use for instructional purposes, numerous reviews of which are readily available.[3] Instead, it is my purpose to examine a series of arguments, positions, and ideologies that are currently being widely diffused and accepted in the educational and film communities but with very little research evidence in their support.

In commenting upon an earlier draft of this paper, Charles Hoban, one of the leading researchers in the use of film in the classroom, questioned the need for such a detailed treatment of the current ideologies of psychological, sociocultural, communicative,

3. The best summaries of this body of research, in my opinion, may be found in Charles F. Hoban, Jr. and Edward B. van Ormer, *Instructional Film Research 1918-1950* (Reprinted by Arno Press, New York, 1972); Hoban, op. cit.; Wilbert J. McKeachie, "Higher Education," in *The New Media and Education* (New York: Doubleday & Co., 1967).

and sensual primacy. He felt then (1971) that these arguments seemed to have little influence in actual educational practice. Since his return from a field investigation of schools, teachers, and media practices in education in the United States (September 1972), he has commented in a personal communication: "These ideologies you discuss in your paper have spread throughout the educational community like wildfire. Their assumptions have not been examined, and the time has come for accountability in the implementation of these film ideologies." This paper is an attempt, then, to begin the process of examining these assumptions.

Three major perspectives are involved in the analysis of the nature and effects of film.

First, there is the psychological perspective that has evolved from the application of the psychology of mind, perception, and art to problems of film. Rudolf Arnheim could be considered the paradigmatic figure in the development of an orientation relating certain psychological theories of perception and art to theories of film. For a variety of sociological and academic reasons Arnheim's orientation and particularly his idea of visual primacy has become the central tenet of what may be referred to as an ideology of film. While this act of adoption may have distorted Arnheim's ideas somewhat, the ideology itself is so important that it merits further examination.

The second perspective is that developed by the artist-critics— most often practicing film-makers or film ideologists who write theoretical and ideological statements about what film is, what place it has or should have in society, how films should be made, or what film's ultimate destiny might be. Theoretical work by film-makers about film has a long and international tradition beginning with the works of Eisenstein [4] and Pudovkin [5] in the Soviet Union in the late 1920s and currently continuing with Pasolini [6] and Bettetini [7] in

4. Sergei Eisenstein, *Film Form* (New York: Harcourt, Brace & World, 1949).

5. V. I. Pudovkin, *Film Technique and Acting* (New York: Lear & Co., 1958).

6. Pier Paulo Pasolini, "The Cinema of Poetry," *Cahiers du cinema* (No. 171, October 1965, pp. 35-43).

7. G. Bettetini, *The Language and Technique of the Film* (The Hague: Mouton Publishers, 1972).

Italy and Godard and Metz[8] in France. America's film-maker–
theorist tradition, although very recent, may be presented through
the work of Gene Youngblood, an American avant-grade film
ideologue, whose book *Expanded Cinema*[9] has taken the place of
McLuhan in the minds and hearts of most young people interested
in film. It is read by film students, recommended by film teachers,
and treated with respect by most younger film-makers in education. It is the most academic of the books by American avant-garde
film theorists and bears the stamp of approval of Buckminster
Fuller.

The third perspective has been developed by the film teachers
—those who teach with film and from film, those who teach about
film, and those who teach how to make film. Film has been used
in grade schools since 1918 and taught in high schools and colleges
in the United States since the 1930s, but its blossoming into a full-
fledged curricular integrated subject was not achieved until the
1960s. Most boards of education now have sections headed by
media specialists who have supplanted in status the old audiovisual
directors. Their job is to help teachers design, develop, teach, and
use film in the classroom. These teachers come from almost every
field of educational specialization, but most seem to come out of
English or language-study departments. Government agencies such
as the American Film Institute support training conferences in film
study for elementary and high school teachers; UNESCO and other
international agencies publish training manuals in film education;
and some churches and many universities have extensive teacher
training programs in what has been called "training for film literacy." An example of this perspective is the latest book by a film
teacher to cross my desk, *Film in the Classroom: Why Use It, How
to Use It*,[10] which reports on the author's work with film in his
own classroom.

8. Christian Metz, *Essais sur la significance au cinéma* (Paris: Editions
Klinchsieck, 1968); idem, "Images et pedagogie," *Communication* 15 (1970):
162-68.

9. G. Youngblood, *Expanded Cinema* (New York: E. P. Dutton & Co.,
1970.)

10. Ralph J. Amelio, *Film in the Classroom* (Cincinnati: Standard Publishing, 1971.)

At the latest conference (October 1972) of the National Association of

VISUAL PRIMACY

Let us start with Arnheim, then. In the 1930s he began to publish his first works on film,[11] describing it as an art form and arguing that it was art precisely because it did not reproduce reality exactly. It was art because and to the extent that it failed to reproduce reality and had the same potential for artistic expression as painting and sculpture. In a series of books and monographs since then, he has moved from what could be considered a limited interest in film as such to the study of the broader aspects of artistic vision. In his latest book, *Visual Thinking*,[12] he has moved from a study of the visual arts to what might be called a general theory of cognition. Basically, he argues that the visual modes of experience and expression have been underutilized and slighted in American education. He argues further that all thinking is basically and primarily imagistic and based upon visual perception. In contrasting words and pictures Arnheim argues:

The visual medium is so *enormously superior* because it offers structural equivalents to *all* characteristics of objects, events, relations. The variety of available visual shapes is as great as that of possible speech sounds, but what matters is that they can be organized according to readily definable patterns of which the geometric shapes are the most tangible illustration. The principal virtue of the visual medium is that of representing shapes in two-dimensional and three-dimensional space, as compared with the one-dimensional sequence of verbal language. This polydimensional space not only yields good thought models of physical objects or events, it also represents isomorphically the dimensions needed for theoretical reasoning.[13] (italics mine)

This quotation seems to me representative of Arnheim's arguments, containing unsupported assertions about the superiority of the visual over the verbal, based upon vague and oversimplified notions of language and assertions about reasoning—equally unsupported—

Media Educators, Amelio's book was singled out as the "kind of book we need more of" and was held up as an example for younger "media educators."

11. Rudolf Arnheim, *Film as Art* (Berkeley: University of California Press, 1957).

12. Rudolf Arnheim, *Visual Thinking* (Berkeley: University of California Press, 1969).

13. Ibid., p. 232.

based upon his previous assertions of the superiority of the visual.

Essentially Arnheim's argument and its appeal to the film buff rests upon the reasonable assertion that visual perception contains or is part of what we normally call "thinking." But he then seems to argue that if visual perception involves thought, all thought is visual.

Arnheim attacks a wide variety of linguists, psychologists, and others, and singles out the art historian Gombrich for special criticism. Arnheim argues that Gombrich "suggests that the world of the senses is an impenetrable puzzle and that images are understandable only when maker and beholder share a set of conventions by which statements about visual reality can be coded and decoded." [14] The linguist Whorf is similarly criticized for his famous view that "segmentation of nature is an aspect of grammar. We cut up and organize the spread and flow of events as we do largely because, through our mother tongue, we are parties to an agreement to do so, not because nature is segmented in exactly that way for all to see." [15] Arnheim argues that these ideas are an "extraordinary perversion" of the true state of affairs, and that those who hold these and similar ideas are responsible for the fact that the visual arts are in such disrepute in educational circles today. He argues further that "we are the *victims* of [these] traditions according to which the senses furnish nothing better or worse than the raw materials of experience." [16] (italics mine)

Arnheim never argues that thinking has *no* relation to language itself, but because of his commitment to certain psychological theories of visual perception which lead him to say that language "serves as a *mere* auxiliary to the primary vehicles of thought" (italics mine), he underestimates or denies the extent to which symbolic systems or conventions mediate our knowledge of the world.

The place of symbolic systems or conventions in human thinking has been powerfully represented by aestheticians and art his-

14. Rudolf Arnheim, "The Myth of the Bleating Lamb," in *Toward a Psychology of Art* (Berkeley: University of California Press, 1966).

15. B. L. Whorf, *Language, Thought and Reality*, ed. John Carroll (Cambridge, Mass.: M.I.T. Press, 1956).

16. Arnheim, "The Myth of the Bleating Lamb," op. cit., p. 137.

torians,[17] psychologists,[18] anthropologists,[19] linguists,[20] sociolin-
guists,[21] and historians of science.[22] Essentially they have shown
that what we see and what we think about is determined *at the
least* as much by our symbolic systems and conventions for representing that universe as by the universe itself. They have shown
that pictures, verbal language, tales, myths, scientific theory, and
speech itself do not depend only upon what is "out there," but
they depend also and in large part upon the structure of symbol
systems that make up the culture.

In his zeal to argue against the idea that language and other
symbolic systems are central to the visual modes of expression and
communication, Arnheim declares, "True visual education presupposes that the world can present its inherent order to the eye
and that seeing consists in understanding this order." [23] Therefore,
the works of such writers as Gombrich, Whorf, and Goodman, for
example, are characterized by Arnheim as a "monumental attempt
to devalue the contribution of perceptual observation." [24] But Arnheim's views similarly devalue the role that language and other

17. E. H. Gombrich, *Art and Illusion* (New York: Pantheon Books, 1961);
idem., *Meditations on a Hobby Horse* (New York: Phaedon Press, 1963);
E. Kris, *Psychoanalytic Explorations in Art* (New York: Schocken Books,
1964); N. Goodman, *Languages of Art* (Indianapolis: Bobbs-Merrill Co.,
1968); H. Wolfflin, *Principles of Art History* (New York: Dover Publications, 1950).

18. U. Neisser, *Cognitive Psychology* (New York: Appleton-Century-Crofts,
1967); Piaget, *Science of Education and the Psychology of the Child*, op. cit.;
idem., *Structuralism* (New York: Basic Books, 1970).

19. F. Boaz, *Primitive Art* (New York: Dover Publications, 1955); C. Levi-
Strauss, *Structural Anthropology* (New York: Basic Books, 1963).

20. E. Sapir, *Language* (New York: Harcourt, Brace & World, 1921); Whorf,
Language, Thought and Reality, op. cit.; N. Chomsky, *Syntactic Structures*
(The Hague: Mouton Publishers, 1957); idem., *Language and Mind* (New
York: Harcourt, Brace & World, 1968).

21. D. Hymes, C. B. Cazden, and V. P. John, eds., *The Functions of Lan-
guage in the Classroom* (New York: Teachers College Press, 1972); W. Labov,
The Social Stratification of English in New York City (Washington, D.C.:
Center for Applied Linguistics, 1966).

22. T. S. Kuhn, *Structure of Scientific Revolution* (Chicago: University of
Chicago Press, 1962).

23. Arnheim, "The Myth of the Bleating Lamb," op. cit., p. 148.

24. Ibid., p. 139.

symbolic systems play in thinking about, organizing, and articulat-
ing man's impressions, perceptions, and thoughts about the world
he lives in—the interior psychological and cultural world as well as
the external objective world. The consequences of this overemphasis on certain theories of mind leave one "at a loss," as Jonas in
his review of *Visual Thinking* commented, as to "where to start
getting straight so much mischief committed by overzeal in a noble
cause." [25]

As we shall see below, this insistence upon visual primacy in
thought and the subservient and even "perverse" nature assigned
to language as a means of ordering the world has been taken as
the unassailable premise for the arguments of the film theorists and
teachers we shall now discuss.

THE FILM THEORISTS

It cannot be denied that a large number of young people
throughout the world and particularly in the United States pro-
fess a deep love for film. A major reason for this, many of them
say, is that they can "dig"—rather than understand—a film easily.
They can just sit there and allow it to envelop them, to "wash all
over" them. No wonder they find Arnheim's thesis—that the world
presents itself to them and all they have to do is keep their eyes
open to understand it—so congenial. It fits a commonly expressed
desire of youth to sit there and be "turned on." It is the world
that presents, not they, not man.

Buckminster Fuller, in his introduction to Youngblood's *Expanded Cinema*, begins by telling us a science fiction fantasy. All
the unborn children in the world are in communication with each
other. They can communicate with each other in a total sense.
These "superborn in the womb" plan to go on strike. They will
not emerge because the world is in a mess created by the outsiders.
If they do emerge, this perfect communication they have with
their fellows will be destroyed. He goes on:

All this brings us to this book by Gene Youngblood . . . the first of the
youth who have emerged from childhood and schooling and social experience sufficiently undamaged . . . [to provide] world-around men

25. H. Jonas, "Review of Arnheim's *Visual Thinking*," *Journal of Aesthetics
and Art Criticism* 30 (1971): 111-17.

with the most effective communication technique for speaking universal language to universal man. . . . Youngblood's book represents the most important metaphysical scenario for coping with all the ills of educational systems based only on yesterday's Newtonian-type thinking. Expanded Cinema is the beginning of a new era educational system itself. . . . Tomorrow's Expanded Cinema University . . . will weld metaphysically together the world community of man by the flux of understanding and spontaneously truthful integrity of the child.[26]

This spontaneously truthful integrity of the child, which exists in the womb where the child cannot see, will be accomplished for those who leave the womb by that great metaphysical welder—the film.

Youngblood says, "Expanded Cinema isn't a movie at all: like life it's a process of becoming, man's historical drive to manifest his consciousness outside of his mind, in front of his eyes. This is especially true in the case of the intermedia network of cinema and television which now functions as nothing less than the nervous system of mankind." [27] Not only does the world present its reality directly through the eyes, but man becomes, man manifests his very consciousness through film. It is nothing less than the nervous system of man. It is the science fiction dream come true.

Youngblood begins by adopting the assumption of visual primacy: "As a child of the new age . . . I am *naturally* hypersensitive to the phenomenon of vision. I have come to understand that all language is but substitute vision. . . .[28] The new cinema has emerged as the only aesthetic language to match the environment in which we live (p. 76)." In pursuing this point he comes to a self-contradiction of which he seems unaware: "We are conditioned more by cinema and television than by nature (p. 54). . . . We have come to see that we don't really see, that 'reality' is more within than without. The objective and the subjective are one . . . (p. 46). The world's not a stage, it's a TV documentary" (p. 78). There is a subtle shift in his thinking that culminates in a strange transformation toward a newer manifestation of visual primacy. "The filmmaker has not moved closer to actual *unstylized* reality

26. Youngblood, op. cit., p. 34-35.

27. Ibid.

28. Ibid., p. 45.

itself but rather a reality *prestyled* to approximate our primary mode of knowing natural events: *Television*" [29] (italics mine). It is not the world out there that presents itself to us but rather a world given to us by television and having the inherent order of the medium itself.

Whereas Arnheim thinks of a structured universe already given, Youngblood posits a stylizing agent that acts upon the universe, that orders and styles what we see. TV is that agent: it prestyles. It is the medium itself that gives order to what we see. "Reality" is abandoned and in its place is the primary giver of reality—television. This is not merely perverse. Although *Expanded Cinema* is replete with humanistic pieties and presents itself as an appeal to make people more human and more related, it is in fact based on an assumption necessary to the visual primacists: the denial of man's activity in the creation of his world. However, the concept of communication as a process by which men share a variety of symbol systems for handling meaning demands a recognition that man orders his films and his television programs, that man stylizes and prestylizes and presents his view of the world. It is only by treating man as a noncommunicator, as an animal that doesn't share any symbol system at all, that it can make sense to talk of reality presenting itself, or of television as a medium prestyling reality. Let us see how Youngblood develops his theme of noncommunication through film.

Because it [Expanded Cinema] is entirely personal it rests on no identifiable plot and is not probable. The viewer is forced to create along with the film, to interpret for himself what he is experiencing. If the information . . . reveals some previously unrecognized aspect of the viewer's relation to the circumambient universe . . . the viewer re-creates that discovery along with the artist, thus feeding back into the environment the existence of more creative potential which may in turn be used by the artist for messages of still greater eloquence and perception.[30]

A man creates. A viewer experiences and interprets. Perception itself is creation and discovery. Skill, taste, thought, meaning, concepts, ideas are absent as indeed, by definition, they must be. For the "unrecognized" is the core material for the formation of "crea-

29. Ibid., p. 80.

30. Ibid., pp. 64-65.

tive potential." Youngblood seems to think that by willingly sacrificing communicative processes for personal, private perception and revelation, he is avoiding the dull, destructive, and uncreative aspects of film. Tyros in the arts always forget that creation and originality cannot even be recognized (or perceived) except within a context of convention and rule-like behavior—*especially* in the arts. It is not within the context of an ordered universe that art exists, but rather within the context of man's *conventions for ordering that universe*. But, for Youngblood, revelation of the unrecognized is creation. If we achieve this, Youngblood continues, "we shall find that our community is no longer a community, and we shall begin to understand radical revolution." [31]

Tomorrow's Expanded Cinema University will (according to Fuller) weld us together in a world community of man by the flux of understanding and the spontaneous and truthful integrity of the cinema child. This is a dream that breeds monsters. Instead of welding us together in a world community, Youngblood's ideas, as he himself tells us, will destroy community.

If these ideas were merely the jottings of Fulleresque, McLuhanite, and Madison Avenue acolytes, we could smugly ignore them as confined to the lunatic fringe. But we cannot ignore them, for they have become embedded in current educational thought. The movement to use film as an educational tool is permeated by these ideas, both to support programs in film education and to justify using film in such ways and for such purposes.

THE TEACHER

Let us turn now to a teacher. Chapter 1 of *Film in the Classroom* [32] is entitled "A Rationale for a High School Film Program." I will quote his five-point rationale in its entirety:

1. Sixty-five percent of today's film audience is 24 years old or younger.
2. For one-fourth or more of their waking hours, from infancy to adolescence, children live in a semantic environment their parents did not create or control.
3. "Sesame Street," the TV program, reaches five million children, almost half of the nation's 12 million children under five.

31. Ibid.

32. Amelio, *Film in the Classroom*, op. cit.

4. Eighty thousand college students are now enrolled in three thousand film courses.
5. For every book the average college student reads, he views 20 films.

Not one of his reasons reflects any educational purpose at all. They are defensive and puerile. Reasons 1, 2, and 5 could as easily be given for studying rock music, sports, and, hopefully, sex. Reason 3, that "Sesame Street" reaches five million children under five, is to me not even clear. Saturday morning cartoon television probably reaches ten million under five, but perhaps "Sesame Street" is chosen because it is labeled *education* and therefore assumed to be education, while Saturday morning television is assumed not to be education. Argument 4, that eighty thousand college students are enrolled in film courses, puzzles me. Over two million college students are enrolled in ROTC and what does that prove? It is not that the arguments are bad or nonexistent, but rather that all too often a case for the study and use of film in the schools is made without the awareness of *any* educational justification for such study or use.

While Arnheim and Youngblood at least present complex arguments purporting to make a case for film and visual primacy, teachers themselves say that "whether the schools like it or not, film is here and it is vigorously affecting our children." Or, "for too many years schools have concentrated on teaching skills in verbal language. As a result, for many students in many schools 'tedium is the method.'"[33] Both Arnheim and Youngblood, as well as many others, argue convincingly for changes in emphasis in the teaching of communication modes. The issue is not whether we have overemphasized words in our educational system, but rather how and for what purpose we should introduce film into the educational process as a substitute for the "debased" verbal language.

In the second section of the book on film language, Amelio proposes to rectify what he considers to be the prevalent student attitude toward words: "Purpose: To train the student to become aware that the medium can be the message."[34] The reasoning seems to be: Children are bored with school, the medium is the message,

33. Ibid.
34. Ibid., p. 37.

children watch movies, children do not read; ergo, teach film. Based on these reasons one can honestly ask, why not teach hopscotch, or why not abolish school altogether?

Film as a Process of Communication

It is almost with relief, therefore, that I find a place to state my own position. Film *is* a means of communication and instruction. Our problem is not in deciding that. The problems to which educators and communication researchers must address themselves are rather to describe (a) how film as a process of image-making in our culture comes about, how and under what conditions it becomes a form of communication, how one person can use it to articulate meaning about something, and how others who see the film can make meaning or sense of it; and (b) how knowledge of this process enables us to understand and to use film in the very process of education itself.

Education must be thought of as a special case of acculturation —the complex process by which a culture manages to ensure that almost all of its newly born become viable members of the group. In our culture, film, like television, books, newspapers, and other message systems, is institutionally organized and supported. Like school, it is a part of the acculturation process. Like verbal language and other symbol systems, film could not be a part of the acculturation process if it were not also capable of being used to communicate. In this sense, communication requires that members of a social group share the meaning of the symbolic forms they use.

Film communication may be considered as a *social process* whereby a transmitted signal is received primarily through visual receptors (often plus sound receptors) and is then *treated as a message* from which *content or meaning is inferred*. Film, as a symbolic form, is a process of communication that employs film, the medium, with its technology of optics, emulsions, and cameras to produce a piece of celluloid with a variable density silver nitrate surface. It is man who creates film communication. This definition suggests that a piece of film in and of itself is meaningless—that meaning exists only in a special social and cognitive relationship between a film-maker and a viewer. This relationship occurs when a viewer *chooses* to treat a film not as mere signals triggering per-

ceptual awareness and biological responses, but as message units
that have been put together intentionally and from which meaning may be inferred.

I suggest that in simplified form the process works something
like this. First the film-maker puts together or articulates a set of
images in a nonrandom fashion in order to "tell" someone something, or in order to make someone "feel" something. The process
of putting these film-image events together is a complex, inten-
tional act requiring skill, knowledge, and creative ability. This
organizing process takes place not only in planning, but in photographing the actual images, and in the selection, rejection, and sequencing that make up the editing process. At some point he decides to "release" his film. It is now no longer a personal act but
a public and social one; it is a symbolic form available for participation in a communication process.

When another person sees this film, he must (depending on
how one talks about such acts) receive it, decode it, or re-create it.
Since meaning or content does not exist within the reel of acetate,
the viewer must re-create it from the forms, codes, and symbolic
events in the film. This definition of film communication would
exclude films made, for example, by blind men who pointed a
camera at random and sequenced their images in editing without
being able to see them. For communication to occur, meaning must
be implied by the creator and inferred by the viewer or re-creator.

The use of film in education, then, must be understood to mean
film communication: a method of image-making involving a set of
conventions through which meaning is transmitted between people
by a process of implication and inference. The piece of acetate in
itself is not a communication, a panacea, a method, an instruction,
or an education.

Those who wish to use film and to understand how film is or
can be a part of the communication process must therefore address
themselves to the problem of describing exactly how and in what
contexts viewers assume that the film-worker intends to express
himself, to deliberately make implications from which viewers will
infer his meaning.

A host of questions can now be raised which have until the
last few years received very little study by those interested in film.

How do people make implications with film? Is there a code—the schemata that Gombrich suggests? Is there a system? How do people make inferences from film? Do they know the code? How does one describe it? Is it like a language? Do all people across cultures, language barriers, and social groupings use the same code? If not, are there different codes used by different cultures? And most important for those who are involved in the process of education: How do people *learn* to make statements in film, and how do people *learn* to make inferences from film? [35]

Film in the Classroom

There are two predominant uses of film in the classroom. First and most frequent is the substitution of films for books or lectures —that is, teaching *through* film. Second, and growing in popularity, is teaching *about* film. Teaching through film has been used since the invention of film itself. Films of "strange dances" by "primitive peoples" were made by German anthropologists and used in German gymnasiums in 1905. Films of animals and humans in motion were used by zoologists, anatomists, and artists to teach their various subject matters in universities, medical schools, and art schools as early as 1907. All of us must have seen many films describing such things as "other lands, other people," "community helpers," and so on. One need not review the variety and quantity of such films. They number in the tens of thousands and represent the allocation of hundreds of millions of dollars.

What is important to note, however, is that the media entre-

35. For a fuller explanation of the concept of implication/inference in communicative interpretation see S. Worth and L. Gross, "Interpretive Strategies in Communication" (in preparation). Briefly, one "implies" through film when one organizes images in such a conventionalized manner that a viewer can infer meaning from the organization or structure of the film, justifying his interpretation by calling into evidence some formal properties of the film itself. For example, "In that sequence the film maker means that the policeman is a pig because first he shows a close-up of the policeman and then shows a close-up of a pig." Or, as in the case of *Birth of a Nation*, "Griffith means to say that people in the North and people in the South faced the same problems because he has a long shot of the woman in the northern city waving goodbye to her husband, then a long shot of the woman in the southern city doing the same, then a close-up of the first woman tearing a lace handkerchief in grief followed by a close-up of the second woman doing a similar thing. When you have similar shots of different people it always means you have to put them together in your head."

preneurs, both those engaged in the production of films for the classroom and those engaged in the development and production of the hardware that these films use, act on the assumption that teaching through film is a preferred method, proven and accepted by the educational establishment. The points these entrepreneurs talk about in their brochures, conferences, and books are those of ease of use, availability of large collections of materials, and instant acceptability to the student. Educational administrators who buy and demand funds for these materials accept the basic premises on which the audiovisual industry operates. In another paper in this volume, Gross[36] makes clear that there is a genuine question whether the use of film or pictures as a teaching device is effective in achieving any of the commonly stated goals of education.

At best, film used this way has one massive advantage. It allows schools to perform a custodial function more easily. Film "to teach through" can be administered, like mass injections, at the will of the school administrator. Unlike a book, which a student must read on his own, a film can be administered to hundreds and even thousands at a time in classrooms and assemblies. The only problem is getting the student to stay awake and hence the development and use of advertising commercial techniques—as in "Sesame Street"—that will keep his eyes glued to the screen.

In recent years there has been a movement toward the recognition of this deficiency of the so-called teaching through film. Not only are these films not particularly suited for developing intelligence (in the Piagetian sense to be discussed later) but they do not address themselves to what this new movement has called "film literacy"—teaching *about* film.

The film literacy movement, developed in England after World War II and expanded in the United States since the middle 1950s,[37] takes as its aim the development of abilities in the child that will enable him to understand the techniques and "language" of film.

36. L. Gross, "Modes of Communication and the Acquisition of Skills and Competencies" (Paper prepared for Panel III of the International Symposium on Communication: Technology, Impact and Policy, Annenberg School of Communications, University of Pennsylvania, Philadelphia, Pennsylvania. March 23-25, 1972).

37. A. W. Hodgkinson, *Screen Education* (New York: UNESCO, 1964); J. M. L. Peters, *Teaching about Film* (New York: UNESCO, 1961).

By and large, however, the movement is devoted to showing commercial films, having the children learn a new terminology consisting of words such as *fade, dissolve, truck, pan, zoom,* and *cut,* and discussing the films they have seen as examples of literature, history, plot development, mood, emotional experience, and so on. Amelio suggests that "the student can learn how film differs from other art forms, how important the director is, and why film editing is an art. Thus our goal is to develop in the student a basis for criteria for aesthetic awareness so that he can evaluate film." [38] The films shown in his lesson plan range from *Potemkin* through *This is Marshall McLuhan: The Medium Is the Message* to *How to Use the Griswold Splicer,* not neglecting *Citizen Kane* and other "classics."

The goal is exemplary. The question is whether we know the answer to such questions as "why is film editing an art," or whether watching films and discussing them is the best way to teach students a basis for aesthetic awareness. An even more cogent question is whether this approach will lead toward the research and analysis necessary for educators to understand how film works and what potential uses it has for education.

It is not only that film and television pervade our culture and help us form our attitudes, values, and ways of organizing experience, but that this happens in ways that are very poorly understood, either by the researchers or by the children and young adults whose attitudes are thus formed. If film literacy were needed only as an antidote to film itself, it would still be worthwhile to understand it and to teach it. But an understanding of this mode of communication has much deeper implications for the very concept of education itself.

Many authors [39] have shown that understanding the process of thought itself requires an understanding of a variety of symbolic modes through which we relate to our environment, become hu-

---

38. Amelio, op. cit., p. 37.

39. Gombrich, *Art and Illusion,* op. cit.; idem., *Meditations on a Hobby Horse,* op. cit.; Kris, op. cit.; D. R. Olson, *Cognitive Development* (New York: Academic Press, 1970); Gross, see chap. 3; S. Worth, "The Development of a Semiotic of Film," *Semiotica: International Journal of Semiotics* 16 (1969): 282-321; S. Worth and J. Adair, "Navajo Filmmakers," *American Anthropologist* 72 (1970): 9-34.

man, and become members of our culture. It is clear that thinking is a multimodal symbolic process that uses much more than words. It is not necessary to argue that words are inferior, debased, or unnecessary to make the point that more than a knowledge of verbal language is involved in education. It does not necessarily make sense to argue for the primacy of the visual any more than it does to argue for the primacy of the mathematical, the verbal, or the musical. What is needed is to show how a knowledge of the use of a particular mode can help in the development of the thinking and behaving capacity of the human organism.

The ability of the child to function as a creative human being in his society rests on his ability to organize his experience—while he both perceives it and thinks about it—and to articulate his attitudes, judgments, statements, and inventions about himself and his universe in such a way as to be understood by his fellows. Education is a process not only by which we learn to take in an environment, but in which we develop ways to communicate about it to others—by choice and by intention.

Of course, men "say" things by pictures and by film—things, it is important to note, that they could not and did not *choose* to say by music, by dance, or by verbal language. Film is one mode in which people can record image events, *organize them to imply meaning*, and through them communicate to others.

Making a film not only can help a child learn how films are made or why they are art, but can help him to learn how to manipulate images in his head, how to think with them, and how to communicate through them. I have used the phrase "making a film" as opposed to "studying film" or "learning film literacy" to emphasize what I consider to be the crucial aspect involved in the use of film in education; of course one can learn to some degree how to achieve a certain effect by watching as well as by making films.

Making a film can be part of a process of teaching children how to understand and to use the visual mode in thinking and communication. Listening alone is not the best way to teach people to play the violin or to compose symphonies; neither are looking and talking the best ways to teach people to use the visual mode.

Gross has summarized much of the research in the acquisition of competence in symbolic modes:

All competence in a skillful mode is acquired on the basis of constant practice and repetition. . . . One achieves competence in a medium by slowly building on routines which have been performed over and over until they have become tacit and habitual. . . . It is on the basis of a repertoire of often repeated actions that the child can begin to introduce and perceive slight variations and thus extend the range of his perceptual-intellectual competence to more complex forms of organized behehavior.

The acquisition of competence in modes of symbolic communication entails the learning of the "vocabulary" for representing objects and events proper to a particular mode, and of the "grammatical" and "syntactical" operations, transformations, and organizational principles which are used to structure these into conveyors of meaning and intention.[40]

Film-making, like other modes of expression and communication, must be done to be understood fully.

New Directions in the Use of Film in Education

Communication and perhaps all social behavior require that the initiator of such behavior must put himself, whether consciously or not, into the role of the receiver. Social behavior does not occur just because people are there; it occurs between people who relate to the symbolic nature of their behavior in some shared way. It is social because we have made it so, no matter how deeply embedded such behavior may be in primary biological processes. Seeing a tree bend in the wind and making attributions from that observation to the probability of rain in the future is different from showing in a film a close-up of a tree bending in the wind. In the latter case the film-maker is using the image of the tree to imply something in the context of other images he has put together. He—the film-maker—assumes in the potential viewer a *shared* ability to perform certain perceptual, cognitive, and interpretative procedures upon the film. He places himself in a viewer's shoes and is able to test the viewer's behavior by checking it with his own, by assuming that they have agreed in some way to think about things in the same way. As I write this, I read it over,

40. Gross, see chap. 3.

and place myself in the reader's position in order to judge whether what I am writing can be understood as I want it to be. I attribute to the reader a set of mental operations and skills similar to my own.

Conversely, when one reads, one places oneself for a moment in the position of a writer. One assumes intention, judgment, choices, meaning, and other things on the part of the author. If I didn't assume that a book was meant to communicate to me, I could read it for only one purpose—to use it as a stimulant for my own purposes. It would cease to be a *social object* and would become a piece of the environment to which I might respond as to water, sunshine, marijuana, or a toothache.

So with a film. When a viewer sees a film, he may, for a variety of contextual and cultural reasons, assume intentionality, purpose, meaning, and order. If so, he will treat it as a possible communication. If he does not assume an intention to communicate, he can only respond as one does to the inanimate universe. A viewer assumes, for example, that if a shot of a wind-bent tree occurs, it was put there, and he may further assume that as in a story it is there for some purpose. The child will assume, for example, that some films tell "a story," and further he will "know" how stories are formed in his culture and will place the images he sees into story forms that "make sense" to him.

In our culture, however, most knowledge that children and adults have of film is viewer knowledge. It is difficult for them to place themselves in the role of the film-maker. Most of us don't know what a film-maker does when he puts a film together. A vague notion that films are "true," are "worth a thousand words," and somehow just come to be underlies our own behavior toward film. It is true, as Arnheim has pointed out most forcefully, that education has ignored pictures, and truer (if that usage of "true" makes sense) that education has ignored teaching how films make sense.

Two educational questions emerge: First, can everyone be taught to make films? Second, are there indeed rules that govern the organization of the pictured world for communicating through film?

Research by Worth,[41] Worth and Adair,[42] Chalfen,[43] and others has answered the first question. Almost anyone who can hold a camera and has the cognitive dexterity to type, for example, can learn to make a film. Children in the United States and England as young as eight have made 16-mm movies. In our own research, black and white girls and boys who ranged from lower-class dropouts to middle-class high school students, and from eleven to twenty-five years of age, have learned to make professional-looking 16-mm movies. In a detailed research program we have taught Navajos ranging in age from sixteen to sixty, some of whom spoke no English, to make such movies. All of these people learn easily, are extremely motivated, and are able to deal with complex and creative ideas.

It is the concept of sequence—the ability to arrange many image events in an ordered fashion to produce implications—that contains within it the major significance for education in visual symbolic manipulation and articulation. Educational programs could reasonably aim at developing and strengthening the child's skills in organizing his visual world for purposes of both thinking and communicating. Film offers a new means or mode of cognition and communication that stands parallel to the established modes; hence, it does not deny the intellectual, creative, and social values upon which our society is based. Giving up the dependence on words alone does not necessitate throwing out either verbal language or the cognitive skills associated with the ability to speak, read, and write.

For research purposes, at least, it is reasonable to give movie cameras to people of varying ages and cultures, show them how to use the equipment, and study and analyze how they behave when they organize themselves as film-makers and how they organize the images they make by editing. Our own research[44] is

41. S. Worth, "Film as Non-Art: An Approach to the Study of Film," reprinted in *Perspectives on the Study of Film*, ed. J. S. Katz (Boston: Little, Brown & Co., 1971).

42. S. Worth and J. Adair, *Through Navajo Eyes: An Exploration in Anthropology and Film Communication*. (Bloomington, Ind.: Indiana University Press, 1972).

43. R. Chalfen, "A Sociovidistic Study of Film Communication" (Doctoral diss., University of Pennsylvania, 1973).

44. Worth and Adair, *Through Navajo Eyes*, op. cit.

an attempt to discover if there are rules and codes of communication that all people, or at least groups of people, share when they attempt to make movies. We want to find out how communicating by means of movies relates to the verbal language and culture of various peoples. A question remains whether there are different patterns, rules, structures, or even "languages" that people use when they make and view films. Related to that question and perhaps even more important is the question of how children in a particular cultural context learn these rules.

The use of film in education therefore depends not upon the naïve assumption that nature or reality presents itself directly, but rather upon a more elaborate conception of intelligence.

The problem of intelligence, and with it the central problem of the pedagogy of teaching, has thus emerged as linked with the fundamental epistemological problem of the nature of knowledge: does the latter constitute a copy of reality or, on the contrary, an assimilation of reality into a structure of transformations? The ideas behind the knowledge-copy concept have not been abandoned, far from it, and they continue to provide the inspiration for many educational methods, even, quite often, for those intuitive methods in which the image and audio-visual presentations play a role that certain people tend to look upon as the ultimate triumph of educational progress.[45]

Piaget—and here it is worthwhile reminding ourselves of the arguments presented in Section I—describes the functions of intelligence as consisting "in understanding and in inventing, in other words, in building up structures by structuring reality." The process of film-making is precisely such a process. It is a process of structuring reality because a film-maker must collect a set of image events on film and must build up a set of structures by ordering and organizing these image events into a communication sequence. The cognitive patterns, structures, rules, or "languages" involved in making implications with and inferences from film are precisely the means of structuring reality afforded by the process of film-making.

In our research[46] Navajos were told that they could "make

45. Piaget, *Science of Education and the Psychology of the Child*, op. cit., p. 28.

46. Worth and Adair, *Through Navajo Eyes*, op. cit.; Worth and Adair, "Navajo Filmmakers," op. cit.

movies of anything they wanted in any way they wanted." They were taught the use of motion-picture equipment but not the "right" or "appropriate" way to photograph, what to photograph, or how to structure the image events they had recorded. Would the Navajos use the cameras at all and, if they did, what images would they take? What rules for organizing images would evolve? Was this ordering process by which they structured their reality through filmed images related to their language, narrative style, myth form, or other modes of communication?

The Navajos learned to use the cameras easily. On the first day of instruction they learned how to operate a Bell and Howell triple-lens turret movie camera, how to load it, how to take exposure readings and how to use the lenses for viewing and shooting. On the second day they were given a hundred feet of film and told to "use the camera—for practice— to do anything you want." Almost all of our six Navajo students "discovered" the editing process in the first days of working with film. One of the students wondered whether if he "put film of pieces of a horse (close-ups) between pictures of a whole horse (long shot), people would know that the pieces belonged to the whole horse." He thought about this, shooting "pieces" of the horse one day and shooting "whole horses" at a squaw dance the following week. He then spliced the pieces "in between" the whole horse, and after he looked at the result on a projector he declared, "When you paste pieces of a horse in between pictures of a whole horse, people will think it's part of the whole horse. That's what I think it is with film." It is difficult to know how Johnny "learned" this rule, but no matter how he learned it, Johnny after two days "knew" that people infer that a close-up acts as a modifier of a long shot in certain circumstances. Further, he not only assumed that one could manipulate film by sequences and spatial organization (close-up and long shot), but also seemed to know that certain shots "had to go" with others while certain other shots "didn't go" with others.

We were also able to show that the Navajos organized certain sequences in their films in conformity with the rules of the Navajo language. That is, certain classes of objects in the "real" world were connected by the Navajo language to special grammatical structures, and the Navajos assumed that images of these same classes of objects had to be connected in a film sequence in ways similar to the ways they were connected in speech. Specific sequences were often organized according to Navajo linguistic rules. Also, the very images and methods they used when they chose to tell a story on film were similar to the images and methods they chose when they told myths and stories in words.

It might be thought that the Navajos, or other film-makers, would depict on film the reality they ordinarily experience. This also was shown to be an oversimplification. When an act or a sequence of actions in a film comes into conflict with that culture's rules of narrative organization, it is often the case that "reality" and "history" are changed to conform to "how stories are told." The same film-maker had a Navajo silversmith in his film mining silver to make jewelry. When confronted with the fact that the Navajos never mined their own silver, he replied, "It has to be that way—that's how you tell a story on film." In Navajo myth and religion, all things have to start at their origin. It was not a question of reality presenting itself to Johnny. It was Johnny manipulating and ordering reality in order to structure the world in a communicable manner.

Many of the editing techniques that the Navajos used were unfamiliar to us, or "wrong." The Navajos frequently cut in ways that had people jumping around the screen as if by magic. A boy who was walking toward a tree from the left would suddenly jump to the right side of the screen on the other side of the tree, or a man kneeling would suddenly appear walking. When asked whether these sequences looked "funny" or had "something wrong" in them, the Navajos were at a loss to answer, even though they knew they had made a "mistake" and they wanted to give the right answer. Finally we had to ask point-blank, "Doesn't it look funny to have Sam suddenly go from kneeling to walking?" The film-makers answered, "Oh—of course not! Everyone knows that if he is walking, he must have got up." Or in the case of the boy and the tree, when we asked a similar question: "No, it's not funny—that's not wrong—you see—why should I show him behind the tree? Everyone knows that if he's first here and then there, he got there. When he's behind the tree you can't see him walking anyway."

It might be said that this represents a lack of ability on their part, or that all beginners make "mistakes" like that. On the contrary. For example, black youngsters in Philadelphia, aged eleven to fourteen, were taught in the same way as the Navajos[47] and produced a film that was edited as smoothly as any half-hour television series film. The black youngsters had "learned" how to structure the universe "our" way, either by merely being a part of our culture that "sees" that way, or by having been brought up on movies and television that structure that way.

These studies detail many levels of such structuring, ranging from the different things that people of different cultures choose to photograph and make films about to the specific ways that certain sequences are organized and manipulated to imply meaning according to tacit cognitive rules that these film-makers employ.

In current research, Larry Gross and I[48] are exploring the developmental process by which children learn to interpret visual symbolic events. At what age, for example, do children learn to make inferences from a film? That is, at what age do they begin to say that their responses to a film come from what the film "says" rather than from what they already know? In the former case, children are inferring; in the latter, they are attributing. When a child says, "The doctor in the movie was a good doctor because doctors help people and that's good," and yet the doctor in the movie didn't help people, the child is not inferring but attributing meaning to an image. However, another child says, "The doctor is not a nice man." You ask him how he knows, and he replies, "Because you showed him, in that picture, not helping a man hurt in an accident." This child can be said to be making inferences from the film. How does this development occur? When does a child learn to deal with the film structure of his society? How does one teach him? What structures help him to become creative and to make inferences, and what structures encourage passivity and attribution? Does film competence develop in a way

47. Worth and Adair, *Through Navajo Eyes*, op. cit.

48. See especially chapter by Gross in this volume.

analogous to linguistic competence? An understanding of this structure and its acquisition is necessary not only for the production of an artistic product, but also for the development of children's intellectual skills. In film, as in verbal language, man develops his capacity to communicate to the extent that he learns to structure reality by symbolic means.

It is not that film is language or is structured in the same way as verbal language,[49] but rather that all of man's cognitive abilities are related. When a child learns the concept of metaphor in language, he is all the more able to use it in other modes, both in implication and inference. When the child develops his ability to create structures as he learns to talk, he is developing the ability to create them in pictures and in film. It may even be true, as Arnheim[50] states, that "the thinking on which all learning is based takes place at the source. . . ." I assume that by "the source" he means the eye in its first contact with an object. But that is certainly not where education and instruction must stop. Arnheim completes the sentence, ". . . and continues to draw on it." It is not the source that we must deal with and continue to draw upon, but rather the child's ability to do something with it. It is literally inconceivable that one mode of symbolic thought operates with a presented universe that arrives ready-made to man's brain, while other modes somehow require the mind to manipulate and to structure. Film, like verbal language, like gesture, mathematics, music, painting, and dance, is a method by which different people articulate their experience and present themselves to one another. What we need to know is more about how this is done across modes, across codes, and across cultures.

What kinds of problems and questions, then, must we set before ourselves in order to understand how to teach film and what to teach with it?

Research for the Future

The research that I have briefly outlined is clearly only the very beginning of such study. We need to know more about how

49. Worth, "The Development of a Semiotic Film," op. cit.

50. Arnheim, "The Myth of the Bleating Lamb," op. cit., p. 148.

audiences in different cultures and with different social positions in one culture make inferences from film and how these inferences may differ across cultures.

Let us now consider the institutional implications of developing in our children the ability to utilize pictures in a way similar to that in which they speak, read, and write their verbal language. Are we preparing them for the encounter with the other cultures that will become possible through film and satellite television distribution? That world will be a place where almost anyone can produce verbal and visual images, where individuals or groups can edit, arrange, and rearrange the visualization of their outer and inner worlds, and where these movies or TVs (or "tellies," a marvelous word coined from television and connoting the verb "to tell" so subtly as almost to be overlooked) can be instantaneously available to anyone who chooses to look.

Imagine a world where symbolic forms created by one inhabitant are instantaneously available to all other inhabitants, where "knowing others" means that others frequently know us and we know them through the images we all create about ourselves and our world, as we see it, feel it, and choose to make it available to a massive communication network hungry for images to fill the capacity for its coaxial cables.

Imagine this place—so different from the society within which we nourish our middle-class souls—in which symbolic forms are not the property of a "cultured," technological, or economic elite, but are rather ubiquitous and multiplying like a giant cancer (or, conversely, unfolding like a huge and magnificent orchid) and available for instant transmission to the entire world.

It is technologically feasible right now, through the use of cable television and communications satellites, for a moving image with its accompanying sound to be broadcast from any place in our solar system and to be simultaneously received in hundreds of millions or even all homes attached to the wire. It is further possible for all homes to have their choice of the hundreds of messages that are simultaneously available.

We have passed the stage in our educational processes where the teacher had to present "our" views of the strange antics of "others." We are now at the point where the teacher should know

how to teach us to "tell" others about ourselves visually through
movies and television. The teacher must also know how to analyze
new symbol systems, for other people will be creating new forms
for their old myths about themselves and our own children must
be taught how to do that also. In the past, teachers could ignore
the goals of visual literacy while pursuing those of verbal literacy.
But now it is impossible to ignore the fact that people all over the
world have learned and will continue in great numbers to learn
how to use the visual symbolic mode. Communication researchers
must begin to articulate the problems that will face us in trying to
understand others when their point of view is known to us primarily through movies distributed by broadcast television and
cable. How can we help our students and future teachers to overcome the inevitable tension between the world they will study
and their own cultural backwardness in the face of mass-distributed
visual symbolic mode?

It is necessary to develop theories and methods for describing
and analyzing how men show each other who they are and how
they are. Theories of vidistics [51] must be developed to supplement
other linguistic, psychological, anthropological, and educational
theories, in order to comprehend how people who organize their
film in ways different from ours are understood or not understood. In a world in which people of other cultures are being
taught to make movies and television, in a world in which our
own children are learning to make movies and are being increasingly acculturated and educated through film and television, can
the teacher afford to remain a "blind mute"? For a blind mute
can never have anything to say to a person who respects visual
"speaking" and whose culture demands social interaction through
pictures. What I am suggesting for the teacher, then, as a first step
is the development of the capacity to express himself through film,
as an artist if possible, but primarily as a simple "speaker" in this
new mode of communication. But the teacher cannot rest with the
"speaker in film" ability alone. The native speaker has no need to
articulate how he knows how to speak and understand his language. The teacher of film and visual communication must know

51. S. Worth, "Cognitive Aspects of Sequence in Visual Communication,"
AV Communication Review 16 (1968): 11-25.

more than how to speak; he must know how he knows how to speak and how others speak. He must, in fact, not only be taught to make movies as children, Navajos and others, all over the world will be taught; he must learn *how* to teach others and must formulate theories about *what* to teach others.

It is when we begin to think about the problem of teaching film and television to others that we must face a host of ethical problems. In teaching people to read we implicitly teach them *what* to read. In teaching people to speak or as is the case with most people when they learn to speak, they also learn what to say and what not to say, and to whom and on what occasion. The use of a mode of communication is not easily separable from the specific codes and rules about the content of that mode. Speaking is something that most people do anyway; we do not have to teach it. Film and television are not something that most people do— at this time. Someone has to teach it. Whoever teaches it will have a large and powerful impact upon the culture and intellectual development of the people using it and viewing it.

Up to this point in the development of our educational institutions, teachers have concentrated on reading, writing, and arithmetic, without great concern for the underlying political issues. Who controls the mass media that children, through the development of these skills, are getting access to? With the advent of a wired planet, a planet in which movies and television produced by diverse peoples are available to almost all, teaching *about* film must include teaching how film and other visual modes are produced, distributed, and controlled. Is it enough for the teacher to concentrate only on individual cognitive processes when he teaches and trains others to teach film-making, or must he also concern himself with how these media influence other people and institutions as well?

Further ethical problems exist. Some of our studies, in which we compared films made by black, white, and Navajo young people, show clear differences in these groups' social organization around film-making, thematic choices of material and subject matter, and attitudes toward the use of film. For example, it seems to be the case, from analysis of our current studies, that blacks prefer to manipulate *themselves as image*; they want to be in the film.

Whites prefer to manipulate the image of *others,* as producers, directors, or cameramen. While the films made by black groups involve behavior close to home and neighborhood, the white teenagers' films are often about the exotic, the distant, the faraway. They rarely show their own block, their own homes, or their own selves.

Hence the use of film in education and communication involves more than teaching our children about film or how to make film. It will require the sensitive guidance of teachers who know how to teach about film as communication so as to foster the development of personal intelligence and cultural sensitivity.

With the advent of a wired planet, control of the use of film in education not only means understanding how to teach *through* films, how to teach *about* films, and how to *make* films; it consists also in knowing how to control the use of educational film and television in the mass media themselves. "Sesame Street" and other programs using it as a model are now part of the educational system. By such programs our children are being "educated" to consume rather than to create. Educators themselves constitute the largest and only group of professionals involved in the making of educational film, in television, and with teaching machines who have no training *at all* in the use or the analysis of film as a process of communication. Hence it is mandatory that we teach teachers the very things that I have argued have to be taught to children.

Some Concluding Comments

The major concern that I have voiced in this paper relates to the reasons and theories upon which an increasingly large number of people in education rest their case for the use of film in educational practice. Certainly film and visual communication should receive greater attention from schools and educators. My disagreement lies with the assumptions underlying the arguments for this greater emphasis. The assumption of visual primacy with its attendant uncritical film ideology gives an unfortunate bias to research problems, to teaching methods, and to curricula as well as to theories of education and public policy. It is *not* that the visual is psychologically, culturally, and sensually the primary way of experiencing and knowing the world, but rather that the visual mode of communication, along with other modes, permits us to understand, control, order, and thus articulate the world and our experiences. The process of becoming intelligent is the process of "building up structures by structuring reality." Film-*making* could become one of the important tools by which we allow and help the child as well as the adult to develop skill in building cognitive structures and in structuring reality in a creative, communicative way. Although we can teach *through* film, we must begin to understand how the structure of film itself and the visual modes in general structure our ways of organizing experience. Salomon,[52] for example, has shown that exposure to short, choppy sequences as in "Sesame Street" has a profound effect on a second grader's perseverance.

Film, as Youngblood and Fuller seem to indicate, may be the way we can destroy community. The way we study visual communication, the questions we ask, and the way we teach people to make films and to look at films may very well determine this larger social question. It is my hope therefore that this paper may lead some to question current theories, ideologies, methods, and research approaches in the uses of film in communication and education.

52. G. Salomon et al., "Educational Effects of 'Sesame Street' on Israeli Children," mimeographed (Hebrew University of Jerusalem, 1972).

CHAPTER XII

Formative Research in the Production of Television for Children

EDWARD L. PALMER

There is currently in the United States unparalleled interest in the systematic use of broadcast television to promote the social, emotional, and intellectual growth of young children. Support for this movement lies in the recognition that television is ubiquitous, reaching into 97 percent of all U.S. households; that young children are exposed to upwards of thirty hours of television fare each week; that while they learn a great deal from what they watch, there have been far too few significant attempts to plan program content in order to address important areas of learning and development systematically; and that no other approach can promise to deliver so much to so many at so small a unit cost.[1]

An important feature of this movement is its emphasis on "formative" planning and research. First, important objectives are clearly identified, then systematic audience tests are carried out in order to evaluate progress toward their achievement during the actual course of a program's production. Formative research is typically contrasted with summative research, which is concerned with follow-up testing to determine the educational effect of new products and practices when actually put into use.[2] What follows is a description of the approaches to formative planning and research taken by the Children's Television Workshop (CTW) in the production of "Sesame Street" and "The Electric Company."

1. Joan G. Cooney, *Report: The Potential Uses of Television in Preschool Education* (New York: Carnegie Corporation, 1967).

2. Michael Scriven, "The Methodology of Education," in *Perspectives of Curriculum Evaluation*, AERA Monograph Series on Curriculum Evaluation, ed. R. W. Tyler, R. M. Gagne, and M. Scriven (Chicago: Rand McNally & Co., 1967).

Although an effort is made throughout to discuss these approaches in ways that will suggest their potential usefulness in the development of other new educational products and practices, this paper is not a compendium of research for the general guidance of producers of educational materials; it is, rather, a case study of the use of a powerful new technology for the achievement of planned educational effects. As a case study, it focuses on the overall operational framework within which CTW's formative research proceeds, on the strategies and rationale for the design of formative field research methods, on organizational and interpersonal conditions, and on similarities and contrasts between the functions and the methods of formative research on the one hand and those of more traditional research approaches on the other.

The Children's Television Workshop was created in 1968 to produce a series of 130 hour-long broadcast television programs for preschool children that placed special emphasis on the needs of the urban disadvantaged child. The result, the now well-known "Sesame Street" series, completed its third broadcast season in June of 1972. The formative research methods developed and applied in the production of "Sesame Street" have been reapplied and extended by CTW in planning and producing its second major program series, "The Electric Company," which is designed to teach selected reading skills to children from seven through ten years of age.

At the beginning of the "Sesame Street" project, the functions formative research could serve and the field methods it could apply were not at all clear. There were no precedents of sufficient scope and generality from either the field of educational technology in particular or the field of educational planning and research in general to provide clear guidelines. What has been learned about the formative planning and research process at CTW has come about under quite unusual circumstances, and since it is unlikely that these conditions will ever be duplicated in substantial detail, it remains to be seen what sorts of new or modified approaches will be required in different situations. What is presented here certainly cannot be construed as a dependable recipe that will assure the success of other like ventures.

Among the unusual circumstances associated with the Workshop's productions, some, no doubt, had quite a direct bearing on the effectiveness of the formative research. For instance, the two Workshop projects were well funded; each was budgeted in its first season at upwards of seven million dollars for production, research, and related activities. This level of support made it possible to utilize high-level production talent and resources and to make extensive use of expert educational advisers and consultants. In addition, both projects enjoyed unusually long periods of time—in each case, approximately eighteen months—for prebroadcast planning and research. Time and resources were available to plan their curricula carefully and to state their educational objectives in very explicit terms. This meant that producers and researchers alike, as well as the independent evaluators who were carrying out preseason and postseason achievement testing projects, could proceed without ambiguity of purpose and in a coordinated fashion. Had there been ambiguity in terms of either the particular objectives to be addressed or the commitment of the producers to direct each segment toward the achievement of one or more of those objectives, the formative research could not have been useful, for there would have been no clear criteria for evaluating a program segment's effectiveness.

Also unusual in the CTW case was the policy followed in production recruiting and the organizational and interpersonal relationships between the in-house research and production staffs. All of the key producers came from commercial production backgrounds. None had formal professional training in education or experience in educational television production. Yet they were given the responsibility for final production decisions. They did not work under the researchers, nor did the researchers work under them. The intended function of the formative research was to provide information which the producers would find useful in making program-design decisions relating to both appeal and educational effect.

To the extent that the formative research worked, it worked in large measure because of the attitudes taken toward it by producers and researchers alike. The producers were committed to experimenting with the cyclic process of empirical evaluation and production revision and tended to have the ability not only to see the implications of the research, but also to carry these implications through into the form of new and revised production approaches. Accordingly, the usefulness of CTW's formative research has depended not only on the qualities of the research itself, but also on the talents of those who put its results to use. Moreover, the producers never expected the research to yield full-blown decisions; they recognized that its function was to provide one more source of information among many. From the research side, because the responsibility for final production decisions resided with the producers, it was necessary to develop and apply only methods which provided information useful to the producers. Accordingly, the producers were involved from the outset in all research planning. No observational method was ever persistently applied, and no specific study was ever taken into the field without their participation.

At this time, there is no tradition of accumulated knowledge in the area of formative research practice. This is partly because so little research of this type has been done, but it is even more a result of the fact that it has only recently come to be recognized as a distinct and systematic field of endeavor. While important contributions to the explicit and systematic conceptualization of the field have been made [3] and while some formative research studies are directed to the improvement of specific educational programs,[4] the present scope and depth of the formative research literature is in no way commensurate with its promise for education. The promise of the approach is that it will provide designers of educational products and practices with empirical data far more directly pertinent to their respective media, materials, and learning conditions

3. Lee J. Cronbach, "Course Improvement through Education," *Teachers College Record* 64 (1963): 672-83; J. Thomas Hastings, "Curriculum Evaluation: The Why of the Outcome," *Journal of Educational Measurement* 3 (1966): 27-32; Scriven, op. cit.

4. George L. Gropper and Arthur A. Lumsdaine, *Studies of Televised Instruction* (Metropolitan Pittsburgh Educational TV Stations WQED-WQEX and American Institute for Research, 1961); Walter Dick, "A Methodology for the Formative Evaluation of Instructional Materials," *Journal of Educational Measurement* 5 (1968): 99-102; Roger O. Scott and Morris F. Martin, "The 1969-70 Classroom Tryout of the SERL Instructional Concepts Program," SWRL Technical Memorandum TM-3-70-4, June 9, 1970; Roger O. Scott, Jennifer Castrup, and Emily Ain, "The SWRL Kindergarten Art Program," Southwest Regional Laboratory Technical Memorandum, May 18, 1970.

than are the results of traditional, more basic, research. For the field of educational television in particular, it offers ways to help bring about planned effects. With mass broadcast distribution making it possible to reach hundreds of thousands or even millions of viewers (in the case of "Sesame Street," the weekly audience is estimated to include more than eight million children), it behooves the producers to employ every reasonable means for ensuring in advance that the programs will achieve their objectives.

The CTW Operational Model

The principal activities undertaken in the production of "Sesame Street" have come to be viewed by CTW as a model, and this model was again applied in the production of "The Electric Company." If there is a single, most critical condition for rendering such a model of researcher-producer cooperation effective, it is that the researchers and the producers cannot be marching to different drummers. The model is essentially a model for production planning. More specifically, it is a model for planning the educational (as opposed to the dramatic) aspects of the production— and formative research is an integral part of that process. In the case of "Sesame Street" and "The Electric Company," at least, it is hard to imagine that the formative research and curriculum planning could have been effective if they had been carried out apart from overall production planning, either as a priori processes or as independent but simultaneous functions. The activities included in the model are presented below in their approximate chronological order of occurrence.

BEHAVIORAL GOALS

As the initial step toward establishing its educational goals, CTW, in the summer of 1968, conducted a series of five three-day seminars dealing with the following topics:

1. Social, moral, and affective development
2. Language and reading
3. Mathematical and numerical skills
4. Reasoning and problem-solving
5. Perception

The seminars, organized and directed by Dr. Gerald S. Lesser, Bigelow Professor of Education and Developmental Psychology at Harvard University, were attended by more than a hundred expert advisers, including psychologists, psychiatrists, teachers, sociologists, film-makers, television producers, writers of children's books, and creative advertising personnel. Each seminar group was asked to suggest educational goals for the prospective series and to discuss ways of realizing the goals on television. The output from the initial seminars was then systematically organized, refined, and made operational by the CTW staff and board of advisers. This work resulted in specific goals stated in behavioral terms. These behavioral objectives served as a common reference point for the program producers and the designers of the follow-up achievement tests.[5] Essential coordination of production and evaluation was thus assured.

EXISTING COMPETENCE OF TARGET AUDIENCE

While the statement of goals specified the behavioral outcomes which the program hoped to achieve, it was necessary to ascertain the target audience's existing range of competence in the chosen goal areas. In its initial formative research effort, the Workshop research staff therefore compiled data provided in the literature and did some further testing of its own to determine the competence range. The resulting information helped guide the producers in allocating program time and budget among the goal categories and in selecting specific learning instances in each goal area.

APPEAL OF EXISTING MATERIALS

To be successful, CTW had to capture its intended audience with an educational show whose highly attractive competition was only a flick of the dial away. Unlike the classroom teacher, the Workshop had to win its audience, and it had to hold their attention from moment to moment and from day to day. At stake was a potential variation in daily attendance which could run into millions. Measuring the preferences of the target audience for existing television and film materials was therefore crucial in the design of the new series.

5. Samuel Ball and Gerry Ann Bogatz, "The First Year of 'Sesame Street': An Evaluation" (Princeton: Educational Testing Service, 1970).

EXPERIMENTAL PRODUCTION

Seminar participants and CTW advisers had urged the use of a variety of production styles to achieve the curriculum goals adopted. Research had confirmed the appetite of the target audience for fast pace and variety. Accordingly, the CTW production staff invited a number of live-action and animation film production companies to submit ideas. The first season of "Sesame Street" eventually included the work of thirty-two different film companies.

Prototype units of all film series produced by or for the Workshop were subjected to rigorous preliminary scrutiny and empirical field evaluation. Scripts and storyboards were revised by the Workshop producers on the basis of recommendations from the research staff, further revisions were made after they had been reviewed by educational consultants and advisers, and finished films were tested by the research department with sample audiences. Some material never survived the process. Four pilot episodes were produced for a live-action film adventure series entitled "The Man from Alphabet," but when the films were shown to children they failed to measure up either in appeal or educational effect, and the series was dropped. Sample video-taped material went through the same process of evaluation, revision, and occasional elimination.

By July of 1969 a format for the program had been devised, a title had been selected, a cast had been tentatively assigned, and a week of full-length trial programs had been taped.

Completed prototype production elements were tested by the research staff in two ways: (a) the appeal of the CTW material was measured against the appeal of previously tested films and television shows, and (b) the CTW material was tested for its educational impact under a number of conditions. For instance, field studies were conducted to determine the effect of various schedules of repetition and spacing, of providing the child with preliminary or follow-up explanation, of presenting different approaches to a given goal separately or in combination, and the relative effectiveness of adult versus child voice-over narration. Extensive observation of children watching the shows provided information about the child's understanding of various conventions of film and television techniques. When each research study concluded, the results were reported to the producers for their use in modifying the show components tested and for their guidance in producing subsequent elements. It should be noted that this progress-testing also served a formative research function for the Educational Testing Service staff by field-testing the instruments and administration procedures that were to be employed in later summative evaluation.

THE PROGRESS TESTING

The evolution of "Sesame Street" did not end with the first national broadcast on November 10, 1969. Formative research continued throughout the six-month broadcast season. During this time, it became possible to begin examining the cumulative impact of the series. Accordingly, the research staff instituted a program of testing the show's effectiveness, using the summative evaluation instruments designed by the Educational Testing Service (ETS) of Princeton, New Jersey. A sample of day-care children, predominantly four- and five-year-olds, were pretested prior to the first national telecast. One-third were tested again after three weeks of viewing the show, the same one-third and an additional one-third were tested after six weeks of viewing, and the entire group was tested after three months of viewing. Comparisons between experimental (viewing) and control (nonviewing) groups at each stage of the testing gave indications of strengths and weaknesses in both the execution of the curriculum and the production design. Other independent formative studies of program appeal and of the responses of viewing children also influenced production decisions during this period.

SUMMATIVE EVALUATION

The summative research and evaluation carried out by the Educational Testing Service on each of the program's first two seasons followed a plan developed in consultation with CTW staff and advisers.[6] Participation of ETS representatives in all the main phases of prebroadcast planning helped to ensure that program development and follow-up testing were coordinated.

For the first-season study, ETS developed and administered a

6. Gerry Ann Bogatz and Samuel Ball, "The Second Year of 'Sesame Street': A Continuing Evaluation" (Princeton: Educational Testing Service, 1971).

special battery of eleven tests covering the major CTW goal areas to a sample of children from Boston, Philadelphia, Durham, and Phoenix. The groups included three-, four-, and five-year-olds from middle- and lower-income families in urban and rural settings and in both home and day-care situations. A special side study related to children from Spanish-speaking homes. Other measures assessed home conditions, parental expectations for the children, and the like. In instances where the results of the first season's summative research were fed into production decisions for the second season, they took on a formative function. For example, the summative data indicated that the children's knowledge and skills before viewing the programs had been underestimated in some goal areas and overestimated in others. This was taken into account in programming the second season of "Sesame Street."

THE WRITER'S NOTEBOOK

As the producers and writers began to develop scripts, animations, and live-action films addressed to particular behaviorally stated goals, it became apparent that the goal statement was not a wholly adequate reference. After having been given several successive assignments in the same goal area, they began to express the need for extended and enriched definitions which would provide creative stimulation. Gradually, through trial and error, a format for the Writer's Notebook was developed which the producers and writers found useful.

The Notebook emphasized four criteria:
1. To focus on the psychological processes involved in a particular form of behavior
2. To exploit and extend the child's own experiential referents for such behavior
3. To prompt the creation of various similar approaches by the producers and writers themselves by presenting them with highly divergent examples
4. To provide suggestions free of any reference to particular characters or contexts from the television program, so that the ways in which the suggestions could be implemented would be left as open and flexible as possible

These features of the Writer's Notebook may be highlighted

through an example. In the broad area of "symbolic representation," the word-matching objective was stated as follows: "Given a printed word, the child can select an identical printed word from a set of printed words." To implement this objective, the Notebook encouraged the producers to use words with different numbers of letters, to vary the location within the word of the letter or letters which fail to "match," and to present various matching strategies—such as comparing two given words letter by letter, moving words which were initially separated into physical superimposition, and spelling out each of two given words and comparing to see if one has made the same sounds both times. Another recommended approach was to make use of the "sorting" format, already familiar to viewers, wherein three identical things (in this case, words) and one odd thing are presented simultaneously along with a standard song which invites the viewer to find the one which is different. Still another was to construct a letter-by-letter match for a given word by choosing from a large pool of letters. To encourage still other approaches, another recommendation was to present pairs of words which matched in one sense but not in another—for example, pairs in which the same word is presented in different type faces, or in which one of the pair is the upper- and the other lower-case version.

The producers and writers asked that similar suggestions be developed for other goal areas. Again, suggestions were solicited from advisers and consultants. In addition, the Notebook provided a place and a format for collecting the ideas of the in-house research staff and helped to ensure that these ideas would be seen and used.

A Model for Research on Presentational Learning

Learning by way of televised presentations does occur, and the objective of the formative research at CTW is to discover principles of program design by which this type of learning can be improved. In the specific case of "Sesame Street" and "The Electric Company," the research seeks principles of presentational learning appropriate to their particular educational goals, audiences, and production techniques. However, there are more basic objectives also, one of which is to create generalizable formative research methods and practices. Another is to discover generalizable principles of presentational learning.

In pursuit of these objectives, a model for research on presentational learning is being developed. A summary outline of the model is given in figure 1. One point highlighted by the model is the

MAJOR PROGRAM ATTRIBUTES (Categories of Independent Variables)	VIEWER OUTCOMES (Dependent Variables)	PRINCIPLES OF PROGRAM DESIGN (Statements Linking Specific Independent and Dependent Variables)
APPEAL	Visual orientation, attention, attitude, channel selection, etc.	Within each major attribute category, any number of specific features may operate to affect viewer outcomes. Statements linking specific and well-defined program features to learning outcomes belong in this column.
COMPREHENSIBILITY	Comprehension	
ACTIVITY-ELICITING POTENTIAL		
a) Potential to elicit motor and psychomotor activity	Verbalization, gross physical acts, imitation, direction-following, etc.	
b) Potential to elicit emotive activity	Arousal, attitude, etc.	
c) Potential to elicit intellectual activity	Synthesizing or integrating, forming concepts or principles, generalizing, comparing, evaluating, predicting, etc.	
INTERNAL COMPATIBILITY OF ELEMENTS	Attention to signal vs. noise, integration of elements (visual-visual, auditory-visual, auditory-auditory), etc.	

FIG. 1. A model for research on presentational learning. Major attribute categories are very general dimensions of the televised presentation. Viewer outcomes represent the effects of the presentation on viewers. Within each attribute category, any number of specific program features (variables) may operate to affect viewer outcomes. Principles of program design are hypothesized or well-validated relationships between program features and specific viewer outcomes.

need to identify and rigorously define features of program design (independent variables) which are reliable predictors of learning and learning-related outcomes among viewers (dependent variables). The statements which relate program-design features to empirical outcomes are principles of presentational learning, which are potentially generalizable to other televised presentations and to other media. Moreover, they are seen as principles which will have to be taken into account within any comprehensive theory of presentational learning.

The model is tentative, intended more as a point of departure for further exploration than as a fixed scheme. However, as it stands, it plays a central role in guiding CTW's formative research studies and in organizing their results. It features four main categories of program attributes, including Appeal, Comprehensibility, Activity-Eliciting Potential, and Internal Compatibility of Elements, Activity-Eliciting Potential presently has three main subcategories: (a) motor and psychomotor activities, including imitation, (b) emotive activity, and (c) intellectual activity. Each subcategory in turn encompasses a number of program attributes. The subcategory of intellectual activity, for example, includes those program attributes responsible for such viewer outcomes as *integrating* (putting together the audio and visual portions of the presentation, or the successive elements of an unfolding plot, etc.), *generalizing* (relating the presentation to past experience or to future possibilities), *anticipating* (predicting possible upcoming events in the presentational sequence), to forming new concepts and principles, imputing the motives and intentions of characters or the program's producers, and evaluating—as in assessing the credibility of the plot, message, or character premises, judging the quality of the performance or the technical quality of the production, and the like. The main attribute categories contained in the model and some of the research methods employed within each are discussed more extensively later. But first there needs to be a clarification of the intended role of the model in the formative research process.

The development of this model is not so much an outgrowth of the formative research process as an integral part of it. It was developed in its present form with a number of specific objectives in mind. First, it is intended by virtue of its highly simplified form to serve as a convenient checklist for both producers and researchers, suggesting program attributes which they need to take into account in creating new segments or designing new formative field studies.

It is also intended to serve a number of useful organizing functions. For example, the various field research methods are organized according to the categories of attributes to which their results relate. This is important in that the various methods within a given attribute category tend to elucidate complementary sets of program-design features and viewer outcomes, and their organization within broad attribute categories tends to highlight this complementarity.

Still another intended function of the model is to bring together within a small and therefore convenient number of attribute categories the great number of hypothesized program-design principles growing out of the formative research.

Finally, the model is open-ended in that it necessarily falls short of presenting an exhaustive list of program attributes and audience outcomes. This open-endedness gives rise to another of the model's potentially valuable qualities: it invites researchers and producers to identify other potentially significant program attributes, audience outcomes, research methods, and principles of program design. To cite an example of this effect, CTW researcher Dr. Joyce Weil, while participating in research planning for a new adult television series on health, extended the categories of the model to encompass two variables considered important in developing such a series, namely, credibility, on the independent variable side, which relates to belief, and memorability, which relates to long-term recall and to factual distortion.

The principles of presentational learning which would appropriately appear in the third column of figure 1 were characterized earlier as statements which relate features of the presentation to empirical outcomes. One important consideration in establishing these principles is the need to define program variables with enough precision that they yield high interrater reliability, i.e., two or more raters ranking the same program segments according to a given definition will produce the same or nearly the same rankings. Another consideration is that the principles of presentational learning based on these definitions need to possess predictive validity, i.e., the rankings assigned to segments in terms of a given program variable should yield better than chance predictions of their effectiveness.

CTW is exploring a number of procedures for identifying program-design variables and linking them empirically to their effects on viewers. A procedure being developed by Rust has been applied to data on program appeal.[7] In this procedure, empirically derived

7. Langbourne A. Rust, "Attributes of 'The Electric Company' That Influence Children's Attention to the Television Screen," in press.

scores on a program's appeal are determined for each 7.5-second interval throughout its presentation. The scores for the various intervals are converted to unit normal (z-score) form, then lists are made so that highest and lowest scoring segments are displayed separately. These are then scanned by researchers and producers in an attempt to define the program-design variables which appear to differentiate the high from the low. The definitions of variables so derived are then tested for interrater reliability and improved if necessary. Finally, the definitions are applied a priori to new segments and evaluated for their power in predicting the appeal measured for those segments. The procedure may be applied with other program attributes as well.

Another procedure is currently being explored for CTW by Dr. Gavriel Salomon of the Hebrew University in Jerusalem. In Salomon's procedure, each segment is scored according to a number of different program-design variables which may contribute to the measured outcomes. As with Rust's procedure, it is important that the definitions of these program-design variables possess high interrater reliability. Through the application of multiple and partial regression analyses, Salomon then can evaluate both the individual and interactive contributions of the predictor variables (the program-design variables) toward producing the measured outcomes.

A third method, currently being explored by Lewis Bernstein, a CTW researcher, is an attempt to apply Guttman's facet analysis procedures to the same general problem.[8] This approach differs from the others mentioned above primarily in the range of alternative models, both parametric and nonparametric, which it offers for relating program features to outcomes.

FORMATIVE RESEARCH ON APPEAL

Appeal research bears on a wide range of program decisions. It reveals the effects of various forms and applications of music, e.g., not surprisingly, that segments with music tend generally to be high in appeal, that a sudden transition into loud, lively music will

8. For perhaps the best presently available discussion of facet analysis, see Dov Elizur, *Adapting to Innovation* (Jerusalem: Jerusalem Academic Press, 1970).

usually recapture attention when it has strayed, and that music can help sustain the appeal of program segments designed to be repeated many times, such as those designed to give repeated drill and practice. It can be useful in the auditioning process, not only for helping to identify most liked characters, but also most liked activities in which characters can engage, such as one person's guiding another through a difficult task in a supportive versus demeaning manner; in the resolution of interpersonal conflict through the arbitrary use of power versus through cooperation; and in the portrayal of an individual's personal struggle to achieve a goal or to improve on his own past performance versus receiving a lecture, to mention a few.[9] It also indicates the relative appeal, in general, of films, animations, and live performances, as well as the most and least popular types of each. Animation, of course, is nearly always popular, but so are other forms which contain some of its features, such as fantasy, ludicrous events, noncluttered backgrounds, an economy of words and actions in playing out the plot, "banana-peel" humor, and a high ratio of visual to verbal communication.

Appeal research also helps to indicate how long attention can be maintained under the various conditions, the optimum amount of variety, the optimum pacing of events (with the "Sesame Street" audience it was exceedingly rare for attention to remain high for more than three or four minutes without a change in format), and the ability of a segment to bear up under exact repetition (in this respect, segments vary widely according to a number of different factors, but they usually hold up if they are high in technical quality from a production standpoint, or if they contain music and jingles, and fall down if the interest resides exclusively in the punch line, if the segment is too long, if it is moralistic, or has too much verbiage and too little visual action). In addition, research on appeal can show the effectiveness of special technical effects, such as fast and slow motion and unusual camera angles. One such effect, pixilation, which deletes selected frames of a film and thus portrays the antics of characters in a rapid, jerky fashion, appears, surprisingly, to be both as high in appeal and as reliably appealing to young children as animation. Monologues and dialogues rarely sustain attention when presented in the form of talking heads. How-

9. E.g., see Rust, op. cit.

ever, voice-over narration by unseen commentators describing or asking questions about a visually presented event are frequently effective. This tends to hold true particularly when the verbalizations are sparse and pointed rather than sustained. There is also a clear and general preference for incongruity, surprisingness, and fantasy, as compared with straightforwardness, predictability, and realism; for episodic versus linear styles of continuity; and for familiar (but not necessarily realistic) versus unfamiliar conventions and symbols dealing with time, sequence, and interpersonal relationships. Finally, this type of research can be used to investigate characteristic individual or group preferences vis-à-vis such program design features.

Since both "Sesame Street" and "The Electric Company" were designed according to a magazine format, with successive brief segments addressed to very explicit educational objectives, it was important to maintain high program appeal on a moment-to-moment basis. Accordingly, a method (referred to as the distractor method) was introduced which yields appeal data throughout the course of a program. The distractor method consists of placing one child at a time in a simulated home-viewing circumstance. A black-and-white video-taped recording of a television program is presented and at the same time a color slide show is flashed at 7.5-second intervals on a rear-projection screen equipped with an eighty-slide carrousel. The rear-projection screen, which is approximately the same size and height from the floor as the television screen, is placed at about a forty-five degree angle from the child's line of vision to the television screen. The child is seated in a chair three to four feet away from and facing the television but is free to move about within the confines of the room at any time. A continuous record is kept noting when the child's eyes are directed toward or away from the set. For each viewer, the eighty-slide carrousel is started at a different slide so that the stimulus competing with a given 7.5-second interval of televised presentation is different for each viewer. Composite graphs of the results help the researchers and producers identify the elements of program content responsible for high and low appeal.

A frequently used complementary form of appeal testing consists of taking observations on successive groups of viewers, where each group typically contains from three to five viewers. Usually, four to six such groups are observed in testing a program. A detailed record is kept according to predefined categories of visual, verbal, and motor behaviors. The visual behavior of children in viewing groups provides a cross-check on the distractor results. The record of verbal and motor responses, in addition to reflecting upon program appeal, helps to identify the program approaches which are most and least effective in eliciting active participation. The fruitfulness of this particular approach is very much a function of the training and the creative interpretive skills of the researcher.

Audience surveys can provide much additional material on program appeal, as can structured interviews. Both enable researchers to determine the salient and lasting as opposed to the immediate appeal of various program features. The lasting appeal of an element is particularly important where it is necessary to attract a voluntary audience day after day.

FORMATIVE RESEARCH ON COMPREHENSIBILITY

Once attention is assured it becomes critical to assess the information extracted. What did the children grasp of the intended instructional points? Can they interpret the motives or intentions of the characters?

Comprehensibility testing, while useful in evaluating a viewer's understanding of the dramatic action, is undertaken primarily to point up program design features important in producing instructional effects. It gives producers an empirical check on their assumptions about the comprehensibility of the program design features they are employing, and even limited amounts of field research can help them to maintain a generalized sensitivity to this important attribute.

Although CTW's research in the area of comprehensibility has just begun, the ultimate objective is to identify and set down specific program-design principles. These principles include the use of production approaches which can help to clarify the relationship between an event occurring on the screen and the theme, the plot line, or the logical progression of the dramatic component, or between the instances and noninstances of a concept, the referents and nonreferents of a term, or the most and least effective of a set of proposed solutions to a problem.

The unique conventions and capabilities of the televised medium are frequently used to convey special meanings. The manner in which these conventions are used determines their comprehensibility to the viewer and thus their effectiveness in communicating the meanings intended. These conventions include the flashback technique, special lighting effects, combinations of music and lighting, various camera perspectives, fast or slow motion, pixilation, and the matched dissolve between objects. They also include the juxtaposition of events to establish a metaphoric or analogic relationship and elements of fantasy, such as presenting puppets and cartoon characters who move and talk like humans. Still other conventions include the creation of "magical" effects, such as making an object suddenly appear or disappear from a scene or grow smaller or larger, and exaggerating motions and consequences, as with slapstick and "banana-peel" humor. Among other conventions which can be used in more or less comprehensible ways are the speech balloon and the rules for playing of games and for reading, spelling, performing mathematical operations, and interpreting maps. Still others include timing, sequencing, and the use of redundancy, as in repeating an event exactly or with an illuminating variation, restating a point from alternative perspectives, and making use of introductions or reviews. The list could go on indefinitely, a fact which helps to suggest the significance of this attribute in educational television research.

Again, as with appeal testing, testing of comprehensibility employs not one but a family of complementary research methods. One very useful approach is to present a program via a portable video playback system to an audience of one or more children, to stop the presentation at predetermined points so as to "freeze the frame," and then ask the viewers what events led up to or are likely to follow from the pictured situation.

If the research concern has to do with a premise about a character or his motivation, the viewer might be asked, "What kind of person is he?" or "Why did he do (say) that?" or "What do you think he will do next?" "Why do you think that?" and so on. In one segment designed for "The Electric Company," a musical rock group made up of children—The Short Circus—sang a song which contained the letter combination *ow* dozens of times. Every time the group sang a word containing the letter combination *ow*, a printed *ow* was superimposed on the screen. The intention was to provide repetitive practice in associating the spoken and printed forms of this particular letter combination. By using the method of freezing a single frame, it was possible to evaluate the extent to which members of the target audience actually perceived the speech-to-print correspondence. In this case, the letter combination was frozen on the screen at a point late in the song and, as the experimenter pointed to the printed letter, the subjects were asked such questions as "Why is that there?" "What does it mean?"

In a related method, a program or segment is played through once or twice. It is then presented again but this time without the sound (or, in a variation upon the method, with the sound but without the picture), and the viewer is asked either to give a running account of what is happening or to respond to specific questions.

Other methods useful for evaluating comprehensibility include observing the spontaneous responses of children watching a program, testing them for achievement gains following their exposure to a program or program segment, and having them role-play scenes they have viewed.

A strength of comprehensibility testing relative to traditional forms of summative evaluation is the opportunity it provides for discriminating between the most and least effective of the many segments devoted to a particular achievement objective. A possible but largely surmountable limitation is the tendency for these methods to produce biased results. Because this kind of testing is done while the program is being viewed and the viewer knows he will be questioned, there is typically an overestimation of a segment's effectiveness. While this bias can be subjectively discounted, it must further be weighed against the possibility that segments which produce no measurable learning when presented in isolation may be effective in combination or when presented along with an appropriate introduction or review. However, this limitation does not detract seriously from the usefulness of such methods. The bias can in fact be turned to an asset, as when it can be shown that a segment of questionable value fails to make its point even when it is evaluated by means of a liberally biased method.

A frequently expressed point of view about the potential of television for instructional purposes is that due to passivity of the viewer, the medium is virtually powerless to produce learning. However, since it is patently obvious that television does teach, it seems desirable to explore how this capability comes about and in what proper and constructive ways it can be exploited. The position taken here is that in spite of the apparent passivity of television viewing, the medium's activity-eliciting potential is perhaps the chief basis for whatever instructional value it possesses.

One significant form of activity television can elicit is intellectual activity. It can also elicit verbal behavior and gross physical acts, from modifying the viewer's performance on tests of attitudes and achievements to encouraging him to imitate televised models. It is important to note that the concern of the medium can be either to exploit these effects as instruments of instruction or to foster them as instructional objectives in their own right.

Some examples of intellectual activities include integrating separately presented items of information, anticipating upcoming events, forming new concepts, imputing motives and intentions to characters, following progressively developed dramatic and instructional presentations, and guessing answers to questions. The viewer may also take an active role in evaluating relationships between premises and conclusions, between information given and interpretations made of it, and between behavioral ideals and the actual behaviors carried out by the performers, or he may relate televised information to his own previous experiences and his future plans.

Tentative indices from formative research on the activity-eliciting capabilities of the medium suggest that many of its assumed limitations may be at least partially surmountable. For example, on the premise that one-way televised presentations permit neither reinforcement nor feedback that can be tied to the learner's actions, it is often assumed that learning through trial and error or through trial and reinforcement cannot occur through this medium. This is not a trivial issue from a practical standpoint, since vast amounts of money may be spent studying the use of two-way communication systems for this purpose; yet—at least conceptually—it is also possible to effect this kind of learning through one-way television, simply by the use of "if" statements. That is, the viewer may be offered a choice among alternatives, given time to make his choice (his point of most active involvement), and given reinforcement—an accuracy check of the form: "If you chose thus and so, you were correct (incorrect)." Empirical studies may or may not support the viability of such an approach, but it certainly deserves further investigation.

The notion that certain activities containing a motoric component can be learned only through direct experience is also questionable. For example, learning how to construct alphabetical characters may be more dependent on practice in scanning over the configuration of the letter, on extended or repeated exposure to the letter, and on having an occasion to make and correct the more common errors than on motor activity itself. But all of these are features one-way television can either duplicate or simulate. We need to know more about the possibilities television offers for simulation of learning conditions in which direct, "hands-on" experience has traditionally been considered essential. We also need to know more about the entry skills required for learning to occur and about the possibilities for employing simulation to facilitate subsequent performance in hands-on learning contexts.

All this is not an argument in favor of a widespread substitution of television for physical activity among children, by the way, nor is it intended to deny the great importance of extensive direct experience in learning, especially in early learning. It is intended, rather, to urge open and positive consideration of some of the possible but not yet systematically explored capabilities of the television medium.

FORMATIVE RESEARCH ON INTERNAL COMPATIBILITY

Internal compatibility is a program attribute which has to do with the relationship of different elements appearing within the same segment. The basic strategy underlying both "Sesame Street" and "The Electric Company" is the attempt to effect instruction through the use of television's most popular entertainment forms.

To this end it is essential that the entertainment and educational elements work well together. Without the entertainment, attention strays, and without the education, the whole point of the presentation is lost. In segments where these elements are mutually compatible, the educational point is an inherent part of the dramatic action and is often actually enhanced in its salience as a consequence. In other segments where the entertaining elements predominate, they may override and thereby actually compete with the educational message. The relationship of elements is also of concern in areas which have to do with auditory-visual, auditory-auditory, and visual-visual compatibilities.

The objective of formative research on internal compatibility is to shed light on the program-design features which make for a high or low degree of compatibility. In one method used for assessing compatibility, a panel of judges, using a predetermined set of categories, is asked to rate each segment of a program according to the extent to which the entertainment element either facilitates or competes with the instructional content. Working from each segment's compatibility score, which is a composite of the ratings given by the various judges, it is possible to identify sets of high-rated and low-rated segments and to present the producers with an interpreted list of each type. The interpretations identify program-design features to be emulated, revised, or avoided.

Another method involves eye-movement research, which has proved especially useful in the case of "The Electric Company" because of the extensive presentation of print on the screen and the desire to find ways of motivating the child to read it. In most segments, the print appears on the screen along with competing stimuli. By reflecting a beam of light from the cornea of the viewer's eye and recording the result on a photographic device for later interpretation, it is possible to identify the conditions under which the viewer reads or does not read the print. Once again, the results indicate program-design features worth emulating and approaches which need to be revised or avoided.

Among the important program features focused on by this method are the location of the print on the screen, the effect of various ways of animating print and of the exact repetition of segments upon the elements attended to, and the usefulness of special motivational devices, such as telling all but the punch line of a joke and then presenting that in print. Methods for measuring eye movement obviously have implications also for assessing other program attributes, such as appeal and activity-eliciting potential.

EXTENDING THE METHODS AND FINDINGS
OF FORMATIVE RESEARCH

The search for ways to improve the contributions of formative research is a continuing process at CTW. Suggestions for new research methods and critical appraisals of current methods are forthcoming not only from the CTW research staff, but also from a wide variety of outside consultants (e.g., Rust; Mielke and Bryant; and O'Bryan).[10] Although it is not a primary mission of CTW, the staff also has a high interest in relating the ever expanding body of formative research findings to more general theories of learning. An excellent contribution has been made by Gerald Lesser.[11]

Organizational and Interpersonal Factors

As technologically sophisticated forms of instruction come into increasing prominence, it will be necessary to make increased use of production teams whose members possess a diversity of highly specialized talents. In anticipation of this trend, we need to know more about related organizational and interpersonal conditions. These conditions deserve attention in any attempt to establish a working partnership between television-research and production groups, and they play a role which is even more prominent in the formative research context than in the context of more traditional approaches to educational research.

An important factor in CTW's case has been the opportunity for the members of the two groups to learn about each other's areas of specialization during an eighteen-month prebroadcast pe-

10. Ibid.; Keith Mielke and Jennings Bryant, Jr., "Formative Research in Comprehension of CTW Programs," in press; Keith Mielke and Jennings Bryant, Jr., "Formative Research in Attention and Appeal," in press; Kenneth O'Bryan, "Report on Children's Television Viewing Strategies," in press.

11. Gerald S. Lesser, *Lessons from Sesame Street*, forthcoming.

riod. Furthermore, every new formative research approach is treated as an experiment to be continued or discontinued depending on its evaluation by the producers themselves.

The fact that CTW's researchers and producers possess not the same but complementary skills is also significant, largely because it makes for clear and distinct functions on the part of each group. Still another factor is that the producers, before joining the project, made the commitment to try to work with formative research. This advance commitment helped to support the cooperative spirit through the early, more tentative period of the effort. Also, research never takes on the role of adversary to be used against the producers in winning a point or pressing for a particular decision. On some matters, the producers must hold the final power of decision and be free to ignore research suggestions if production constraints require it.

In all, the factors consciously dealt with in the interests of researcher-producer cooperation have ranged from the careful division of labor and responsibility to housing the two staffs in adjacent offices and from patience and diplomacy to occasional retreat.

The Distinctive Role and Functions of Formative Research

Formative research is distinguished primarily by its role as an integral part of the creative production process. It is important to maintain a clear distinction between this type of research and summative research—that is, research undertaken to test the validity of a theory or the measurable impact of an educational product or practice. Research undertaken in the context of scientific validation is concerned with effects which have been hypothesized a priori within the framework of a broader deductive system, with the use of empirical and statistical procedures well enough defined as to be strictly replicable (at least in principle), and with the highest possible degree of generalizability across situations. While research carried out within the formative context can possess these same characteristics, it need not and typically does not. The main criterion for formative research recommendations is that they appear likely to contribute to the effectiveness of the product or procedure being developed. It is neither expected nor required that they be validated by the research out of which they grew. Establishing their validity is the function of summative research.

As this view implies, to achieve the objectives of formative research it is often necessary to depart from traditional research practices and perspectives. This is not to say that experimental rigor has no place in the formative context. However, even where strict experimental and control conditions have been maintained, there is seldom anything to be gained by using tests of statistical significance. The creative producers often prefer to work directly with information about means, dispersions, and sample size. Also, whereas matching of experimental and control groups on the basis of pretest scores is discouraged where inferential statistics are to be used, because of the conservative effect on the usual tests for the significance of the results, such matching can be very useful in the interests of efficiency and the maximization of the reliability of information based on small samples. In the area of sample selection, it also can be useful to depart from the traditional practice of including all age and socioeconomic groups for which the educational materials are intended. Time and effort may often be saved by selecting a sample of average performers, of performers from the high and low extremes, or, where the intent is mainly to upgrade the lowest performers, a sample only of those. In general, where biased methods of sampling and biased methods of testing are more efficient than unbiased methods, and where the objective is not to make accurate population estimates, it is often useful to exploit the very biases which quite properly would be avoided in other research situations.

In practice, it tends to be difficult for researchers trained and experienced in traditional approaches to adopt an appropriate formative research point of view. In the formative situation, their first responsibility is to improve a specific product or practice and not to contribute to a general body of knowledge (though the two objectives certainly are not incompatible). In such instances, studies must first address the information needs of the product designers and not the special theoretical interests of the researchers. Where it is economically impossible to cover a wide range of empirical questions and to rigorously report or establish careful experimental conditions, and where the usefulness of the results is not unduly compromised as a consequence, the former course may deserve priority. Quantitative indices, such as percentages, and highly detailed item-level data, if they communicate most effectively with the creative producers, are to be preferred over those which conform to standard practice for research reports. Broad, speculative interpretations of empirical results are typically more useful than interpretations limited to the more strict implications of a study. And, as indicated earlier, biased methods of sample selection and testing often can be employed to good advantage. However, in following these departures from standard research practice, there is a risk of producing misleading results. Accordingly, it is essential that resulting production recommendations be appropriately qualified.

Formative research, in my view, is properly eclectic and pragmatic. In these respects, it is highly compatible with the current trend toward defining instructional objectives very explicitly, then developing through systematic trial and revision instructional systems for achieving them. This approach, incidentally, in no way diminishes the traditional role of the behavioral sciences in education or the usefulness of existing theory and knowledge. Rather, it holds that a useful step between basic research and educational practice is additional research of a formative sort, directly concerned with specific combinations of educational objectives, instructional media, learners, and learning situations.

This is not to say that formative research is exclusively concerned with putting theory into practice. It has the equally valid function of starting with practice and transforming it into improved practice. It also has the function of providing hypotheses for further research and theoretical development. This is, incidentally, what is coming to be the dominant conception of the technology of education—a commitment not to teaching in the older audiovisual tradition, but to achieving a planned educational effect.

One long-standing point of view in education holds that theories and results growing out of the "mother" disciplines of psychology, sociology, anthropology, and the like, will filter into effective educational practice if enough educators have been trained in these basic disciplines. While this approach has been useful to a degree, it has not produced broadly satisfactory results. Meanwhile, creators of new educational products and practices have proceeded largely without the benefits of measurement and research. This is partly because skill and training in these areas have been linked to the process of theory construction and validation and partly because there has been an inappropriately rigid adherence to traditional research practice within the product development context. Formative research procedure promises to help in creating a mutually constructive relationship between these two overly isolated realms—the science and the technology of learning.

CHAPTER XIII

The Potentials and Limitations of Television as an Educational Medium

T. R. IDE

The Educational Context

EDUCATIONAL AIMS AND EXPECTATIONS

Any statement of the potentials and limitations of television as a means of expression, communication, and education is necessarily tentative, given the rapid changes in this powerful technology.

A brief historical review of the aspirations, failures, and reverses of educational television (ETV) development may provide initial insight into its educational potential. In the 1950s television in the United States was seen to be a partial solution to some of education's logistical problems: (a) increasingly large numbers of students to educate, (b) crowded facilities, (c) increases in the amount of information to disseminate and in the number of educational tasks to fulfill, (d) limited human and financial resources. The capabilities which television systems seemed to offer were seen as strategic assets. Clarence H. Faust[1] echoed the concern expressed by an increasing number of educators in suggesting that an appraisal be made of television in the light of existing educational purposes:

If our purpose is the development of intelligence, if the essential function of education is the development of the mysterious ability of men to reflect, to take thought, to judge, and to weigh, then we certainly need to look hard at the new means of communication available. . . . We need to consider what new possibility exists because of television for confronting the students with the most exciting minds of our day, when new materials not otherwise possible in the curriculum may be intro-

1. In 1950 Clarence H. Faust served as vice-president of the Ford Foundation and President of the Fund for the Advancement of Education.

duced by it and, not least of all, what curricular reforms will result
when we begin to examine and readjust our means of education.[2]

As a result of the injection of large sums of money for experimental and developmental purposes from various foundations such
as the Fund for Adult Education, Twentieth Century Fund, Payne
Fund, and the Ford Foundation ($76.4 million was contributed by
the Ford Foundation up to 1962), a number of projects appeared
across the United States.

Studies undertaken for the most part focused on (a) teacher
education and curriculum improvement, (b) acceptability of
television in relieving classroom and teacher shortages, and (c)
economic feasibility. Despite the enthusiasms with which the task
of introducing television into education was undertaken, the results in most areas were disappointing. Teachers and students,
while apparently willing to accept the new medium, were far
from enthusiastic in their measured responses, and studies designed
to test the effectiveness of TV as a teaching instrument or technique did not show it to be significantly better than the conventional techniques. In a critical study in the United States[3] the lack of
technical excellence and the fragmentation of effort and financing
were seen as reasons for the apparent failure of ETV—or ITV
(instructional television) as it came to be known as—to live up
to early expectations. Remedial action was undertaken and by 1968
production had become increasingly centralized and networks of
ETV stations began to be formed. Whereas in 1962 almost 78
percent of ITV programming was locally produced, in 1968 this
figure had fallen to 35 percent.

Professional broadcasters were soon brought in either to produce or to advise on the production of programs. Although school
broadcasts remained largely dedicated to direct teaching, which
tended to duplicate classroom techniques, more and more programs designed to enrich the curriculum began to appear. The
early tendency to photograph teachers presenting material in a
simulated classroom situation and designed as a substitute for a

2. Clarence H. Faust, "Educational Philosophy and Television," *Educational
Record* 35 (1958): 44-51.

3. Judith Murphy and Ronald Gross, *Learning by Television* (New York:
Fund for the Advancement of Education, 1966).

regular presentation was modified to permit more programs similar to the documentary film to be used. Television began to be viewed as an additional yet important source of information for teachers.

As mentioned earlier, during the period from 1965-70 a distinction between ETV and ITV found increased acceptance. The term *instructional television* generally applied to the interaction of a learner with television resource material regardless of whether or not it was received via broadcast television. Systematic, developmental instructional goals were sought. Use was made of ITV for direct instruction in many subject areas, either by total television teaching or as a supplement to existing courses. Instructional television practice, however, had for the most part been on the periphery of ordinary schooling, teacher education, the budgeting of educational institutions, and innovative curriculum planning.

Following the 1967 report of the Carnegie Commission[4] on ETV, the connotation of education was deemphasized and slowly replaced by the concept "public television." Broadcast agencies with ETV in their names converted to the public television label. Emphasis was now to be openly placed on public affairs and cultural programming. Edwin Cohen described his view of the emergence of three public broadcasting functions: namely, public affairs, culture, and education (preschool, school, postschool). The purpose of cultural programming is "to cause changes in behavior affecting the cultivation of taste and appreciation in the arts, providing a sense of contemporary culture and its heritage"; the purpose of public affairs is "to cause changes in behavior to help Americans make informed decisions on crucial domestic and foreign policy issues"; and the purpose of educational broadcasting is "to cause specified and verifiable changes in aesthetic, informational and skill behavior." [5] One result of this reconceptualization was that ETV was directed less to working through the schools and directed more to working with the public itself.

In contrast to the American experience, ETV in most European countries developed under the auspices of national broadcasting

4. *Public Television, A Program for Action,* The Report of the Carnegie Commission on Educational Television (New York: Bantam Books, 1967).

5. Edwin Cohen, "Continuing Public Education Broadcasting: Today and Tomorrow," *Educational Broadcasting Review* 4 (February 1970): 5.

agencies. In Great Britain, for example, the British Broadcasting Corporation was responsible for broadcasting information, *education*, and entertainment. A school broadcast division was established to provide programs to enrich the curriculum and supplement the work of teachers. The BBC and, later, companies of the Independent Television Association produced, under the direction of personnel recruited from professional broadcasting and the educational community, many high-quality, school-oriented programs which were much closer in their approach to the documentary film.

The development of ETV in Britain, however, was also disappointing, but for different reasons. Centralized productions, while of high quality, appeared to lack relevance to the individualized curricula of local education authorities, and by 1964 demands began to be expressed for systems under local control that would more effectively involve the classroom teacher in development, presentation, and utilization.

To overcome problems presented by inflexible broadcast schedules and rigid timetables in the secondary schools, the local authorities increased the repeat factor and planned for additional channels. The locally produced programs, however, were not unlike those of the earlier American model. The same problem of restricted resources and lack of experienced production personnel encountered by the U.S. pioneers forced the responsible officials in Britain to depend upon productions centered upon a teacher supported by such graphic material as could be prepared or produced by the limited staff available. It was a curious anomaly that while in the United States the trend was away from locally produced material and toward centralized production and network distribution, in Great Britain the movement was in the opposite direction. Clearly, neither approach seemed to promise that the early hopes for the medium would be fulfilled.

An examination of the early approaches to the utilization of ETV in other countries, while of academic interest, is of only limited help in determining the potentials and limitations of the medium for the purposes of education. In most cases the experiences reflected the particular cultural, physical, and political requirements of the region concerned. Lack of qualified teachers, combined with a disturbing degree of illiteracy among parts of the population, determined the approach taken by Telescuola in Italy; physical remoteness from educational institutions led to the establishment of the correspondence senior high school by NHK in Japan; and in countries such as France where a strong centralized government existed, development was left largely to the national broadcasting system in cooperation with the Ministry of Education. In Canada, by contrast, early efforts on the part of the Canadian Broadcasting Corporation to supply ETV programs for the schools were hampered by the difficulty of providing relevant material for more than ten distinct and different curricula. As a result, although many programs were of high quality, little use was made of ETV until local municipalities and provincial departments of education began to take an interest in developing their own systems in the mid-1960s.

With varying emphasis in individual countries, the key role for educational television ranged from providing learning opportunities to those who lived great distances from schools and universities or to those not able to make use of conventional educational institutions to providing a medium that permitted inexperienced teachers to observe experienced teachers in action and become familiar with examples of new curricula to enriching or supplementing existing educational practices, all within the context of the established formal approach to schooling.

In general, expectations had been that television would help to organize and process information, to move, distribute, and provide access to limited resources, and to disseminate a changing curriculum to the classroom. Whether the early approaches taken and the programs produced tapped those qualities of television which represent its greatest potential is now seriously questioned.

More recent experiences may provide more encouraging results. It has become increasingly clear that if television is to play an important role in education, it will only do so either outside existing institutions or within those which have been so altered as to make best use of it and the other technological media. The most ambitious attempt to date took place at the university level when early in 1971 the Open University in Great Britain enrolled some twenty-four thousand adults who began studying on a part-time basis one or two of an initial four foundation courses. The new university had worked out a cooperative arrangement with the British Broadcasting Corporation, which established a separate entity dedicated to the development of courses in conjunction with university personnel. Basic components of each course included radio and television broadcasts, correspondence packages, counselling sessions and summer seminars. No formal entry qualifications other than that of age (twenty-one) were required and hence anyone could earn a university degree upon the satisfactory completion of the required course work (six course credits for a general B.A.). Results of the first year were considered highly satisfactory by an academic committee which reported directly to the government minister responsible.[6]

RESEARCH FINDINGS

Literally hundreds of studies have been carried out pertaining to the effectiveness of educational television. The early investigations were almost wholly aimed at providing evidence of the value of television as a substitute for traditional teachers or as a demonstration of the equal or superior value of television instruction as compared to conventional classroom teaching. Measurement in most cases was based on the extent of factual recall. Other studies were undertaken to determine attitudes, motivation, acceptability, and factors of interest of students, teachers, and administrators.

Schramm provided some insight as a result of an exhaustive look at the early studies:

There is no longer any reason to raise the question whether instructional television can serve as an efficient tool of learning. This is not to say that it always does. But the evidence is now overwhelming that it can and, under favorable circumstances, does. . . . The effectiveness of television has now been demonstrated . . . at every level from pre-school through adult education, and with a great variety of subject matter and

6. The academic committee which is independent of the Open University was chaired by Professor Hilde Himmelweit of the London School of Economics and consisted of a number of prominent British educators. She indicated to the author that of the 24,191 originally enrolled in January 1971, 19,033 paid the registration fees required by March. Fifteen thousand eight hundred twenty-three wrote the final examinations and 14,667 earned one or two credits. Forty thousand candidates enrolled for the 1972 academic year. The British Government began to receive requests to lower the twenty-one-year minimum age requirement.

method. The questions worth asking are no longer whether students learn from it, but rather (1) does the situation call for it? and (2) how, in the given situation, can it be used effectively? [7]

Roberts and Schramm[8] and Twyford[9] reported that the effective use of television seems to be related more to good teaching than to anything else. Television instruction is successful when the program content is well organized, meets high pedagogical standards, and is presented in a learning context.

Allen, in a summary of findings, emphasized the nature of various studies conducted:

The predominant finding from the hundreds of evaluative studies in instructional television is its overall equal effectiveness when compared with face-to-face instruction. That students learn from televised teaching cannot be doubted, but the conditions under which such learning takes place and the specific characteristics of televised presentations that bring this about are yet to be determined, and most research ignored such questions.[10]

Research concerning the preschool "Sesame Street" series did consider characteristics of televised presentation. The application of a variety of production techniques reported in tests submitted to the Children's Television Workshop in New York indicated significant instructional impact. The uses of humor and incongruity were identified as effective production techniques for gaining attention, encouraging language play, and motivating thinking and learning processes. Constant repetition of short program elements often resulted in reinforcement of learning in that children would repeat verbal messages away from the viewing situation. The observation of overt verbal imitation and anticipation of instruc-

7. Wilbur Schramm and Godwin C. Chu, *Learning from Television: What Research Says* (Final Report, Contract OE 4-7-0071123-4203 U.S. Office of Education, Stanford: Stanford University Institute for Communication Research, 1967), p. 177.

8. Donald F. Roberts and Wilbur Schramm, eds., *The Process and Effects of Mass Communication* (Urbana: University of Illinois Press, 1971), p. 605.

9. Loran C. Twyford, Jr., "Educational Communications Media," *Encyclopedia of Educational Research*, 4th ed., ed. Robert L. Ebel (Toronto: Collier-Macmillan Canada Ltd., 1969).

10. William H. Allen, "Instructional Media Research: Past, Present, and Future," *AV Communication Review* 19 (Spring 1971): 10.

tion led researchers to conclude that "self-programmed individualization of learning is a feasible feature of one-way televised
instruction." [11]

Specific cause-and-effect relationships have generally been
difficult to identify in respect to the television communication
process. Halloran [12] directs attention to the multitude of variables which contribute to effects. Individuals receive messages
through a selective and subjective process in terms of their personal
needs, values, and beliefs and in concert with ideas, values, and
experiences of peers and cohabitants within a social structure. He
suggests that viewers seldom assimilate messages without reference
to social groups.

Caution as to possible broadcast information overflow is noted
by Lazarsfeld and Merton, who refer to "the 'narcotizing dysfunction' of mass media and deal with the possibility that exposure to
a flood of information may serve to narcotize rather than to
energize the average reader or listener." [13] In light of the existence
of these intervening variables, to depend upon broadcast television
as a means for enhancing cultural standards on a massive scale
seems somewhat unrealistic. Enthusiastic expectations are dampened
upon study of research concerning the narcotizing effects of
cumulative television viewing reported by Halloran:

Lyle, Schramm and Parker find few signs that television is raising
taste—on the contrary, they feel it may be hardening taste at a level
based on its own common-denominator standards. Their findings, together with those of Himmelweit, that children learn to like the programmes available to them, although ordinarily they would not select
these programmes, will be regarded with concern. . . .[14]

Similarly, some of the early enthusiasm for the potential massive
impact of educational television has been dampened by reports of

11. S. Y. Gibbons, Jr., and E. L. Palmer, "Pre-Reading on Sesame Street"
(Paper taken from a report to the Committee on Reading of the National
Academy of Education, June 1970), pp. 76-78.

12. James D. Halloran, *The Effects of Mass Communication with Special
Reference to Television*, 4th ed. (Leicester: Leicester University Press, 1970),
p. 34.

13. As cited in ibid., p. 23.

14. Ibid., p. 16.

the lack of mass appeal in education and through the identification of problems in coordinating broadcasting with traditional school timetables or integrating broadcast television within established educational programs.

Characteristics of Television

THE VISUAL AND AUDIO TELEVISION PHENOMENON

An inventory of the characteristics of television as an electro-magnetic phenomenon provides a base for ascertaining its significance within the teaching-learning process. Some attributes and properties are peculiar to television alone, some are related to general mass-media traits, while others are inherent in television systems.

A television picture seen on a receiver fundamentally consists of patterns of light and shade "painted" on a phosphorus screen by means of a continually scanning beam regulated by varying electrical currents. These signals correspond to the light distribution at the source which has been converted by means of cameras and associated electronic equipment for transmission and reception. The illusion displayed in North American TV systems is a result of sixty one-half pictures scanned every second which the human eye conveniently blurs together by persistence of vision. The picture is relatively low in visual data but of sufficient quality for normal viewing. The sound signals are picked up at the source through microphones and audio equipment for separate but related transmission.

A fundamental characteristic of television, then, is that it is capable of taking light from a variety of sources by various means and transmitting it in combination with sound to various reception points. This manipulation of light can be used to create an infinite variety of visual images or symbols such as a dissolve, a split screen, a corner insertion, a fade, or a superimposition of images. Light, intensity, color, and shade are arranged through electronic means into patterns which alone or in combination with sound can present meaningful displays. Millerson[15] described visual and sound

15. Gerald Millerson, *The Technique of Television Production* (New York: Hastings House, 1961), pp. 210-11.

images as being factual and atmospheric. Factual sounds or icons reveal information directly as close to reality as possible whereas atmospheric images offer selective aspects of reality which modify meaning, or fantastic arrangements which distort the actual or create new symbols in an attempt to solicit viewer imagination through association. The functions of sound and picture in television, according to Millerson, have been to refer directly to actuality, to establish context, to interpret, to imitate, to identify, to recapitulate, to couple, to interplay. A number of tasks have been identified which can be accomplished visually or in combination with audio. Some of these include:

1. Directly contrasting or comparing two ideas, situations, etc.
2. Linking a variety of subjects through common association
3. Juxtaposing apparent incongruities
4. Deliberate . . . distortion
5. Associative selection
6. Deliberate overstatement or understatement
7. Repetition
8. Irony
9. Personification
10. Metaphorical transfer
11. Successive comparison
12. Sudden revelation [16]

Although opinions vary as to the difference between film and television as a means of expression, two distinct differences are apparent. Television has become a mass medium available to most people in their homes, and it brings a sense of immediacy to the screen through its transmission in real time—an illusion which appears to persist even when the broadcast is delayed through the use of video tape. The immediacy of live television is said to motivate a concentration of visual attention and give a feeling of participation. The sense of suspense is a key in this regard. In addition, by using high-quality lenses and microphones it is possible to gain a fuller perception of an event than might be obtained by personal attendance. Exploration of personal spaces through use of extreme close-up lenses can be made in real time without giving the viewer the sense of discomfort present had he moved in such

16. Ibid., pp. 213-17.

intimate association with the camera's subject in reality, or the sense of unreality when the similar technique is used on film and projected on the large screen of the cinema.

The home-viewing environment can offer considerations of comfort, informality, intimacy, and small-group interaction or distraction. Certain programs have acquired a personal quality as illustrated by Paddy Chayefsky's television plays which direct attention on a small screen to subjective, intimate, inner manifestations of one or two of his characters' actions or thoughts; as seen on "informal talk shows" which capitalize on the attractiveness of amiable personalities; and as revealed by the one-to-one relationship sometimes achieved through a presenter's style and eye contact with each viewer.

Imbued with a high visual capacity for presenting process, motion, and event, the interplay of process and growth of forms of all kinds can be illustrated through the medium. It also has the capacity to present large amounts of material as a coherent whole. This capacity presents a problem of redundancy. Means of determining the proportion of redundancy to the amount of information in a given space and time is an area in need of investigation.

From the layman's point of view audio and visual signals are not significantly changed in the process of their transmission through school cable systems, community antenna or commercial cable systems, 2500 Mhz systems, satellite relay, and UHF or VHF direct broadcasting. Access to programs from a remote source is only a part of the context in which television is seen in education. In addition to these broader aspects of broadcast television systems, individual video tape or video cassette equipment, single cameras and related accessories, all of which can be dynamically controlled in real time by the learner, are components of the inventory.

THE NATURE OF TELEVISION AS AN ART FORM

There appear to be only threads of agreement among philosophers and artists as to what constitutes a work of art. Most would concur, however, that it is the product of human activity, it is original, it embodies excellence, and it is "larger than life," i.e., it adds a new dimension to our understanding. A new reality is presented in a superrational visional manner in symbolic or metaphorical terms. A work of art serves a communication function, using conventions and symbols to express ideas, emotions, attitudes, and values. A television production is in essence a display of human interpretation, a symbolized substitution of reality. Television has not yet been recognized as an art form largely because of its relative youth and the fact that in the early days it was used for transmitting visual images and sound in a purely representational manner with little attention given to the television program form.

As a vehicle of transmission it has represented life, but it has not created new experience. To do this, there is need for a focus on and expansion of its tools. Only recently has work been done to explore the artistic possibilities of television. The establishment of the National Center for Experiments in Television associated with KQED-TV in San Francisco is a pioneering step in this direction. Artists have been brought to the center to work:

> . . . with the television monitor as the prime surface of aesthetic occurrence rather than as the conventional display of photographed reality. Center artists seek to understand and formalize principles of composition with electronic images and sound. Here broadcast television, and the theatrical motion picture and journalistic histories which have comprised it, are set aside, and the medium's unique characteristics—electrical energy, two-dimensionality in a fixed aspect ratio, time-dependence—are applied in studies of shape, movement, tension, volume, plasticity, texture, and duration.[17]

In some areas of artistic expression it is not always clear as to who the artist is. One person is usually identified when we are talking about literature, sculpture, painting, musical composition, choreography, and still photography, but it becomes more complex when we attempt to identify the artist in the theater. Here we have to acknowledge the role of the director, writer, actor, designer, and others. Depending on the production, any one individual might play the dominant role. Film adds further complexity, for the roles of the cameraman and editor must also be considered.

In television the role of the cameraman, while still important, is somewhat reduced, for the director has direct control during production for selecting the images actually seen by the viewer.

17. National Center for Experiments in Television, KQED-TV, San Francisco (A brochure, 1971).

It appears likely that in the future more attention and emphasis will be placed on the producer-director as a principal artist among a number of contributors. It is he who molds moving patterns of picture, spoken language, sound, and music within controlled time and space, as the program "New Guinea Mosaic" [18] illustrates.

Television is still in its early years of development at a stage where not nearly enough is known about its potential. Recognition has been given to it, however, as a unique medium for artistic exploration. As such, it promises to offer to education not only prepackaged materials but also a means of imaginative expression for students of all ages.

Treating TV as an art form brings into focus the central educational concerns of children's expression, appreciation, and criticism. The development of portable, battery-operated cameras and video tape recorders has already led a number of schools to permit pupils to experiment with production techniques; nevertheless, TV is at present too expensive for such expression via production by children on a mass scale. It is, however, immediately practical to utilize aesthetic and artistic criteria in viewing the medium with respect to conventional analysis and meaning.

THE EVOLUTION OF A LANGUAGE OF TELEVISION

Systematic analysis and description of languages in terms of traditional grammar or from a structural linguistic orientation are recognized, and specific codes with lexical, structural, and social-cultural significance have been identified in a formal manner. Berlo observed that "as yet, we have little systematic knowledge of the syntax and vocabulary . . . of radio-TV production . . . there is no recorded grammar for . . . its code." [19]

Although a grammar as such has not been identified and accepted, a number of textbooks and journal articles have appeared which attempted systematically to explore the elements and techniques of television production. It is in a film entitled *Heartbeat*,

18. The Ontario Educational Communications Authority, "New Guinea Mosaic: 7, Middle Sepik I (A video tape, Toronto, 1972).

19. David K. Berlo, *The Process of Communication: An Introduction to Theory and Practice* (Toronto: Holt, Rinehart & Winston, 1960), p. 58.

however, that the language of television has been formulated in terms of eight elements which are used in television advertising to build to a moment of sensory impact.[20] These elements are movement, time, space, color, facial images, spoken words, natural sounds, and music. By electronically structuring these elements of light and sound energy, reality can be duplicated or enhanced. Music, motion, and color can build an emotional response without tapping the viewer's own experience per se. It is also possible to create an emotional environment which can be easily identified with a product without the use of the spoken word. It is further observed that the dissolve, the fade, the close-up, the long shot, motion, image, and sound have become more meaningful than the dot, dash, exclamation mark, italics, or the still photograph in four colors.

Although symbolic systems such as music, written or spoken language, painting, and dance can be displayed directly through television, there is still some question as to the extent to which permutations are created in the process and whether any changes are indeed of significance. Whereas structural groupings of words which convey certain meaning are differentiated in written language by graphic signals of intonation and pause, in a similar fashion meaning may be conveyed in television by image groupings distinguished by the use of a defocus or dissolve. Beyond conventional use of the medium, the devices which enable the mixing of images and sounds, special electronic effects such as the simultaneous display of many pictures, various screen-wiping patterns, etc., make possible certain original symbols. While synthesized images and sounds may develop as unique ingredients of an expanded television language and a catalogue of effects of various production techniques is developing to the point where it can be exploited for dramatic, educational, and commercial purposes, there is some question as to the fruitfulness of a search for a language of film or television which would be analogous to that of ordinary language.[21]

20. Television Bureau of Advertising, *Heartbeat* (A film, 1962).

21. See comments elsewhere in this book by Howard Gardner, Vernon Howard, and David Perkins, as well as by Sol Worth.

Learner-Television Interaction

CHARACTERISTICS OF THE LEARNER

Among the characteristics that distinguish a competent person are the literary skills which permit one to interact successfully with others both present and at a distance, both interpersonally and with the materials as coded within documents and institutions. There is, however, growing opinion that there are other kinds of intelligence than that reflected by an individual's ability to handle the printed word. There is even some question as to the necessity for the use of language, as we commonly understand it, to enable effective thinking to occur. Schools throughout the 1960s and early 1970s have continued to be print-oriented, designed and organized in such a fashion as to enable easy progress to be made by people who read and write effectively. Intelligence tests generally imply a degree of literacy. While it is true that Wittgenstein and the later philosophers of the British analytical school have emphasized the importance of words and the ability to decipher precise meanings of words as the critical factor in a person's ability to think, the role of intuition is being increasingly mentioned as a major factor in the creative and inventive mind. Television's role in the development of nonverbal intelligence has yet to be ascertained.

Further, because it is primarily a visual medium and because of differing human perceptual capacities, particularly in the pictorial realm, television may well become an effective means of accommodating individual differences. To a greater extent than is likely in the case of the written word, different people may enjoy a picture on different levels of sophistication and each may profit from the experience. If different perceptual learning styles can be individually identified and classified, the development of learning materials corresponding to these styles and preferences would be a distinct possibility. These observations require further in-depth study, but what is immediately apparent is the challenge for new approaches in the production of learning resources which take individual preferences and variations in learning styles into account.

The determination of goals which are closely related to actual learner needs is a process essential to ETV's success. Whether or not television should be used depends upon the readiness, attitudes, and social climate of the target audiences—factors not sufficiently dealt with in most broadcast and nonbroadcast ETV enterprises. The investigation of needs and opinions of specifically defined groups of adults and youth prior to ETV program-planning is a process which should be given more attention. While attempts to do so have been undertaken in the last few years,[22] the effectiveness of such searches is limited because those people who evidence the greatest needs tend to be those least likely to be strongly motivated. Most individuals who are highly motivated are likely to equate needs with interests and hence are eager to utilize learning materials designed to satisfy their requirements. In cases where an individual has real needs and interests, but there is a low degree of motivation, a decision is usually made to postpone, perhaps indefinitely, the use of specially prepared learning materials.

Surveys of learner needs and wants provide guidelines for programming for large numbers of individuals who are willing both to indicate their particular requirements and to take advantage of programs that have been prepared in response to them. The problem of the unmotivated and the intellectually disadvantaged, however, calls for more highly specialized research. It may be that investigation into the area of nonverbal intelligence, touched on earlier, will be a promising field for study in this regard and one in which television would likely play a prominent role.

ASPECTS OF THE TELEVISION-LEARNING PROCESS

The type of system available to the learner determines the flexibility of his access to programming and the nature of his interaction with television resources. Different applications have been recognized for broadcast television as opposed to closed-circuit systems. There is a place for each, depending upon capacity, economics, and specific educational requirements.

Broadcasting over large geographic areas is the most economic and efficient method for primary distribution of a signal. While community antenna systems do provide excellent signals to schools

22. *Study of Educational Needs and Interests in the Channel 19 Coverage Area* (Toronto: Ontario Educational Communications Authority and Ontario Institute for Studies in Education, August 1971), p. 2.

and homes, the most economical means of sending programs to the head ends of the various systems is by broadcast. One cost analysis carried out for the Channel 19 signal area in Metropolitan Toronto, Canada, indicated that the cost of distributing video tape directly to fifty CATV head ends was over three times that of distribution by broadcast.[23] An additional benefit, not feasible by cable at that time, was the availability of the broadcast signal to rural areas.

On the other hand, one of the important arguments for closed-circuit television is the capacity for providing audiovisual information on demand. An information retrieval capability has long been the dream of educators concerned with the development of the individual as an independent and critically aware person. A number of experiments in this vein have been conducted to date, of which probably the most advanced was a twelve-channel system developed primarily for schools of the Ottawa School Board in Canada. This project provided films and video tape programs on demand via cable with remarkable efficiency. Nearly all teachers who had access to the information retrieval television system were of the opinion that it was an effective audiovisual aid and an important advance in the use of television in education.[24] Nevertheless, problems were encountered in building up a large enough library of programs relevant to the curriculum to fully tax the available channels, and the costs involved in extending the system to all schools under the jurisdiction of the board were such that the original concept was modified and a less ambitious distribution system substituted.

The high degree of interest sparked by such information retrieval experiments reflects the frustration of those concerned over their inability to select those programs they want to see at times they want to see them. This reaction is of course understandable; nevertheless, it is important to recognize that there are certain advantages as well as disadvantages to the relatively inflexible schedule associated with off-air reception. A very real attribute of

23. Harry K. Davis, *Report on the Functional Parts of ETV Distribution Including Methods and Costs* (A report submitted to the Ontario Department of Education, Educational Television Branch, November 1969).

24. G. Harry MacLaughlin, *Teachers View IRTV* (Ontario Institute for Studies in Education, November 1970), p. 2.

broadcast television is the opportunity it gives to large numbers of people for "browsing." People are prone to select friends, books, and periodicals that share or reflect their personal views and biases, yet through television, often owing to inertia, audiences may be exposed to different and challenging ideas. It is obviously important for the student to encounter ideas that are new to his experience or in conflict with his convictions. The browsing function ascribed here to broadcast television parallels to a degree the type of experience enjoyed in a library where, as a result of wandering among the shelves, books are discovered which stimulate new and unexpected areas of interest. Where the educational television programming is of high quality, departures from conventional and established routines can often be rewarding.

The usefulness of ETV is often questioned by those who have been conditioned to think of television as a medium of entertainment or as an electronic distribution system to facilitate the multiplication and magnification of the conventional teaching situation. Implicit in their skepticism is the assumption that television is a mass medium and that the viewer is necessarily passive. It is becoming increasingly apparent, however, that with the development of the video cassette and multichannel cable system, the medium can appeal to specific audiences of various sizes. It is obvious also, as Ryle[25] points out, that the exercises of learning can be either overt or covert. Simsonson[26] discusses approaches an individual can take in viewing which lead to different degrees of accomplishment. He suggests that the individual can view as a passive onlooker with little involvement or retention; as an appreciative viewer with perhaps some emotional interplay; as a critical judge who weighs what is before him in terms of predetermined criteria; as an intellectual monitor who carefully stores and processes new data; or as a creative percepter who engages in a profound intellectual, sensitive, creative interaction.

It is important as well for the individual to understand the craft of the producer and not to limit his critical involvement to the message itself, for production and editing techniques have become

25. Gilbert Ryle, *The Concept of Mind* (Penguin Books, 1949), p. 46.

26. Solomon Simsonson, *Crisis in Television: A Study of the Private Judgment in the Public Interest* (New York: Living Books, 1966), pp. 163-73.

so sophisticated that it is often difficult for the viewer to separate reality from fantasy. This is not an easy task, for the art form is developing so rapidly that few instructors, even in communications courses, have acquired the visual fluency to design the necessary learning experiences. Nevertheless, students with serious intent to learn, who understand how to approach learning through television, and who have acquired basic skills in listening, viewing, and interpretation in the nonverbal realm should reap substantial benefits from a critical study of both the medium and its messages.

One current problem in using televised material for individualized instruction is the lack of a system of classification of both the programs and the material found in them. Most scholarly books have been classified and indexed so that the learner may select specific information he may wish to know without reading the entire book. The educational video tape, however, has not been indexed in a similar fashion and, therefore, despite a technology that will permit the viewer to look at any selected segment of the tape almost upon command, it is virtually impossible for the learner to identify those portions which may be relevant to his needs. With new material being recorded at ever accelerating rates, the lack of an early attempt to come to grips with this problem may well prove to be the biggest obstacle preventing the use of the medium for individualized learning.

Conventional broadcast and cable distribution systems limit individual user control on a nonsequential basis, that is, to interact by stopping, starting, returning to points previously explored. Remote access and control devices for several individuals have not been put into operation. With the advent of portable video tape recorders and certain video cassette machines combined with an adequate index and classification system, this interactive dimension becomes possible.

TEACHER COMPETENCES

The traditional function of the teacher in respect to television has been as the manager of the instructional process, a partner of the studio teacher, a supplementary research person for a televised course of study, or as a proctor where a televised course is complete within itself. Too often, the teacher has been merely a passive onlooker, a person who directs when the set is to be turned on and off and, if engaged at all, is involved only in conventional pre- and post-telecast activities. Not understanding the nature of the medium and the need for flexibility and changes in roles according to specific learner needs and the programs used, teachers may become dissatisfied. It is perhaps because of its newness in education and because of its role in entertainment that TV has developed a certain mystic quality. The creators of the television program are thought to belong to a kind of private club to which only a few are admitted; the remaining members of the profession stand aside and are asked to accept what is presented without enjoying a sense of personal involvement. While the teacher may not be a professional writer, she knows how to write and hence her appreciation of the book is at a deeper level than that of the television program. Available to combat this teacher estrangement due to visual fluency and lack of personal involvement are the portable camera and record and play-back equipment—tools enabling self-expression in this new medium. This use of television on an individual basis has been explored in many schools. Examples of approaches and practices vary according to curriculum focus and to the capabilities and interests of students.

In a "videopak" handbook prepared for elementary school teachers, examples are given to show how such portable equipment can be an important mode of expression and an indispensable tool of discovery.[27] Through a series of developmental assignments or contracts, teachers and students alike learn to exploit the versatility of the vidicon camera. Beginning by capturing shapes and rhythms in nature and their man-made environment, they learn the basic elements of a picture. Later, by approaching subjects from different points of view, they discover how to manipulate phenomena to make the strange familiar and the familiar strange. After achieving a sense of confidence and competence, the individual or group may use the equipment for projects relating to their normal courses of study. The consequence of exposure to the medium is related most directly to what the learner does, to what internal events take place within the mind. Both attitude toward the task

27. James Moriarty, *The Third Eye* (Toronto: Ontario Educational Communications Authority, 1972).

and skill in dealing with it are vital. Just as individuals learn to read, write, and use the book, they must discover how to communicate by television. It is this expression that Bruner and Olson have related directly to intellectual ability (see chapter 6).

Recent projects to establish production workshops for teachers have had as their objective the development of a new kind of literacy, a dispelling of the glamour and mystique. Only through such a process can the effective function of the teacher and student within the TV-learning situation be realized.

The Characteristics and Qualities of Programming

Integral to the success of any program or series of programs is the planning approach taken by the ETV production organization. The Children's Television Workshop, the Open University, and the Ontario Educational Communications Authority have all relied heavily on planning teams which incorporate individuals actively engaged in instruction within a given discipline, media specialists, and educational technologists who are particularly knowledgeable about research techniques and utilization procedures.

In answering the theoretical question, "What will happen to educational television?" Bruner stated in 1963:

Most of its weaknesses, except those of youth, exist because we have neglected its potential and failed to exploit it to its fullest. Most of the other weaknesses arise because the medium aspires to *self-sufficiency*— failing to join skillfully with other media and techniques. For the future of ETV, the greatest mistake could be to put it to work sanctifying the traditional.[28]

Since that time, more and more educational broadcasters have accepted the view that television cannot stand alone in the educational process and hence will be utilized most successfully in a mix with other media. The term *multimedia* has come into common use and not without justification.

A number of projects have in effect employed television as one element in a learning system. In most of these, such as the Open University in Great Britain, the Television Technical College in

28. Jerome S. Bruner, "Imaginative Uses of Educational Television," in *Inquiry: Implications for Televised Instruction* (Washington, D.C.: National Education Association, 1966), p. 58.

Poland, Telekolleg in Bavaria, the Television College in Chicago, and TEVEC in the Province of Quebec,[29] TV has been used in a fairly conventional way to present lectures and documentary material complementary to the course textbooks, correspondence elements, summer sessions, and such other components that may be particularly relevant to special situations. In others, however, a number of innovations have been tried that are worth noting in a consideration of the potential of the medium.

Overt responses by viewers to televised material were sought through the use of simulation game techniques. In 1968, WGBH-TV Boston developed a series entitled "Cabinets in Crises," [30] which called for political judgments to be made based upon identification with representatives of various nations and an understanding of their policies. In a more recent example, "Operation Moon Vigil," [31] the O.E.C.A. attempted to involve primary and junior school pupils in the creation of social institutions in reaction to a simulated crisis on the moon which found the participants temporarily unable to return to earth as a result of a technical breakdown. The object was to provide the students with an unusual insight into the relatively abstract concept of institutionalized society. The television element consisted of eight ten-minute highly realistic broadcasts and was supported by kits containing procedure manuals, space food units, other aids, and debriefing guidelines.

Tapping the ability of television to create the emotional environment as well as to provide an overview of the depression

29. The objectives of and the approach taken in the TEVEC experiment were somewhat different from the others. It was designed for an underprivileged region in the Province of Quebec to enable adults to complete ninth-grade studies. This multimedia course involved social animators who worked within various communities and homes, home study kits, group viewing and discussions, visiting teachers, counseling sessions, and mail-in questionnaires. Approximately 15 percent of the population took part in courses in French, English, mathematics, economics, social studies, and special programs. Attempts were made in the television productions to relate subject matter to events and situations that were familiar to the viewers and in line with contemporary life. Between eight and nine thousand students wrote the ninth-grade examination in the first year and in general the project was considered by the government of the Province to be successful.

30. WGBH-TV, "Cabinets in Crisis" (A television series, Boston, 1968).

31. Ontario Educational Communications Authority, "Operation Moon Vigil" (A video tape series, Toronto, 1972).

years, a production team representing the Ontario Institute for Studies in Education and the ETV Branch of the Ontario Department of Education developed a system which included tape recordings, still pictures, reproductions of source documents, and selected articles. The principle objectives were to provide a learning environment that would reach students on many fronts across lines separating various disciplines and to maximize opportunities for the individual to proceed at his own pace and in accordance with his own interests. An evaluation report indicated that:

The effectiveness of "concerted" media was remarked upon by many observers. Ingredients such as television programs and films brought an emotional dimension to the study of the Thirties that would have escaped some students if they had been confined to print.[32]

Challenged by the problem of helping new Canadians to learn English, R. J. Handscombe, designed a multimedia package which combined paperbacks, audio cassettes, pictures, self-help materials, and TV. The television element consisted of a series of programs which used the "soap opera" format, entertaining in itself, to provide characters and situations with whom and with which the particular audience could identify. He comments:

How is it possible to design a programme that encourages people to move away . . . from the "classroom," and put themselves at risk in the community? Part of the answer is . . . to consider the programme as only a segment of the whole, and to provide . . . a "multi-media" presentation. The community itself then falls into place as another extension of the package."[33]

The explicit statement that the program was designed to move away from the classroom reflects a growing dissatisfaction with traditional educational institutions that began to be manifested in the late 1960s and early 1970s. If the trend toward nonsequential learning outside the schools, colleges, and universities continues,

32. John H. Syrett, "A Review of the History of the Project," *Evaluation Report on the Multimedia Project on the Thirties: Age of the Great Depression* (Toronto: Ontario Department of Education, Educational Television Branch, 1969), p. 1.

33. Richard J. Handscombe, "Castle Zaremba: A Multimedia Approach to Learning Canadian English as a Second Language," *English Quarterly* 4 (Fall 1917): 34.

then media such as television will obviously be freer to play an integral role than it does at present.

Projects such as these are perhaps the forerunners of a kind of programming approach incorporating an orchestrated system which facilitates learning even more. New program concepts will no doubt develop as persons involved in educational television gain broader and more profound understanding of the nature of the medium. At the moment, too little is known about whether or not the producers' expectations are realized in the viewing experience and the extent to which unintended effects are of consequence. Even though increasing use is being made of pilot pretesting, it is difficult to measure the emotional dimension and the extent of attitudinal change. Yet it may well be that it is in this area that educational television has its greatest potential.

The lack of research in this area is disappointing. In the colleges and universities, where research facilities are strongest, production resources are generally meager. First-rate programs are extremely expensive and, with one or two exceptions, organizations with the necessary funds do not build this kind of research function into their operation.

Toward the Realization of Television's Potential

It is difficult to draw firm conclusions regarding the potential and limitations of television as an educational medium when to date it has been primarily used as a stopgap treatment for deficiencies within the system. Marshall McLuhan made this point in his introduction to *Understanding Media* when, in describing the culturally disadvantaged child as a TV child, he stated, "One strategy of cultural response would be to raise the visual level of the TV image to enable the young student to gain access to the old visual world of the classroom and the curriculum."[34] McLuhan is obviously not enthusiastic about this approach and rightly so, for this is what has been attempted with ETV in various ways ever since the early experimental years, and ETV has yet to be established as an integral element in the formal learning process.

Unlike commercial enterprises which modify structures and

34. Marshall McLuhan, *Understanding Media: The Extension of Man* (New York: McGraw-Hill Book Co., 1964), p. x.

procedures to take advantage of advances in technology, the edu-cational establishment seems simply to superimpose a new tech-nology on an existing structure. This naturally results in uneco-nomic and inefficient applications. The complaint is often heard that the television schedule is inflexible. This may be true but it is also true that the school schedule is equally so. In this era of rapid change, no institution, educational or otherwise, can afford to ig-nore the new priorities which are being continually placed upon it by a restless society.

Whatever the specific reasons, educational institutions have placed increasing stress on the needs of the learner as an individual, and except for a brief reaction against the "progressiveness" of the early and mid-thirties, schools have become more and more child-centered and discovery-oriented. Students have asked for and have been given, particularly at senior levels, a voice not only in choos-ing courses but also in the formation of the curriculum. Although perhaps desirable in theory, the new approaches have placed heavy demands upon the time, patience, and ingenuity of teachers. As a result, the profession has pressed not only for higher salaries, but also for lower teacher-pupil ratios. Education costs have risen sig-nificantly and public opposition to increased educational spending has hardened considerably. All the while, children's response to schooling has, if anything, deteriorated—a deterioration McLuhan has attributed to the low participation permitted the participation-oriented TV child.

It is obvious that a different approach to the problems facing the schools is needed. We can no longer afford to use ETV as just an aid to enrich the curriculum managed by the ordinary class-room teacher. Yet, its original application as a substitute to solve teacher shortages following World War II was singularly unsuc-cessful. It is with this background in mind that educators and spe-cialists in educational communications are coming together to analyze the learning experience. If a way can be found to involve the learner himself in the planning process, the prospects for success will be considerably brightened.

There is no question, however, that television is a superb instru-ment for the attainment of motivational goals in education and that the acquisition of certain skills and knowledge can be equally if not better facilitated through its use. Dieuzeide in an interesting switch of the traditional view regarding the teacher and television commented, "We should ask ourselves what it is that the teacher should do that the machine cannot do."[35] This is a challenging question for it implies a new approach to curriculum planning and an equally new approach to the design of educational communications materials. It recognizes the essential human qualities of the teacher and suggests that it is only through the analysis of learning objectives that the respective roles of teachers, schools, and media can be designed.

To determine which educational concerns can best be developed by television will require not only research, but also specially designed learning systems. The experimental programs are found to be expensive. First-year costs of "Sesame Street," designed for a predominately out-of-school audience, have been reported at about $8 million. The Open University systems in Britain required annual expenditures of £7 to 9 million. Neither of these involved any disruption of the conventional process, and any threats, imagined or real, to existing institutions were minimal.

Much more resistance can be expected, for example, to a proposal made to the O.E.C.A. to design a new environment-for-learning experience around an existing secondary school course in sociology. In effect, students would acquire knowledge about the content of the course through printed and televised materials made available to them in their own homes or libraries or resource centers and then meet periodically in small groups with teachers in schools or study centers to exchange and defend ideas. Not only would initial expenditures be high, but school schedules could be seriously disrupted. The only justification that would make sense to the responsible education officials would be not only the promise of eventual increases in the quality of learning, but also the expectation that such an approach, if successful, would reduce education costs through more effective use of facilities, personnel, and time. While there will be a natural reluctance to embark on such an ambitious experiment, it seems apparent that this step is inevitable if we are, in fact, going to utilize the medium of television in an appropriate manner. Fortunately, other changes in philosophy and

35. Henri Dieuzeide, "Educational Technology and Development of Education" (Paris: UNESCO, 1970), p. 10.

approach within school systems are taking place concurrently. These changes are directed toward ensuring a more flexible and open system and hence will enable experiments to be carried on with greater ease than in the traditional school.

Television has proved itself a powerful medium of communication which has had profound effects on all aspects of society. The early expectations that it would revolutionize educational practices have not been realized, and many critics still charge that it is an expensive frill that the schools can ill afford. In too many jurisdictions, however, little thought has been given to its special qualities as a medium. The tendency has been to use it either as a substitute for the teacher or as an audiovisual aid not significantly different from the documentary film. On the other hand, as increasing attention has been given to the nature of intelligence and the learning process itself, a number of educators have begun to experiment with learning systems designed to provide improved opportunities for students of all ages. In particular, preschool programs such as "Sesame Street" offer renewed hope for the disadvantaged child; projects such as TEVEC and the Open University provide new avenues to learning for adults, and various multimedia experiments supply stimulating experiences which challenge schools to find more effective methods for ensuring that pupils acquire deeper insights into traditional subject disciplines.

Television appears to be the single most important resource for dealing with contemporary concerns for open enrollment in classes, for nonsequential educational experiences, and for coping with the high costs of such programs. Despite some recent advances, little is known about television as an art form, about its language, and its capacity to communicate in other than the most conventional manner. The importance of television, both viewing and producing, in the intellectual development of children has yet to be confirmed. It is critically important for those responsible for educational television (and for organizations created to provide learning experiences using a variety of media) to incorporate research-oriented units into their structure. Only in this way will it be possible to ensure that adequate resources will be available for the continuing investigations which must be carried on if television is to become a significant part in the education of man.

CHAPTER XIV

Man and Computer: The Impact of Computer Technology on the Development of Psychological Processes

O. K. TIKHOMIROV

Computers are a manifestation of the scientific and technological revolution; their actual creation, utilization, and further development cause new theoretical and applied problems in psychology and in education.

Does the computer influence human psychological activity? If it does, what is the nature of its impact? Can this impact be exploited for educational purposes? To answer these questions one has first of all to analyze the interrelation of human activity and computer performance in solving one and the same problem: does computer performance duplicate human activity? An answer to this particular question provides the basis for analysis of the relation between man and computing machines. Our argument will be based primarily on a consideration of existing computers. As far as future computers are concerned, we shall confine ourselves to an evaluation of actual projects aimed at developing computer-functioning possibilities.

During recent years drawing an analogy between thought (and behavior of organisms in general) and principles of computer performance has been widespread. Special emphasis was placed on the so-called *heuristic programs* of Newell and Simon.[1] The term *heuristics*, while it denotes any principle or tool which contributes to reduction of average number of trials in problem-solving, reflects a certain stage in the development of task-programming

1. A. Newell and H. A. Simon, "GPS: A Problem That Stimulates Human Thought," in *Computers and Thought*, ed. E. A. Feigenbaum and J. Feldman (New York: McGraw-Hill Book Co., 1963).

theory. Heuristics are mechanisms which guide the search and make it selective. It is important to note that this meaning of the term does not correspond to the broader one ascribed to Papp.[2] The term was interpreted by him as "problem-solving skill" and had been used before the sciences of human thought were differentiated. The content of the term was rather indefinite and was considered to include methods of analysis and synthesis.

How does the human process of searching for solutions interrelate with that of the machine? Are search-guiding mechanisms (i.e., heuristics) adequate? Let us approach the problem by considering a concrete human activity, chess play, which has frequently served as an object for simulation in cybernetics. The actual level of computer play—in other words, the interrelation of the objective results of human thought and computer performance —is essential in comparing human thought with machine performance in this case. Despite the fact that at present the level of computer play is low in comparison to that of an expert, from a concrete psychological point of view man-machine chess games are of great interest.

These games, which have been held both in Moscow and in Cambridge, are interesting mainly because they provide an opportunity to clarify what actual activity components are reproduced in a computer chess game. They include not only elementary game rules and elementary tactics, but also a two-stage organization of machine-move succession; that is, some of the moves establish the precondition (for example, a sacrifice) for advantageous achievements and others realize the achievements.

The following is our general answer to the question, What is the interrelation between the objective results of human thought and the objective results of computer problem-solving? Some relatively elementary results are equally attainable by man and by machine. It is difficult to state the source or origin of such results; it is difficult to state whether they have been created by man or by computer. In any case, things re-created nowadays by computer represent only a minor part of the achievements shown by man in the specific activity of a chess game.

2. D. Poja, *Kak rešat'zaddaču* (Moskva: Učpedgiz, 1961). (*How to Solve a Problem* [Moscow: Učpedgiz, 1961])

However, even these few and limited facts (i.e., the computer's ability to solve problems which could be solved in the past only by man) drove some scientists to the conclusion that the computer program is nothing but a theory of human thought; that the computer's potential to re-create some function is the criterion of correctness or incorrectness of a psychological interpretation given to an activity; that a negative answer to the traditional question of whether a machine can think is nonscientific and dogmatic because comparison of man and machine behavior often gives identical results.

According to this approach, the impact of the computer on thinking activity is actually interpreted as implying the substitution or replacement of man by computer in every field of mental work. This is the theory of *substitution*. In order to provide the validation of this approach one should carry out detailed investigation of the heuristics guiding the search process when man and computer are set to solving equivalent problems.

Our laboratory carries out experimental psychological studies of chess games and chess problem-solving. The thinking-aloud method is being used in the study, as well as visual search registration (which has been shown to reflect essential links of problem-solving), tactile activity registration of blind chess players, and the registration of indices of emotional activation—GSR (galvanic skin response), pulse, expressive components of verbal reasoning.

Let us use results of these investigations to discuss the foregoing questions. Heuristics are used by both man and computer (in the case where the latter works according to a heuristic program). Heuristics as used by machines are usually described in the same way as in psychology. The terms used denote certain structural components of human activity; this fact fosters the illusion that the actual processes exercised by man and machine in problem-solving are the same. Actions which are "goal directed," that is, those that involve working back from the solution, heuristics of choice, functional heuristics or "means-end" analysis, and planning, are often regarded as heuristics in both man and machines.[3]

3. O. Tikhomirov, *Struktura myslitel'noj dejatel'nosti čeloveka* (Moskva: MGU, 1969). (*The Structure of Human Thought* [Moscow: Moscow State University, 1969])

Let us illustrate the comparison of man and machine heuristics with the example of means-end analysis. Does human activity contain means-end analysis that falls within the category of heuristics? Yes, it does. The problem is to bring into correspondence means-end analysis in machine performance with what is denoted by the same term in human activity.

Analysis of existing chess programs shows that the term *goal* denotes certain criteria for concrete actions included in the program. Each of the criteria includes a set of certain limited and strictly fixed attributes, the presence or absence of which determines if a criterion is applicable or inapplicable. The consecutive application of these criteria to the objectively possible actions in the next concrete situation allows for the acceptance or rejection of a given move either as a final move or as a move liable to further, more detailed examination.

Thus, *goal* in machine performance is a criterion of selection, and *means* is a concrete action based upon the attributes which are fixed in the criterion; *means-end analysis* here is an application of the criterion to some concrete action. Goals are fixed in the program, that is, they are given before the beginning of the game and are not altered during the game. Usually a program contains a number of selection criteria—in this case there is a fixed succession in the application of criteria, which have a fixed hierarchical interrelation or preferred order.

Experimental study has shown that means-end analysis in human thought is considerably different from the process given the same name in machine performance. The main difference lies in the fact that particular human actions and the selection criteria for judging them can be formed in a concrete situation. Subjects try to find a concrete action that serves as a means of gaining the goal by establishing various attitudes to the formal requirements (or search needs). Means-versus- end distinguishing is rather relative in human activity; at a certain stage of search, a concrete action may present a means of gaining the goal; at the next stage, the same action may perform the goal function. Therefore, we may say that means-into-goal transformation is one of the ways of goal formation. This kind of transformation makes human thought considerably different from machine performance, in which a sequence of "goals" is given by the program. A number of conditions have been found under which one starts forming goal activities in terms of the concrete situation (but this does not occur in every situation). We mean here, first of all, the failure of the actual situation to coincide with the predicted one. In those cases where "goal" appears as "given," it is possible to trace its formation process in previous situations, which consequently are combined, in some sense, into groups.

Therefore, concrete goal formation, the dynamic transformation of means into goals, and the search for concrete actions that are realized by the mechanism which creates these search needs represent specifically human aspects in the heuristics of means-end analysis. Sameness of man and machine heuristics is nothing but illusion. A more general conclusion is that search processes of human and computer problem-solving do not coincide in their organization.

When we regard planning as heuristics, the term *plan* is often understood as just a "group of subtasks" which appear as the result of some main task division and which provide for search reduction. This interpretation is far from adequate. It can surely be applied to an already formed plan of human activity, but, as has been shown by many studies, human activity plans in game situations include the prediction of the opponent's actions and the distinguishing of the most probable conditions for further activity on the basis of that prediction. Sense of actions which do not coincide completely with their objective meaning has been shown to be an experimentally controlled variable which determines the direction and level of detail of complex search activity. The plan structure depends on values the subject gives to the success or failure of his prediction.

Action choice carried out according to the maximum reduced scheme (like the matching of a situational alteration to the formation of the hypothesis or final decision) is the result of an extensive preceding analysis which includes both the prediction of the opponent's intentions and one's own action planning. Thus the group-of-subtasks interpretation of the term does not cover the mechanisms which govern human search activity; nor do we see in machine performance any processes analogous to the development of a sense of the elements in a situation—sense of the situation in general or of earlier attempts at solution. Hence it appears that the direction and the level of detail of search at different stages of problem-solving is determined by means of correlating these different sense formations.

The study of emotions is expected to provide further improvement in machine programs. For this reason recent computer literature has given much attention to that phenomenon.

Our studies show clear and steady correlation of emotional activation with the processes of goal formation, that is, of finding some applicable problem-solving (or decision) principles and of finding that the objectively true decision is indeed the "correct" one. Emotional states appearing in the course of problem-solving are an essential part of the problem-solving process. The activation regularly precedes the naming of a decision principle; it prepares the individual for finding still unknown decision principles or final solutions.

The finding of a decision principle may be divided into two stages: (a) picking out some approximate field in which the principle might be found, and (b) finding the principle as such. Emotional activation is related to the first, preparatory stage, which we may say determines the subjective value of that or another search direction.

The appearance of emotional activation (which is frequently experienced by the subject as "assurance") changes the whole of the problem-solving process: the field of further search is strictly bounded, activity becomes directed, capacity for search activity is reduced, and some emotionally colored points are picked out, to which (although not in the initial situation) the search is sent back in the case of failure. The very character of search activity is altered by this restriction on the process of sense formation. These facts give us reason to conclude that emotions perform a certain regulating function, namely, the function of heuristics.

Empirically, a shift in the search zones that accompany emotional activation has been found, as well as a shift in their hierarchic relations—the activity in one zone serves as preparation for the appearance of another. Parallel to the use of emotional experience in hypothesis formation we could observe the transformation of emotionless action-naming into emotional naming of the same action in later trials. A kind of cumulation of earlier emotional coloring of the action takes place. Alteration of the subjective values or the significance of one and the same action may occur; this results in alteration of emotional coloring. Thus the emotional state is the expression of alteration in emotional coloring. At the same time, subjective values often emerge as the reflection of objective values of elements. Apparently it is this very reflection that makes complex problem-solving possible for the subject.

We have pointed out some conditions related to the process of hypothesis origin and formation: it has been shown that emotional activation is a necessary precondition for productive intellectual activity. Emotions do not just "replace" data search but adjust the search process itself; emotions turn out to be not "generators" of random decisions but factors in search trends.

Acknowledged limitations of the so-called heuristic programs have made computer scientists interested in human emotions, and this has resulted in attempts to reproduce emotional functions in machine performance. However, analysis of existing work shows that emotional functions have been oversimplified: sometimes they are related only to reproduction processes and to starting mechanisms instead of to creative activity as such, and sometimes they are interpreted as a "program of reactions."

Emotion-to-program analogy (even if we take a program of some special kind) distracts from the dynamic and variable nature of emotions that has been clearly shown by our studies. Being dynamic regulators of decision search in problem-solving, emotional states are not given a priori but emerge and change in the course of concrete problem-solving. In a certain sense emotional states are alternatives to "programs." When a decision is found, the direction is clear and the goal may be gained without periods of emotional activation. The scale of human emotional values, which alters during problem-solving, is directly opposite in nature to the fixed evaluation function of the machine program. Put another way, the results of experimental psychological investigations show that human heuristics do not coincide with present heuristics programs. The majority of mechanisms controlling human search are not represented in present computer programs at all. In the cases where computer heuristics somehow resemble human ones, they appear to be much simplified and are not in fact comparable. Computer reproduction of some of the results of human activity is carried out without reproduction of the process, that is, without reproduction of the human heuristics.

On the basis of the foregoing facts, we may conclude that *the replacement conception does not reflect the actual relations of human thought and computer performance, nor does it express the impact of the second on the development of the first.*

It seems hardly possible to answer the question about the impact of the computer on the development of mental processes without discussing the problem of human thought as such—without pointing out the essential stages of its development before computers emerged. We must understand these stages in order to attack the problem of computerization from the broader perspective of history and the development of human culture.

We consider it necessary to contrast *psychological* theory of thought with *informational* theory of thought. This latter theory (which has at present much popularity) is often interpreted as a description of thought at the elementary level of information-processing. It deals mainly with the nonquantitative characteristics of informational processes.

The main point of the informational theory of thought is that every behavior, including thought, can and must be studied in relative independence from its neurophysiological or biochemical or any other such basis. Even though mind and computer are structurally different, there is a certain resemblance in their functioning. The fact that *complex thought processes consist of elementary symbol manipulation processes* is considered the main reason for interpreting human thought in terms of information-processing. These elementary processes may be described in general terms as follows: read the symbol, write the symbol, copy the symbol, wipe the symbol off, and match two symbols. Here also is included the ability to "take different activity lines according to the results of matching." If the two symbols compared turn out to be identical, information-processing takes one line of activity: performs one complex of elementary processes. If they are different, the system performs another complex of processes. The only problem, then, is to develop a regulated succession of these basic processes. It is quite easy to see that "elementary informational processes" or "elementary processes of symbol manipulation" are nothing but elementary operations of computer performance. Thus, the demand to study thought at the level of "elementary informational processes" actually implies the demand to interpret human thought exclusively in terms of the system of concepts attached to computer performance.

The main working notions of this conception are information, information-processing, and information model. Information is essentially a system of signs or symbols. Information-processing is sign transformation of different kinds in accordance with given rules (or "symbol manipulation," according to some authors). The information model (or "problem-model space") is data about the task that are either represented or being generated in the storage of the problem-solving system. The idea that the essence of human thought and behavior is a complicated but limited and sufficiently definite complex of information-processing rules has become a kind of a bias or statute which is used even to differentiate "scientific" from "nonscientific" (i.e., mysticism-assuming) approaches.

If we admit the informational theory of thought (with its analogy to computer performance), then there is only one answer to the question about computer impact on human thought: increasing capacity and speed of computer processing adds to human information-processing abilities. This point of view may be called a *theory of addition*. Within the bounds of the theory, the correlation of man and computer (if they are combined in one system) is the correlation of two parts belonging to one whole—information-processing. Working together with the computer, man performs much more information-processing. He does the job more quickly and possibly with greater accuracy. That is to say, a purely quantitative increase in his abilities takes place. Bearing in mind that the theory of addition is directly connected with the informational theory of thought, it is, we think, critical to examine its acceptability.

What does thought mean psychologically? Does the information approach to human thought attach to or disengage itself from the most essential characteristics of human thought? We find answers to these questions not through making models of the psychological process, but through the theoretical and experimental analysis of thought processes and problem-solving that has accumulated in psychology.

From the psychological point of view, thought often appears as problem-solving activity and under certain conditions is usually interpreted as goal-directed. However, the goal is not always "given" from the very beginning. Even if it is formulated from outside (as happens in school tasks), it often appears to be rather indefinite, allowing multiple interpretations. Even the conditions in which the goal is set are not always "definite"; goals need to be extracted from the general environment of activity on the basis of some orientation, on the basis of an analysis of the environment. A problem, as a specific goal under a definite set of conditions, needs to be formulated. Thus, thought is not just problem-solving: it is problem-forming activity as well. Therefore, goal formation or goal supposition is the most important manifestation of thought activity.

What do the problem conditions include? What does man deal with while solving a problem? It may be real objects or things, or even people, in the case of the so-called visual-practical thought; it may be signs, in the case of verbal thought.

Does it suffice to say that human verbal thought manipulates signs in order to express essential aspects of thought? No, it does not. Following Vigotsky, in the sign, we mark out the sign proper, the attachment to an object, and the meaning. When manipulating signs, man manipulates meanings, and through them, in the end, he manipulates objects of the real world. Thus, if we interpret human thought only as manipulation of signs, we shall be distracted from the principal psychological content of thought, which is related to man's concrete activity. This omission is characteristic of the informational theory of thought.

Real objects or named objects that are included in problem conditions possess additional characteristics, such as value. Actions with these objects (i.e., situation transformation) possess various values as well. There exist different sources of value formation for one and the same situational element, as well as different interrelations among these values. Furthermore, problem conditions may include a certain scheme or plan that is expressed in one form or another.

Reflection of reality given in the formal presentation of a problem, such as a graph or a list, must be abstracted from objective or contextual characteristics of the problem, such as the form used by the problem composer, the values of the various elements involved, and the ways of transforming the situation. These characteristics, which are neglected in the formal presentation, not only exist in reality but also determine, sometimes from the outset, the course of problem-solving. Psychological and informational characteristics of the problem do not coincide. When generated by man, the result of mental activity not only leads to the goal but also often appears in the form of signs (naming a plan of action that leads to goal achievement, for example), which possess some definite meaning and some value.

The achievement of this or that result through thinking usually comes about after a search process that is greatly expanded in time and detail. Sometimes this process may be objectively studied only with the help of special methods, since it may be concealed from the subject.

Control over the search process is being realized with the help of special functional mechanisms, or heuristics. These heuristics are of two kinds: (a) those possessed by the subject before solving a concrete problem, and (b) those formulated by the subject in the course of problem-solving. Mental problem-solving appears to be a process of complex functional development.

The significance of complex problem-solving manifests itself not only in heuristic formation, but also in the change (sometimes repeated) of heuristics as well. This change of heuristics (or overcoming of some "cognitive-psychological barrier") presents one of the characteristic features of the most complex forms of creative thought. The search for a solution is based upon the perception of the situation, but that is altered by the very search activities carried on in the course of problem-solving. The structure of problems influence man not only through their absolute characteristics, but also through their relative ones. Take, for example, the relative value assigned to elements of a given concrete situation. The lack of correspondence between absolute and relative values stands out most clearly in game problems, and the more experienced the man is in a given field, the greater the discrepancy we observe.

A situation is always perceived by man as being of some definite type, that is, as taking some place in his formulated schemes and plans (and in conflict situations, projected in schemes and plans for another as well) and in his scale of emotional values, which essentially influence the character of further transformations. Task-condition transformations as such (in the form either of concrete attempts at a solution or of reexaminations of the situation) are characterized not only by their consequences but also by their assimilation in some definite scheme (not necessarily being verbalized); the matching of scheme and results determines the direction of further analysis.

In the course of the solution of one particular problem, these sense formations may be repeatedly changed. It is their complex correlation that determines the dynamics of the whole process. Briefly, then, the characteristics of problem-solving that mark off the psychological theory of thought are:

1. The solver's operational sense of a situation, his sense of concrete attempts at solution, his sense of their reexamination, and his sense of the individual elements of the situation in contrast to their objective meaning
2. The processes by which the sense of the elements of a situation and of the situation as a whole arise and develop at different stages
3. The processes of interaction of predicative phenomena (e.g., interaction of the nonverbalized sense of an element with the sense of reexamination) and the role of predicative phenomena in the organization and scope of the search activity
4. The processes by which search needs arise and are satisfied, changes in the subjective values attached to the elements of a situation and in actions as reflected by change in their emotional coloring (with constant motivation), the role of a changing scale of subjective values in the organization of a search, the formation and organization of the personal meaning of the problem situation and the role of that meaning in the organization of problem-solving activity

In human problem-solving, such real, functional formations as one's operational and personal sense and the subjective values of objects are not just added in a neutral way to informational characteristics of the material; they take a direct part in the control of the processes of problem-solving activity. This qualitative peculiarity is the principal fact distinguishing human mental activity from the processes of information-processing by machine. Whether this is taken into account differentiates psychological and informational theories of thought.

Thus, in discussing the problem of computer impact on the development of human mental activity, we cannot accept the theory of addition because the informational theory of thought upon which it is based does not correspond to the actual structure of human mental activity. However, without having formulated our attitude toward current work on artificial intelligence we cannot attack the problem.

Works on cybernetics usually deal not only with highly specialized problems but with problems of general theoretical value as well. The analysis of approaches to these problems actually aims not only at evaluating the ideological problem created by the computer scientists but also at predicting some further developments in certain branches of cybernetics.

Cybernetics, which Wiener took to be the theory of control and communications in organisms and machines,[4] was divided in the course of its development into a number of branches, including self-organizing systems, simulation of human thought, and creation of artificial intelligence. The last of these approaches has become the leading one in a number of countries, mainly because the development of the first branch raised considerable difficulties, while the second and the third have been largely combined into one.

Artificial intelligence is not just a belles lettres theme but a genuinely scientific trend that demands the most careful analysis from the psychological point of view. Let us dwell on the interpretation of that approach taken by Minsky,[5] McCarthy,[6] Simons,[7] and those who share their view. Artificial intelligence, according to a widespread definition, is the science that develops methods

4. N. Wiener, *Cybernetics* (Cambridge, Mass.: M.I.T. Press, 1948).

5. M. Minsky, ed., *Semantic Information Processing* (Cambridge, Mass.: M.I.T. Press, 1968).

6. J. McCarthy, "Progress with Common Sense," in ibid.

7. H. A. Simon, *The Science of the Artificial* (Cambridge, Mass.: M.I.T. Press, 1969).

whereby machines can solve problems that, when being solved by man, demand mind. At the same time, the term *artificial intelligence* is frequently used to denote the functional possibilities of computers; we say that the machine is intelligent if it solves human problems. At first, problem-programming for computers developed on the basis of a differentiation or even an opposition between two scientific approaches: artificial intelligence and the simulation of psychological processes. As it emerged, this differentiation was as follows: (a) "artificial intelligence" meant writing programs for computers that disregarded the way these problems would be solved by man, (b) "the simulation of psychological processes" meant writing programs that attempted to reproduce human ways of problem-solving. The border line between these two views has now practically disappeared. Representatives of the second approach appear to be discontented with the term *to simulate*, which has the connotation of imitation or the purely external similarity of the two objects, a description that does not reflect the aspirations of the authors. On the other hand, adherents of the first approach emphasize the fact that in order to make machine programs more sophisticated, it is necessary to take into account human experience in problem-solving. Therefore, artificial intelligence has gained in popularity and is now being interpreted differently than it was five or ten years ago. *A closer tie between machine ways of problem-solving and human ways is the strategic goal of work concerning artificial intelligence.* It is always stated as well that there already exist no limitations on the bringing together of program possibilities and human abilities.

The strategy thus formulated touches upon a number of philosophical and methodological problems. It is considered, for example, that the positive answer to the traditional question of whether a machine can think is necessarily connected with materialism.[8] A similar idea has been expressed by Neisser: the man-computer analogy is based, in his mind, on materialism.[9]

It is sometimes claimed that the creation of artificial intelligence

8. H. Borko, *Computer Application in the Behavioral Sciences* (New York: Prentice-Hall, 1962).

9. U. Neisser, *Cognitive Psychology* (New York: Appleton-Century-Crofts, 1966).

would reduce man's self-esteem and destroy his illusion of human uniqueness. Some believe that its influence on man's view of himself would be even greater than, say, the influence exerted by his learning of the minor rank that our planet has in the galaxy or of the laws of our evolution from more primitive forms of life. Some other authors write about "a blow to egocentric conceptions of man." At the same time, peculiar prognoses of our future machine "outlook" have begun to be offered. According to Minsky, when intelligent machines have been built, we should not be surprised at their being analogous to man in having false beliefs concerning psychics, matter, conscience, free will, and so on.

Sometimes it is supposed that the creation of intelligent machines will throw light upon the everlasting problems of soul and body interrelation and the role man plays in the universe as well. According to Slagle,[10] the existence of intelligent machines would support the "mechanistic conception"—for man is nothing but a machine—and the answer to the psychophysiological problem would supposedly be that only the body really exists.

Conceptions of mechanistic materialism are sometimes intentionally formulated as the methodological basis of works on artificial intelligence. Such a basis fails to recognize the distinction between mechanistic and dialectical materialism: the latter is ignored and the former is given out as the only form of materialism.

When analyzing a program in artificial intelligence, it is necessary to drop the content that has been assigned to such traditional philosophical and psychological categories as "thought," "knowledge," "problem-solving." Usually, in the context of works in artificial thought these terms are interpreted in the following way:

1. Knowledge is the ability to answer questions; hence, if a system answers a question, this is an indicator of its possessing "knowledge." This is the so-called empirical definition of knowledge.
2. Introspection during the process of self-education is man's way of "exposing" knowledge that he needs for solving some given class of problems.
3. Human thought is the process of algorithm realization.

10. J. R. Slagle, *Artificial Intelligence* (New York: McGraw-Hill Book Co., 1971).

4. The source of information about human thought with which computer performance is being matched often appears to be just a dictionary of definitions.

Each of the four statements may be directly applied to the science of human thought (to psychology, namely) and therefore it is reasonable to consider the extent to which scientists in the field of artificial intelligence take into account concrete scientific investigations. In order to evaluate the recent trend, this consideration seems necessary.

That knowledge divides into formal knowledge and meaningful knowledge has been known in psychology for a long time. For example, a good teacher will hardly be pleased with his pupil's progress if the pupil mechanically reproduces what he has been taught. True knowledge is the reflection of some essential relations of objects in the outer world. It is a system of generalizations. When man learns mechanically, he sets relations between the question and the answer only. But when man learns meaningfully, he incorporates the data he acquires into a system based on man's past experience. Therefore, the formalism inherent in the scientific approach to artificial intelligence has only surface similarity to human knowledge.

Further, the method of uncovering the processes involved in man's problem-solving (by observing one's self-education) put forward by adherents of this scientific trend appears to be extremely limited. Any action of man consists of verbalized and nonverbalized components, including generalizations. It has been known for a long time that human interaction with objects results in practical generalizations that, though not fully verbalized, are active participants in the process of solving a certain class of problems. Without taking this into account, the answer to the question, What knowledge is used in human solving of a certain class of problems? is far from adequate.

The organization of search processes in human problem-solving, as our studies have shown, is much more complex than the analogous computer processes. These studies show mainly that the actual process of the human search for a solution to a problem is not simply an algorithm realization. At its best, it appears as a product of human creative activity. Here the comparison of human thought and computer performance based on defining dictionaries seems rather archaic.

It is interesting to note some of the ways in which the comparison of thought and computer performance is criticized. Slagle[11] refutes only one thesis—that the computer can do only what it has been told to do, while people can do more than that. According to him, in a sense, man also can do only what he has been told to do. Man's heredity supposedly tells him what to do and determines the ways in which he gains experience from the environment. On this basis the author comes to the conclusion that the arguments which claim that computers are in principle less intelligent than man are false. However, Slagle's counterargument is not completely convincing. It is widely known that even at the level of so-called instinctive animal behavior, hereditary factors do not predetermine a fixed orientation to the environment.

The arguments in defense of "machine thinking" are based on the following line of reasoning: if a technical system solves the same problems solved by man and man uses thought in problem-solving, the technical system too possesses thought. However, the scientific concept of "thought" fixes not only the resultative but also the functional aspect of man's cognitive activity. Hence, a technical system could be said to possess thought only if it solved the same problems solved by man and did so in exactly the same way. There is no more reason to call the problem-solving of a machine "thought" than there is to call an airplane a bird.

The above analysis shows that the initial preconditions and assumptions of the scientific trend named *artificial intelligence* are built upon oversimplified conceptions of thought, knowledge, and their interrelation. This gives us ground to be doubtful about the possibility of achieving the final goal—creating an automatic machine that reproduces all human thinking abilities. Evaluation from this perspective leads us to conclude that there is no reason to think that the methodology of dialectical materialism, which is the development of a system of sciences, must give up its place to a mechanistic picture of the world.

How, then, shall we treat "artificial intelligence"? As a scien-

11. Ibid.

tific trend, artificial intelligence is a theory of programming problems for computers. The term in itself is nothing but a metaphor recalling the romanticism of (for example) Minsky and Papert's book *Perceptrons*.[12]

At present, psychological science has rather original ways of development. We shall consider how the problem we are interested in may be put into the framework of the tradition of Soviet psychology. The historical approach to the development of human mental processes has become the traditional in that psychology. A great part in the assertion of that principle was played by Vigotsky.[13]

In analyzing practical activity, psychologists point out that tools are an essential component of human activity; they are the components that create the qualitative peculiarity of human as compared to animal behavior. Tools are not just added to human activity; they transform it. For example, in one of the simplest actions carried out with the help of a tool—chopping wood—not only is it impossible to achieve the result without using an axe, the axe by itself cannot give that result. The expression *tool action* gets its meaning from that synthesis of motor activity with man-made device. The tool, in itself, appears as an extra human organ created by man. Human activity mediation is clearly seen in analyses of practical activity of humans.

One of the central ideas of Vigotsky was that the psychological processes of man change in the same way as do the processes of his practical activity; that is, they are mediated. The role of that mediated link is played by signs (language, mathematical signs, mnemonical tools), of which the most significant is language.

Using auxiliary tools and signs (for example, notching a tree as a reminder), man alters external things; but afterwards these alterations influence his internal psychological processes. By changing the environment, man can regulate his own behavior and control his own psychological processes. Mediated mental processes

12. M. Minsky and S. Papert, *Perceptrons* (Cambridge, Mass.: M.I.T. Press, 1969).

13. A. Vigotsky, *Razvitie vysšix psixičeskix funkcij* (Moskva: Izdatel'stvo APN, RSFSR, 1958). (*The Development of Higher Psychic Functions* [Moscow: APN Publishers, RSFSR, 1958])

initially appear as functions shared by two men, then they become an internal psychological function of a single man. The development of mediated psychological processes means at the same time the development of new forms of functioning. The appearance of logical thought as opposed to situational thought, mediate memorizing as opposed to immediate memorizing, voluntary attention as opposed to involuntary attention—all characterize the development of higher psychological functions.

Written language is the artificial memory of mankind; it is the reason for the immense advantage of human over animal memory. With the help of speech, man gains thought because the very formulation of speech contains logical processing of perceived impressions.

When we consider the computer's place in this traditional historical approach to human activity, we see that computers together with other machines present to us organs of mind created by human hands. Just as the development of gasoline engines provided a tool for human physical activity, so the development of the computer provided a tool for human mental activity. Mental activity preserves its mediate structure, but the tool itself is new. So, the question of computer impact on the development of human mental processes must be formulated as follows. What is the difference between mediating mental processes by computer and mediating them by signs? Does this new look contribute new properties to the *structure* of mental processes? Is it possible to distinguish this new stage in the development of higher mental processes in humans?

The transformation of the traditional forms of human activity and the appearance of new ones are a result of using computers; this is one aspect of the scientific-technical revolution. Bibliographical references, bank calculations, machine design, complex management systems, medical diagnoses, air traffic control, scientific investigation, education, creative work—all these are built on a new basis. Proposals for "man-computer" systems are being put forward and actually developed. The creation of such systems touches upon many scientific problems in such areas as the technical, the logico-mathematical, the sociological, and the psychological. We shall dwell in detail on two of these.

First, what peculiar human activity occurs in man-computer systems and not in other forms of activity? Generally speaking, a man-computer system cannot function without at least one man and one program in computer storage. Consequently, the question deals with the forms of human activity that cannot be accomplished without the participation of a computer. (This does not include the cases of computer use where human participation is limited to maintaining the mechanical functioning of the computer itself.)

One characteristic of human activity in the systems under consideration is the immediate reception of information as to the consequence of action. The principle of reafferentation, the mechanisms for sensory corrections which provide the necessary means for the adjustment of activity, was described in the early works of Anohin[14] and Bernstein.[15] Later, the mechanism of feedback as a universal principle of control was formulated in the works of Wiener.[16] The transformation of this adjustment in human mental activity is just one expression of the impact of the computer. These transformations of the feedback mechanism make the process more controlled.

Let us compare the processes of controlling human activity by means of ordinary speech commands and by means of the computer. Evidently there is some resemblance between the two, yet there exists an essential difference: the "immediateness" of computer operations may be exploited for certain purposes or adjusted to conditions. Moreover, the computer may produce and evaluate data about intermediate results of human activity which are not perceived by an outside observer (for example, the change of states displayed by EEG).

Thus, as far as the problem of regulation is concerned, not only is the computer a new tool for mediation of human activity,

14. P. Anohin, "Novye dannye ob osobennostjax afferentnogo apparata uslovnogo refleksa," *Voprosy psixologii,* 1955, No. 6. ("New Data on the Peculiarities of the Afferent Apparatus of the Conditioned Reflex," *Questions of Psychology,* 1955, No. 6.)

15. N. Bernstein, *Očerki po fiziologii dviženij i fiziologii aktivnosti* (Moskva: "Medicina," 1966). (*Essays on the Physiology of Movement and the Physiology of Activity* [Moscow: "Medicine," 1966]).

16. Wiener, op. cit.

but the very transformation of this activity is different from that which occurs with the application of the tools analyzed by Vigotsky.

Secondly, what specific mental activities are altered when a man works in a man-computer system? As a rule, this alteration is described as a release from technical and executive components of mental activity. What specifically does the executive component of mental activity involve from a psychological point of view?

Let us consider in detail a man's performance in a man-computer system. Suppose that the computer has the algorithm for solving two-move chess problems. The man wants to know the solution of a given problem (say, the list of successive actions that will lead inevitably to checkmate). It is sufficient to set a certain goal for the computer and to write the description of the requirements of the concrete problem in order to obtain the necessary plan of action. Is it possible, then, to say that the computer has saved the man from knowing or working through the algorithm? The answer is negative, for the man may still not know the algorithm. A more appropriate psychological interpretation here would be that the man has been saved from the necessity of problem-solving. As special psychological experiments have shown, the solution of a chess problem is often a really creative activity that includes those complex mechanisms of search that we have described above. Consequently, in this example, the man is saved not from the mechanical but from the creative work. In a more general way we may state that the computer may save man from the creative forms of search when he deals with problems where he does not know the algorithm or where the algorithm is so complicated that its application appears to be impossible.

At first it seems that our conclusions prove the replacement theory: creative activity is replaced by computer performance. In fact, this replacement may occur, but only in a definite class of problems—namely, those problems for which an algorithm has actually been written. As far as this class of problems is concerned, the structures of the mental processes of the user and the programmer will be essentially different.

An algorithm is a completely formalized procedure for solving some definite class of problems. In using the computer to answer his question, a man might not know the concrete algorithm required for the solution of the problem. But if the problem can be solved by computer, the algorithm will have been written by some one else and preserved in computer storage. Therefore, user activity is mediated by this formalized procedure and has the character of external mediate activity.

At first this activity looks absolutely analogous to that occurring when any message is given to another. For example, instead of solving a problem on my own, I ask my fellow worker to do it. The difference is seen when we notice that he solves the problem without an algorithm. So we are dealing here just with the case of handing the problem over from one man to another, not with any transformation into some formalized process. We may conclude, therefore, that a new form of human activity is involved when a person's problem-solving activity is mediated by a heuristic procedure which he has not assimilated.

Now we shall consider psychological peculiarities of programmer activity. The programmer develops an algorithm for solving the chess problem and puts it into computer storage. He is then given a new two-move task. The solution of such a task may be achieved in two possible ways: without using the algorithm and the computer, in which case it would not be a completely formalized process, or by using the computer, in which case it would be a completely formalized procedure, specially written for the computer beforehand. Is it possible to say that man would save himself from a completely formalized process in the first case? No, because the programmer when working without the computer does not solve problems in a purely formal way. A programmer will use, in the second case, formalized processes which save him and other people from the necessity of solving a definite class of problems. The machine may then carry out "executive" or "mechanical" work by transforming into mechanical work non-mechanical work that has been carried out beforehand.

The statement that computerization saves man from technical and execution components is true only in the cases where the sophistication and division of labor of the activity has led to its being formalized—that is, when it is composed of monotonous, reiterative actions performed according to strictly fixed rules. The activity is never purely mechanical (in the full sense of that word), but comprehension of the activity may cease to be essential to its performance. In that case, computerization may mean the assignment to the machine of what was earlier formalized in the human activity.

However, cases where the computer on its own solves some problems which in any case, no matter how, have already been solved by man are of less interest than cases where man and computer jointly solve a problem—a relationship that may be called *complementary*. Man-computer systems and not artificial intelligence represent, from our point of view, the future of computerization.

Creative thought is impossible without the use of available knowledge, which is kept in what Vigotsky has called the "artificial memory of mankind" (manuals, encyclopedias, journals, books, and the like. At the same time, data accumulation leads to data search in the artificial memory, and this search presents a separate problem sometimes so complex that it distracts from the solution of the main problem. This search activity often appears absolutely impossible; some people say that it is easier to make a discovery than to check whether it has already been made by others. Computer usage for storing the information is a new stage in the development of the "artificial memory of mankind," and the effective use of the computer for data search in that storage transforms human activity. It makes it possible to concentrate on creative problem-solving itself. Other systems for linking the resources of the human mind with those of the computing machine are developing on several fronts—computer graphics, transformation of images, continuous data transformations, and other forms of exploring events.

Thus the computer, far from replacing human thought, serves as a new tool for mental activity and thereby transforms thought. *This transformation theory is compatible with the actual facts of historical development first traced by Vigotsky and stands in marked contrast to the theories of replacement and addition.* The computer is a tool for amplifying rather than replacing human mental processes. Finally, let us consider the impact of the computer on the ontogenesis of mental development and on education.

The theory of human development has come to focus upon the acquisition of social experience as the most fundamental aspect of human development. Formal education, of course, carries major responsibility for this acquisition. The development of the computer changes both the form of storing social experience (in "electronic brains" rather than in libraries) and the acquisition of that social experience. Teacher-pupil relations are coming to be mediated by computer; the computer modifies both the content that is acquired and the process by which it is acquired. Hence we may state that a new stage of ontogenetical development of thought is being formed as the result of computerization.

Psychological investigations show that complex problem-solving in man involves the use of many optional stages and mechanisms. With functional development, different options are exercised at different points in the solution of a problem; for example, intuitive guesses precede strict logical verification of these guesses, and the feeling of solution-nearness precedes the logical analysis of the solution. How does the use of the computer change this process of functional development? By transforming the formalized activity components of problem-solving into the form of an external mediate link, the computer leaves man free to concentrate on the intuitive thought components. It leaves man free to do what he does uniquely and best, namely, to generate the hypotheses. Without the computer, the complexity of the job of verifying a hypothesis often suppresses the intuitive thought components; with the computer's aid, we are free to make a guess and the computer assumes the responsibility for formally checking it out. The functions of man and computer are complementary. Hence, we may conclude that there are functional changes in man's mental processes when he solves problems with the aid of the computer.

In developing his theory of higher psychological functions, Vigotsky drew a parallel between historical and ontogenetic development. A child acquires signs that have been developed by mankind. In both cases the external mediation was interpreted by Vigotsky as a stage on the way to internal mediation of activity; speech, once internalized, is the basis of discursive thought, involuntary memory, rehearsal of attention, and so on.

The new type of mediation provided by computers is not a

new stage on the way to internal mediation. It is a further development of external mediation or (according to Vigotsky) of interpsychological functions that influence the development of the intrapsychological functions. Here we face another peculiarity of these new forms of mediate mental activity.

In the preceding pages we mainly dwelt on the way in which the computer alters the structure of human mental activity, but data memorizing, storing, and search (reproduction) are being transformed as well. As man-computer communication, especially the creating of languages similar to natural ones, is a new form of communication, we may state that communication is being altered. Beyond that, computer usage mediates human relations. It makes it possible for human activity to acquire a more perfect structure. But these possibilities will be realized only by observing technical, psychological, and social criteria as well. Technical criteria mean that the computer must be sufficiently developed; psychological criteria mean that it must be adjusted to human activity and that man must adjust to computer conditions of work; social criteria mean what the goals of computer usage are in a given social system. The social basis for computer usage requires a concern for the increased creative aspects of the labor of men.

But, as the preceding pages should make clear, our understanding of the relationship of man to computer is just beginning. More serious is the fact that the disciplines of neither psychology nor pedagogy are presently organized to study the psychological aspects of computerization. None of the relevant branches of psychology—labor psychology, engineering psychology, human factors psychology, social psychology, and pedagogic psychology—has direct concern with the array of problems and possibilities created by the invention of computers and their use in man-machine systems. These issues have their closest ties with the concerns of general psychology for activity, communication, thought processes, and personality. At the same time, one need only look through a course in psychology to realize that man-computer problems have not yet found their place in general psychology. The investigation of the transformations produced in man's mental, mnemonic, communicative, and creative activity as a result of computer usage, as well as the optimization of these transformations, must constitute, from our point of view, the content of a psychological branch of science. We propose to term this branch the *psychology of computerization.*

The elaboration of this new branch of psychological science would provide for a more complete exploration of the possibilities in both the functioning and development of human mental activity that are obtainable with computers and would also lessen the possible incidental negative consequences of technical progress in that field.

CHAPTER XV

What Is Learned and How It Is Taught: The Interaction between Media, Message, Task, and Learner

GAVRIEL SALOMON

Media Functions in Education: Three Basic Distinctions

The conceptions of the roles media play in education have been extremely diverse. With changes have come many shifts of emphasis —from evaluative work to basic research, from audiovisual development to system development, and from uncritical adoption to deep disappointment. Since the AV movement has yielded little in terms of consistent findings or conceptual guidelines, more attention has been given recently to instructional technology in either one of two senses. It has become either the application of tools or, in the direction led by Lumsdaine,[1] the application of learning theory— the alleged underlying basic science of education—to the problems of media.

The Commission on Instructional Technology[2] sensed this distinction between the machinery and the total-system approach. Yet it preferred to view this area from the more traditional point of view—that is, from that emphasizing the tools of communication.

Media seem to have been lost between the two technologies, unless they are viewed as nothing more than technical gadgets. Utilization and development have of course continued with ever increasing momentum, but attempts at conceptualizing the major

1. A. A. Lumsdaine, "Educational Technology, Programmed Learning, and Instructional Science," in *Theories of Learning and Instruction*, Sixty-third Yearbook of the National Society for the Study of Education, Part I, pp. 371-401 (Chicago: University of Chicago Press, 1964).

2. *To Improve Learning.* A Report to the President and the Congress of the United States by the Commission on Instructional Technology (Washington: Government Printing Office, 1970).

components of the field have gradually disappeared. It is, as Allen[3] remarks, that "the objective observer can't help but feel that media research today is in a state of suspension, ready to move but lacking an activator" (p. 11).

The major question is that of media functions in education. To say that media can motivate, reinforce, inform, guide, assist in recall, enhance retention, and the like, is to say only that media can be used in instruction. But we are left with the open question of what media characteristics facilitate instruction on what kinds of tasks and for what types of learners. Aside from a large number of educated guesses and fragmentary experiments, little has been done to guide us in answering that question. The purpose of the present chapter is to provide the outlines of a conceptual framework for examining both the existing and the developing functions of media in educational contexts.

The use of media in education involves several factors. A particular symbol system is selected to transmit to learners particular messages with certain characteristics so that some kinds of educational objectives will be attained. The factors that thus underlie the use of media are *the symbol system, the message, the learner,* and *the educational task.* Even when there is no particular educational goal in the producer's mind, the educator may ask if the film, model, or TV show has any educational value. It does when the message is appropriate to the learner's requirements and those requirements are relevant to some educational goal.

The four factors interact with each other in rather complex ways. However, before attempting to describe these interactions, three basic distinctions need to be made. These distinctions should aid us in identifying the educationally most significant features of media.

MEDIA, TECHNOLOGY, AND SYMBOL SYSTEMS

Media differ in terms of technologies of transmission and in terms of available symbol systems. The development of a new technology leads, after a certain period of time, to the development of a new symbol system which, partly at least, is uniquely suited to

3. W. H. Allen, "Instructional Media Research: Past, Present, and Future," *AV Communication Review* 19 (1971): 5-18.

that technology. With the development of the new symbol system, added information potentialities also open up. The new symbol system, or language, offers a range of new expressive and communicational possibilities. Moreover, as E. Carpenter[4] maintains, the symbol system affects to a large extent the nature of the messages and their meanings. Thus, for example, the meaning of a film will undergo changes when its plot is verbally told.

In instruction, when it comes to the question of "what difference makes a difference," the answer appears to be that when they can be differentiated, *the symbol systems sampled from, rather than the technologies of transmission, are critical.* When East Africans were found to misidentify objects in drawing or to misinfer depth from them,[5] they were facing difficulties with the symbolic *codes*, not with the technologies. Whether the drawings were printed or projected seemed immaterial. Similarly, the mental processes or skills required in map-reading are determined by the grammatical and syntactical nature of the medium rather than by the technical way it is presented.[6]

Unfortunately, the typical experiment in which the effectiveness of one medium is compared with that of another is in actuality a study of different technologies. When live teaching is compared with televised instruction, the real difference between the two is one of transmission rather than anything inherent in any particular symbol system. Thus, it is not surprising that the vast majority of such studies reveal no significant differences. Similarly, one is led to distinguish between cases of media communication in which a specific "language" of a medium is deliberately called upon to serve unique instructional functions and cases in which only the technology of transmission is used. Hence the difference between a *television* lesson and a *televised* one. It is the symbol system rather than the technology of transmission that is crucial for instruction.

4. E. Carpenter, "The New Languages," in *Explorations in Communication,* ed. E. Carpenter and M. McLuhan (Boston: Beacon Press, 1960).

5. E. French, "A Background of Nonreference," *Makerere Journal* 5 (1961): 3-10.

6. G. Salomon, "Cultural Differences in Reading and Understanding Geographic Maps" (Paper presented at Annual Meeting of the American Educational Research Association, Chicago, 1968).

INHERENT AND IMPOSED ATTRIBUTES OF MEDIA

The inherent characteristics of a medium are its defining attributes. These are the symbols and combinations thereof selected from the symbol system that was developed in connection with the specific technology of transmission. On the other hand, situations of exposure (even if typically associated with the medium as in the case of the darkened theater hall), teachers' instructions, or even the didactic structure of the presentation, are *imposed* attributes.[7] They are imposed simply because one could easily remove them, apply them differently, or apply them to another medium. They are *at best* correlates of the medium. Thus, for instance, when C. R. Carpenter[8] studied the use of programmed instruction via TV transmission, no inherent characteristic of TV was dealt with. Programming a lesson is unrelated to the question of media; it can be done through any given medium.

This is not to say that imposed attributes are unimportant. The claim is made, however, that little knowledge about the utility, let alone the unique potentiality, of media is gained by dealing with imposed factors. Take, for instance, the question of the learner's active participation in an instructional session, a question that has kept many a researcher busy for a long time. Asking whether learning from a film is facilitated by asking the learners questions while they are viewing the film is to deal with a problem unrelated to *film*. It would be quite surprising if active responses to questions built into the film did *not* result in better learning. There is no reason to hypothesize that the body of knowledge relating active participation and learning should suddenly be suspended because film is involved.

It is, therefore, important to distinguish between the inherent attributes of a medium, particularly its symbol systems, and the imposed ones, among which we find situational and instructional variables. It is the former that may entail the greatest promise for instruction.

7. C. Pryluck, "Structural Analysis of Motion Pictures as a Symbol System," *AV Communication Review* 16 (1968): 372-402.

8. C. R. Carpenter, "Adopting New Educational Media for Effective Learning of Students," in *Instructional Technology*, ed. F. G. Knirk and J. W. Childs (New York: Holt, Rinehart & Winston, 1968).

EFFECTS AND EFFECTIVENESS

A caricature, as McLuhan[9] suggests, makes one fill in the necessary missing information. A wide screen, according to Perrin,[10] makes one feel involved in the presented events. A series of non-redundant visual elements put side by side or quickly interchanged arouses processes of comparison, as Gropper[11] argues, and a well-edited film calls for processes of mental fusion of single elements.[12] All these are real or alleged *effects* in the sense that certain psychological processes and states are affected by the modes of presentation.

For researchers in either psychology or mass communication, discovering the effects may be the end of the trip. Thus, Berlyne[13] focused on the psychological effects of complex, ambiguous, and incongruous stimuli, and Feshbach and Singer[14] concentrated their efforts on the study of the cathartic effects of TV programs showing aggression. For education, however, there is an added criterion. Education is a purposeful undertaking in which means are selected to serve particular ends. The psychological effects of a mode of presentation must, therefore, be considered in terms of the contribution they make to definite educational objectives. The same effect may be of value in one case but not in another. Thus, while *effect* is related to the interaction between mode of communication and the person communicated to, its *effectiveness* depends on the desired goal and outcome.

An important implication of this distinction is that the search for one universal instructional medium or mode of presentation is

9. M. McLuhan, *Understanding Media: The Extension of Man* (New York: McGraw-Hill Book Co., 1965).

10. D. G. Perrin, "A Theory of Multiple-Image Communication," *AV Communication Review* 17 (1969): 368-82.

11. G. L. Gropper, "The Design of Stimulus Materials in Response-oriented Programs," *AV Communication Review* 18 (1970): 129-60.

12. G. Mialaret, *The Psychology of the Use of Audio-Visual Aids in Primary Education* (London: George Harrap & Co., 1966).

13. D. E. Berlyne, *Structure and Direction in Thinking* (New York: John Wiley & Sons, 1965).

14. S. L. Feshbach and R. D. Singer, *Television and Aggression* (San Francisco: Jossey-Bass, 1971).

based on invalid assumptions. Another implication is that the distinction between instructional media and mass media rests on shaky ground. Only after one has learned about the psychological effects of unique, inherent attributes of media qua media can one ask about their utility for instruction. Thus, no purpose is served by forming a general class under the label of "instructional media." It is only when the question of instructional utility of particular media effects is raised that instructional issues become relevant. Our concern is therefore with the effects of specific *media characteristics* on specific individuals and with the functions they accomplish, given particular instructional tasks.

The Interaction between Media, Messages, Tasks, and Learners

EFFECTS OF MEDIA ATTRIBUTES

The preceding section suggested that elements of a medium's symbol system (its inherent attributes) have particular psychological effects. These, in turn, may or may not be functional in a given educational setting, depending on its psychological requirements. This line of thought calls for some elaboration.

Rothkopf[15] suggested the term *mathemagenic responses* to represent covert mediating activities that make a nominal stimulus into an effective one as well as determine what is learned from a given instructional document. These covert responses augment the effective stimulus by responses that are evoked by it. They include covert activities such as internal labeling, internal rehearsal, comparison, analysis, calculation, selection, and the like.

Media, in the sense of selections from qualitatively different symbol systems, can be assumed to function along the same lines: they activate different types of mediational activity or mental skills. It is these specific mediating activities that have to be affected if the intended information is to be extracted and processed. We may conceive of them as specific media-related skills. In their absence we speak of one's "illiteracy" in handling messages from a particular medium.

15. E. Z. Rothkopf, "The Concept of Mathemagenic Activities," *Review of Educational Research* 40 (1970): 325-36.

Olson[16] provides a more detailed description of "media" effects, which may be useful here. For him, a medium is a range of *performatory activities* such as drawing, speaking, counting, and the like. Performatory acts in such media have their peculiar sets of alternatives that determine the kind of information that must be extracted from a stimulus presentation in order to yield a correct performance.

However, performatory activities include not only overt but also *covert* activities such as differentiating, comparing, contrasting, visualizing, hypothesis-generating, and the like. These covert mediational activities or, more appropriately, mental skills are differentially affected by the inherent attributes of media. The information that is extracted and processed, then, is a function of the perceived or inferred alternatives encountered in carrying out that activity.

The differential effects of words, pictures, and words plus pictures in recognition tasks exemplify this line of reasoning. Jenkins, Neale, and Deno[17] and others have shown repeatedly that recognition is superior when presentation and testing are done via pictures, as compared to other media. Apparently, a picture, which employs a very dense symbol system (see chaper 2), arouses more activity for the selection of cues, which are subsequently transformed, at least by adults, into one or more internal verbal descriptions. A word, when presented, allows a far more restricted selection, while setting off, in many cases, a chain of private image-associations. The information extracted from pictures is consequently different from that extracted from words. No wonder, therefore, that in such studies, recognition of a picture, when the original presentation is a word, is inferior.

Similar differences of effect occur as a result of varying the spatial arrangements of visual presentation. Putting two visual displays side by side tends to activate comparison and discrimination. The information picked up in such a case is quite different from that gathered when the visuals are presented successively.

In conclusion, it is possible to postulate that different modes of

16. D. Olson, *Cognitive Development: The Child's Acquisition of Diagonality* (New York: Academic Press, 1970).

17. J. R. Jenkins, D. C. Neale, and S. L. Deno, "Differential Memory for Picture and Word Stimuli," *Journal of Educational Psychology* 58 (1967): 303-7.

information extraction and processing are activated to the extent that different media "code" information in different ways. Where critical information is presented via symbolic features unique to a medium, unique information is extracted and hence unique cognitive effects may be expected.[18]

This latter generalization needs, however, to be qualified. Inherent symbolic media attributes vary as to the generality of their effects. Some appear, as a rule, whenever a particular medium is involved (e.g., movement in film, or linearity in language), while others—which are more complex—are employed on rare occasions only (e.g., specific relations between sound and vision in films). This, then, ought to lead to some taxonomy of media attributes which is paralleled by a hierarchy of effects on cognition. Possibly, one will find, at the top of the taxonomy, overriding media attributes unrelated to content. Their cognitive effects are quite universal, given a particular culture. They could be taken as the most fundamental categories of the major symbol systems (see chapters 2 and 3), such as prearranged objects and events, iconic systems, analogue symbolic systems (e.g., movement in ballet), and digital symbolic systems (e.g., language, and number systems). Further down on the taxonomy one would place basic coding elements, such as dimensionality, iconicity, movement, simultaneity, and the like.[19] Below them we might find features of the "secondary coding system,"[20] such as ways of editing and juxtaposing, sequencing, and so on. Then, still further below, explicitness of information, complexity, redundancy, and ambiguity would be found. Note, however, that as one moves down from the top of the taxonomy, more specific attributes are found. Notice, too, that the more specific the attributes, the more specific the cognitive effects are assumed to be. Thus, as Snow[21] suggests, the hierarcy of human abilities could be paralleled by one of media attributes.

18. C. Pryluck and R. B. Snow, "Toward a Psycholinguistics of Cinema," *AV Communication Review* 15 (1967): 54-75.

19. G. M. Torkelson, "Educational Media," in *What Research Says to the Teacher*, no. 14, pp. 1-33 (Washington: Association of Classroom Teachers of the National Education Association, 1968).

20. Pryluck, op. cit.

21. R. E. Snow, "Research on Media and Aptitudes," in G. Salomon and R. E. Snow, eds., "Commentaries on Research in Instructional Media," *Viewpoints* 46 (1970): 63-91.

MESSAGES: THE EXTRACTION OF INFORMATION

The mental skills brought to bear upon a presentation, as we have indicated, guide and shape the extraction of information from the presentation. But it should be added that this is in actuality a circular process. Information that is extracted has a feedback effect on the mental activities: gaps detected in the information, incongruities, or emotion-arousing components set off another chain of cognitions. This circular process may cease when the learner feels that he has obtained enough information for his purposes. As these purposes vary with age, children of different ages show different degrees of inquiry when given Piagetian tasks of conservation. The younger children detect fewer gaps in the information and thus search for fewer additional cues.

This leads us to the question of *how much information can be extracted from a message.* Information is "that which enables us to make a selection from a set of alternatives or narrow the range of possibilities about which we are ignorant."[22] Thus, as Olson[23] points out, an utterance (and, for that matter, any act of communication) "partitions a set of alternatives . . . it specifies different aspects or distinguishing features of the perceived referent." In this respect the symbol system of language carries with it more information than, say, pictures. The same is true when a map is compared with an aerial photo. With both language and maps more accurate selections can be made between alternatives than with pictures and aerial photos.

However, when it comes to the *number of issues* about which information can be extracted, language and maps are at a relative disadvantage. There are more issues—i.e., unrelated elements—that can be dealt with in a painting or a photo than in a verbal statement. The painting is far more ambiguous than a verbal statement, in the sense that the painting leaves us with many more alternatives, or uncertainty. It offers us a wider choice of elements from which we can extract at least some information. It provides us with more opportunity for inquiry.

One implication that emerges from these differences is that since

22. D. MacKay, *Information, Mechanism and Meaning* (Cambridge, Mass.: M.I.T. Press, 1969).

23. D. Olson, "Language and Thought: Aspects of a Cognitive Theory of Semantics," *Psychological Review* 77 (1970): 257-73.

no inquiry can take place without a state of uncertainty, all media are not equally appropriate for this kind of goal. The visual-pictorial media serve this function far better than the verbal ones. On the other hand, for purposes of conveying large quantities of information, the verbal medium is far more appropriate. Another implication is that "a picture is worth a thousand words" only when these have been uttered before the picture is seen. If "advance organizers"[24] aid in learning written material, they are even more important when preceding visual communication, given that the goal is exclusively that of conveying large amounts of information.

Second comes the question of differences between media in terms of the qualitative meanings extracted from their messages. It may be claimed that any type of information can be conveyed (and thus extracted) by any medium. But there are at least two issues involved.

Representation of critical features. A symbol system associated with a particular technology of transmission will be better suited to convey a particular domain of ideas and events than other domains, although symbol systems overlap to some extent. Why is that? The answer is that the better a symbol system conveys the *critical features* of an idea or event, the more appropriate it is. But critical features of an event change, depending (in an educational setting at least) on the goal, that is, on the new differentiations the learner is expected to learn. Thus, for example, if the simultaneous operation of valves in an engine is taken as the critical feature, language would not be the appropriate medium to convey that sort of information. Moreover, if the knowledge to be extracted is supposed to be a mental representation of a simultaneously occurring set of events, a lineal message would require additional reencoding on the learner's part. Similarly, if the learner is expected to extract from the message information about the interrelations between two entities, a set of pictures would necessitate additional covert processes in which we may not be interested.

The question thus hinges on the explicitness of the presentation of the critical features relative to the knowledge or skill we wish to develop in a learner. It is possible to give a verbal description of a landscape. How many additional steps of reencoding and trans-

24. D. P. Ausubel, *Educational Psychology: A Cognitive View* (Toronto: Holt, Rinehart & Winston of Canada, 1970).

forming the message would the learner have to apply before the desired outcome has been attained? A map "skips" many of these steps, but it represents the critical features more explicitly by means of spatial relations than temporally organized sentences could.[25] We are led to conclude that the qualitative "fitness" of a medium to convey specific information is not entirely an attribute of the medium but depends both on the nature of the educational task and on the receiver's skills and knowledge as well.

This implies that certain domains of events and ideas cannot be conveyed in the same way to all groups of learners. For instance, small children fail to extract the critical information from a verbal description of a territory. They fail likewise when confronted with a map. While they could learn something about a territory from visiting it, such a form of experience is necessarily restricted. The more abstract or relational knowledge of a domain is linked to the more abstract symbolic systems.

Symbol system's effect. The second issue involved in the question of qualitative content differences between media is closely related to the preceding one. When roughly the same idea is represented in two different symbol systems, is the *same* meaning obtained from the messages? There are no clear research findings on this point, although comparative work on words and pictures provides us with some leads.

From daily experience, one knows that it is virtually impossible to convey via words the information that can be conveyed by a painting. Similarly, it is rarely the case that a filmed novel conveys the same meaning as the written one (see chapter 3). What accounts for the differences are the mental processes or skills involved in the extraction of the information from the different symbol systems. When the same point or idea is conveyed through two media, the more different the media, the more different will be the obtained meanings.[26] Olson and Bruner (see chapter 6) show that even in the case where the contents of two different messages

25. I. H. Sigel, L. M. Anderson, and H. Shapiro, "Categorization Behavior of Lower and Middle-Class Negro Preschool Children: Differences in Dealing with Representation of Familiar Objects," *Journal of Negro Education* 35 (1966): 218-29.

26. See Richards, chap. 5. The example of the nonequivalence of a statement such as "A point is beneath a line" and (one possible) visual representation such as /. bears out this point.

are roughly synonymous, the skills assumed and/or developed in the two cases may be radically different.

A medium may be more appropriate for the transmission of certain information to a particular learner because it utilizes a symbol system that is isomorphic to the symbolic mode of that learner's thinking. Using another symbol system would require additional mental transformations to bring the information to the learner's preferred symbolic mode. While these operations would add to the difficulty of the task, these added transformations would lead to the extraction of other types of information. A case in point is when mathematical questions are stated in verbal form.

LEARNING TASKS

Let us now return to the utility or function of the information that is extracted. This, of course, depends on the nature of the learning task. Indeed, as mentioned earlier, not all cognitive or motivational effects are educational. While the effects may exist and lead the learner to extract some particular information, the task may require something else altogether.

Salomon and Sieber[27] have shown that a randomly spliced film leads students to generate many hypotheses about the meaning while limiting their memorization of content details. The converse is true when a well-structured film is shown. These results are to be explained by the facts (a) that a randomly spliced film arouses states of uncertainty which in turn lead the learner to extract information concerning possible interpretations of the film, and (b) when the film is well organized, it provides a structure for remembering the details. The educator's goals, then—making hypotheses versus remembering details—would determine the method to be used.

Another illustration of the interaction between media and tasks is seen in the debilitating effect of pictures on learning basic reading, as summarized by Samuels.[28] Obviously, pictures facilitate learning, in some cases, where a ready-made image is a necessary

27. G. Salomon and J. E. Sieber, "Relevant Subjective Response Uncertainty as a Function of Stimulus-Task Interaction," *American Educational Research Journal* 7 (1970): 337-50.

28. S. J. Samuels, "Effects of Pictures on Learning to Read, Comprehension and Attitudes," *Review of Educational Research* 40 (1970):397-408.

mediator of learning. But learning to read does not require such a medium. In fact, the picture serves too well; it allows the child to guess the word from the (familiar) picture without looking at the (new) letters at all.

The problem we are facing here is that superficial operational differences between tasks are not directly related to the more important underlying differences in mental activity of information extraction.[29] Take, for instance, the case of the "association." Contiguity, an externally manipulated condition, disguises a rather complex internal activity of relating, inferring, and comparing.[30] The task of forming an association is not to be equated with the final outcome, the association between two terms. Thus, it is necessary to distinguish between the observable nature of the learning task and the mental operations that underlie it. After all, it is those mediating operations that one wants to affect via the differential use of media; affecting them will lead to the desired learning outcome.

The question is one of matching the medium with the requirements of the task. More specifically, it is the match between the mental activity of information extraction and processing, on the one hand, and the nature of the requirements of the task on the other. But since both the requirements of task and the effects of media differ, *there uan be no best technique, method, or medium for the attainment of a general educational objective.* The search for the "best" mode of presentation for such general goals is therefore bound to fail, as indeed it has failed in the past.

LEARNERS

To complicate matters further, the nature of learners needs also to be considered. If media in instruction are considered in terms of the mediating activities of information extraction and information-processing, then the question of learners' abilities, attitudes, patterns of motivation, and the like, becomes of utmost importance. There are major theoretical reasons, accompanied by a rapidly

29. A. W. Melton, "The Taxonomy of Human Learning: Overview," in *Categories of Human Learning*, ed. A. W. Melton (New York: Academic Press, 1964).

30. S. E. Asch, "A Reformulation of the Problem of Associations," *American Psychologist* 24 (1969): 92-102.

growing body of empirical evidence, to indicate that no media variable, minute or gross as it may be, affects all groups of learners in one and the same way. Hence, one type of "treatment" cannot achieve a common instructional outcome. Consider two reasons for this: learners have different levels of competence and they have different goals.

All of the messages conveyed by any medium are coded in terms of symbolic systems, which children must master before they can extract those messages. Given the necessary levels of skills or competence, different media features, as it has been argued, will tend to produce particular effects. But, obviously, all children do not have the same skills. Cross-cultural research shows large group differences in this respect. For instance, children of Moslem background, who have little experience with pictorial and schematic media, do not possess the necessary skills with which to extract the critical information from maps.[31] Similar differences were found among subcultures in the U.S.[32] But even within a given cultural group there are large individual differences that make one learner profit more than another from a specific mode of presentation.

Intelligence, as Olson[33] maintains, is skill in a medium. Being skillful or intelligent in this sense means having available the process required for the proper handling of the symbol system represented by any medium. Obviously, individuals differ from each other with respect to their mastery of media-relevant skills, and they differ therefore in the extent to which they extract the "intended" messages.

What learner aptitudes are relevant? Traditionally, programmed instruction, computer-based instruction, and instructional technology considered *rate of learning* as the most relevant aptitude variable. General ability was also considered an important dimension by many. However, if recourse is to be made to specific media components, which are supposed to have specific effects on cognition, then specific aptitudes also need to be considered. These

31. Salomon, op. cit.

32. D. H. Feldman, "Map Understanding as a Possible Crystallizer of Cognitive Structures," *American Educational Research Journal* 8 (1971): 485-503.

33. Olson, "Language and Thought,"op. cit.

may differ from case to case, varying in nature and specificity in accordance with the nature of the media effects and task requirements. A high level of reading ability is required to learn history from a textbook. Similarly, when a program like "Sesame Street" is considered, quite a number of different aptitudes—ranging from the most general to the most specific—could interact with the presentation. Thus, aptitudes, such as perseverance and impulsivity, and, particularly, initial general knowledge may determine the amount learned from the program as a whole. However, when more specific media variables are considered, such as "zooming-in" on details and relating them to contexts or connecting discrete temporal segments, far more detailed aptitudes become relevant. It has been shown[34] that students with low ability of this kind fail to infer the appropriate relations between part and whole. Thus, a "zoom-in" may not activate in them the processes that would ensure the extraction of the information required by the producer's objectives.

Further, cognitive styles tend to interact with media. Koran, Snow, and McDonald[35] found that less field-dependent students benefited more from a likelike visual presentation than did the more field-dependent ones when learning to ask analytic questions. The latter benefited more from written material. Apparently field-dependent learners are less skillful in decomposing a complex situation and reencoding it, a skill required for processing complex visual displays. The written presentation provides a ready-made verbal coding system that compensates for the learners' difficulty in doing it on their own. Given such an effect, a written presentation accomplishes for them a "supplanting" function—it supplies them with operations they cannot perform for themselves.

Generally speaking, a low degree of literacy in any medium severely restricts the information a subject can extract from any symbolic display. However, individuals differ not only in terms of literacy in media, but also in terms of concerns and interests and

34. G. Salomon et al., *Educational Effects of "Sesame Street" on Israeli Children*. Final Report, Jerusalem, 1972.

35. M. Koran, R. E. Snow, and F. J. McDonald, "Teacher Aptitude and Observational Learning of a Teaching Skill," *Journal of Educational Psychology* 62 (1971): 219-28.

intentions at any given moment. What one sees depends upon what one is looking for or upon one's perception of the task. For this reason, it becomes difficult to predict accurately what information a particular learner will extract from a display in a realistic learning situation.

As the preceding discussion implies, the domain of media in education is a rather complex one, entailing four major factors that interact with each other. Having described some of these interactions, it now becomes possible to suggest a general conceptual structure that can be brought to bear upon questions of media utilization in instruction. This structure can be described in terms of a general hypothesis as follows:

The attainment of an educational objective by a specific learner is facilitated to the extent that the medium or one of its inherent characteristics (a) affects particular mental activities, (b) leads to the extraction of the critical information, (c) matches the requirements of the educational task, and (d) matches the characteristics of the learner. As we have maintained, it is in the overlapping area of the four factors that instructional effectiveness of media is maximized; the broader the overlap, the more a specific medium "makes a difference."

What Is Learned and How It Is Taught

One implication that emerges from our hypothesis is that there is no direct and simple correspondence between that which is taught and that which is learned. It is therefore erroneous to assume that the use of some particular medium will necessarily solve all instructional problems. When media are used because of their unique symbolic qualities, a whole new array of complexities emerges, but with them come aspects of a solution.

How, then, is what is learned related to how it is taught? An answer depends upon recalling the distinction between *knowledge* and *skills* as described and analyzed by Salomon[36] and by Olson and Bruner (see chapter 6). What is learned from any educational

36. G. Salomon, "Can We Affect Cognitive Skills through Visual Media? Explication of a Hypothesis and Initial Findings," *AV Communication Review* 20 (1972): 401-23.

experience must be considered in terms of both of these categories. Although any use of instructional media in principle serves these goals simultaneously, let us consider the major effects of *informing* and *developing mental skills* in turn.

Transmitting function of the medium. The first kind of media usage and the most common one associated with the mass media emphasizes their *transmission* quality. It is obvious that certain media bridge distances over space by their distribution or dispersion qualities and, over time, by their record-keeping qualities. Very often these functions of media are taken as the prime justification for their use in instruction. The "front-row view" approach assigns media only a transmitting function. The medium involved is taken to be but an envelope and as such it is not expected to have an influence on the transmitted messages. That is, the unique symbol system associated with the chosen technology is largely overlooked. Hence the classroom-like appearance of most current instructional materials that are transmitted and diffused on a wide scale.

The most common function served by this use of media is the acquisition of knowledge. Toward this end, the selection of symbolic elements to carry the messages is restricted to the most common ones so that as many learners as possible will be able to handle the messages. No particularly well-developed media-specific skills are called upon. Such restrictions on the use of a medium, while facilitating the acquisition of knowledge, limit greatly what can be accomplished in terms of improved skills in the use of that medium. One must reconsider, for example, the assumption underlying the "translation" of the classics into simple English. Do the classics serve to convey critical information (that is, knowledge) or to develop one's use of the language?

Exploiting unique aspects of symbol systems. The second use of a medium deliberately exploits the unique aspects of the symbol system available to it but, again, for the purpose of increasing the learner's knowledge. The assertion is that some kinds of information can be conveyed more appropriately through one medium than through another. Again, one must consider not only if that particular aspect of a medium is appropriate to that particular type of information, but also if that information is relevant to the task at hand and the particular style and competencies of the learner.

The selection of a certain code permits the representation of a specific phenomenon which it can uniquely code. The history of technology is a record of the achievement of these effects. In instructional contexts one may capitalize upon these unique capabilities. Thus, when one is to teach about the relationship between waterways and urban development in Europe, maps and graphs will probably be used because this is the unique content-knowledge they specify. Similarly, when one is to teach how an internal combustion engine works, a slow-motion film may be used because it will focus on the simultaneously occurring operations; film is used here because its coding system is better suited to handle this type of information.

Media, particularly the visual media, are often claimed to serve the function of "concretization." That is, one assumes that the learner needs to evoke mental processes with which he will generate an image of an event or a process to complement verbal information that would otherwise remain abstract. Without this image, the learner's comprehension of the material is limited. A presentation through media of such an image is thus expected to assist the learner by formulating a spatial or visual representation that he is incapable of generating on his own.

An example of this process would be where students learn about the relations among various governmental functions and are then given a flow chart to describe their relations in summary form. The spatial-visual representation of such interrelations is generally found to facilitate the learning of the material. But while the provision of a ready-made chart exploits some aspects of spatial organization, it does little or nothing to encourage the *development* of the student's own ability to cast his experience into spatial terms.

The use of any particular symbolic code for instructional purposes makes some demands on the learners, namely, that they understand the code being employed. Different learners have different degrees of competence, and instruction must thus be tailored to their competencies. This, however, is only one side of the consideration in the use of a medium for instructional purposes. *It justifies the use on the basis of what message is presented, what knowledge is conveyed—not on the basis of how that content information is extracted, what skills are involved in processing that information.*

The second consideration, developing mental skills, justifies the use of the medium not only because it is better suited to represent the desired information, but also because mastery of the code itself has important consequences: *the use of a particular medium for learning is justified because its code is isomorphic in some way to the learner's symbolic mode of thinking.* The ways in which information-processing skills are affected and the quality of the processes so affected must be a primary determinant in the choice of a medium for any particular learning task.

The media can affect mental processes or skills in at least three ways. First, they arouse certain general attentional processes. Without the arousal of attention and some mathemagenic responses, no effective communication can take place at all. As mentioned earlier, particular modes of presentation arouse typical mental processes such as comparison, analysis, relating, and the like. The activation of such processes facilitates the extraction of the intended messages. It is well known that the viewing of a film or still pictures can serve an important role in creating interest in and concern for almost any educational topic.

A second aspect of skill development via media is that of elaborating the symbolic system utilized by the medium in order to permit better use of or more critical appreciation of the medium. In other words, the medium means teaching the symbolic code as it is, so that one will be better able to read a map, extract meaning from a film, or apply caution in interpreting statistics. High school and university courses on film have this as their primary objective. Wide reading combined with wide movie-watching is perhaps the most likely way to develop the broad range of skills termed *media literacy*. Possibly the only better way would be actually writing the books or making the films. The effects of the alternatives discussed above are not konwn, although Gardner, Perkins, and Howard (see chapter 2), Gross (chapter 3) and Parker (chapter 4) all emphasize the latter method.

The use of media for that purpose is based on the assumption that exposure familiarizes the learner with the coding system. However, the objective of improved "media literacy" entails more than meets the eye. If a medium has its relatively unique domain of information, then familiarization with its coding system makes that domain of information more accessible. Learning the "language" of ballet may, therefore, allow the learner to extract information that he could not have extracted before and that he could not have encountered before in a different medium. If "intelligence is a skill in a medium," as has been maintained, then learning a new coding system would involve an improved ability to use the medium whose code is being learned, as well as access to new domains of information. This is presumably what Olson and Bruner have in mind when they talk of media as exploratory devices (chapter 6).

The third and perhaps most fundamental way in which media affect information-processing skills is based in part on McLuhan's[37] description of how exposure to media affects perceptions, cognition, and the social order. Underlying the use of media in this capacity are three assumptions: (a) symbolic codes serve for both communicational and representational purposes; (b) external coding systems that serve for communication purposes can be incorporated or internalized to serve in a representational capacity; and (c) the codes, once internalized, can be schematized (i.e., detached from their original contexts) and thus serve as schemes of thought. Olson and Bruner[38] discuss this process of recoding one's experience in terms of a symbol system as "deuteropraxis."

Language acquisition and internalization serves as a prime example. The categories of ordinary language become the predominant categories for the assimilation of experience. Language be-

37. McLuhan, *Understanding Media,* op. cit.

38. See Olson and Bruner, chap. 6. See also J. S. Bruner, "The Course of Cognitive Growth," *American Psychologist* 19 (1964): 4-16; J. S. Bruner, R. R. Oliver, and P. M. Greenfield, *Studies in Cognitive Growth* (New York: John Wiley & Sons, 1966), p. 56.

comes the means of reworking that experience out of context. If that occurs for a spoken language, it may also occur for other media. However, while internalizing a natural language, the child is both an encoder and a decoder. Can the same be said about the "language" of film, for which most of us are only viewers, not producers? The prototype of this effect would be that after seeing slow-motion or time-lapse photography one could imagine these transformations. Some preliminary evidence suggests that internalization of media codes is possible, apparently through the mechanism of imitation and internal rehearsal. In a series of studies, specific mental operations or skills were made explicit through film on the assumption that viewers would internalize what they saw explicitly portrayed for them.[39]

More specifically, in a series of experiments it was found that learners became better visualizers of transformations in space, better analyzers of complex displays, and less field-dependent after they were exposed to films that overtly and explicitly specified the relevant operations. Thus, students who saw films that entailed zooming-in on details of paintings were found subsequently to be better able to attend to cues, more sensitive to complexities, and better able to absorb more information from one display. Similarly, students who saw films that repeatedly "spread out" in numerous ways the components of complex displays showed increasing "field independence" afterwards.

One interpretation is that these students *internalized* the operations shown to them, schematized them, and then applied them to entirely new instances. While there must be limits on the skills one can acquire from viewing—watching the Olympics will never make one a great athlete—these limits are not clear for mental skills. Although some of the "modeled" operations were not necessarily part of the filmic coding system, still the implication is that these skills thus portrayed can be, at least to some extent, internalized.

A large-scale investigation of the effects of "Sesame Street" on Israeli children[40] who had had little or no exposure to TV indicated that their viewing resulted in a marked improvement in their

39. Salomon, "Can We Affect Cognitive Skills," op. cit.

40. Salomon et al., op cit.

ability to extract the intended information. Indeed, when specific skills were called upon repeatedly, children who had already mastered some of the necessary medium-related skills showed improvements. The children showed continuous improvement in abilities that were modeled explicitly on the screen, such as viewing an object from different points of view, or relating a single element to a complex array. Not only mental skills changed as a result of explicit modeling. Perseverance, a trait more than a skill, changed as well; as children watched more of that mosaic-like, nonnarrative program, their tendency to persevere decreased.

The experimental assessment of the techniques that are most powerful in developing these skills is just beginning. One parameter that would seem to be important is the degree of explicitness with which particular operations or transformations are carried out by the instructional medium. Assume that S_1 is the initial state of knowledge, while S_n is the final state, the goal to be acquired, and that tr_{1-n} are the mental operations leading from S_1 to S_n. A fully explicit presentation would include all three components: $S_1 \rightarrow tr_{1-n} \rightarrow S_n$. Since it details the transformations or operations, it may indeed facilitate the mastery of the skills specified as the goal. However, because the actions are performed by the tutor, in whatever medium, the learner is not required to perform them for himself but to imitate and internalize them. No wonder, therefore, that only learners with initially poor mastery of the skill benefit from such a presentation.

Let us designate any presentation that *skips* the mediating step as *short-circuiting*. With short-circuiting, those learners who already possess a sufficient degree of competence will improve in their mastery of the skills as much as the less able students who are given the explicit presentation. Evidence for this contention comes from a recent series of studies [41] in which some learners were given either highly explicit or short-circuiting presentations of solid objects and layouts of them, i.e., with or without seeing the transformations linking the two. Children with higher visualizing ability were capable of visualizing the transformations with the result that they developed even higher-level skills because of seeing

41. Salomon, "Can We Affect Cognitive Skills," op. cit.

one short-circuiting film. Lower-ability children benefited likewise from the more explicit films.

On this basis, we may postulate that as the number of different communicational coding systems increases, the mental capacity increases. With the acquisition of each coding system, one becomes able to think in a new way, while also being better able to handle more domains of information.[42] These internalized skills serve as mental tools. Whether their development is permitted only by education in the arts—making, not observing—remains to be seen.

Summary

Media were conceived by us as composed of three major components: symbol systems, messages, and technologies of transmission. Of these, the symbol systems are most important in that they appear to have different effects on mediating activities of information extraction and processing. These processes affect also the acquisition of some particular content. Both the common and peculiar effects of media, however, have a relevance only when they map on to specific educational objectives to be attained by particular learners.

This four-way interaction between medium, message, task, and learner enables media to accomplish two superordinate functions: informing, and developing mental skills. These two basic functions may be further differentiated to indicate six types of uses in education:

1. Media as "indifferent" channels of transmitting already coded information
2. Media as coding systems whose use should have specific cognitive effects while the information is transmitted
3. Media used to short-circuit specific mental operations for better acquisition of information
4. Media used to arouse or activate specific mental operations deemed relevant to the task, which in turn can then be developed

42. W. D. Rohwer, Jr., "Children and Adolescents: Should We Teach Them or Let Them Learn?" (Invited address to the American Educational Research Association, Chicago, April, 1972).

5. Media to teach coding systems so that learners will be better able to extract information from media and to handle new domains of content

6. Media as sources of coding systems to be internalized and schematically used as mental tools

We must consider finally what kinds of objectives instructional media may be expected to serve for particular individuals. Educational decisions regarding instruction fall into the foregoing six categories. Even if the message is the *only* concern, the medium is highly relevant; educators would choose on the basis of quality, efficiency, cost, individual preference, and so on. However, such "content" goals are no longer central to most general education programs. If particular skills are the goals of education—literacy, visual imagination, etc.—educators have no alternative to employing the medium involving the particular symbolic system. These symbol systems may then be best acquired through the arts, giving students adequate opportunity for performance and exposure. Because such programs are expensive and depend so largely on expert tutoring, indirect means are being considered. ("The Electric Company" is an example.) Literacy, however, means skill in the arts of reading and writing. Print must then appear on the TV screen. It does, with startling if well-known effects. It seems likely that children who learn to read off the TV screen will also read off printed surfaces.

The large percentage of instruction, however, falls between those roles. Knowledge acquisition is the goal but the processing skills are highly valued as well. Hence, instructional decisions should be made within the parallel constraints—maximizing the knowledge acquired and the skills developed. Both of these must be tailored to the level of skill and knowledge of the individual learner.

TECHNOLOGY AND INSTITUTIONS: THE NATURE OF EDUCATION IN A CHANGING CULTURE

CHAPTER XVI

The Magic Lantern: Metaphor for Humanism

BRUCE R. JOYCE

A century devoted to the rationale of technique was also a century so irrational as to open in every mind the real possibility of global destruction. It was the first century in history which presented to sane and sober minds the fair chance that the century might not reach the end of its span. It was a world half convinced of the future death of our species, yet half aroused by the apocalyptic notion that an exceptional future still lay before us. So it was a century which moved with the most magnificent display of power into directions it could not comprehend. The itch was to accelerate—the metaphysical direction unknown.[1]

Mailer's statement captures the paradox of our times. Technology, including our media of communication, teases us with the possibility of creating new and more satisfying modes of life. It promises to stretch our possibilities for personal growth and common action. Concurrently, it frightens us by making us potentially more dangerous to one another in terms of both our possibilities for violence and our possibilities for controlling one another.

The potentials of technology for enhancing our society are also much in evidence. As we seek to solve the problems of our cities, computer simulation helps us apprehend complex processes and reduce them to manageable terms. Information storage and retrieval systems help us see past prejudice in the current facts of a situation. Human relations techniques help us work together more effectively and overcome our conflicts.

Paradoxically, as we develop technology and learn to use it to solve problems, we sometimes find that it exaggerates certain defects which have long been with us. The tendency to violence is one such example. In education, technology increases the potential

1. Norman Mailer, *Of a Fire on the Moon* (Boston: Little, Brown & Co., 1971), pp. 47-48.

for both good and bad schooling. Trivial content, taught in a more powerful way, becomes menacing. Unfair testing practices—standardized, automated, and administered too rationally—become nightmarish.

To find ways in which communication and technology can enhance society without exaggerating its defects is one of the tasks in education, as in other domains. The fact that we have developed powerful communications media and that these media have affected all aspects of our lives is not at issue. Nor at issue are the facts that we have only scratched the surface of applying communications media to education and that the power of the media makes the selection of content and process even more critical than previously. Until 1960 most educational technologists expended their energy trying to get teachers to employ some of the newer media, such as filmstrips and motion pictures, in the classroom to augment their instructional modes. Media technologists in education generally feel that these efforts were relatively unsuccessful. However, while attempts to increase the use of media in the classroom have not been very effective, experimenters have used media to create new modes of education. Experiments with open- and closed-circuit television, the creation of multimedia instructional systems in conventional and new curriculum areas, and the expansion of the concept of the library as a multimedia information storage and retrieval system have all created new educational possibilities.

Many of these newer modes have not yet touched the lives of the majority of children. One reason for this is that the school environment has not been conducive to many educational forms involving media. For example, most secondary schools are organized into sets of forty-five to fifty-minute time periods. Manufacturers of films and filmstrips, audio tapes, and of other devices have been required to tailor them to these time periods. Thus, motion pictures made for schools have generally been held to between ten and twenty minutes, which still barely leaves time to orient the students to the film, show it to them, and then have discussion afterwards. This type of constraint has greatly affected the kinds of topics that can be treated and has also resulted in considerable superficiality in the treatment of complex topics. Despite some successes, closed-circuit television broadcasts have been very difficult to use in the classroom. As Guba and Snyder [2] pointed out, the classroom use of broadcasts from the Impati system was very poor, chiefly because closed-circuit television paces instruction, requiring teacher and students to accept the flow of the broadcast medium. More exotic uses of media, in which constraints of time and organization are ignored, have been infrequent. Elaborate game-type simulation, for example, is barely used at all.

The thesis of this paper is that the application of communications media to education requires a general design, one that can both guide the development of alternative educational forms and create a congenial institutional framework in which these forms can be applied. *The structure of the school is in many senses the medium of instruction*—it facilitates certain kinds of learning modes and inhibits others. The home, for example, has turned out to be a most suitable place for broadcast television at the nursery school level, as exemplified by the programs from the Children's Television Workshop. Programs such as "Sesame Street" would not have anywhere near the effect they are having if there were not television sets in most homes and if the parents were not delighted to have the children occupied before them. The same programs have been used successfully in schools that have been willing to put aside the time and to manage the pupils while they watch television. While many schools have utilized the programs, many more have not.

Well-organized "dial access" educational systems, which permit students to select films, television tapes, audio tapes, and other mediated segments from a bank of options are a powerful support to student inquiry. Dial access, however, is not used unless the school is modified so that the students have time to use it and unless its use in the instructional framework is legitimized (as, for example, in the West Hartford High School and the Dallas Baptist College). Clearly, we cannot simply design applications of media to education—we have to design the institution as well.

A general design technology will have to accomplish three related tasks:

1. *A description of educational models.* A design technology needs

2. Egon G. Guba and Clinton A. Snyder, "Instructional Television and the Classroom Teacher," *AV Communication Review* 13 (Spring 1965): 5-26.

to specify the alternative educational models (educational purposes and processes) in which media might be applied. These models provide the designer with descriptions of the range of educational environments in which media might play a role.

2. *An array of media potential.* Concepts have to be developed about the media themselves and their potential functions in a variety of learning models. Such a conceptualization will provide a basis for the potential relation of media to various educational purposes and means; it gives the designers an array of media potential.

3. *The generation of institutional forms.* Finally, concepts are needed to generate the institutional forms in which educational models and media capability can be linked. These institutional forms become the elements of the school.

Thus we need a design that will permit us to characterize educational models, to apply media to these models, and to design institutional forms that will be conducive to the convergence of media and models. If this is done, it will be possible to apply the media to education in a vast variety of ways.

The Array of Education Models

Media relate to education productively by enhancing the learning process, by becoming part of an educational environment which is created to facilitate certain kinds of student growth. An educational model—a model of teaching or learning—is the specification of an educational environment which is likely to bring about pupil growth. Potential educational goals and processes exist in large numbers and types and rest on competing theses about what kinds of learning are most desirable and what are the best kinds of environments for achieving growth. The characterization of educational models which follows was developed by Weil[3] from earlier work by Joyce and Weil.[4] Models of learning may be divided into four families, each of which is appropriate to some distinctive educational goal.

3. Marsha Weil, unpublished paper, 1972.

4. Bruce Joyce and Marsha Weil, *Models in Teaching* (Englewood Cliffs: Prentice-Hall, 1972).

PERSONALISTS

The family of "personalists" focuses primarily on the individual's construction of his own reality. Thus they emphasize the development of the individual and speculate on the environments which might affect his personality or his general ways of relating to the world. Therapists, especially, tend to share a concern with the distinctive ways each person constructs his world; they see human nature in terms of the individual person. These models are directed towards helping the student develop in terms of his own style.

SYNERGISTS

The second family focuses on the processes by which groups and societies negotiate rules and construct social reality, sees education as a process of improving the society. Many developers of synergistic models have suggested an ideal model for society and procedures for creating an education which can help to bring that model into existence.

Others who emphasize social behavior have concentrated on interpersonal relations and the dynamics of improving them. The approaches to education in either case have a distinctly social character. These models are directed towards the development of human relations skills—the ability to work together for common social purposes.

INFORMATION-PROCESSING

The information-processing category is concerned with affecting the information-processing system of the student. It includes those procedures which are designed to increase general thinking capacity (as the capacity to think abstractly or to think inductively). It also includes those models which focus on ways of teaching students to process information about specific aspects of life. For example, many educational theorists believe that a major mission of education is to develop approaches to the teaching of the academic disciplines, so that the student learns to process information in the ways that the academic scholar processes it, thereby achieving the intellectual power of scholarship. These models, then, are directed to the development of new ways of thinking.

CYBERNETICS AND BEHAVIOR MODIFICATION

The fourth group focuses on the processes by which human behavior is shaped and reinforced by external factors. The major theorist leading this group is Skinner,[5] and their major efforts have been devoted to understanding how the shaping of human behavior occurs and how education can be built on an understanding of this process. These models are directed towards the shaping of both simple and complex modes of behavior.

In general, these families of models of teaching and learning represent the alternative design forms which can be employed to organize learning centers and to control the development of the informational support and instructional systems which comprise their major elements.

Models can be combined in many ways to generate educational programs. Some models within each family are appropriate for only a few educational goals whereas others are quite general in application. It is even possible to develop an entire school program around one broadly applicable model. (Summerhill exemplifies a personalist model.)[6] It seems more reasonable to build a school around a large variety of learning centers which employ combinations of models. (The Parkway School exemplifies a pluralistic model.)[7]

Very few present-day schools have been designed with self-conscious selection of specific models of learning. Attempts at design usually involve an intuitive collection of models. In practice, a "recitation" model has dominated most elementary and secondary schools throughout most of history.[8]

An important design question is how to shape educational pro-

5. B. F. Skinner, *Verbal Behavior* (New York: Appleton-Century-Crofts, 1957).

6. A. S. Neill, *Summerhill* (New York: Hart Publishing Co., 1960).

7. John Bremer and Michael von Moschzisker, *The School Without Walls* (New York: Holt, Rinehart & Winston, 1971).

8. James Hoetker and William P. Ahlbrand, Jr., "The Persistence of the Recitation," *American Educational Research Journal* 6 (1969): 145-68.

cesses to provide students with increasing control over their own behavior. This is less a question of how individual teachers should teach (which has been the traditional way of approaching the problem) than of "How can we design the entire education milieu so that the learner obtains increasing control over his behavior?"

One fundamental purpose is to help the learner develop a degree of competence with each of the models of learning, which he can then exercise for his own purposes. The really helpless learner is not simply one who is controlled from outside but one who is unable to control his behavior because his own personal repertory of models is limited. If a student has a degree of competence in these basic learning models, then he is in a position to construct his own education. If he does not have these, eventually he will fail to learn because he does not have the flexibility to solve a wide range of learning problems and create learning opportunities for himself. As the student comes into possession of a repertoire of models for learning he obtains greater control over his education, for he uses his skill to shape the environment which sustains him.

The Array of Media Support Possibilities

The communications media can be used to support models of learning in two basic but overlapping ways. Either they become a part of the environment into which the learner dips as he inquires or they are arranged to lead him through learning tasks. In some models of learning, the former type of support, both by teachers and media, is predominant, for the learner takes a great part of the responsibility for selecting and shaping his goals and learning processes. In other models, teachers play a greater role in shaping the environment. The distinction is one of use rather than the form of the media. A multimedia educational game, for example, can be part of a storehouse from which the learner or the teacher selects. The game and the storehouse are similar, the difference is one of use. It is no paradox that media designed on one model (as a political game built on cybernetic principles) can be used to support learning processes guided by another model (to simulate political processes during a group inquiry).

Our task in this section is to identify the characteristics or potentials of the array of media which can support learning across a variety of educational models. To build the array, we must consider media type, function, and style of use. The types of media we shall consider include: motion picture, television, still flat photographs, graphic representations, microfiche, transparencies, audio tapes, phonograph records, and the like.

There are vast differences among these media which have been considered in other chapters of this volume. Much research is needed to determine how they can be employed optionally for instructional purposes, for information transmission, and as artistic forms. However, it is clear at present that each of them has great versatility and together they represent a capability which has barely been tapped for public educational purposes. Roughly speaking, however, they can be employed in both the two general types of educational support systems—as storehouses of data and artistic products and as parts of instructional systems which themselves can be stored as an array of instructional possibilities.

FUNCTIONS OF MEDIA FORMS IN SUPPORT SYSTEMS

Consider three major functions of media in support systems that run across a variety of models for teaching and learning.

Task presentation. Any medium can be used to present learning tasks appropriate to a variety of learning models.

Feedback message. Almost any medium may be used to give feedback to the learner as to the consequences of his acts. The kind of feedback depends upon the symbol systems employed by the medium in question; hence, different kinds of tasks are more appropriate to some media than to others.

Substantive information source. Any medium can be employed to store information units, but the message is affected by the medium which is chosen.

STYLES OF ARRANGEMENT OF MEDIA

Three styles of arrangement of media which differ in degree of control by the learner can be identified. Various models of learning and various characteristics of students determine which of these different styles are suitable.

Random access. This concept represents pure storage, with

tasks, feedback messages, and information units being stored in categories from which they can be withdrawn in any order. The more random the arrangement of tasks, feedback messages, and storage, the greater the active role of the learner in shaping his own educational environment.

Linear. This concept represents a sequential ordering of media types in terms of various functions. For example, a programmed sequence orders the tasks, feedback messages, and information sources according to a plan to induce sequential learning. The more linear the arrangement, the greater is the control of the system over the behavior of the student.

Dynamic interactive. This concept represents the arrangement of media functions within a communication system which provides tasks, feedback, and substantive information in a pattern which permits instruction to be regulated according to learner performance and motivation. A pilot simulator and a language laboratory are examples of dynamic systems.

Dynamic arrangements are suitable for complex areas of learning where specific training is necessary, but differences in learner behavior require great adaptability of the system so that each student can increase or decrease his practice of specific skills and integrate several skills into a complex behavioral pattern.

These three styles of arrangement of media may be cross-classified with the three primary functions of media to yield an array of instructional media possibilities.

THE ARRAY OF MEDIA POSSIBILITIES

When we consider the media types and the functions to which they can be put, we obtain an array of media possibilities rather than an analytic set of concepts which distinguishes one medium from another. Each medium may be used in the multiple ways outlined above. That is, each medium can be used for each of the functions in one way or another. Motion pictures, for example, while generally used for linear information transmission, can be used for random access information transmission, especially when a series of motion pictures on a particular topic is stored under a category system to which the student has random access. Motion pictures can be used to present tasks as they are in pilot simulators, and the tasks can either be within a closed system or a task can be selected by the learner. Similarly, feedback can be provided by motion pictures as it is in the driver simulator where a learner who turns the wheel to the right or left sees an image which provides him with the information he needs for corrective action. In the teacher simulation developed by Kersh[9] and his associates at the University of Oregon, motion pictures are used for reinforcement. When a teacher behaves in a certain way, he receives the reinforcing film, and when he behaves in a different way, he receives the punishing film. In addition, motion pictures represent an art form and the art itself can become the subject of study. All of the media can be be employed in all of these ways. This does not deny in any way the capabilities of the media. The purpose of this analysis is to present alternatives rather than to analyze differences and similarities among media.

THE TEACHER AS MEDIUM

The human teacher or "training agent" should be considered a medium analogous to other communication media and technologies. His possibilities and limitations should be considered in the same way we consider the possibilities and limitations of any other media. For example, if we wish to build a highly sequenced curriculum over defined content, tasks can be presented to the learner by the training agent or by some other medium. Feedback can be provided to the student through the training agent or any other communications medium. The design problem is to determine the particular roles in the creation of the educational environment to be played by each of the media, including the training agent. For example, the human teacher can apprehend the emotional responses of the students to instruction in a way that no communications technology can. Similarly, although he has considerable capacity for processing the results of instruction and feeding it back to the students, through augmented information-processing systems, he has a higher capacity to handle certain kinds of feedback with large numbers of students. Communications media can present human relations tasks to students and present models of good human

9. Bert Y. Kersh, *Classroom Simulation* (Monmouth, Oreg.: Teacher Research of the Oregon State System of Higher Education, 1963).

relations behavior. However, media cannot interact with students as the training agent can, by helping them generate activities which emerge from the synergy of the group. The teacher can be a relatively effective information storage and retrieval system in certain ways but he has only one terminal. A multimedia storage and retrieval system can contain more information than any human training agent can possibly embrace and can have many terminals through which students can have access to the information. Furthermore, the human training agent is responsible for the creation of an effective social system within the school. The teachers working together create the community of the school. The possibilities of that community are greatly affected by the types of media and learning models which are made available, but it is essentially a human responsibility. Warmth and lovingness of a teacher simply cannot be replaced by media. A general design, then, needs to compare the teacher's capabilities with those of the other media and to use the teacher for what he can do very well that media cannot do and avoid wasting him on activities which media can do nearly as well or possibly even better.

Designing Institutions: Bringing Media to the Model

As we discussed previously, the early literature on audiovisual instruction made much of the different capabilities of various media. The relevance of most of these distinctions has been greatly reduced by the invention of the concept of multimedia system. This is not to say that the concepts of media differences were not extremely useful or that distinctive uses of particular media will not emerge as practice and research generate more direct comparisons in the years to come, but they were developed largely during a time when the teacher was seen as the primary mediator of instruction, and it was important to teach teachers that they might use graphics and motion pictures (in addition to the chalkboard, textbooks, and oral communication) as primary media of teaching. Thus many of the concepts which distinguished, for example, the characteristics of overhead projectors, 35-millimeter slides, the chalkboard, and motion pictures were invented in order to encourage teachers to make wise use of a wider variety of media.

The development of multimedia instructional and support systems has provided the tools for creating learning centers in which a very large number of models of learning can be actualized over a great range of content with considerable variation in complexity. By employing our media technology as support systems, we can offer to the student a very great number of ways to learn a large number of things. In addition, we can give him much control over his learning so that he can develop himself in a number of possible directions unthinkable even twenty years ago.

What multimedia systems promise is a form which permits the delivery of a range of instructional supports and informational supports. Multimedia systems are not restricted to a single type of learning or instructional model—they represent support for a range of them. It is a common fallacy to associate technology with restrictive models of learning and the human training agent with the more "open" models. Each is compatible with a wide variety of models and, as was stated above, it is the human training agent who most often in practice employs restrictive models.

The capability of multimedia systems is markedly greater than that of ordinary classroom practice in creating a variety of learning models. The achievements of industry and the military are perhaps the clearest examples here because of the investment which has enabled elaborate development to take place, but these are by no means the only examples. To make the point, however, let us consider the creation of the flight simulator.[10]

This device is striking because it provides the opportunity to learn exceedingly complex skills which are related to sets of diverse and precise theoretical knowledge bases. It uses a variety of media which are brought together with a series of learning tasks which can be paced by an instructor or by the student, with the aid of tracking systems which provide feedback about learning to either the external training agent or the student acting-as-agent.

In a flight simulator the student is presented with a mediated simulation of flight conditions. In the variation which simulates a flight from origination to destination it presents to the student a sequence of tasks which commence at his entrance into the simu-

10. James F. Parker, Jr. and Judith E. Downs, *Selection of Training Media* (Washington, D.C.: Office of Technical Services, U.S. Department of Commerce, 1961).

lated cockpit, continue through his communication with simulated flight-control agencies, his take-off and piloting of the vehicle, and conclude with his landing with simulated radar guidance. As he engages in the tasks, he receives feedback messages on the basis of which he can modify his behavior. If he has difficulty performing some tasks, the relevant phases of the simulation can be repeated until he masters the requisite skills.

On a much simpler scale, Joyce and his collaborators[11] have developed a learning center based on a set of data banks which store information about a variety of communities representing the diversity of human societies. This learning center can be used in relation either to models of learning which respond to learner direction or which provide structured learning tasks and systematic instruction. The array of data banks represents alternative information sources to which the student can be related or relate himself according to a large variety of educational purposes.

The development of multimedia systems has made the distinctions among various media (motion pictures, television, print, etc.) less striking than the possibilities for the design of complex systems in which an array of media are used in appropriate combinations to support the effort of the learner. A single instructional or support system utilizes a combination of media, as in the instructional systems developed by Joyce, Gulliow, Weil, and Wald.[12]

The development of multimedia educational systems permits many models of education that otherwise are inconceivable as long as we think of the classroom and the teacher as the primary mediator of instruction.

THE RECIPROCAL RELATIONSHIP BETWEEN MODEL AND MEDIUM

There is a reciprocal relationship between model and medium that may be exploited for educative purposes. Game-type simulation, for example, mediated largely through broadcast television as in the case of "Cabinets in Crisis," is very different from a game-

11. Bruce Joyce et al., *The Teacher-Innovator*. A Report to the U.S. Office of Education (New York: Teachers College Press, 1969).

12. Bruce Joyce et al., "Teacher Innovator System for Analyzing Skills and Strategies" (Unpublished paper, Teachers College, Columbia University, 1972).

type simulation mediated by closed-circuit television, as in the case of "Moon Vigil," and both are different from even the same game mediated by print media, as in the case of "Internation Simulation." The first of these is much more linear and structured than the latter two which are more randomly accessible. The process of education is composed of the medium, the process, and the substance which interact together in ways which are at persent only dimly perceived. When any model of learning, such as behavior modification or information-processing, is mediated differently or is even supported by different media, the model is transformed. Thus it would be a mistake to think that we simply apply media to a curriculum without changing that curriculum, a point made by Ivins and McLuhan.[13]

ON ORGANIZATION: THE LEARNING CENTER

To replace the concept of the classroom in educational design we have developed the concept of multimodel or multisystems approaches to educational design. Rather than designing classrooms, we can design learning centers which employ different models of learning supported by various multimedia systems. These centers can serve various educational functions and be arranged so that the education of any given student can be fostered by relating him to appropriate combinations of learning centers.

The capability of multimedia systems combined with the multimodels of learning provides the base on which we can create a new educational technology aimed not at improving the classroom but, rather, at the creation of a flexible array of centers for learning. Education need not take place in specific, multipurpose institutions called schools, but rather can be organized in terms of a set of learning centers, each devoted to particular educational goals, to which people would have a lifelong relationship. These learning centers can be directly related to the needs and purposes of a contemporary education.

By providing a variety of learning centers, each implying its unique model of learning, we present to the students an array of ways for developing productive modes of learning while at the

13. William Ivins, *Print and Visual Communication.* (Cambridge, Mass.: Harvard University Press, 1953); Marshall McLuhan, *Understanding Media* (New York: Signet Books, 1964).

same time giving them the human support to help them reflect on their goals. Second, we create a variety of ways for students to reach one another and to explore the possibilities of their communication. Thirdly, such learning centers provide a contemporary media ecology within the provinces of schooling that will permit students to explore the nature of communication and media.

Once institutions are organized around specific educational functions rather than around classrooms and teachers, we need no longer use a language designed to exhort teachers to use more media. Rather, we will need to work with a concept of multimedia systems in which a variety of media are combined to perform various functions with respect to any educational purpose.

Suppose, for example, that we wish to design a system to teach mathematics to children. We can combine the various media to provide both random and sequenced access to information, to provide both designed and emergent activity initiation, to provide informational and value-referenced feedback, and to arrange media so that students can operate on and with them. For any given aspect of activity, several media may function simultaneously or be very closely integrated to one another. We need not design a curriculum so that all of instruction in any given area is provided through any one medium or by the human agent.

In fact, the greatest change this is going to generate is that in the future a small proportion of instruction will be primarily agent-mediated, with the other media playing very small roles. In the future we can expect much greater proportions of the instructional load to be carried by media in various combinations. Our major question will be which learning models to use and in what combinations, and which media to use and in what combinations to support those learning models. In the past we have wasted the energy of the human agent in many roles for which he is not well suited. The schools of tomorrow will find human teachers very much in the picture, but in no area will education be limited simply to what that agent can or will do at any given point of time and he should not be wasted on roles better suited to mediated agencies.

The Design of Learning Systems

An institution consisting of a set of learning centers would teach as much by its form as by its substance. Students who, by managing their learning, become competent in the learning models and who work with a complex of communication systems will have an opportunity to develop competence in the form of contemporary communication and to learn to comprehend and cope with life in an advanced "technetronic" society. By participating in the planning of their own education, they are practicing the arts of governance which can prepare them to achieve control over the future shape of society. Because they would actually create their education from a vast array of proffered components, they would learn that most needed of habits—that of controlling technology to re-create the forms of society.

To sharpen the issues, let us take a visit to a mythical school of the future, the design of which communicates the primary message of this paper. Our school is not housed within a single building. It is organized as a series of learning centers which occupy a variety of physical locations. These centers which reflect the primary models of learning are independently organized, although they share some technical support systems. In fact, a general storage and retrieval system is designed so that students can retrieve information and instructional systems in several media from both their homes and from the learning centers.

The learning centers are designed to serve several major purposes, which purposes give their names to the respective centers as follows: skills centers, academic centers, performing arts centers, social ecology centers, and idiosyncratic centers. Let us consider these centers in turn.

THE SKILLS CENTER

The skills center employs diagnosticians who assess students' communications and other basic skills and then refer them to appropriate instructional systems and to tutors. Whereas the younger child spends considerable time in the skills center, persons of all ages return to the center to improve their old skills or learn new ones.

Communications skills in all media are included in the center. For example, making and viewing film is as prominent in the center as is writing and reading. At the advanced levels, seminars on form and substance, as well as training in the comparative analysis of media and symbol systems and their role in the culture, would be pursued.

The skills center would also include training in the use of the support systems which facilitate each of the learning systems. Training in the use of multimedia instructional systems, information storage and retrieval systems, and diagnostic and management systems are embedded in the center. The acquisition of these skills facilitates self-education and thereby complements the function of the idiosyncratic center.

ACADEMIC CENTERS

In the academic learning centers, devoted to the humanities, aesthetics, sciences, and mathematics, students join groups of other students for three types of courses. One type is survey courses in specific areas, conducted by teachers with support from the instructional systems center. These are followed by inquiry courses in which students work with academic teachers to try out the modes of inquiry of the disciplines. Advanced students relate to academic tutors who help them construct plans of personal study and to relate to groups of similarly advanced students. These centers are housed in laboratories which are especially constructed for the disciplines (as physics laboratories, art workshops, etc.) and are supported by the library and instructional systems centers in the same way as are the other centers.

THE PERFORMING ARTS CENTERS

Music, drama, television and film production, dance, athletics, and the other performing arts are housed in a network of laboratories, workshops, and little theaters throughout the community. Students relate to the performing arts centers in a variety of ways, some for an initial survey experience, others for recreation, some for skill development, and others as a long-term, expressive venture.

The school contains other learning centers, but the number described thus far is probably sufficient to provide a concrete idea of the concept on which it is developed. The primary goal of such centers is the child's acquisition of a variety of models of learning that would serve as strategies in the child's further self-education.

Matching models such as Hunt's [14] would be used by counselors to help students locate the learning models which would most facilitate their development. Learning centers and support systems would be always changing to meet emerging educational needs while maintaining the coherent, warm, and facilitative social system needed to provide stability to the student. Although a comprehensive design is still in the future, we have discussed some elements of such a design that can support a variety of educational means and ends.

THE SOCIAL ECOLOGY CENTERS

The social ecology center is devoted to the process of improving the society. It is organized to facilitate problem-solving groups who study social issues and problems, examine and improve their own interpersonal behavior, and generate social action to alleviate social problems and initiate improvements in societal relations.

The library, data bank, instructional systems centers, and the academic center provide support, but the social ecology center employs a series of simulators and an information retrieval system based on the "social situation of planet earth" as essential supports. An urban simulator supports the study of community problems, an internation simulator provides service to the study of international problems, and an "earth resources" simulator is used to study biological support systems.

The teachers in the social ecology centers are group leaders, for the most part, skilled in human relations training and the use of teaching models which facilitate dialogue on social problems and the organization of social action.

Students relate to the social ecology center from the earliest years, but at first they concentrate only on neighborhood problems and face-to-face human relations. Gradually they increase their scope, studying ecology, urbanization, government, and the creation of an international community. The simulators enable them to study social processes and to try alternative modes of social behavior. Human relations exercises help them to explore ways of

14. David E. Hunt, *Matching Models in Education* (Toronto: Ontario Institute for Studies in Education, 1971).

reaching out to one another and organize themselves to improve social life in day-to-day relations and in the generation of action to improve societal patterns.

IDIOSYNCRATIC CENTERS

Idiosyncratic centers serve the students on their own terms. They are staffed with counselors and facilitators who relate to students as equals, helping them formulate their goals and procedures. The facilitators-teachers help the students relate to a wide variety of part-time teachers—members of the community who serve, largely on a voluntary basis, as tutors, resources, advisers, and teachers of short courses. In addition, they help students relate to the other centers where other teachers and tutors can serve them. The center for the performing arts, for example, serves individuals who wish to relate to activities in that center, as does the social ecology center and the academic study centers.

The idiosyncratic centers are also supported by a multimedia "library" and data bank, most of which is automated and which employs microfiche and microfiche copymaking units to give access to virtually all the material available in the Library of Congress. Many of the automated storage facilities are shared by all the schools of the region. The library supports all activities of the other centers.

The center is also supported by the instructional systems bank, which consists of an array of self-administering multimedia instructional systems in the most common areas. A modular plan permits students to select among the offerings and assemble sequences of them to serve specific purposes.

Thus, the idiosyncratic centers consist of counseling areas, where students (of all ages) make contact with counselors-facilitators who help them define their own goals and procedures and relate to the support services they need to achieve personal growth and enhanced individuality.

Phasing in Change

The politics of educational reform have always been heated and bifurcated. The organic relation of school and society makes it inevitable that any change in schooling will create some dislocation and resistance; these are necessary concomitants of reform in any social institution in a complex society.

However, this paper rests on the proposition that the type of design which utilizes multimedia systems, learning systems, and instructional and informational support for a variety of learning models is more in line with the demands of the postindustrial society than is the conventional school. In fact, all of the learning center options described here have real-world examplars which can be interpreted as the beginnings of adjustment of the school to contemporary society.

Thus, the proposals in this chapter have to be distinguished from proposals which would use education to reform society. In this case we are trying to create an educational design to reduce the distance between educational form and an already changed society.

To phase in change, one might well begin with those types of learning centers which represent familiar educational purposes (reading and other basic symbolic skills), follow with those which provide badly needed social adjustment (continuing vocational education), and proceed with the more unfamiliar and less comfortable types.

The question of definition of purpose is a serious one, communities can elect to emphasize idiosyncrasy, social purpose, and so on, but not to choose is to leave the choice to the mindless workings of administrative pragmatism.

CHAPTER XVII

Educational Technology for Developing Countries

H. DIEUZEIDE

Most assessments of the spectacular expansion of world education are on the whole scarcely encouraging. They tend to show quality sadly lagging behind increasing quantity, inadequate output, both internal and external doubts, and moral crisis. Attention is also drawn to the growing rift between the educational system and a society which is (a) breaking the school's monopoly as the source of knowledge, (b) developing through communication media new relationships between man and the world, and (c) obliging all men to continue their education throughout their professional and civic life. Developing countries, by seeking disorderly linear expansion of their already existing school systems, have only succeeded in multiplying indefinitely existing monopolistic forms of conventional education, based on the historic, rigid models of the West, thus heading rapidly toward economic disaster and social bankruptcy.[1] Since the human and financial resources allotted to education have now practically everywhere reached (and often exceeded) their limit, improvement in educational output must depend on a distribution of resources geared to a revision of targets and a widening of the educational establishment.[2]

The institution of new, flexible, and more productive educational patterns demands that a certain number of pseudotheorems which at present block all educational progress must be strictly and searchingly examined. For instance, educational research has never been able to establish a relation between the *number* of

1. Philip H. Coombs, *The World Educational Crisis: A Systems Analysis* (New York: Oxford University Press, 1968).

2. E. Faure et al., *Learning To Be* (London: Unesco, Harrap, 1972).

pupils in a class and the *effectiveness* of the instruction they receive. It appears that the "ideal" formula, "one teacher for twenty-five pupils," has no scientific justification anywhere.[3] In fact, it merely serves as a prop for archaic educational practices, since the sole aim it proposes is to reduce group numbers of pupils *in the hope* of improving efficiency in the educational process. We may ask whether it would not be more appropriate to equip teachers with materials and methods which would increase their efficiency.

The next step is to increase ways to incorporate scientific advance and introduce modern methods and techniques into teaching. The ideal of this untouchable sector, the sanctuary of the "direct relationship," has always been the widespread adoption of the tutorial principle. There is a current demand everywhere by pupils and parents, often supported by teachers, for more "live" teaching and more humanity in relationships, not for more machines. Wherever attempts have been made, even very timidly, to use machines for communication or analysis in education, they have been most of the time condemned by students, teachers, and parents alike as dehumanizing and robot-producing.

These refusals, fostered sometimes by generous utopianism and, among teachers, by fear of unemployment resulting from technology, deliberately disregard the importance which the new technologies have acquired, not merely in physics and mechanics, but also in human life (through medicine) and social relations (through communications). Scientific methods of analysis and organization have developed everywhere. They have been transforming industrial organization, political power, and military operations and have given an unprecedented impetus to scientific research. Information, publicity, and political propaganda have devised and brought new and more effective symbol systems into general use, leading to deep social transformation. Finally, the breakthrough of cybernetic thinking, combined with new ecological approaches, has encouraged developments of technological configurations away from

3. The recent report *International Study of Achievement in Mathematics: A comparison of 12 countries* (1967) shows that, in general, "size of class is not related to mathematics achievement. . . ." When a difference is observed, it will be seen that larger classes operate to advantage for younger children whereas smaller classes suit older students better. "To the average teacher, a class of 25 may mean much the same as a class of 35 or 45."

purely mechanistic systems into more flexible homeostatic models.

There is, however, growing anxiety in some quarters because education remains the only major human activity in which technology may not increase man's potential. Voices rise to denounce the strange and pernicious paradox whereby the educational institution is required to change the world without any concession that it must itself be transformed. More and more in developing countries, specialists like the author are pelted with fundamental questions from anxious educational authorities. To what extent can present advances in communication and organization be used to improve processes of learning, memorization, and transfer of knowledge? What patterns of human and material resources will produce better and more economic teaching of more individuals? Where positive results have been identified, can they be introduced generally into all educational activities, formal and informal, and can they be applied in the developing countries? Are there already strategies by which new technological contributions could be introduced into existing educational systems, taking into consideration the technical difficulties and human reluctance that they raise?

The present state of emergency in which educational systems of these countries are plunged does not make it easier to answer such questions, as description is too often confused with prescription in this field. One tends to forget that research on what takes place during communication can make clear what happens but does not necessarily tell what to do to make it happen again. The following remarks must therefore be construed as an attempt to bridge the gap between science of facts and techniques of action in the applied field of communication for learning.

Recent bibliographies list hundreds of titles of publications issued during the past ten years dealing with the use of audiovisual equipment, new methods of learning, communication networks, systems analysis and computer sciences, and the latest developments to rationalize the learning act within machine-man systems.[4]

Provisionally we shall use the term *educational technology* to include intellectual and operational efforts made during recent

4. The *Bulletin of the International Bureau of Education* in its December 1970 issue (no. 177) lists, in addition to 450 books, 24 basic bibliographies on the subject, all published in the preceding five years.

years to restructure and systematize the application of scientific methods to the organization of new sets of equipment and material so as to optimize learning processes. Using the new apparatus and techniques of communication as well as new methods of organization and application may make it possible to *change* the quantitative or qualitative output of school systems, to spread their influence to new publics, and, occasionally, to set up new institutional structures.

However much talked about as the new models for educational technology are, too few are in use to be significant. The report to President Nixon by the commission of inquiry into instructional technology [5] shows that in the United States less than 4 percent of educational expenditure is devoted to educational materials, including textbooks, laboratories, and teaching materials of every kind, whereas over 70 percent of the budget is allocated to teachers' salaries. For Great Britain, "in 1968 less than one percent of total expenditure of schools went on books; on all kinds of teaching materials the allowance for each child in a secondary school was set at £5; the cost of teacher per child was just under £90. This reflects the degree to which our secondary education is teacher-based." [6]

The developing countries today may well ask whether six school years are absolutely necessary to achieve the aims of primary education, whether education must be organized on the basis of academic subjects rather than of tasks and problems, whether categories of individual textbooks must be multiplied indefinitely, and whether it is necessary to build and equip school complexes which are unused for almost six months of the year and to run radio and television equipment or computers at a quarter or a third of their capacity. Should not the introduction of new technologies in education enable developing countries to free their schools, while there is still time, from the educational models which belong to the past of the developed countries and which the former imitate, not merely the structure but also the implicit or explicit objectives?

5. *To Improve Learning* (A report to the President and the Congress of the U.S. by the Commission on Instructional Technology [Washington: U.S. Government Printing Office, 1970]).

6. L. C. Taylor, *Resources for Learning* (London: Penguin Books, 1971).

The continuing fragility of the educational systems of the developing countries is an additional reason for inquiring whether they should consolidate organization and equipment which will be obsolete in a few years' time or invest in new structures likely to endure and develop. Such change should take place before the systems become blocked by the hypertrophy which is now appearing in many developed countries.

Technologies of Communication in Education: The Example of Developed Countries

A survey of the evolution of educational technology in the developed countries should be instructive as to the tasks to be accomplished, the magnitude of those tasks, the approach to be selected, and the tactics to be employed.

THE CRAFT APPROACH

New techniques have been very slow in finding their way into schools of industrialized countries and only then after long proof of their practical value in daily home life. Their increased use has been due to the individual initiative of certain teachers anxious to establish a new relationship with their pupils and not to the educational authorities. Therefore, these techniques have generally been used for fringe activities of extreme diversity: Gramophone records and radio in preprimary schools; projectors to illustrate history, geography, and general-knowledge lessons; tape recorders for improving oral expression, correcting pronunciation, and narrating stories; films for the teaching of science, technology, and arts subjects; radio for the teaching of music, presenting linguistic models, and pronunciation drills; television for civics and the introduction of current affairs and contemporary history into traditional education.

There is some evidence that such uses have helped in clarifying concepts, stimulating group and individual activities, developing a collective critical awareness, changing attitudes, (sometimes) imposing a new structure or organization on certain subjects, and encouraging originality and creativeness.[7] All too often, however,

7. *Research in Instructional Television and Films*, 34041 (Washington: U.S. Office of Education 1967).

pupils are subjected to sporadic bursts of audiovisual information or halfhearted attempts to apply the techniques to conventional school activities. Intuitive judgment has been relied upon more than measurement of the effects. Use of these aids depends entirely on the teacher and becomes meaningful only when carefully fitted into an educational pattern previously decided upon by the teacher himself. Too often his aim is to produce his own documents for his pupils. He prefers using the tape recorder and the overhead projector in his class rather than relying on mass-produced records, films, and radio and television broadcasts. Very often, uneasy relations develop between traditional systems adhered to by teachers and new symbolic codes brought in by pupils. But the tradition of those generations of teachers who have dictated their lessons with a sublime disregard for the existence of textbooks is thus being continued by these faithful "audiovisual" craftsmen.

From the point of view of improving educational output, what hopes does this approach offer us? The strategy of providing each teacher with specialized equipment, maintaining the equipment, and giving the teachers special instruction in its use is certainly an effective, but slow and expensive, way to improve "craft" methods. The critical mass needed to produce a leap forward in the quality of this output cannot be achieved merely by injecting new messages in small doses. Economists observe that since these methods are not financed by a redistribution of existing resources, they can only represent additional costs. Moreover, there is no certainty that the requisite material will be used to the full, since each teacher decides for himself about using it. If costs per pupil often seem low, it is because they are frequently distorted by the fact that the time taken by the qualified teacher in preparing material is rarely taken into account. In developing countries, the development of robust and inexpensive equipment such as solar projects and silk-screen printing equipment cannot disguise the fact that these are again marginal "aids" to traditional teaching procedures and do not optimize the role of the teacher. However interesting such isolated individual efforts may be, it has to be acknowledged that they have not so far resulted anywhere in adequate methods for achieving the rapid expansion of education which development demands. All this goes to explain why these methods have been so slow to catch on.

There is of course no question of discouraging these experiments which play their part in the gradual improvement of traditional educational systems, but it would be dishonest to claim that they are among the fundamental remedies for the present crisis.[8]

PALLIATIVES AND STOPGAPS

Over the last ten years there has been a tendency to use the resources of educational technology, particularly radio and television networks or new learning processes such as programmed instruction, in an authoritarian manner as emergency treatment for certain defects in the education system, particularly at the secondary level.

In certain cases educational technology has come to be used as a remedy for inherent deficiencies in the system—to offset the teachers' lack of qualifications by regular classroom broadcast demonstrations or drills or by programmed documents for the pupils, to speed up the introduction of new subjects or new education methods, or to take over activities on which the schools have fallen down, using informal methods.

In other cases the aim has been to extend the field of action of the traditional system to cover new sectors of the public which could not be reached by existing institutions, through the creation of informal education structures based on the use of radio, television, correspondence courses, and programmed instruction. The first "extension" courses were on the line of the formal lecturing by TV of the City Junior College in Chicago for those not enrolled in schools. "Replacement education" was developed in areas where the educational establishments were nonexistent, such as the

8. One of the fields in which there seems to be most justification for continuing and developing these experiments, because of their long-term snowball effects, is without doubt that of teacher training: use of language laboratories for modern language teachers, training in programming techniques for use in the arrangement of subject matter, use of the closed circuit for improvement of teacher-pupil communication and relationships. Similarly, radio and television are used to provide teachers with "remote control" in-service training. This form of contact helps to avoid the inevitable falling-off in the teaching standards of serving teachers and to prevent their failure to keep abreast of developments in their profession when they are geographically isolated or become absorbed into the cultural milieu which it is their duty to change. More and more, the main teacher training institutions in developing countries manage to combine the use of radio, correspondence courses, and programmed instruction for teaching, retraining, and upgrading.

Italian Tele-Scuola, designed to provide the young people in the depressed region of the Mezzogiorno with the visualized rudiments of traditional secondary instruction.

There is often a tendency nowadays to pass severe judgment on undertakings of this kind, in which political opportunism has frequently taken precedence over educational needs. Critics are quick to point out that they are superficial and produce only a temporary respite and false economy. It is true that they have often been hurriedly improvised and (because of the lack of time and sufficient forethought) have not always made the best of the technical resources and specific potential of the media. On the plea of urgency, the media have often been put to uses for which they were not designed. For example, television has often been used simply as a vehicle for a verbal message without any visual content, thus reinforcing old-fashioned practices (authoritarian teaching methods, verbal teaching, and the like). There has been some justification to speak of "retrograde innovations" which have tended to displace or disguise problems rather than solve them.

It must be said, in favor of these operations, however, that their very limitations have given rise to some hard thinking about the impact that the use of communication infrastructures or of industrial methods might have on education. Education does not only mean the organizing of microactivities at the level of small groups; it can use the vast resources of radio, television, and programmed material, for instance, to increase its own efficiency. Moreover, the halfhearted combination of technology with a traditional system by stressing to the point of caricature the worst features of the system, like the "chalk and talk" approach, has forcibly emphasized the need to reexamine education's aims and methods. The most positive result of these experiments has probably been that they have brought educators, administrators, and research workers face to face with new concepts and novel technical requirements and have led—sometimes compelled—them to take a fresh look at existing systems, their aims and their operation.

MORE PROGRESSIVE INNOVATIONS

Last but not least, these experiments have, over the last two or three years, made possible new and positive lines of approach which

go beyond short-term provisional measures. All of them irrevoca-
bly link the use of communication machines with a more scientific
organization of school work, transcend the traditional distinction
between school and postschool activities, and seek to reduce inequality of opportunity. Among the most striking examples of late
is the "Sesame Street" program in the U.S., designed to prepare
preschool-age children from underprivileged environments (especially districts without kindergarten) to enter and accept the traditional school.

Radio and television have been used widely within disadvantaged schools too. Unlike distribution circuits of the film-library
type, media networks have made possible the industrial-style production of documents by organized teams of education specialists
and instant, widespread distribution. With their aid a common level
of educational information and activity can be maintained in schools
which do not all enjoy equally favorable circumstances. In Niger,
Hungary, and Cuba, television has introduced simultaneously over
vast territories identical new models of learning, created the conditions for a collective motivation for learning, and regularly distributed instructions for teachers to update their teaching procedures.

Another example is the attempt to achieve a combination of
various communication networks into more coherent and comprehensive organizations that will be more responsive to diversified
requirements. Instances include the new institutions for technical
and secondary education and even part-time higher education
("second-chance" schools) which have been developed recently
in industrialized countries and which combine the distribution of
programmed documents, broadcasting of instruction, information
models and demonstrations on radio and television, information
"feedback" through correspondence courses, the telephone or the
duplex system, face-to-face contact provided by traveling instructors, study in small groups, and supplementary summer schools
(Tele-Kolleg in the Federal Republic of Germany, Tele-Polytech-
nic in Poland). Today the Open University in the United Kingdom has developed a model of multimedia institutional approach
which is already being further developed or adopted in Spain,
Iran, Japan, and Mexico.

Alongside these methods which combine extremely varied resources, we can also see the emergence of complex arrays of integrated installations designed to provide intensive accelerated courses on an individual basis, especially in Japan or USA, for training the staffs of large firms: learning laboratories, television circuits, teaching machines, individual-response control systems, simulation, computers with audiovisual terminals, and so on. This costly apparatus whereby one learns "by appointment" requires, if it is to be an economic proposition, intensive and coordinated collective use. It provides a blueprint in certain developed countries for what great educational centers for intensive courses, on the line of "teaching clinics," could be like.

Equipping Education in Developing Countries

When one turns to the Third World, one finds it characterized by the unequal and mixed development of various technologies. The sometimes desired and sometimes imposed sophisticated technologies exist side by side with antiquated methods; each country has a whole range of possible measures available and the problem is knowing how to succeed in optimizing education in each case.

THE EMERGENCE OF SOPHISTICATED TECHNIQUES

Often these countries which have attained a level of development rendering them accessible to Western techniques adopt, under commercial pressure, some advanced technology: scientific apparatus, films, and so forth. Generally speaking, such technology, which is sporadically introduced and without any overall plan, makes but a marginal contribution to educational development and does not seem to have more real effect on optimizing education in the developing than in the developed countries.

Other direct importation results from the express decision of some governments to make use of new technological apparatus (radio networks, or computers, for instance) with a view to producing a massive effect on the educational system of the country. This generally involves mass communications media employed to overcome the obstacles of distance and number far more than to promote the quality of educational processes; their introduction is sometimes the result of a political choice rather than of an essentially pedagogical decision (this is often the case with television).

The presence of similar prestige apparatus in neighboring countries is often an additional motive for introducing this kind of novelty (for example, computers).

All these recently applied advanced communication techniques (whether educational television or programmed instruction) share the characteristics of requiring heavy investments, industrial production of the contents they communicate, maintenance of a broadcasting and receiving infrastructure, and specialized retraining of the technical and pedagogical staff who are to use them.

Among the recent and significant applications of these media, mention should be made of the Ivory Coast's use of television to reorient its curricula reform and to recast the teacher training system with a view to a better economic and cultural adaptation to the environment. A six-year extension plan, started in September 1971, will make it possible to serve fourteen thousand primary and postprimary rural teachers by 1977. In Spain, a fairly similar objective of radically changing the orientations of the educational system has led to planning a computer-teaching network which, beginning in 1974, should make it possible to train or retrain three hundred thousand teachers in ten years, i.e., the whole body of secondary school teachers. In Indonesia, the systems approach is being used to determine the functions of educational radio in a school system stretching over three thousand islands, and in Latin America a survey is being carried out on the feasibility of organizing a satellite communications system in order to speed up the educational integration of the region.

The general tendency is first of all to assign quantitative goals to educational technology; for instance, an existing service is taken over by a technological apparatus, ensuring equal quality at a lower cost. Still more frequently the aim is to extend educational services to areas previously without them, either at lower costs than those which could be provided by the extension of conventional services or at the same cost as that of conventional ones but with sufficient time-savings to justify using the new techniques. This is, for instance, the case with space communication.[9]

To be sure, qualitative objectives, either manifest or implied, likewise emerge. For instance, the idea may be to introduce new

9. *Communications in the Space Age* (Paris: Unesco, 1968).

contents into an educational system, modify its basic methods, or raise the individual teacher's qualifications. Here again, it will be observed that the desire to democratize education by disseminating information on a large scale takes precedence over the use of apparatus that individualizes learning. Indeed, the general trend is to consider educational technology as a means of speedily providing large doses of education, often as an emergency or alleviating measure, for large groups. The sophisticated techniques for individualizing instruction (learning laboratories, remote access terminals to data banks) corresponding to a tailor-made, by-appointment-only education are seldom given priority.

Nevertheless, the idea is gradually emerging that mass techniques not only increase ways of spreading information, but also make it possible to vary educational opportunities by simultaneously offering several types of education. This in itself constitutes a certain kind of educational individualization. Moreover, in some limited experiments it has been possible to use a combination of individualized and group techniques. Certain combinations of programmed teaching material and television (as used in Singapore, for instance) produce an effective blend of general and analytical learning processes. In Central Africa, experiments of the opposite nature in which the same programmed material, often combined with visuals, is used in a group likewise seem to open up the possibility of solving someday the dilemma of mass, as opposed to individualized, education.

The introduction of sophisticated technology has generally taken place as part of a technical assistance program, which entailed a close link with the countries providing it. In order that no time be lost, material is sometimes introduced directly from developed countries before schemes for its use adapted to the beneficiary country can be worked out. This happens when equipment which has already proven itself, i.e., its research costs have already been covered in developed countries, is used. Exceptions occur when developing countries call directly upon the experience of advanced research laboratories, as in Spain, for example, which is now preparing to use computers in education with the aid of the most advanced American and European institutes in this field. In other instances, the setting up of a sophisticated technological system on a really large scale may have been preceded by a more modest experiment; thus, the Ivory Coast is following the example of an educational television project in Niger, which in five years developed an original system of implementation, utilization, and feedback techniques, spreading over a network of twenty schools.[10] When the technique requires less equipment than development of contents, other solutions have been found. In Asia, the UNESCO regional project on programmed instruction has made it possible to step up production of programmed material in eleven countries by coordinating efforts of institutes partially or wholly specialized in programmed teaching. In Central Africa, a considerable amount of programmed material has been worked up by the teachers of four countries who will be its future users, while they were organized as a production team during intensive practical sessions (the Brazzaville "factory-school").

APPROPRIATE TRANSFER OF TECHNOLOGIES OF
COMMUNICATION

The lessons to be learned from the *technico-economic* difficulties inherent in advanced technology are beginning to be carefully examined: the difficulty of financing costly equipment in tropical countries, the reluctance of officials in developing countries to commit themselves to a heavy drain of hard currency, and an insufficiently high local level of technological resources to ensure the smooth operation of the system. There are other, human, limitations inasmuch as setting up these systems would make considerable demands on the country's supply of qualified technical personnel.

Economic difficulties are not the only ones. One of the most remarkable boomerang effects of sophisticated technological innovation is that priority is given to apportioning economic resources for installing equipment to the detriment of developing content organization and, often, of the technological research needed for effectively adapting the new techniques. Sophisticated technology of communication, when introduced, requires at least as much in the way of human and economic resources for the contents as for

10. *Television in the Modernisation of Education in Ivory Coast* (Abidjan: Secretary of State for Primary Education and Educational Television, 1972).

the equipment (software-hardware balance). Besides, it is through the effort made to work up original software carefully adapted to needs that it becomes possible for a new technique to effectively take root.[11] Mass educational technology is only acceptable when based on industrial production of standardized teaching material of high quality. Only then is it possible to universalize it and justify the expense, as it may take a team of specialists one hundred hours to produce one hour of programmed instruction and up to two hundred hours to produce one hour of computerized instruction (figures are often higher for film-making or teaching packages).

Importing new apparatus and contents as they are is only one step in the use of sophisticated technology. Up to now, attention has mainly been given to the imported technological apparatus whose development and universalization has been paid for in the developed countries. Sometimes the very appearance of this apparatus reflects the aggravating excesses of a consumer society. Neither bright chrome on cars nor luxurious cabinets for television sets contribute to their efficiency. Experience has shown that it is possible to strip down some sophisticated equipment for use in the developing countries by reducing the number of wavelengths a radio or television receiver can pick up, replacing costly studios with light shooting equipment for outside work, and simplifying language laboratory booths, thus cutting costs by half or more.

Moreover, there are many low-cost techniques which require neither elaborate equipment nor a large, highly qualified staff: this is the case, for instance, with slow-scan television, rarely used in the developed countries, by which series of successive still images can be instantaneously and widely broadcast. There has been little exploration of these possibilities because their use in the developed countries is blocked by other more complex techniques.

Unfortunately, research in the developed world is generally directed towards the most elaborate techniques and is ill-equipped for reorienting itself towards low-cost or stripped-down techniques. The latter are to be worked on in the developing coun-

11. *Educational Television in Developing Countries* (Tokyo: Nippon Hoso Kyokai, 1965).

tries which have acquired sufficient mastery of Western techniques (India or Brazil, for instance) to be able to develop new adapted communication models or technological organization. Some advances have already been made. There is the example of India producing antennas from chicken wire for group reception of satellite signals for thirty dollars. Their cost in the developed countries is about three thousand dollars. Unfortunately, very few such efforts are being made and then only sporadically. They should be coordinated through more systematic international cooperation.

The sociocultural problems, however, appear to lie deeper and be less easily measurable. The difficulties met up to the present involve primarily the ill-suitedness of some techniques to the type of society they have been grafted onto or arbitrarily introduced into. When grafted, they disfigure without transforming. When arbitrarily introduced, they tend to have a disruptive effect on the educational systems of these countries, rather than to further their development.

More than one government hesitates to redefine the roles of teaching staff which often constitutes an influential intelligentsia. But there is one definite danger which ought to be stressed: using sophisticated technology can lead to arresting educational development at a particular level if it is done in a way that subjects the system's evolution to technical limitations. For instance, setting up an educational television network should not preclude its later transformation into another more elaborate or differently structured system of telecommunication. The objectives laid down for a system of educational technology must be modular and capable of being integrated into other or more general aims (as was the case with the Ivory Coast ITV project). What is especially original in educational technology is that which makes possible the gradual development of self-organizing and self-regulating units. Through more and more numerous informational and analytic apparatus, increased powers of memory, more and more sophisticated regulating mechanisms, educational technology can enable an educational system to guide itself according to the reactions it provokes and thus to develop, adapt, and grow by keeping control of change. In addition, the sophisticated systems offered to the developing countries could be designed with a degree of openness and flexibility that allows adaptation to the requirements of development.

In another connection it has been seen that it is not enough for a country to reach the level of technological development which ensures that grafting sophisticated technology onto it will succeed. Provision must also be made for effectively integrating and controlling all the consequences of technological innovation. Whether with regard to the Aswan dam or DDT, we have seen that hasty technological development can have consequences difficult to keep under control, both because of their complex nature and because they often do not show up till a later date. The inference is that insufficient foresight, not so much the technique itself, is generally at fault. *The large-scale introduction of sophisticated technology is not a strategy whereby structural changes can be avoided.* On the contrary, it makes them inevitable; just as the "green revolution" requires agrarian reform to reach its aims, so the introduction of technology into education will only make sense if it serves more humane concepts.

Finally, other investigations concern the preservation of local cultures. In this respect it has been found that the greatest difficulties do not always exist as predicted. The "wildcat development" of certain advanced communications media, such as television, has been enough to reduce to their proper proportions the warnings abundantly proffered by specialists regarding the "perceptive incapacities" of some primitive milieux. Today, it appears that the errors made in interpreting visual messages should not be assigned a perceptive origin. They appear to be of a cultural nature (unfamiliarity with the message's codes of reference) and consequently can by training be quickly reduced into appropriate recoding.

But, on the other hand, some people feel that the incongruity between the essential nature of these techniques and the environment in which they are to be applied make the two incompatible and do disservice to the very concept of development. It is not easy to align mass communications transmitted by television with a functional literacy campaign, which is primarily centered on the occupational environment but at the same time strives for self-improvement among illiterates and expresses their desire to step up from the environment. Obviously television could help establish a system of reference for such an aspiration.

Recently, ecological scruples induced European experts in an African educational television project to promote an ecological approach in rural education programs, which resulted in justifying inertia among African peasants rather than encouraging the struggle for the development of agriculture. To the extent education is to serve development, technology of learning has a role to play in it.[12] It is difficult, however, to decide today where the necessary circulation of educational knowledge as a basis of development ends and the danger of foreign cultural invasion and recolonization leading to cultural genocide begins.

It must be regretted that the required instruments to control such forms of communication, especially the indicators of cultural penetration, do not yet appear to have been developed. Only a greater number of studies preparing for large-scale operational undertakings, like the surveys presently being made for the UNESCO/UNDP educational satellite project in Latin America (SERLA), will make it possible to clear up these problems.

In actual fact, the concern shown by the developing countries in this respect is indicative of the difficulties they have had in defining education for a development which does not simply satisfy material needs, but also answers individual and collective psychic needs. The importance of radio broadcasting, the only sophisticated innovation to have spread all over the Third World, should serve as a support to and also as an example of educational development. It became universal the day it reached an adequate technico-economic level: transistors and miniaturization make it possible to produce inexpensive, reliable apparatus adapted to conditions in all countries. At the same time, radio has shown that it answers the cultural needs of societies with oral traditions and unwritten values. But for the moment it is an isolated case and it must be admitted today that all types of technological apparatus

12. R. Jacobs, "Technology as an Agent of Change in Developing Education," in *The United States and International Education,* Sixty-eighth Yearbook of the National Society for the Study of Education, Part I (Chicago: University of Chicago Press, 1969).

446   EDUCATIONAL TECHNOLOGY

do not appear neutral to developing countries. Some technologies are felt to be "cleaner" than others, but, on the whole, least developed countries tend to consider that their presence may introduce a set of Western values and preexisting ideologies. Therefore, economic limitations in some instances and cultural reservations in others have encouraged the development of the concept of "intermediate technology."

THE CONCEPT OF "INTERMEDIATE TECHNOLOGY" AND ITS
ADAPTABILITY TO EDUCATIONAL NEEDS

The concept of "intermediate technology" has emerged in the economics of development objectives. Exportation of sophisticated technology from the developed countries to the developing countries has generally been limited to certain results of industrialization and confined to urban areas, which tends to create cultural conflicts and increase imbalances in development between town and country. Part of the purpose of developing intermediate technology would be to reduce such conflicts and imbalances.[13] The main idea is to start with intensive work, as opposed to an abundance of capital, and seek ways to make better use of the cultural, economic, social, and technical resources available in the environment itself, especially in rural areas. Intermediate technology aims at mobilizing local, particularly human, resources and encouraging the inhabitants to participate in discovering the implements of their own development. In practice, this means that efforts are made to give priority to using locally available raw materials, to further the development of small industries oriented towards the local environment (particularly as regards agriculture), and to systematically modify existing equipment in order to make it more efficient, rather than seek to import foreign equipment and experts.

Undertakings based on these principles have so far covered a very wide range of activities, extending from the search for new energy sources (e.g., the setting up of methane lighting systems using gas produced from household refuse) to the transformation of public services (developing new hospital equipment, including

13. E. F. Schumacher, *Social and Economic Problems Calling for the Development of Intermediate Technology* (London: Intermediate Technology Development Group, 1970).

that which is adapted to local conditions—incubators for maternity hospitals, for instance). In any case, the aim of these efforts is to speed up progress at the local level, ensure participation of the existing labor force, and make the best possible use of available material resources. Specialists are of the opinion that it is probably China that has most actively pursued research of this nature and gone farthest in applying it.

It may be wondered whether education has given this endogenous approach to the development of new techniques all the attention it deserves. Educational technology experts tend to reject the concept of the individual teacher's work as that of a pallitative industrialization of education based on mass production of materials and messages. The structure, organization, and contents of education in the Third World countries are still conspicuously marked by colonial models; education has not yet developed to the point of reaching an adequate stage of critical awareness and technological inventiveness, and it tends to fall back on the "stop-gap" use of educational technology. A further reason would be that the program of intermediate technologies is usually presented in its strictly economic version as a simple attempt to provide work for a greater number of people, whereas the main problem of education today is to increase the efficiency and productivity of personnel already in service. But the employment approach of intermediate technology is only a technical factor, a means and not an end, as the ultimate objective of intermediate technological programs is to encourage technological inventiveness and creativity in archaic cultures (which is in itself an important goal of concern to all educators).[14]

In another respect, the search for *new technological schemes* without heavy investments may open new possibilities for parallel integrated efforts in education. Might not the regrouping of handicraft workshops, as they begin to appear in the economic sector, provide useful models for reorganizing traditional classroom-type

14. "The distinction between 'capital intensive' and 'labour intensive' industries ... does not really make contact with the essence of the problem. . . . The choice of industry is one thing but the choice of technology to be employed *after* the choice of the industry has been made is quite another thing. It is therefore better to speak directly of technology and not to cloud the discussion." (Schumacher, op. cit., p. 5).

work units into more effective collective units, based on a better division of pedagogical labor and leading up to the school factory? It seems likely that if pedagogical thinking started from these analogies, fruitful results would be obtained by devising combined sets of methods and specific techniques answering the needs of a region, state, or even a tribe, subculture, or dialect. These methods and techniques will be intermediate between *standardized national or international industrial production* and the *craftsmanlike* efforts left to the initiative of the individual teacher, alone in his classroom.

Of course, the authorities in the developing countries may not wish to encourage a too diversified technological development, which would necessarily be heterocultural and consequently liable to have a dispersive effect as regards national unity. This diversification will generally be tolerated in regard to primary education oriented towards rural life, but at all other educational levels it may appear to be opposed to the unifying function most developing countries assign to the educational system. Some countries, however, such as India, seem ready even now to adopt a diversified approach at all levels.

The purpose of trying to evolve intermediate technology of communication and organization is to bring educational development into line with preexisting structures. For these largely determine the ability to adopt and adapt an innovation. Japan will serve as an example in this respect. Owing to its preexisting integrated handicraft structures, it was able to adapt television to its own ends, both with regard to production of hardware and creation of software. Far from conflicting with Japanese traditional culture, the media seem to help strengthen it. Thus a better knowledge of local sociocultural structures ought to be able to facilitate development of new techniques and make them assimilable or at least acceptable to existing cultures instead of destroying them.

So far, research on the use of adapted technology in education for developing countries has been scattered and piecemeal. It has been chiefly concerned with pedagogical accessories or aids without any attempt at developing methods and systems. In some research or teacher training institutes, simplified slide projectors have been introduced which are operated by solar energy—some even had a simplified optical system which could be made from the bottoms of beer bottles. Mainly owing to UNESCO, it has been possible to use locally available materials in the construction of elementary equipment for science teaching. In fact, without wishing to cast a slur on the creative merits of their individual work, it may be said that almost all this equipment is a crude substitute for that produced and used in wealthy countries. These poor copies of Western models have generally been developed with a view to serving traditional, imported education. Consequently, it would be difficult for them to provide the basis for a forward thrust towards original and better adapted forms of teaching. This explains their limited expansion so far.

It seems more advisable to encourage, whenever possible, the development of simplified techniques within general learning strategies in order to provide the basis for new educational configurations adapted to the country.[15] Such strategies should include redefining the educational institution which is to serve as the technical unit (neither a large factory nor a group of individual workshops, which waste teachers' time and talent); stressing group work and "teach-another" techniques; utilization of standardized messages and team teaching; appropriate material for group viewing; stepping up the circulation and exchange of teaching material produced by means of simplified techniques (a school press, for instance); development of educational "self-service" facilities comprising sets of simple teaching machines; making each student a producer as well as a consumer of educational materials; installation of uncomplicated educational radio and television systems that could be the basis for work sessions with traveling specialists, and so on.[16]

When defining the elements of an intermediate technology development strategy, a distinction should be made between those countries where development will still require another ten years or more of saving of qualified manpower and those in which such

15. Deliberate restrictions could be used to bring about development of these adapted techniques. It has been seen how the forbidding of large-scale importation of educational materials for economic reasons has resulted in the creating of an "educational vacuum" and obliged some countries to devise their own teaching material (e.g., India). Nevertheless, these restrictions will never be fruitful unless an awareness of the need for new techniques already exists.

16. L. O. Edstrom, *Adult Education and Correspondence Education in Developing Countries* (Stockholm: Almgvist, 1970).

manpower already exists (or will shortly) and where the aim is to provide work for it (as in many Asian countries). According to this strategy, the first efforts should be made with a view to sectoral improvements in the educational system, particularly where costs per pupil justify them and where the optimum combination of investments and manpower would be easiest to achieve—vocational and teacher training, high-level technical training, and higher education. It is only by beginning to work at the microlevels that it can be hoped to apply later these techniques on a larger scale—to rural and primary education.

Such confrontations in a field where there has so far been little systematic exploration are likely to be fruitful. Let it suffice to mention the example of intermediate technology in which all the technical principles are applied but the corresponding equipment is not used. This is the case with the administration of a developing country which has tried to organize the processing of information in its offices according to data-processing principles, employing only the large available labor force. Here, the administration imitates the computer but does not use one. Some of the technological principles of the computer are thus turned to account, while many of its practical advantages, such as rapid calculations, are dispensed with. It may be asked if such an approach is not of particular relevance to education. To come back to the computer, we know that today's generation of computers respond much too rapidly to justify using them in a learning process requiring a machine-student relation. Computers responding much more slowly are quite adequate for such a dialogue. The fact is that in computer teaching it is the concept of the *learning algorithm* which is basic and not the sophisticated technology of the transistor.[17] Probably other areas of education should be considered as activities that can be made more fruitful by technological research without being crushed under the weight of the latter's apparatus.

IS POSTMECHANICAL TECHNOLOGY A WAY OUT?

We are thus led to wonder if the future of educational technology does not lie in *applying principles before using machines*

17. L. N. Landa, "Research on Application of Logic of Mathematics and Theory of Information to Learning Problems," in *Questions of Psychology*, no. 2, Moscow, 1963.

and sometimes in dispensing with the latter altogether. In the sophisticated technologies, methodology up to now has appeared inseparable from a specific apparatus. Would it not be possible to deduce principles from these technologies which could help education in the developing countries without, however, employing complex equipment? Modern technology is indeed on the way to achieving what the mechanical advances of the nineteenth century could not, i.e., organize society on a rational basis. Mumford has shown that machines have often been used to "disguise man's inefficiency" and it will be readily admitted that technology is the subtle and discriminating use of machine principles.

If it is not the teaching machine which is important but the programming principles which make its application possible, then we can imagine an educational technology which would be based on "mock machines," rebuilt according to the functions they are to fulfill. It is thus, for example, that when the mathematician Dienes wants to introduce small children to modern mathematics, he prefers to do it by using "little machines" which have no actual mechanical parts and simply offer new ways of thinking, in the guise of games. A similar approach is adopted in the diagrams commonly used for training in data processing: any allusion to actual operation and utilization of computers is scrupulously avoided.

Efforts along these lines should not be considered naïve dodges aiming at transferring the essence of sophisticated technology while avoiding the necessity of purchasing the apparatus, but as a guarantee that intermediate technology will survive. Unless these theoretical principles are developed and applied to education, intermediate technology runs the risk of becoming a blind alley for development rather than constituting a necessary stage. It is *technological creativity* which, as it outlines new methods, will ensure the indispensable standardization of intermediate technology and consequently its universalization. Such an effort would be justified on the grounds that it would improve educational productivity in a country (for instance, by bringing about quicker ways of making and keeping people literate). But it could also facilitate access of archaic cultures to a higher technological order, not through forced superimposition but by endogenous rediscovery. It could include development of techniques for organizing contents and duties, which should make it possible to universalize systems analysis and programming of a type that future teachers would need practice in their preparation. Cybernetic models and learning algorithms would be used as they deserve to be. Also included would be investigation of the contributions of communications techniques such as information compression (the procedures used to teach speed reading), which would radically alter the present uses of printed educational matter. One should stress here the importance of giving the young experience with the symbol systems divorced as far as possible from the complex technologies involved in their transmission.

Simulation techniques, stripped of their complex operational apparatus, should offer exercises in which events are speeded up and require decisions regarding complex alternatives, just as games, instead of simulating reality, should develop competition and group efforts in the planning of imaginary futures.

It will be noted that only contributions inspired by Western techniques have been mentioned here. Their development in the Third World may raise as many cultural problems as does the use of sophisticated equipment. For instance, with regard to visual communication and programming procedures, experiments in progress tend to show that there is no possibility of their being effective here either, unless forms and contents are adapted to different cultural frames of reference. This is a new challenge, at once anthropological and psychological, to technological creativity. And technological invention is not necessarily tied to a given level of GNP.

Could a "Designed" Education Be Based on Technologies?

Technologies of communication can only play a decisive role if associated with technologies of organization in systematic patterns. It seems that we are presently moving away from thinking about technology in education (i.e., thinking chiefly concerned with equipment, elaboration of ad hoc symbolic codes, and then incorporation into traditional teacher-centered activities) to thinking about the technology *of* education (i.e., rationalizing and optimalizing the chain of processes that each individual has to go through in order to acquire and use knowledge). The aim behind such thinking should be to move away from dispersion of wasted effort or, worse still, the overhasty adoption of technology as a means of patching up shaky educational systems to a full and integrated use of all the resources of the technological age. Hitherto, these areas in education to which technology has been applied have all too often resembled patches of ground strewn with machine parts that no one would attempt to assemble.

Instead of attempting merely to recruit and train an ever increasing number of teachers, the time may have come to try to analyze the various educational functions with a view to redistributing the human and material resources available to wherever in the educational system their potential can be most fully realized. This, of course, implies the acceptance on our part that *instead of continuing to let the machine do only what the teacher cannot do, we should ask ourselves what it is the teacher should do that the machine cannot do.* This further implies the acceptance of far-reaching changes in the organization and hierarchical structures of the educational establishment and in the responsibilities and functions of pupils and teachers alike. There may be some hope that technology will cease to be a miscellaneous collection of new equipment and methods designed to lighten some of the teacher's traditional tasks and will provide education with a coherent set of liberal methods and original concepts of learning and training.

Such are most of the means now at our disposal—new display devices and, more important still, image and sound-recording and reproduction devices, the storage and collective or individual retrieval of image and sound, self-scoring and self-assessment possibilities, the feedback facilities and flexibility offered by some techniques (ranging from the individual-response control system to the computer), and particular methods of presentation (programming) —that modern technology, with its methods of organization and measurement, its evaluation and experimentation techniques, can provide education with the *guiding principles* upon which to base a definition of the relationship (a) between various new techniques and methods and (b) between them and the institutions' content and existing methods of education, which they could help transform from within.[18] The transition from technology *in* education to the technology *of* education involves a thorough reappraisal of

18. Kenneth Richmond, *Educational Technology* (London: Allen & Unwin, 1970).

the existing educational system, of its objectives, and of the means used to attain them before any decision is reached to employ these new techniques for specific teaching purposes. The time has come to consider whether the teacher-turned-technologist could not gradually assume the function of an "educational engineer" whose job it is to increase the output of the entire teaching machine.[19]

THE COMPREHENSIVE APPROACH

Over the past few years experience has shown that educational innovation, technological or otherwise, cannot simply be introduced in the form of a local transplant onto the existing educational anatomy. Such innovations are meaningful and effective only *in relation to their effects upon the body as a whole*. We have recently had the opportunity of seeing the futility of introducing school curricula involving, for example, the acquisition of new knowledge or of new methods of teaching without the involvement of instructors and teachers and the manufacturers of teaching materials. We have similarly learned the absurdity of teaching a particular section of the population to read and write and then not supplying them with satisfactory printed material (local press, occupational handbooks, and so on). The school today is an organic unit in which the teacher is only one teaching agent among others, just as the school itself is only one component of a larger overall educational activity. The need for technological change bids us today to turn the eye of the biologist or the mechanic on the educational system and see it as an organism.

The methods of organization which have developed over the past few years under such names as *operational research* or *systems analysis* appear to be suitable intellectual instruments for an overall critical study of existing systems and for suggesting *new educational configurations* based on scientific principles, in which there would be a place for the resources of technology.[20] Why not apply relevance trees or critical path analysis to the bottlenecks in the educational systems? Would it not be possible to apply the principles of feedback and self-correction to the active functioning of

19. G. Taylor, *The Teacher as Manager* (London: NCET, 1970).

20. *Educational Technology: The Design and Implementation of Learning Systems* (Paris: OECD, 1970).

educational institutions? Again, more generally, how can there be any hope of a rational improvement in educational activities without measuring and analyzing their functioning?

We know that by the term *system*, analysts mean the sum of separate parts acting both independently and on one another to achieve predetermined objectives; the system is, therefore, defined by reference not only to its constituent parts, but to the organization that allows it to function. In any analysis of a system the aim is therefore to measure exactly the objectives to be attained in terms of performance, to define the levels of application, to allow for the constraints under which it operates, and to derive rational operating models. Can this effort, the aim of which is to define logical structures incorporating all the constituent parts and to *marshal the various agents into a unified process in pursuit of maximum efficiency*, be applied to educational process?

In human activities other than education these coherent sets of methods have made it possible to detect the weak points and failings in a given organization, to choose from a range of schemes for improvement, to rearrange the constituent parts of a body in various combinations, or to add new parts to it in order to secure new results. Systems analysis should make it possible to define for any given organization an optimum structure which maintains equilibrium by means of successive readjustments to the environment. True, the experts are ready to admit that education is too complex an overall process to be analyzed otherwise than in terms of probability: education is an *open* system.[21] However, the thing about systems analysis is that it makes it possible to incorporate uncertainty into action. Since the new technologies are constantly coming up with further sources of information and analysis, increasingly powerful memory units, and increasingly sophisticated control mechanisms, it becomes possible to envisage the development or further development of self-organizing and self-regulating educational systems, both at the individual level and at the level of the educational institution.[22] The educational system itself could

21. F. W. Banghart, *Educational Systems Analysis* (London: Collier MacMillan Canada, 1969).

22. K. U. Smith, *Cybernetics Principles of Learning and Educational Design* (New York: Holt, Rinehart & Winston, 1966).

thus steer a more accurate course than at present by means of the incoming reactions and hence be able to evolve, adapt, and grow by mastering change.

AN EXAMPLE OF ANALYSIS: A LEARNING SEQUENCE

First, however, the educational system must be given the means of establishing correlations between the objectives, the learning processes, the means of instruction, and the teacher's functions. The analysis of the various components and various points in the act of learning will then make it possible to use on each separate occasion the situation and the means best adapted to the end in view. In one act of learning we are led to distinguish, for example, an information stage, characterized by research and the collecting of the data that have to be acquired; an exploitation stage, which involves the marshaling, criticism, and processing of the data; an assimilation stage, in which knowledge is fixed; a transfer stage, in which the knowledge is applied; and, lastly, an assessment (or self-assessment) stage.

Only the new technologies of communication allow each of these stages to combine with maximum efficiency. At the first, or "information" stage, technology facilitates acquisition of individual information by means of visual or audiovisual data banks and documentation and information centers (record libraries, film-slide libraries). The acquisition of information may be collective in form and involve mass communication (e.g., the cinema and television). The second or "exploitation" stage is generally characterized by group work and involves the use of individual response control systems. The period of assimilation and fixation may be individual and involve the use of programmed instruction, teaching machines, and learning laboratories and may also involve group work—for example, joint utilization of programmed material or group work on computer terminals. The "transfer" period lends itself to the employment of simulation techniques (closed-circuit television and teaching machines). Response analyzers and testing machines in general can be brought in during the "assessment" segment of the process. Lastly, recording machines and computers make it possible to keep an individual record of the pupil's progress throughout his school career.

Obviously, at each point in the learning process the teacher comes in for each application of a particular technique with a corresponding and different function. Before carrying out any educational operation, he will have to find the teaching strategy required to apply all the various procedures chosen. During the course of the information phase his role is that of the guide who prepares the stimulants and supplies the documentation which he has himself prepared or chosen. During the exploitation phase his role is that of a mediator or of a group leader who motivates the interactions (and who must gradually train the members of the group in group leadership). He sees that the ideas which have been acquired are properly understood and helps to discover and correct misunderstandings. During the assimilation and fixation stage, his role is diagnostic—he prescribes the treatment best suited to the capabilities of the learner. During the transfer phase, his role becomes that of an adviser-cum-guide. During the last phase of the learning process his role becomes one of checking, ensuring that the system of marking is uniform, and seeing to it that continuity is maintained in the assessment process.

The teacher's use of technology will have made him more receptive and will have placed him in a more central position so that pupils more easily approach him with their individual problems. In this connection, it cannot be stressed too strongly that the use of educational technology—far from implying any qualitative decline in the role of the teacher—frees him from certain purely mechanical tasks of exposition and repetition, thus enabling him to devote himself to the noble and irreplaceable functions of stimulation of interest, diagnosis, motivation, and advice.

This, of course, implies a fairly radical overhaul of the existing educational and administrative arrangements, which are based generally on the individual unit or class—reorganization of timetables, the splitting up of groups of classes, full-time use of schools, continuous assessment, the preparation of educational activities in interdisciplinary teams, dividing and distributing work among teachers according to their aptitude and experience, adaptation of buildings to give greater flexibility, responsibility of the pupils themselves for discipline, and the production of a considerable amount of teaching materials. Educational technology can help to reintroduce a certain amount of flexibility into the functioning of the school system, which has been in a rut for decades.[23]

However, it should not be thought that there is any single strategy for scientific reorganization of this kind. The point about systems analysis is rather that it helps to define strategies *differentiated* according to the degree of economic development, resources, and type of educational system. For example, as far as the distribution of educational information is concerned, it is possible to think of the *dissemination* of information in the form of audiovisual broadcasts, either through a restricting and relatively inexpensive system (radio, television), or through a user-controlled system involving the use of telephone lines and computer networks. Systems for the *distribution* of recordings supplied direct, either to educational institutions or to individual students at home, are another possibility. These systems of distribution, which are more complex and slower than the broadcasting systems but which are also more selective and better differentiated, can either be centralized, e.g., in the form of film-loan libraries and correspondence tuition centers, or decentralized in the form of commercial distribution direct to customers (e.g., institutional tape library or personal record library).

In countries where there are fewer industrial and professional resources these new systems could be based upon simpler or more cost-effective equipment, taking into account the needs and objectives of the educational system. In a developing country, therefore, if a system of inertia-free instantaneous broadcasting such as radio or television is chosen, a particular technique must be employed so as to get the best out of it. Where television is available it will be employed *both* for school and out-of-school educational purposes. If it is used to transmit programs for group use, it can also be used to show programmed learning exercises, which would be transmitted by other means (teaching machines) in a country that was better equipped. Television is also used to give instruc-

23. I. A. Richards, *Design for Escape: World Education through Modern Media* (New York: Harcourt, Brace & World, 1968).

tions to the teacher or instructor as to how he should conduct his teaching and how television can be incorporated in it, and provide in-service training.[24] Here a multipurpose one-medium system may prove more effective than a multimedia single-purpose system.

With a systems approach, it is not only possible to coordinate uses and techniques and to organize them rationally on a continuous basis for the individual learner, but also for the group (class or school grade) and the institution, at the regional level. It is therefore possible, proceeding by analyses, to design a complex set of harmonized functions, ranging from the microsystem of the individual learner to the national macrosystem.[25] Although it is generally accepted that the degree of complexity of systems should increase in proportion to the resources available and the difficulties of the learning process (thus the establishment of a complex technological system will generally be more justified in the case of higher education), in practice there is no reason why such a complex system could not be applied to functional literacy.

THE SCHOOL OF TOMORROW—A FACTORY OR SELF-SERVICE
ESTABLISHMENT?

By making it possible to redistribute human and material resources and by lending support to the attempt to find ways and means of increasing the internal output of the educational institution, the development of educational technology opens up the prospect in the years ahead of developing new types of educational institutions radically different in form from the elitist and selective establishments of yesterday. The establishment in which educational technology (audiovisual communication, learning laboratories, data banks) has been incorporated would, according to one model, tend to resemble an enterprise in which educational technology would be used to reduce wastage to a minimum and to optimize the act

24. In a number of African countries, however, experience has shown that certain difficulties can arise as a result of combining too hastily different distribution networks. For example, such a tempting technique as "radiovision" (the projection of slides synchronized with a radio transmission) presents both the disadvantages of being bound by the constraints of broadcasting and the hazards of having to rely on the delivery of the slides.

25. Harry F. Silberman, *The Systems Approach, Technology and the School*, forthcoming.

of learning by establishing precise mechanisms to produce effective individuals by dint of intellectual constraints, fear and the spectre of failure having first been banished from their training.

In contrast to this deterministic model based on efficiency, there would be another model, no doubt using similar means but arranged in different configurations. It would offer a community service of individualized self-instruction for safeguarding individual freedom of action—a complete self-service system adaptable to individual needs, to which the pupils would feel an allegiance based on individual involvement.

The first of these formulas would prove particularly useful in immediate vocational training. However, since the society of tomorrow is to be founded on lifelong education and since the spirit of one's initial training determines the practical interest he shows in his subsequent training, the self-teaching center will, more so than the learning enterprise, be bound up with lifelong education. Teaching is less and less a matter of forcing information upon pupils or exposing them to knowledge, but rather is one of instructing the young by the practice of self-teaching—a method calculated to ensure social mobility—how to shape their education by mastering a system and progressing beyond it. Thus, educational technology will not be confined to increasing the internal efficiency of the school center; it also will increase its involvement with social reality.

Assistance to Strategies of Technological Innovations

In the past, reforming education meant converting from one relatively stable system to another equally stable. Now the time has come for leaps to be made under conditions of permanent instability—from autocratic, fixed, closed, and ponderous systems to planned, open, flexible, and self-adjusting ones that will admit of the possibility of forecasting and integration.[26]

It seems that there are three different strategies for technological innovations: The *first* is to change everything at the same time, but so far there has been little instance of this having been undertaken successfully. The *second* one involves modifying the existing

26. Henri Dieuzeide, "Educational Technology," *British Journal of Educational Technology* 2 (1971): 168-87.

state of affairs by introducing innovation at the lowest level in the system and carrying on from there, the new system pushing the old one in front of it; such is the case with the gradual introduction of television year by year, involving, in the case of the Ivory Coast, the transformation of primary education and, in the case of El Salvador, of secondary education. The *third* strategy involves setting up and developing a new system parallel to the old one and capable of influencing it and eventually substituting for it; such as in the case, for example, of educational television for elementary schools in Niger or, at another level, of the Open University in the United Kingdom.

In the long term, this latter strategy is no doubt the most effective, although this is not to say that we should not *optimize* right away the use of technology in education, such as it is, and undertake localized projects without waiting until all the conditions are right. It is not inconsistent with an attempt to *rationalize* the use of educational technology on the basis of models that combine all the data into an integral system. Planning by segment and long-term planning are only two aspects—strategical and tactical—of the same productive effort.[27]

CRITERIA FOR APPLICABILITY

It must be remembered, especially regarding developing countries, that a comprehensive body of experience is lacking and it is still difficult to suggest definite, universally applicable strategies. Sophisticated technologies do not yet offer more than a few really large-scale projects and intermediate technology is still considerably dispersed. It appears difficult at present to give one form of technology precedence over another. For instance, deciding for intermediate technologies probably means renouncing for a long time the possibility offered by the sophisticated technology to keep back the corrosive effects of traditional environment upon innovative projects. It means also replacing a strategy of shock and abrupt change with one of gradual change and abandoning the hope of accelerating evolution by taking shortcuts and reintroducing the time factor as one of the inevitable trammels of development. Might it not be considered, therefore, that each of these technical

27. Richards, op. cit.

choices corresponds to a specific development effort within the framework of a general strategy and in connection with a definite objective? It may appear necessary to give priority to a shock effect and therefore make sacrifices for sophisticated technology (Ivory Coast). Elsewhere, on the contrary, when all available local resources must be mobilized, intermediate technologies will be applied (China).

Decisions can only be reached after establishing the economic alternatives of the various technologies (by means of what configuration can the best instruction be given to the most individuals in the shortest time?), their organizational limitations (training, maintenance, evaluation), and, finally, the learning criteria for selecting a technology—relevance to the general objectives of the system, sufficient power for effecting changes in structures and contents, orientation towards helping the learner rather than the teacher, capacity to remain open and to be developed and adapted. A first attempt at listing some of the required criteria for developing countries based on present development of international assistance programs would appear as in figure 1.

INTERNATIONAL STRATEGIES

Such criteria help in drawing up complex strategies combining these various resources: for instance, radio broadcasting as a low-cost, wide-range medium for mass instruction (primary and rural education), sophisticated multimedia techniques for fields capable of both financing and integrating them (e.g., higher technical instruction and intermediate technologies where priority is given to developing technological creativeness and devising schemes adapted to the environment).

Such systems which can be developed first will probably be in areas less burdened by antiquated structures and therefore present less risk of an abrupt rejection—the out-of-school and informal sectors, "remote-controlled" education, part-time education, or sectors under review because of strong external pressures, such as higher education or technical education. Even at the microsystem level, care will have to be taken to define an operational *critical mass* that is suffcient to bring about a chain reaction leading to renewal. Properly conducted, *technical innovation should be a*

Criteria		Sophisticated technologies, e.g., ETV (mass instruction) or CAI (individualized instruction)	Intermediate technology, e.g., teaching in small groups, cooperative learning	Rational technologies, e.g., programmed instruction, organized learning
Geographical distribution	in relation to the size of population	considerable	none	none
	distance, saving in time, rapidity of result	considerable	some	some
Cultural effects	neutrality or adequation to tradition	middling to none	considerable	intermediate
	springboard to development	considerable (either positive or negative)	considerable	considerable
Pedagogical effects	simplicity	no	yes	yes
	immediate effectiveness	yes	assumed	yes
	long-range	unknown	unknown	yes
Economic acceptability	investment (foreign aid)	considerable	only for R and D	considerable
	operation (local)	considerable	slight	slight
	cost/effectiveness forecast	good	very good	not obvious
Technical feasibility	complexity/operation	considerable	little	little
	maintenance	considerable	small	none
	dependency on industrialized countries	considerable	slight	slight
Level of staff qualifications	training	considerable	average	considerable
	ability to adapt to new situations	considerable	considerable	average
Political implication	advisability expediency	small	considerable	few
	factor in national unity	important	average	slight

Fig. 1. Educational technologies: Some criteria for determining applicability to developing countries

focal point for energies around which could be grouped efforts at reorganization which could not be undertaken otherwise. There have already been frequent instances of the *catalytic effect* of school television or programmed instruction in hastening the reform of school curricula and teacher training. The more limited the resources of the country, the more urgent it will be to identify existing technological resources that could be more fully utilized: broadcasting agencies, printing facilities, data-processing centers, and so on. It will be essential to coordinate the use of such resources in the framework of an overall plan.

An attempt will also be made to improve cooperation between the various occupational groups concerned with the development of education. In order to achieve progress in this direction it is essential that the manufacturers of teaching equipment and program producers rally around explicit educational objectives. In some countries electronics engineers and visual-aid manufacturers, textbook publishers, and the developers of programmed instruction methods are already trying to combine their efforts. Elsewhere, national agencies for the production and distribution of new teaching materials have already been set up (Sweden, Netherlands); and in some countries (e.g., Japan and the United Kingdom) various authorities or ministries have worked together to coordinate their use of the existing communication networks.

Particular care is being taken at present to develop *centers for the promotion of innovation,* whose task it is to produce—or get those concerned to produce—new school curricula, new systems of evaluation and control, and new teaching materials, as well as to form *centers of excellence* and truly experimental establishments based on new organizational principles, with the aim of bringing them together, of linking them, and, if possible, of coordinating them in a flexible manner calculated to ensure mutual benefit and to increase their impact and their capacity for innovation.

Consequently, it is applied research conducted by multidisciplinary teams that should be encouraged. Its results will not be in the form of reports but of *products,* which may be new teaching materials, and also methodological systems or new institutional forms. Research done as a pretext and research of the academic kind with a bias towards theoretical generalization should be avoided. Industry and medicine are standing proof that effective methods can be generally introduced without being given a formal basis in theory.

Lastly, there is need to inform more and train better. We must inform the public since it is the customer of the educational system, and especially pupils' families, whose attitude is often wary. We must train the teachers and change the old patterns they have been used to, in order to prepare them for the new roles that educational technology entails for them, especially their roles as in-school and out-of-school leaders. Such training should be given to in-service teachers as well as to student teachers and this will be possible through the transformation of the professional training institutes into lifelong training institutes having at their command all the resources of modern educational technology. Further, special attention will have to be given to the training of a corps of educational technologists, i.e., specialists of all levels, who, according to some experts, may in twenty years' time account for anything up to 10 percent of the total of all those employed in education: specialists in the revision of objectives and curricula, testing and measurement specialists, administrators of new systems, communications specialists, production and maintenance technicians, and the like.

International assistance programs are also being rethought with a view to the systematic development of innovation, taking due care not to spread resources too thinly or to disperse efforts too widely.[28] New avenues have been opened up by the tentative start on *integrated* educational planning that has been made in Algeria and in Indonesia and is presently being developed in many countries under the guidance of UNDP and UNESCO. Aid should stimulate, not paralyze, communications between the motive elements of innovation within the country concerned (research centers and production centers). For most of the creative efforts will fall to research and development institutes, probably in association with local universities, with local personnel predominating, and with the assistance of experts from the developed countries being reduced to a minimum. The institutes' activities should be oriented towards working up materials, developing critical methods (feedback, evaluation) and elaborating team production techniques (systems analysis and programming).

It seems, therefore, that more serious consideration should be given to the idea of international networks for liaison between these elements throughout the world, involving (wherever possible) the use of the most up-to-date means of communication and exchange (computers and space communication in particular) and making it possible to achieve a better division of assistance work. Some national centers could be formed into support centers to develop educational technology at the regional level, as in the case

28. *Education: Sector Working Paper* (Washington: World Bank, 1971).

of the Institute for Educational Communication in Latin America (ILCE) in Mexico, or of the Asian Center of Educational Innovation for Development (ACEID) in Bangkok. Both are information centers using the most up-to-date communications technology and centers for training and research geared to technological innovation. Such regional networks and centers should be backed by *task forces* made up of specialists who, at the request of the governments, may be called in to help fit new educational strategies based on systems analysis and technology to the country's special needs. These agencies should have a strong anthropological component in order to advise educational authorities on how to assimilate new developments without disrupting the traditional cultural balance.

GUIDELINES FOR ECONOMIC DECISIONS

Since the final purpose of educational technology is not to provide each individual teacher with his own personal audiovisual outfit but to reform the functioning of the educational system, and since its introduction provides the opportunity for analyzing—and perhaps for reorganizing—the existing institutions, it is within the available or foreseeable budgetary provisions of a country that educational technology must be introduced, by adjustment of educational practices to resources and vice versa. In a number of European countries, the establishment of experimental institutions has been rendered possible by an all-out effort to reorganize teaching spaces and to rethink fittings and equipment. Within a given context, this involves a comparison of the effectiveness of the old system with that of the new educational pattern. It is a question of finding out which teaches more subjects best in terms of quantity and quality, in more places and in equal or less time.[29]

29. A good example of a purely additional analysis is given by Vaizey et al. regarding study of cost for training packages for renovation of the curriculum in English secondary schools: "For writing the packages in five subjects—English, math, general science, social studies, French—they have allowed a salary cost equivalent to one teacher in each subject (plus that of a coordinating director and of secretarial staff) for each year's work produced. All ancillary costs in producing, receiving, and using the packages have been included. Suppose costs are spread over 5,000 users, the total cost of education in a secondary school would be raised by 2 percent per child; at 10,000 copies the increase is 1.5 percent. Package-based learning is not impossibly expensive." Quoted in L. Taylor, *Resources for Learning* (London: Penguin Books, 1970), p. 213.

Conversely, the costs of integration of educational technology could be calculated not in terms of *additional expenditure* per capita, but in terms of *overall expenditure* of the redeployed system. This is the case, for instance, of the program that has been undertaken in the Ivory Coast for the incorporation of television into primary education. It is based on a planned reduction by half over a period of ten years in the present dropout rate and on an increase in operating costs of primary education of approximately 8 percent, which would be covered by the estimated increase in national revenue.[30] In assessing unsophisticated versus advanced technologies, economists should be on their guard against concluding too hastily that the utilization of advanced educational technology will a priori weigh too heavily on the economics of the developing countries. Modern communications apparatus, particularly those involving electronics, are among the rare manufactured products whose cost continues to decline rapidly. For instance, a transistor which cost ten dollars a decade ago has today been replaced by an integrated circuit which costs one dollar and does the work that fifty transistors did ten years ago. The cost diminishes as the extensiveness and reliability of the service increases. The cost of the same series of computer operations has become about six hundred times less than it was twenty years ago. Moreover, it has to be admitted that innovation today is a costly affair and that we can hardly choose between whether to innovate or not to innovate. It is a matter of knowing how to innovate at greater or lesser cost and over a longer or shorter period of time. It is then possible to look beyond the individual cost-benefit ratio and to compare costs and performance in global terms. Recent studies by economists would seem to indicate that there is a level for the distribution of resources within an educational system beyond which there is no longer any improvement in the results. It is this state of equilibrium which must be sought and attained and the place of educational technology at last defined.

It has been established that in most countries, whether developing or developed, educational expenditure is tending to mount regularly year in and year out by anywhere from 5 to 8 percent.

30. *Television in the Modernisation of Education in the Ivory Coast,* Republic of the Ivory Coast, 1972.

Most of this increase is accounted for by rising salaries of teachers. The question today is whether priority should not be given to investment that seems likely to have a positive long-term effect on the efficiency of education. The time may have come for educationists to ask—and governments to decide—that some of the increase in national educational expenditure already scheduled for the coming decade (say, half) be devoted exclusively to refining the ways and means best calculated to ensure a rapid increase in the efficiency of the educational system and, more especially, to the rational development of technologies of organization and communication of knowledge.

It may well happen that the developing countries will not be the only ones to benefit from this industrialization. On the whole, international assistance is helping to develop new techniques according to a "shared risk" assistance scheme. The contribution of the highly developed countries to projects of this type is intended to encourage a universal movement towards innovation, but they themselves may benefit from the pedagogical or technological fall-out from these projects. This is particularly the case with regard to the Spanish project of computer utilization, which could lead soon to a counterflow of Spanish technical assistance to the donor countries.

Novissima Verba

Education may indeed be regarded as an economically depressed sphere of activity in all countries. Consisting of activities based more on work than on capital (as can be seen from the size of the staff budget in relation to the whole operational budget of education) and entrenched in its traditions, education resists progress. If it is established that educational systems throughout the world (in the developed as well as in the developing countries) are and will remain an area of general economic and intellectual under-development for a long time, perhaps they should all be subjected to the same thorough and cooperative examination in terms of the respective roles to be played by sophisticated, intermediate, and rational technologies in their development.

True, education, which is concerned with values, cannot be entirely rationalized, if only because the demand for education is in itself an irrational phenomenon. Education has a great many other functions than transmitting acquired knowledge and turning out lucid and effective future citizens. Educational institutions, according to their various levels, function as places for child-minding and protection, as centers in which national unity may be forged and in which a civic education or a premilitary training may be given, and also as places where the individual learns to find his place in society and as a ritual instrument by means of which the individual is initiated into adult life.[31]

The crisis of education is not going to be completely overcome by the introduction of technological principles and communication machinery. But by inducing each educational system to reexamine its functions of production and control, to create for itself a new and more flexible structure, and to generate within itself new roles and new human relations by making it adaptable and flexible, is not technology enabling education to fulfill its other functions better and to reconsdier its ultimate purpose with the requisite lucidity?

31. Carl Bereiter, "Schools Without Education," *Harvard Educational Review* 42 (1972): 390-413.

CHAPTER XVIII

Teacher Image in Mass Culture: Symbolic Functions of the "Hidden Curriculum"

GEORGE GERBNER

"The figure of the schoolteacher," wrote Hofstadter,[1] "may well be taken as a central symbol in any society." But a symbol of what? Searching for an answer is like opening Pandora's box with its host of evils. My examination of the evidence suggests that teachers, schools, and scholars project a synthetic cultural image that helps to explain—and determine—the ambivalent functions and paradoxical fortunes of the educational enterprise in American society. The clues that point to that disquieting conclusion (which also raises questions about anticipated extensions of the present structure of culture-power) have led me to new reflections. These concern the illusions and reality of schooling, the nature of symbolic functions, the lessons of national and cross-cultural research on the teacher-image, and the role of that "hidden curriculum" in social policy.

The basic features of American schools, as of our society, have been fixed for more than a century. Spectacular changes transformed the "quality of life" through unfolding and extending those features into every aspect of existence. Among the most dramatic of the changes has been the rise of institutions of cultural mass production—the mass media—exempt from the laws of public but not of private corporate development and authority. These institutions have taken over many functions performed in the past by the parent, the church, and the school. The media's chief impact stems from their universality as the common bond among *all* groups in our culture. The media manufacture the shared sym-

1. Richard Hofstadter, *Anti-Intellectualism in American Life* (New York: Alfred A. Knopf, 1963), p. 309.

bolic environment, create and cultivate large heterogeneous publics, define the agenda of public discourse, and represent all other
institutions in the vivid imagery of fact and fiction designed for
mass publics. Teachers and schools no longer enjoy much autonomy, let alone their former monopoly, as the public dispensers
of knowledge. The formal educational enterprise exists in a cultural
climate largely dominated by the informal "curriculum" of the
mass media.

New developments in communication technology may both
individualize and globalize the penetration of mass-produced messages into the mainstream of collective consciousness. Before we
can consider what that new transformation might portend for our
schools (and for our culture), we need to take a fresh and sober
look at the omens from the past.

Many of those who would correct the evils of society slowly
and painlessly have long argued for educational extension, improvement, and reform. And, for more than a century, schooling has
been extended, improved, and reformed. Yet it is still compulsory,
unequal, class-biased, racist, and sexist. From the Coleman report[2]
of 1966 through the Jencks report[3] of 1972, study after study
demonstrates that the schools, even when "equal," tend to justify
rather than rectify the child's fate as defined by the culture of the
home, the street, and the television.

Eminent public figures declare schools a "disaster area" and
"a pathological sector of the economy," meaning that even money
cannot cure what ails them (although that remedy has never really
been tried on a large national scale). A few call for their abolition.
Instead of becoming the social corrective that idealistic reformers
sought and democratic rhetoric promised, the more schools change,
the more they streamline their induction of young people into their
places and roles in the existing social structure. The Mason-Dixon
line between the states has been abolished, but its modern equivalent now rings every city and the few bridges busing children
across it may be dismantled. Schools still provide custodial drill

2. James S. Coleman et al., *Equality of Educational Opportunity* (Washington: U.S. Office of Education, 1966).

3. Christopher Jencks et al., *Inequality: A Reassessment of the Effect of
Family and Schooling in America* (New York: Basic Books, 1972).

for the poor, enrichment for the rich, and equal instruction for those with equal economic or political clout.

We are just beginning to understand that these harsh facts result from no accidental abberation or cultural lag. A new generation of "revisionist" historians has exploded "the great school legend." Greer's book[4] by that title shows how the perennial "crisis" of the schools, like the perpetual "problem" of the slums, is in fact more functional to the existing social order than would be its elimination. Katz's book[5] on class, bureaucracy, and the schools documents the recurring phenomenon of school-reform movements that engage the zeal and energies of those who would attack the inequities of society, only to find that each wave of "reform" harnesses their schools to the dominant interests of the times.

Nearly twenty years after the Supreme Court ordered school desegregation "with all deliberate speed," feeble efforts at enforcement bog down in political controversy reminiscent of the parochial school aid controversy that was used to defeat past proposals for massive federal financing. Busing is claimed to threaten the fiber of society when it brings children of different races and social classes together, but not when used to keep them apart, its traditional use. If "campus unrest" is followed by recession and cutbacks, who is to blame? The schools that should redeem us teeter on the edge of bankruptcy. It seems that when citizens consider what is nearest and dearest to them, e.g., children, they are most vulnerable to the deceptions of their culture.

Symbolic Functions

We are keenly aware that messages intended to persuade usually serve the purposes of those who create and disseminate them. Less obvious but perhaps even more crucial are the purposes served by news, fiction, drama, and other storytelling designed with no other obvious intent than just to inform or to entertain. The social tasks to which presumably objective news, neutral fiction, or nontendentious entertainment lend themselves are what I call sym-

4. Colin Greer, *The Great School Legend: A Revisionist Interpretation of American Public Education* (New York: Basic Books, 1972).

5. Michael B. Katz, *Class, Bureaucracy, and the Schools: The Illusion of Educational Change in America* (New York: Praeger Publishers, 1971).

bolic functions. They are the consequences inherent in the way things "work" in the symbolic world of storytelling.

These functions usually do not stem from individual communications or campaigns but from the general composition and structure of the bulk of the symbolic environment to which an entire community is exposed. The consequences typically are not those of change but of continuity and resistance to change. Given a stable social order, the functions are usually to selectively cultivate existing tendencies and perhaps to deepen and sharpen them.

Symbolic functions differ from those of nonsymbolic events in the ways in which causal relationships must be traced in the two realms. Physical causation exists outside and independently of consciousness. Trees do not grow and chemicals do not react "on purpose," although human purposes may intervene or cause them to function. When a sequence of physical events is set in motion, we have only partial awareness and little control over the entire chain of its consequences.

The symbolic world, however, is totally invented. Nothing happens in it independently of man's will, although much that happens may again escape individual awareness or scrutiny. The reasons that things exist in the symbolic world, and the ways in which things are related to one another and to their symbolic consequences, as in a play or story, are completely artificial. This does not make their production any more arbitrary or whimsical than the events of the physical world. But it means that the laws of the symbolic world are entirely socially and culturally determined. A character in fiction "dies" not because he has lived but because it serves a purpose to have him die. Intended or not, that purpose is the only reality of the story. The causal link is not between life and death but between a creator's or producing organization's position in life and society and the significance of that death. No TV badman ever dies a natural death, nor can the hero of a western serial be cut down in the prime of life. To be "true to life" in fiction would falsify the deeper truth of cultural and social values served by symbolic functions.

Whatever exists in the symbolic world is there because someone put it there. The reason may be deliberate and planned, or circumstantial such as an "unrelated" marketing or programming decision, or a vague feeling that it will "improve the story." Having been put there, things not only "stand for" other things as all symbols do, but also *do* something in their symbolic context. The introduction (or elimination) of a character, a scene, an event has functional consequences. It changes other things in the story. It makes the whole work "work" differently. Dynamic symbol systems are not "maps" of some other "real" territory. They are our mythology, our organs of social meaning. They make visible some conceptions of the invisible forces of life and society. We select and shape them to bend otherwise elusive facts to our (not always conscious) purposes. Whether we know it or intend it or not, purposes are inherent in the way things actually work out in the symbolic world. Even when men and institutions lie, they cannot do so without giving off signs of the purposes of their lying, at least in the long run; otherwise, why lie? More problems arise from communicating hidden purposes than from failing to communicate at all.

How things work out in mass-produced symbolic systems, as in all collective myths, celebrations, and rituals, is indicative of institutional interests and pressures. Various power roles within and without the institution enter into the decision-making process that prescribes, selects, and shapes the final product. In the creation of news, facts impose some constraints upon invention; the burden of serving institutional purposes is placed upon selection, treatment, context, and display. Fiction and drama carry no presumption of facticity and thus do not inhibit at all the candid expression of social values. On the contrary, they give free reign to adjusting facts to the truth of institutional purpose. Fiction can thus perform social symbolic functions more directly than can other forms of discourse.

That is why in fiction and drama there is no need to moralize. The moral is usually in the "facts" themselves. For example, if a social inferior (lower class, native, black, etc.) usurps the place of a superior (through marriage, business deal, combat, etc.), he or she can have an "unfortunate accident," thus avoiding overt bias and yet performing the symbolic function of enhancing the superior life chances of "superior" characters. Violence in the mass media—unlike life—is usually among strangers, permitting the lessons of social power (what types stand to win or lose in a conflict) to emerge unhindered by close human ties. Fiction can act out purposes by presenting a world in which things seem to work out as they "ought to," regrettable or even terrible as that might be made to appear.

Characters come to life in the symbolic world of mass culture to perform functions of genuine social import. These functions need not be planned or perceived *as such*. They need not even conform to any overt rationalizations or moralizing. The functions are implicit, not in what producers and audiences think they "know," but in what they assimilate of that which the characters of the symbolic world in fact *are* and *do*.

The "Hidden Curriculum" and Its Effects

The "facts of life" in the symbolic world form patterns that I call the "hidden curriculum." It is the framework that makes the notion of "effects" sensible as those changes that can be observed within a stable structure. The *prior* preoccupation with effects is misleading. However, it only betrays greater concern with marketing tactics than with the basic allocation of values in our society. The post-World War II movement within social science reflected more concern with buying or voting behavior than with meanings that govern *all* behavior. Now, social scientists are taking another look at the relationships between social structures and those general frameworks of knowledge and values that, in turn, shape the meanings and the efficacy of particular messages. As humanists have always known, no society designs its religions or its customs or its schools on the basis of a comparative assessment of the effects of various factual or philosophical statements. That would put the cart of tactics before the horse of basic aims and functions. Any assessment of effects must assume the existence of a standard of measurement against which different or changing quantities and qualities can be measured. That standard is implicit in the value structure of a culture. Should that be immune from inquiry? The contention that the existence or meaning of an action or communication should not be assessed until its effects are established is tantamount to the assertion that the structure of a culture should not be investigated; only its tactics are to be subjected to "scientific" inquiry. Far from being scientific, this is itself a symbolic tactic attempting to define what is "scientifically" reasonable and respectable in a way that serves only the most dominant, pervasive, and taken-for-granted social interests.

The hidden curriculum is a lesson plan that no one teaches but everyone learns. It consists of the symbolic contours of the social order. One cannot sensibly ask what its effects are any more than one can ask about the effects of being born Chinese rather than American. Culture power is the ability to define the rules of the game of life that most members of a society will take for granted. That some will reject and others will come to oppose some of the rules or the game itself is obvious and may on occasion be important. But the most important thing to know is the nature and structure of the representations that most people will assume to be normal and inevitable. Having established some features of the hidden curriculum, one can then ask how its specific lessons are internalized and which of its functions serve what purposes.

Every culture, as any school, will organize knowledge into patterns that cultivate a social order. The fundamental lessons of the curriculum are not just what pupils learn in mathematics, history, physics, etc., but also the fact that *those* are its commonly required subjects and not basketweaving, harmony, or Marxism-Leninism (except where *that* is required). One cannot ask about the effects of that pattern of required learnings except by comparing it with the functional dynamics of other patterns. The structures themselves and most of their symbolic functions are inevitably assimilated if there is to be anything like a relatively stable social order. Culture *is* that system of messages that makes human society possible. After grasping the implicit agenda of discourse, scale of priorities, spectrum of valuations, and clusters of associations that most members of a culture come to assume as the overall framework for most of their thinking and behavior, we can begin to observe the fluctuations and reversals within that structure. Only after that can we ask the "effects" question.

The question of effects, properly phrased, inquires first into individual and group selectivities by dipping into the currents and cross-currents of the cultural stream. Secondly, "effects" research can investigate the contributions that particular types of messages make to the processing of particular conceptions within given frameworks of values and knowledge. We are a long way from being able to answer the second question. The answer will be of strategic significance once we know more of what the game is about.

The prior need is to examine the framework implicit in the hidden curriculum. We must first go beneath the explicit and fragmented significance of individual images available to casual personal scrutiny and find the symbolic patterns and functions that entertain (in every sense of that word) the collective morality and the dominant sensibilities of the social order.

The image of schools and scholars is that part of the hidden curriculum in which all members of society learn about learning itself. Its symbolic functions relate images of learning (and of the formal institutions of learning) to basic human values and to the locus of power in society. I think that the figure of the school teacher is a central symbol of the uses and control of popular knowledge. Its most telling features touch upon questions of vitality and self-direction, social relations, morality, and power.

Historical Images

When he is not the Ichabod Crane of literature (scared out of town by the virile males of the community, with a pumpkin smashed over his head), the typical teacher in American novels is "stooped, gaunt, and gray with weariness. His suit has the shine of shabby gentility and hangs loose from his undernourished frame." [6] So it is, until class is out and memory rings the school bell when we say a nostalgic "Good Morning, Miss Dove" or bid a tearful "Goodbye, Mr. Chips."

In his study of the college professor in the novel, Belok [7] noted that American fiction uses teaching to "unsex a woman." Even being a teacher's wife may be unenviable. Theodore Dreiser characterized Donald Moranville Strunk, A.B., Ph.D., professor of history, as having had "one of the homeliest women for a wife I ever

6. Arthur Foff, "The Teacher as Hero," in *Readings in Education,* ed. Arthur Foff and Jean D. Grambs (New York: Harper & Bros., 1956).

7. Michael Victor Belok, "The College Professor in the American Novel, 1940-1957" (Doctoral diss., University of Southern California, 1958.)

saw." College students responding to a survey [8] characterized the school teacher as a person "who cannot even command an attractive wife." Love eludes even the attractive, eager "Our Miss Brooks" and the owlish but smart "Mr. Peepers"; sex degrades the neurotic Miss Brodie and destroys Professor Rath of *The Blue Angel.*

For Americans, the prestigious title "professor" resounds with mock deference. *The Century Dictionary and Cyclopedia* for 1899 gave as one definition of professor ". . . any one who publicly teaches or exercises an art or occupation for pay, as dancing-master, phrenologist, balloonist, juggler, acrobat, boxer, etc." From there it was not too far to the piano player in a brothel or, as Henry L. Mencken euphemistically recorded in *The American Language* (Supplement II), "a house musician." In time the usage mellowed to permit any prominent orchestra leader to be called "professor," as those who remember Kay Kyser will recall.[9] Recent media fare is replete with such phenomena as the movie *The Nutty Professor,* TV's "Professor Backward," the cartoon "Professor Wimple's Crossword Zoo," and Pat Paulsen's "Laugh-In" professor.

Belok could find only about two hundred novels since 1900 in which college professors appeared as characters. Major American novelists, wrote Lyons,[10] either have avoided the "academy" or have written novels that are basically anti-intellectual. An English reviewer of the American scene observed, however, that the college novel is now a "cottage industry." "And so it seems," commented Shapiro,[11] noting the entry of writers into the universities, "as book after book assaults us with tales of assorted hypocrisies committed under the name of higher education."

Hofstadter has also observed that the American teacher has not become an important national figure, worthy of emulation. His-

8. Donald D. O'Dowd and David C. Beardslee, *College Student Images of a Selected Group of Professions and Occupations,* Cooperative Research Project No. 562 (8142) (Washington: U.S. Office of Education, April 1960).

9. Robert L. Coard, "In Pursuit of the Word 'Professor'," *Journal of Higher Education* 3 (1959): 237-45.

10. John O. Lyons, *The College Novel in America* (Carbondale: Southern Illinois University Press, 1962).

11. Charles Shapiro, "The Poison Ivy League," *Saturday Review* 46 (1963): 37.

torical reasons may partly account for the fact that the scholar, as Wecter also noted in his *The Hero in America*,[12] "has never kindled the American imagination."

Before the industrial and national revolutions and even after the influences of those movements were operating in Europe, teachers were likely to be recruited from among the misfits of society. When the common schools were established in Russia, the theological seminaries dumped their "undesirables" to be the teachers. In the Prussia of Frederick the Great, it was the army that disposed of its invalids by their appointment as schoolmasters. "The low opinion of the rank-and-file schoolmaster in Europe spread to the New World, and a seventeenth-century rector of Annapolis recorded that on the arrival of every ship containing bondservants or convicts, schoolmasters were offered for sale but that they did not fetch as good prices as weavers, tailors, and other tradesmen."[13]

The national revolutions of Europe had a popular cultural character. Many of the leaders were writers and poets rising through the ranks of the intellectuals closest to the people—the teachers. W. G. Cove, the British teacher, strike leader, union president, and member of Parliament, once wrote: "At the head of every continental revolutionary movement, or near the head of it, stands an ex-teacher."

Until perhaps the emergence of the black liberation movement, which for reasons peculiar to American culture seemed to propel clergymen rather than teachers into leadership, there has been no comparable historical force to add a heroic dimension to the traditional image of the American teacher. The forced pace of industrialization in the nineteenth century and the consequent pressure for extending public education created the monitorial schools, according to Wittlin, "to fit the early state of industrial civilization."

"Pupils were cheaply mass produced, down to $1 per year. The scholars, who first learned their lessons from the teacher, conveyed exactly the same lesson to other children, ten to a monitor. . . . In 1916 a book appeared in Boston on *Public School Administration*, by E. P. Cubberley, in which it was stated that ". . . the schools are, in a sense,

12. Dixon Wecter, *The Hero in America* (New York: Charles Scribner's Sons, 1941), p. 478.

13. Alma S. Wittlin, "The Teachers," *Daedalus* 92 (1963): 750.

factories in which the raw materials are to be shaped into products to meet the various demands of life." According to this philosophy the educator was allotted the modest role of the copyist of patterns."[14]

During the ensuing years, the cultural forces that shape the common images of society became largely mechanized, centralized, and commercialized. Teacher-power emerged as an organized force and education became a political battleground. But the social function of the teacher image in the new culture remained the traditional one: to cultivate mistrust of the intellect on the loose.

Teacher and School in U.S. Media

There are 2.5 million teachers in the public schools in the United States. They range from twenty-two to over sixty-five years of age and come from all states, classes, religions, and ethnic groups. Of course, they have some characteristics as a group: they average thirty-nine years of age, twelve years of professional experience, and about nine thousand dollars a year in salary. Two out of every three are women. Teaching is the largest profession; its members run the gamut of human types.

But not in popular fiction and drama. The raw facts of life are not the truth of social and institutional purpose. Frequency of symbolic representation is not the reflection of census figures. The casting of the symbolic world has a message of its own.

Studies of the representation of occupations by mass media characters (see DeFleur,[15] Gerbner[16]), celebrities (Winick,[17] Hazard[18]), and even movie titles[19] agree that teachers, the largest pro-

14. Ibid., p. 751.

15. Melvin L. DeFleur and Lois B. DeFleur, "The Relative Contribution of Television as a Learning Source for Children's Occupational Knowledge," *American Sociological Review* 32 (1967): 777-89.

16. George Gerbner, "The Film Hero: A Cross-Cultural Study," *Journalism Monographs*, no. 13, American Association and Departments of Journalism, 1969.

17. Charles Winick, "Trends in the Occupation of Celebrities: A Study of News-Magazines Profiles and Television Interviews," *Journal of Social Psychology* 60 (1963): 301-10.

18. Patrick D. Hazard, "The Entertainer as Hero: A Problem of the Mass Media," *Journalism Quarterly* 39 (1962): 436-44.

19. James Verb, "An Analysis of Movie Titles with the Intention of Finding the Occupations Which Are Listed in Them and the Words Which Are Most Commonly Associated with Them" (Unpublished class paper, University of Illinois, 1961).

fessional group in life, are among those least represented in the media world. Only about 2 to 3 percent of all identifiable professional references or characterizations go to media teachers. DeFleur's classification of occupational roles found the same number of educators as taxi, truck, and bus drivers in the televised labor force.

Most of the literary studies delineate a teacher image created for elite audiences. Except when mellowed by misty memories of childhood, it is generally cruel and unsympathetic, as if in revenge for the intellectual and social pretensions of the hired hand. Much of that image found its way into the mass media, somewhat relieved by the populist fantasy of the "good" if not too enviable teacher.

Studies of media images were conducted by a group of researchers at the University of Illinois; the work is continuing at the University of Pennsylvania. For a number of years our focus was the portrayal of teachers, students, and schools in the mass media. Some studies dealt with one medium, like Schwartz's study of Hollywood movies [20] and Brown's study of magazine fiction;[21] others ranged more widely. The U.S. Office of Education supported my analysis of over fourteen hundred feature films, television and radio plays, and popular magazine stories featuring twenty-eight hundred leading characters in the mass media of ten countries.[22] The National Science Foundation, UNESCO, and the International Sociological Association jointly sponsored a study that I did of the "film hero" involving one year's feature film production in six countries.[23] I will draw on the summaries of these and other studies to piece together some basis for reflecting upon the symbolic functions and social role of the image of the "teacher" in mass culture.

20. Jack Schwartz, "The Portrayal of Education in American Motion Pictures, 1931-1961" (Doctoral diss., University of Illinois, 1963).

21. Roger L. Brown, "The Fictional Presentation of Education in *The Saturday Evening Post* and *Woman*" (Master's thesis, University of Illinois, 1963).

22. George Gerbner, "Mass Communications and Popular Conceptions of Education: A Cross-Cultural Study," Cooperative Research Project no. 876 (Washington: U.S. Office of Education, 1964); idem, "Images Across Cultures: Teachers in Mass Media Fiction and Drama," *School Review* 74 (1966): 212-29.

23. Gerbner, "The Film Hero," op. cit.

Schwartz's study [24] of Hollywood movies found that the presence of a teacher tips the odds three to one in favor of the movie being a comedy. Mass media teachers, creatures of private industry depicting public agents, suffer from signs of a cultural power conflict in which the media have the upper hand. The study's comprehensive review of research concludes:

> Teachers in books, drama, magazine cartoons, and films were depicted as tyrannical, brutal, pedantic, dull, awkward, queer, and depressed. The few attractive teachers remained in the profession only long enough to find a mate. Teachers had a difficult time getting and staying married. One investigator noted that two-thirds of the teachers were portrayed as emotionally maladjusted. Another writer noted that "to succeed as a teacher one must fail as a man or woman." [25]

LOVE AND THE TEACHER

Love and sex are dramatic symbols of vitality and power. How a profession fares in love in the mass media is a good measure of its symbolic stature.

The mass media teacher pays a price for professional success. The price is impotence, and worse. The "schoolmarm" image hits women especially hard. Love and marriage are women's chief media "specialities" and typical reasons for existing in the stories at all.

Female characters in the world of mass fiction and drama are limited to a narrow range of parts. That is why media males not only dominate media females (except in the home where males *prefer* to be incompetent) but also vastly outnumber them. The average ratio is four men for every woman. But the proportion varies by theme. Love, marriage, and bringing up children are themes that utilize women characters in parts that do not require special explanation.

Studies of school-related stories in all media [26] found both women teachers and love playing prominent parts—but rarely together. Almost half of all media teachers are women; this is a high female ratio for the media, but still lower than the two-thirds of

24. Schwartz, op. cit.

25. Ibid., p. 4.

26. Gerbner, "Mass Communications and Popular Conceptions," op. cit.

all real-life teachers who are women. The school stories are more likely to feature romance than are stories in general. But the romance rarely involves the teacher—and least of all the woman teacher. Typical is Miss Dove, who is so devoted, so selfless, so excruciatingly *good*, that she passes up her opportunity to marry in order to pay back $11,430 her dead father has "borrowed" from the bank where he worked.

Nearly half of all media adults but only 26 percent of male teachers and no more than 18 percent of female teachers are married. Despite all the romance and happy endings in the stories, teachers rarely inspire love or fall in love, especially with each other. The most common condition of love is that the teacher find a partner outside of education. The typical pattern has her quitting a New England high school and a biology teacher fiancé to "find herself" and a *man* in New York. Or it has him leaving a dull musical chair at a western college and a straitlaced professor girl friend, to be taught something about music and love in Tin Pan Alley.

Failure in love and defeat in life permit most media teachers to be fully dedicated to the profession. The media teacher leaving for another specific occupation knows the road to success in the media world. Five times out of six the road leads to show business.

POVERTY OF THE SCHOOLS

In the film study, 25 of the 470 movies portraying some aspect of education show the financial plight of the schools. The deficiencies are usually in extracurricular activities such as entertainment and sports. There is never a need for more teachers or laboratories or classrooms. Profits from sports events and successful musical shows and unexpected bequests of the rich are the usual solutions to academic poverty. Only two films show schools to be public responsibilities, publicly financed. One deals with support for West Point and the other depicts the building of a school in a remote New Zealand village.

Only one film shows the financial problem as one of low salaries for teachers. A wealthy Texas rancher is shocked to find his son trying to raise a family on the meager salary of an instructor. He secretly negotiates with a local butcher to sell his son meat at half price. He also tries to prevent his son's promotion, confident that if not promoted he would return to the ranch. When he does not, the father solves the problem by donating enough money to the school to provide a pay increase for all teachers.[27]

An analysis of teacher characters in *Saturday Evening Post* fiction found them in more frequent financial "pickle." This was usually explained by showing that they strive less than the other characters. About one-third of the magazine's teachers solve their financial problems by quitting the profession. No teacher is ever given a salary raise. No student is supported on a public scholarship. No community takes the initiative to raise taxes or to build or improve the schools. When there is a suggestion of improvement in the finances of the schools, it is likely to be a private solution such as finding a rich donor or holding a fantastically successful show or sports event.[28]

THE SCHOOL SPORTS STORY

School sports is an arena of "early male socialization."[29] Extensive friendship ties are linked to participation in games. The winning team is also a symbol of an institution's ability to attract talent and display power. Winning scores have been found to relate to legislative appropriations and certainly to alumni giving. An article in the *Philadelphia Magazine* (May 1972) quotes the head of the alumni society as saying that "the Alumnus in Oregon or Texas is going to read about Penn's basketball team in his hometown paper, not some professor's finding old ruins in England."

There is no doubt that the most frequent appearance of schools and colleges in the American press is on the sports page. The magic words of American higher education are Ivy League and Big Ten. *Saturday Evening Post* readers loved the stories of George Fitch. The first of these, published in 1908, began:

Yes, sir, it's been seven years now since old Siwash College has been beaten in football. . . . We've shut out Hopkinsville seven times—pushed them off the field, off the earth, into the hospitals and into the discard. We've beaten six State universities by an average of seven touchdowns,

27. Schwartz, op. cit., pp. 49-50.

28. Brown, op. cit.

29. Alan Booth, "Sex and Social Participation," *American Sociological Review* 37 (1972): 183-92.

two goal kicks, a rib, three jawbones and four new kinds of yells. We put such a crimp into old Muggledorfer that her Faculty suddenly decided that football developed the toes and teeth at the expense of the intellect and they took up intercollegiate beanbags instead. And in all those seven years we've never really been scared but once. . . .

The school sports story, with its violent terminology, strong group spirit, and concern over the rules of the game, is the most likely vehicle for community enthusiasm, teamwork, and the mixing of different classes and races in a common cause. It generally demonstrates the ethics of skill and power among those who achieve equal status. (This can be contrasted with the symbolic functions of the crime or spy story displaying the game of power among those of unequal status or those who do not play by the same rules.)

A sketch of boys' sports fiction [30] describes its symbolic functions as integration into the virtues of unquestioning participation, hero worship, inviolable hierarchy, sorting winners from losers, and a sharp sense of authority, belonging, and superiority. The school becomes society and the game the system at its dramatic best. As the English novel of life at Rugby, *Tom Brown's School Days*,[31] which introduced the genre to American boys in 1870, pointed out quite explicitly: "Perhaps ours is the only little corner in the British Empire which is thoroughly, wisely, and strongly ruled just now." A hundred years and several new media later, the functions are the same, even though the tactics are a bit more sophisticated.

The film study shows sports to be the central theme in twice as many movies as those that deal with study, science, or research, and to depict virtues never seen in a portrayal of scholarly activity. The school sports story serves its symbolic functions in three ways: (a) as the means by which youths from different walks of life find acceptance in the group; (b) as the chief symbolic unifier of students, faculty, parents, and alumni; and (c) as teaching the importance of passing a realistic test of social and ethical "maturity."

30. Walter Evans, "The All-American Boys: A Study of Boys' Sports Fiction," *Journal of Popular Culture* 6 (Summer 1972): 104-21.

31. Thomas Hughes, *Tom Brown's School Days* (New York: Harper & Bros., 1870).

The largest single group of stories concentrates on the third, the socioethical lesson. The films warn that romantic illusions lead to cynicism and despair. They counsel realism and vigilance lest "alien" ideologies take advantage of and subvert "our" flexible rules for "their" purposes.

Of the portrayal of sports in education by motion pictures, Schwartz reported:

> The most common presentation of sports was that it was a much less glamorous and honest activity than student-players were at first led to believe. . . . For the sake of victory, schools were shown to sacrifice their honor by depending upon extra-collegiate sources for both personnel and financial support. This dependence upon outside sources was not portrayed as unethical in all films dealing with sports—in fact, several films portrayed this dependence in a vein of lighthearted comedy which, if not condoning the practice, did not take the unethical aspects of the situation seriously. However, in the films to seriously treat the unethical practices of the sport and their demoralizing consequences for students, the portrayal of school sports was likened to a *rites de passage*. Sports were shown as analogous to the battleground upon which a young initiate experienced teamwork and struggle, despair and disillusionment, victory and defeat.[32]

The typical school sports story is a morality play that shows a sort of pragmatic "democracy in action." The rules will bend within reason and anyone can play, as long as the game is just a game and the prime source of power is clearly understood. Abuse the rules and the tone changes. In one group of films, gangsters try to manipulate players and even faculty to reap large gambling profits. In another, radicals "disguised as students" (described in a contemporary *New York Times* review as "namby-pamby, bushy haired, and wearing tortoise-shell glasses") plan to overthrow capitalism, beginning with the college football team. The local hero falls briefly under their spell, but recovers in time to win the "game of the year" and the respect of "normal healthy Americans."

COMMUNITY AND POWER

When they cannot relate to "the game," in which students play the lead, teachers usually do not "belong" at all. Typically presented as alien to the community in which they live and work,

32. Schwartz, op. cit., p. 59.

and often in conflict with its values, teachers may be seen as well-meaning and kindly if impotent, or dangerous and evil if powerful, but rarely both good *and* effective.

Studies by Bowman,[33] Boys,[34] and Springer[35] trace community conflict and antagonism through fifty years of magazine publishing, general fiction, and Broadway drama. Brown's study[36] of *Saturday Evening Post* fiction found that teachers "act differently" even when trying to conform. The film research concluded that all but six of the twenty-eight films touching upon relations between school and community portray a teacher as the target of hostility, ridicule, or ostracism. The offending teachers are usually shown as "outsiders . . . with their own set of values often aiding in isolating them from the community." [37]

Nonconformist media teachers usually come to see the error of their ways. One movie depicts a socialistically inclined economics professor striking it rich. He changes his mind about radical causes and returns to his job a millionaire.

Most instances of unreconciled conflict between teachers and community involve the cardinal sins of trying to change society rather than the schools (usually labeled communism) or of finding a source of wisdom outside the approved community context (usually represented as atheism). Sex often appears as a malignant obsession when sought by such unlikely characters as teachers. A cynically explicit portrayal in a 1937 movie shows a southern mob lynch a "yankee" teacher convicted of assaulting an attractive student. The district attorney does not believe the teacher guilty but prosecutes vigorously because of the political value of the case for his own career.

In casting about for occupations to delineate hero types who

33. Claude C. Bowman, "The Professor in the Popular Magazines," *Journal of Higher Education* 9 (1938): 351-56.

34. Richard C. Boys, "The American College in Fiction," *College English* 7 (1946): 379-87.

35. Roland A. Springer, "Problems of Higher Education in the Broadway Drama: Critical Analysis of Broadway Plays, 1920-1950" (Doctoral diss., New York University, 1951).

36. Brown, op. cit.

37. Schwartz, op. cit., p. 40.

are both right and mighty, mass media authors rarely pick teaching. Smythe's analysis[38] of television drama found teachers outstanding among all TV occupations in being the cleanest and the kindest. But they were also rated the weakest, the softest, and the slowest. The more potent teacher risks turning into that symbol of evil intellect—the mass media scientist. On television, the scientist was rated as the most deceitful, cruel, and unfair of all professional types.

Personality ratings used to assess students' images of real-life teachers tapped mass-cultural stereotypes. O'Dowd and Beardslee[39] found that the student image of the school teacher is that of an unselfish, uninteresting, unsuccessful, and effeminate person. The scientist, on the other hand, presents the image of the cool, cruel, hard-driving intellectual and often a loner who cannot be trusted.

Similarly, Gusfield and Schwartz[40] concluded that the teacher image presents "the sharpest contrast between elements of esteem and status, on the one hand, and those of power and income on the other." The teacher ranks as the most honest and second most useful of fifteen occupations and also the weakest and lightest. The scientist again appears to be cool, tough, and antisocial as well as irreligious and foreign.

PUBLISH AND PERISH

It is not surprising that the dramatic uses of scholarship and research contrast sharply with those portraying sports and other entertainment. Academic research leads to murder in nearly half of the twenty-five films found to portray teachers conducting the research. Film teachers invent poisons, revive prehistoric monsters, or train other creatures to do away with suspected enemies. One famous movie of the 1950s shows a psychology professor hypnotizing gorillas to murder the girls who rejected his advances. The typical plot has some obsession drive the demented intellect to in-

38. Dallas W. Smythe, *Three Years of New York Television, 1951-1953* (Urbana, Ill.: National Association of Education Broadcasters, University of Illinois Press, 1953).

39. O'Dowd and Beardslee, op. cit.

40. Joseph R. Gusfield and Michael Schwartz, "The Meanings of Occupational Prestige: Reconsideration of the NORC Scale," *American Sociological Review* 28 (1963): 270.

vent an instrument that gets out of control and destroys its maker, to the relief of all mankind.

In a group of nine films dealing with research, the experimenting teacher or professor falls victim to his own delusions and exposes the stupidity or hypocrisy of scholarship. Typical is the movie in which the professor of Egyptology incorrectly deciphers an ancient tablet and the false message sends him on a series of comic adventures.

Research and experimentation fare better in the hands of amateurs. Student scholarship is usually foolish but never evil or selfish. Incidentally, classroom scenes hardly ever exhibit learning or scholarship. They are used to display problems of authority and discipline. The teacher struggling for discipline in the school is often brutal and sadistic. In films of more recent vintage, students (as if representing the avenging forces of society) strike back in kind. The "class struggle" is one in which the teacher rarely comes out on top.

Images Across Cultures

Through a series of cross-cultural comparative studies we tried to understand our own images better by comparing them with those of others.[41] Four countries of Western Europe and five countries of Eastern Europe (including the Soviet Union) provided our comparisons. A plot sketch from several countries' samples will give something of the flavor of the material.

"Red Castle" is what townspeople call the new headquarters of the Teachers' Recreation Center. It was a baron's palace before the revolution. A priceless collection of jewels is still stored in the castle. One day a precious stone is missing. The shadow of suspicion falls on Professor Zach, a frequent visitor at Red Castle. But the clever deductions of his students(turned amateur detectives) vindicate the professor, and the real culprits are caught. (Czechoslovakia)

Word gets around that the attractive new teacher is carrying on with the well-known high school "jock." And in the

41. Gerbner, "Mass Communications and Popular Conceptions," op. cit.; idem, "Images Across Cultures," op. cit.

locker room, too. She is nearly ruined before it develops that the student, himself the victim of psychopathic, scandal-mongering father, only tried to rape her in an unguarded moment. (U.S.)

The tactlessness of a dry and dogmatic school director drives one of the students of the elementary school of Borsk into the clutches of a religious sect. The teachers' collective is dismayed. A timid young instructor is drawn into the struggle against the sect. Emboldened through her efforts to demonstrate that religious dogmatism defeats the goals of free education, she realizes the great role of the teacher in public life. (USSR)

The humane methods of the new teacher in an East End slum school lead to disaster. "Spare the rod . . ." gloat the hardened old disciplinarians. The teacher is about to give up and leave when a glimmer of student response at the end of the term gives him second thoughts. (England)

The impoverished peasants of a village refuse to work for starvation wages on the count's estate. But the gendarmes have a firm grip on this treasonous activity. The peasants are ordered to the railroad station to welcome the arriving count. They come. But they come to pay respects to the departing teacher, who is being run out of town as the chief troublemaker. (Hungary)

A utopian idealist teaching in a lyceé becomes so involved in his pacifist schemes that he neglects his family. Reality finally deals him a tragic but sobering blow: his daughter has a lover, has taken part in a robbery, and is about to run away. (France)

Orphaned, hungary, and demoralized, a gang of boys terrorizes the countryside at the end of the war. A former partisan leader, now teacher, turns them into useful citizens. (Poland)

TEACHER GOALS AND FATES

We found that the Russian and other socialist media teachers are depicted as more learned, democratic, and manly than those of the West. Eastern mass media stories of schools and teachers stress the ideals of service to community and nation more than three times as frequently as American and other Western media.

United States media portray a higher proportion of women

teachers on all levels of education than do the media of other countries. Our media also depict a composite image of the teacher as less professional and less likely either to advance or to slip on the social ladder than the media teacher of other countries. The U.S. media teacher is more easily frustrated and victimized by the much higher level of violence and illegality prevalent in her world than is the media teacher of the other countries.

Teachers are quitting the profession in about 28 percent of U.S. and Western media and in 14 percent of Eastern media stories. The main reasons for giving up teaching in Western media are the frustrations and conflicts of the job and marriage. Eastern media teachers leaving the field of education are most likely to be fired, retired at the end of their service, or advanced to positions of higher leadership.

Teachers stand out everywhere in seeking intellectual values more often than do the other adult characters in the same fictional environment. But Eastern European media characters, and especially teachers, are different from those of other countries in their much more frequent pursuit of goals of social morality (justice, honor, public service, a better world).

We analyzed the barriers that stand in the way of achievement and found that the one major difference between the problems of U.S. media teachers and those of the other countries lies in the teachers themselves. Only in U.S. media are teachers more likely than other adults to be depicted as handicapped by their own weaknesses and fears. The fears may be justified. Over one-third of all U.S. media teachers commit violence and nearly half fall victim to it. This is low by U.S. media standards, but it is roughly twice the mayhem found in media of Western Europe and about six times that found in the media world of education in Eastern Europe.

A happy ending is symbolic insistence that justice triumphs despite all troubles. American media stories are the most insistent. Conditions of success, however, are more indicative of its functions than frequency alone. We compared the goals of unambiguously successful characters with those who clearly fail.

Only in American media are successful teachers depicted as less likely to pursue aims of social morality than are teachers marked for failure. Many U.S. media teachers who do tackle social goals are naïve, comic, and even mad, and most are crushed by some misfortune that fictional fate throws in their paths.

THE ROLE OF STUDENTS

Being a student is a long and varied stage in life. The range of opportunities for portrayal is great. The institutional and social forces that shape the representation of teachers in the mass media also affect the depiction of students. But the potential diversity of the student image leads to extraordinary differences in scope and function.

American mass media are unique in not earmarking significant resources to young people. They treat children as a low-income, high-profit, quick-turnover market where the message of social power (police, violence) can be sold in its cheapest and crudest forms. As if to underline the analogy to the slum, the trade journals call the children's program segment on television the "kidvid ghetto."

Market considerations also account for the fact that children and youth (as well as old people) in leading roles make the product a "specialty story." They presumably fragment audience appeal and need special exploitation. American youths become universally employable for dramatic purposes (as otherwise) when they *leave* school.

An international study of the "film hero" [42] classified students as an occupational group. Entertainers head the list of occupations with 18 percent of all leading characters. Students are next to the last with 4 percent. (The last were laborers.) The Western European pattern is similar, although students are more numerous than in U.S. films.

The films of Eastern Europe offer striking contrast. Students are in *first* place on the same list of occupations, with percentages ranging from 20 percent in Poland to 24 percent in Yugoslavia and 28 percent of all leading characters in Czechoslovakia.

The diversity of the portrayals permits few generalizations. Focus on childhood and adolescence in American media requires specialized story values. They are often found outside the regular

42. Gerbner, "The Film Hero," op. cit.

social context. Several stories are about mentally ill, retarded, and physically handicapped youngsters. One revolves around a little boy playing Cupid. Another deals with a sadistic teen-age gang leader. A sociology student's research requires her to pose as a prostitute. Youngsters complicate life for attractive widowed fathers or mothers. A hard-boiled manager of a gambling house finds himself the guardian of a six-year-old orphan. A good-hearted mute befriends a homeless prostitute and her little daughter. Six homeless waifs camp out in an unused shack on the Connecticut estate where a glamorous but exhausted star seeks peace and quiet.

Students in the media of Eastern Europe are not only more numerous but also move in the thematic and moral mainstream of their symbolic world. This is a world in which a mountain youth pressed into hard labor by the lord of the manor joins the outlaws to fight injustice—as his father had done before him. A crippled and lonely student finds amusement in shooting birds from his wheelchair, until he downs a homing pigeon awaited by a little girl and her fishermen friends and begins the slow, painful road to recovery for both the pigeon and himself. Three boys on a school outing steal away into the woods and come upon a partisan hideout; their teacher demands an explanation for their absence, but he is the local commander of the native fascist militia! A theft of puppets from the school theater sends a group of youngsters on a wild chase involving an unpopular boy who plays detective, unaware that his schoolmates suspect *him* of the crime. A school girl's vacation love affair, her first, sets her on a course of competition and conflict with her attractive aunt. A school boy longing for a bicycle stumbles upon lost money—and discovers the difficulty of making a moral choice. A group of classmates decide to expose the hypocrisy and stealing going on at their collective farm—but what to do when they find some of their own parents among the culprits? A student poses as a German sympathizer in order to obtain information for the Resistance; the anti-Fascist patriots are out to kill him, but his mission demands that he maintain silence. A young pupil is falsely accused of having stolen his classmate's pencil and confesses to escape the ridicule of his accusers—only to make matters worse.

In these stories, school is often the center of social and moral struggle. Behind the authority of the teacher stands the power of the state. Analysts rated the media schools of Eastern Europe as "related to real life" and learning as "of immediate benefit" about twice as frequently as in the media schools of the West. Eastern European media students are shown as "interested in knowledge," as "leaders and organizers," and as "participating in community affairs" from two to three times as often as those of the West. East European media students are depicted as taking examinations three times as frequently as U.S. media students, but the latter were observed "dominating classroom activity" four times as frequently as the former.

Knowledge and Its Control

An episode of the television serial "Wild Wild West" features a geology professor who, imbued with noble if (naturally) impractical ideas, goes West in the employ of a rich prospector in order to alleviate his own genteel poverty. But the prospector lets him down. Feeling betrayed (with some justification), he becomes obsessed with thoughts of revenge. His knowledge, now out of control of an employer, becomes a menace to society. He plots to destroy the state through a series of earthquakes triggered by dynamite blasts at critical points in the fault line he mapped through the area. "I have turned the tide," he cries, "employed nature for my own use—now I want my reward." Brawny agent West and his brainy sidekick (!) make sure that he gets it. We last see him scrawling equations on a chalkboard as he holds "class" alone in his jail cell.

All societies suspect what they need but cannot fully control. Symbolizing such uneasy symbiotic relationships are ambivalent images of oracles, eccentrics, witches, alchemists, and others "possessed" of independent knowledge, as well as teachers. The teacher image is likely also to fall short of the mandarin ideal or to suffer from the human tendency to denigrate "outgrown" authority.

Beyond such similarities, however, differences in mass-mediated symbolic functions reveal and cultivate significant social distinctions. As we go from West to East, teachers stand out in their own fictional environments as more distinguished in learning and in qualities of personal and social morality. The terms of this morality are not necessarily comparable across cultures. The ethic of individualistic liberalism is not the same as that of socialist morality or the Soviet concept of the moral development of the child, even if some of the same terms are used. Nevertheless, the image of the teacher in the socialist media reflects a happier fate and a more stable, purposeful, and socially meaningful existence in its own fictional world than it does in the West.

Differences in social organization account for some of these distinctions. Mass media are cultural organs of industrial society. Their ownership, management, and clientele—extending the institutional order into the cultural sphere—shape their outlook and functions. The organizational and client relationships of Eastern European media interlock with other public institutions, including the schools, the party, and the state itself. The hidden curriculum serves the same institutional interests as the overt one; both are agencies of planned social transformation. This places media images of schools, scholars, and the knowledge they symbolize in the mainstream of the symbolic world undergoing a cultural revolution. In performing their symbolic functions, socialist media can take advantage of their legacy of intellectual leadership in nationalist and proletarian movements in which teachers have had a prominent place for centuries.

Organizational and client relationships of American media also reward development of a particular selection from prevalent cultural patterns. The selection manifests the dual character of private-enterprise views on public enterprise. On one hand, the school is a necessary cost factor whose value is limited to its direct usefulness to the investment in current products, practices, and outlooks. On the other hand, schools represent political capital and popular aspirations for mobility, equality, and social reform. The concept of knowledge and its role in and control by society are caught in the cross fire. The most enduring and pervasive images of teachers in American mass culture are those that humiliate and depress them. Failure in love and impotence in life permit them to be "good." Or they can be vigorous but evil or perhaps only ridiculous.

Poverty is normal and probably desirable for a dependent institution that should not develop a strong power-base of its own. When cut loose from corporate, military, law enforcement or other established power, even the "miracles of science" turn into "mad scientist" horrors.

No school or culture educates children for some other society. Giving teachers a messianic mission and having schools soak up all the dreams and aspirations citizens have for their children doom the enterprise to failure. No social order can afford to make good such a promise. The illusion itself contains the seeds of the "noble but impractical" image. It becomes only "reasonable" and "realistic" to show teachers full of goodness but sapped of vitality and power. Turn on the power and the impotent figure becomes a monster, only confirming the doubts and suspicions inherent in the ambivalent image.

Unlike the army and the police, the schools do not appear to be a major public responsibility at all. They are shown as places of controversy and conflict, except when the goal is winning for "the team." The school sports story provides a dramatic framework for learning the rules of order and life in a community dedicated to skills directly applicable to competitive power.

American media scholars symbolize the promise of learning on behalf of noble and idealistic goals and undercut that promise by being strange, weak and foolish and generally unworthy of the support of the community. The hidden curriculum cultivates the illusion of social reform through education and, at the same time, helps pave the way for the perennial collapse of its achievement. As things work out in the symbolic realm, the bankruptcy of the schools is their own fault. The invidious distinction between *teaching* and *doing* is maintained. The promise of a productive society to place the cultivation of a distinctly human self-consciousness highest on its scale of priorities is again betrayed.

American media are cultural arms of private enterprise in the public sphere. The images they project have a dual character. They attempt to be serviceable (or at least not inimical) to the commercial and other interests of private enterprise and, at the same time, represent those public ideals that give them universal attraction, currency, and credibility. That is why the study of capitalist mass media and their symbolic functions presents a particularly complex and challenging task. The task is to discover the actual laws of symbolic behavior in a field of conflicting institutional interests

and to assess their real contributions to the cultivation of human
conceptions and social policy.

I doubt that the nature of education, the role of knowledge,
and the prospect for real changes in school policy can be fully
grasped until that assessment is well under way. New developments
in communication technology have the potential of altering social
patterns of knowledge, as did the "old" developments. The question is whether they will merely extend the scope and reach of
the existing structure or begin to change them. That, of course, is
not a technological question but an institutional one. Institutions
use technology in communications and culture for their own purposes. The image of the schoolteacher in the hidden curriculum of
the mass media may continue to be a useful indicator of those purposes.

Index

Abilities: acquisition of, 142; experience in relation to, 126
Ability vs. knowledge, 126
Abstraction, uses of, in images, 209
Academic learning centers, description of, 425
Adair, J., 292
Alberti, Leon B., 228
Allen, R. R., 158
Allen, William H., 384; quoted, 336
Alternatives, exploration of, in research on symbol systems, 44
Anderson, Richard C., 154
Annenberg School of Communications, 14, 23
Anohin, P., 376
Appeal (media), formative research on, 316
Aristotle, 12, 82
Arnheim, Rudolf, 65, 239, 274, 277, 281; discussion of chapter by, 18; quoted, 276, 278, 279, 297
Artificial intelligence: assumption of, 373-74; definition of, 369-70; see also Computer
Art and science, differences in domains of, 34-35
Artistic vs. scientific education, 54-55
Arts: place of, as peripheral studies, 91-92; use of organizing principles of sensory modalities by, 87; use of sensory modalities of, 98
Asian Center for Educational Innovation for Development (ACEID), 466
Association, two types of, 109
Attention, relation of movement to, 191
Attneave, Fred, 223
Audio and visual cultures, bridges between, 82-83
Audiovisual equipment, literature on, 439; see also Media Audubon, John J., 183
Audubon, John J., 183
Authenticity, notion of, in visual materials, 207-8

Bacon, Francis, 166
Bandura, A., 131
Beardslee, David C., 488
Beethoven, Ludwig von, 31
Behavior: changing of, as concern of man, 86; search for psychology of, 124-25; see also Learning
Behavioral goals, establishment of, for CTW, 307-8
Behavior modification, cybernetics in relation to, 414-15; see also Learning
Bell, Alexander G., Graphophone of, 4
Belok, M. V., 477
Bereiter, Carl, 141
Berlo, David K., quoted, 342
Berlyne, D. E., 387
Bernini, Giovanni, 195
Bernstein, Lewis, 316
Bernstein, N., 376
Bever, Thomas G., 160
Birdwhistell, R., quoted, 67
Black, Hillel, 173
Bloom, Richard D., 175, 176
Bower, T. G., 160
Bowman, Claude C., 487
Boyle, Robert, 36
Boys, Richard C., 487
Bradbury, Ray, 164
Brain organization, symbol systems in relation to, 38-41
Branch, M. N., 139
Brown, Roger, 481, 487
Bruner, J. S., 17, 112, 131, 157, 393, 402; quoted, 13-14, 350
Buhler, Karl, 242
Bryant, Jennings, Jr., 325

Cable systems, programs through, 340; see also Media
Caricature, a peculiarity of, 42-43
Carnegie Commission, report of 332
Carpenter, C. R., 386
Carpenter, E., 13, 385

Informative displays, variety of, 213-26

Innovation: approach to, in developing countries, 454-56; criteria for determining strategies for, 462-65; development of centers for promotion of, 464

Institutions, designing of, in view of media, 419-23

Instruction: conditions for improvement of, 9-10; symbol systems in relation to, 385; three forms of, 134-35

Instructional decisions, constraints upon, 406

Instructional materials, printing in relation to, 2; see also Media

Instructional television (ITV), 332

Instructional technology, definition of, 12

Intelligence, relation of to skill in a medium, 396

Intermediate technology, concept of, 446-50; use of, in Japan, 448; see also Developing countries

Internal compatibility (film), formative research on, 323-25

International Sociological Association, 481

Ivins, William J., Jr., 68, 76, 249

Ivory Coast: use of television in, 439; project of, 443; see also Developing countries

Jakobson, Roman, 105; quoted, 62, 99, 106, 109, 118

Janzen, J. C., 127

Jencks, Christopher, report of, 471

Jenkins, J. R., 389

Johnson, Samuel, 36

Jonas, H., 279

Jones, Sheila, 140

Joyce, Bruce, 412, 421; discussion of chapter by, 22

Joyce, James, 83, 147

Jung, Carl G., 259

Kant, Immanuel, 28

Katz, Michael B., 8, 472

Keil, C. M., 71

Kennedy, John B., 19, 239; discussion of chapter by, 18-19; quoted, 229

Kersh, Bert Y., 418

Klee, Paul, 88

Knowledge: acquisition of, 132-35; attack on goals of, 126; centrality of education in, 126; contribution of linguistics to, 55; dependence of, on purpose, 127; empirical definition of, 371; questioning of, as primary goal, 149-50; technical modes of, 61; treatment of control of, in media, 494-97

Knowledge and skills: distinction between, 398-99; relationship between, 129

Kolers, P., 50

Kopferman, Hertha, 223

Koran, M., 397

Korzybski, Alfred, 119, 120, 121

Krauss, Reinhard, 269

Kris, Ernst, 264

Kulhavy, W., 154

Langer, S., 29

Language: acquisition of knowledge in relation to, 131; advantages of, 161-62; advertiser's use of, 102-3; characteristics of, 157-58; conveyance of knowledge by, 100-1; factors determining primacy of, in learning, 176-78; functions of, 242-43; playwright's use of, 101-2; pornographer's use of, 103-4; relation of, to thought, 162-63; temporal problems with, 158-62; use of, as instructional medium, 138-9; use of, by educators, 99-101; use of, in aural and visual cultures, 83-84; use of, in poetry, 104-5

Language vs. direct experience, 153-58

Language vs. direct experience, 153-58

Latin America, satellite educational project in, 445

Lazarsfeld, P. F., 337

Learners: characteristics of, 344-45; nature of, in relation to media, 395-98; research on use of media with, 403

Learner-television interaction, 344-50

Learning: print in relation to, 176-79; verbal fallacy in relation to, 73-74; visual representation in relation to, 148; see also Presentational learning, Problem-solving

Learning centers, organization of, 422-23

Learning experiences, classification of, 172-73

INFORMATION CONCERNING
THE NATIONAL SOCIETY FOR THE STUDY OF EDUCATION

1. *Purpose.* The purpose of the National Society is to promote the investigation and discussion of educational questions. To this end it holds an annual meeting and publishes a series of yearbooks and a series of paperbacks on Contemporary Educational Issues.

2. *Membership.* Any person interested in the purpose of the Society and in receiving its publications may become a member by sending in name, title, address, and a check covering dues and the entrance fee (see items 4 and 5). Graduate students may become members, upon recommendation of a faculty member, at a reduced rate for the first year of membership. Dues for all subsequent years are the same as for other members.
Membership is not transferable. It is limited to individuals and may not be held by libraries, schools, or other institutions, either directly or indirectly.

3. *Period of Membership.* Membership is for the calendar year and terminates automatically on December 31, unless dues for the ensuing year are paid as indicated in item 6. Applicants for membership may not date their entrance back of the current calendar year.

4. *Categories of Membership.* The following categories of membership have been established:

Regular. Annual dues are $10.00. The member receives a clothbound copy of each part of the yearbook.

Comprehensive. Annual dues are $20.00. The member receives a clothbound copy of the yearbook and all volumes in the current year's series on Contemporary Educational Issues.

Life Membership. Persons sixty years of age or above may become life members on payment of a fee based on the average life expectancy of their age group. Regular life members may take out a Comprehensive membership for any year by payment of an additional fee of $10.00. For information apply to the Secretary-Treasurer.

Graduate Students. First year dues for the Regular and Comprehensive membership are $8.00 and $18.00 respectively, plus the $1.00 entrance fee in either case.

5. *Privileges of Membership.* Members receive the publications of the Society as described above. All members are entitled to vote, to participate in meetings of the Society, and (under certain conditions) to hold office. The names of members are printed in the yearbook in alternate years.

6. *Entrance Fee.* New members are required to pay an entrance fee of one dollar, in addition to the dues, for the first year of membership.

7. *Payment of Dues.* Statements of dues are rendered in October for the following calendar year. Any member so notified whose dues remain unpaid on January 1 thereby loses membership and can be reinstated only by paying the dues plus a reinstatement fee of fifty cents ($.50).

School warrants and vouchers from institutions must be accompanied by definite information concerning the name and address of the person for whom the membership fee is being paid. Statements of dues are rendered on our own form only. The Secretary's office cannot undertake to fill out special invoice forms of any kind or to affix a notary's affidavit to statements or receipts.

Cancelled checks serve as receipts. Members desiring an additional receipt must enclose a stamped and addressed envelope therefor.

8. *Distribution of Yearbooks to Members.* The yearbooks, normally ready prior to the February meeting of the Society, will be mailed from the office of the distributor only to members whose dues for that year have been paid.

9. *Commercial Sales.* The distribution of all yearbooks prior to the current year, and also of those of the current year not regularly mailed to members in exchange for their dues, is in the hands of the distributor, not of the Secretary. Orders may be placed with the University of Chicago Press,

Chicago, Illinois 60637, which distributes the yearbooks of the Society. Orders for paperbacks in the series on Contemporary Educational Issues should be placed with the designated publisher of that series. The list of the Society's publications is printed in each yearbook.

10. *Yearbooks*. The yearbooks are issued about one month before the February meeting. Published in two volumes, each of which contains 300 to 400 pages, the yearbooks are planned to be of immediate practical value as well as representative of sound scholarship and scientific investigation.

11. *Series on Contemporary Educational Issues*. This series, in paperback format, is designed to supplement the yearbooks by timely publications on topics of current interest. There will usually be four of these volumes each year.

12. *Meetings*. The annual meeting, at which the yearbooks are presented and critiqued, is held as a rule in February at the same time and place as the meeting of the American Association of School Administrators. Members will be notified of other meetings.

Applications for membership will be handled promptly at any time. New members will receive the yearbook scheduled for publication during the calendar year in which application for Basic Membership is made. New members who elect to take out the Comprehensive membership will receive both the yearbook and the paperbacks scheduled for publication during the year in which application is made.

KENNETH J. REHAGE, Secretary-Treasurer

5835 Kimbark Avenue
Chicago, Illinois 60637

PUBLICATIONS OF THE NATIONAL SOCIETY FOR THE STUDY OF EDUCATION

NOTICE: Many of the early yearbooks of this series are now out of print. In the following list, those titles to which an asterisk is prefixed are not available for purchase.

Distributed by

THE UNIVERSITY OF CHICAGO PRESS, CHICAGO, ILLINOIS 60637

1974

Please direct all orders for books to the University of Chicago Press.

Series on Contemporary Educational Issues

1971

Accountability in Education (L. M. Lessinger and R. W. Tyler, eds.)
Farewell to Schools??? (D. U. Levine and R. J. Havighurst, eds.)
Models for Integrated Education (D. U. Levine, ed.)
PYGMALION *Reconsidered* (J. D. Elashoff and R. E. Snow)
Reactions to Silberman's CRISIS IN THE CLASSROOM (A. H. Passow, ed.)

1972

Black Students in White Schools (E. G. Epps, ed.)
Flexibility in School Programs (W. J. Congreve and G. L. Rinehart, eds.)
Performance Contracting—1969-1971 (J. A. Mecklenburger)
The Potential of Educational Futures (M. Marien and W. L. Ziegler, eds.)
Sex Differences and Discrimination in Education (S. Anderson, ed.)

Please direct orders for the above titles to:

Charles A. Jones Publishing Company
Worthington, Ohio 43085

1974

Crucial Issues in Testing (R. W. Tyler and R. M. Wolf, ed.)
Conflicting Conceptions of Curriculum (E. W. Eisner and E. Vallance, eds.)
Cultural Pluralism (E. G. Epps, ed.)
Rethinking Educational Equality (A. T. Kopan and H. J. Walberg, eds.)

Please direct orders for the 1974 titles to:

McCutchan Publishing Corporation
2526 Grove Street
Berkeley, California 94704

DATE DUE

NO 14 '84	NOV 14 '84		
DE 07 '84	NOV 29 '84		
SE 23 '87	SEP 4 '87		
GAYLORD			PRINTED IN U.S.A.